Postwar Politics in the G-7

Postwar Politics in the G-7

Orders and Eras in Comparative Perspective

Edited by

Byron E. Shafer

THE UNIVERSITY OF WISCONSIN PRESS

The University of Wisconsin Press
114 North Murray Street
Madison, Wisconsin 53715

3 Henrietta Street
London WC2E 8LU, England

5 4 3 2 1

Printed in the United States of America

Library of Congress Cataloging-in-Publication Data
Postwar politics in the G-7: orders and eras in comparative
  perspective / edited by Byron E. Shafer
    336 p.   cm.
    Includes bibliographical references and index.
    ISBN 0-299-15100-X (cloth: alk. paper).
    ISBN 0-299-15104-2 (pbk.: alk. paper)
    1. Comparative government.   2. World politics—1945–
I. Shafer, Byron E.
JF51.P65   1996
320.9—dc20   96-18066

For Gabriel Almond & Seymour Martin Lipset,
classic and intuitive comparativists

Contents

Contributors

Andrew Adonis is a reporter and analyst for the *Financial Times* of London.

Stephen J. Anderson is Inforum Project Director, Center for Global Communications, International University of Japan.

Miriam Feldblum is Professor of Political Science at the University of San Francisco.

J. Jens Hesse is Founding Director of the European Center for Comparative Government and Public Policy Research in Berlin.

Richard C. G. Johnston is Professor of Political Science at the University of British Columbia.

Carol A. Mershon is Professor of Political Science at the University of Virginia.

Byron E. Shafer is Andrew W. Mellon Professor of American Government, Nuffield College, Oxford University.

Postwar Politics in the G-7

1 *Byron E. Shafer*

Introduction

This is an exploratory venture in comparative political analysis. It begins with a set of nations possessing a previously formed identity, the nations known collectively as the "Group of Seven." And it begins with a period of time possessing widely recognized bounds, the period from the end of the Second World War to the end of what became known as the "Cold" War. To organize the politics of these nations across that period, this venture applies a simple and straightforward conceptual framework, involving political eras and political orders. From this application, it seeks comparative insights, both the previously unperceived similarities which are the conventional product of comparison and the idiosyncratic distinctions which prove so important in one or another nation at one or another time.

The "story line" for such an enterprise encompasses some remarkable events and developments. In the chapters that follow:

1. Germany is divided, the Berlin Wall goes up, and the Berlin Wall comes down, while an economic recovery with nationally distinctive institutions is fashioned and chugs away underneath;
2. France attempts to return to an older era, meets the sharpest challenge to democratic governance of any of the G-7 nations during this

period, with the Algerian crisis, and moves to entirely new constitutional arrangements;

3. Britain undertakes implementation of the most sweeping single effort at a comprehensive welfare state in all these nations, and ultimately sees the long-delayed counterattack;
4. The United States does sustain a prewar order, then leaves it abruptly to inaugurate a pattern of split partisan control of government, a pattern destined to acquire at least echoes everywhere in the G-7;
5. Canada exits a long period of multiple but suppressed conflicts, for one where ethnocultural divisions sweep everything into their vortex, with national continuity itself occasionally in the balance;
6. Japan builds not just a world-class economy but a durable political order beneath it, such that the steering mechanisms to both can change *without* much challenge from changing public issues;
7. Italy constructs and maintains a much more highly stylized system of elite negotiations, where major institutional "safely valves" are integral and important but where continuity always seems more problematic.

Accordingly, a focus on the G-7 nations in the postwar years does not lack inherent surface drama. Yet such an enterprise also requires—and such a listing only underlines the need for—some single but consistent and comprehensive framework. At a minimum, such a framework is needed to facilitate the exploratory nature of the project. But beyond that, it is also needed to extract larger (and underlying) relationships and distinctions among these nations, while simultaneously disciplining the more dramatic individual examples, so that they become just that, "examples", which fit within (and contribute to) a more general understanding. Imposed successfully, such a framework even raises the possibility of moving to a deeper analytic level, in which additional driving influences—but also the inherent *limits* on any comparison—eventually emerge.

In any case, two simple notions are at the heart of the framework used here: political eras and political orders. A *political era* is, quite simply, a period in which politics revolves around roughly the same continuing substance. It may well be—the chapters that follow certainly suggest—that conflicts over this substance can be additionally grouped, into two further clusters. One of these involves what are essentially issues of national integration. These "cultural and national issues" tap concerns for the character of domestic social life and its relationships with the wider (non-national) world. The other of these involves what are essentially issues of material (re)distribution. These "economic and social-welfare issues" tap concerns for the material well-being of individuals, groups, or social categories.

A *political order* is then a set of key structural elements which shape political behavior—politicking—aimed at influencing these substantive concerns. Again, the chapters which follow would suggest that these influential structures can be found in three general places. The first is the underlying social base for politics, including such traditional aspects as social "cleavages" and social coalitions, as well as less usual elements like geographic and residential dispersion. The second is the intermediary organizations of politics, including political parties and party systems along with major interest groups, but also less usual elements like the organizational focus of social life more generally. And the third of these structural categories is the formal arrangement of governmental institutions themselves, both their electoral systems and their policymaking procedures.

From one side, political eras are unlikely to come into existence, that is, underlying concerns are unlikely to characterize politics for an extended period, if they do not acquire regular and recurrent structural supports. From the other side, the structures which go to constitute a political order—its social divisions, for example, or its party system, or even its basic policymaking arrangements—are not by themselves sufficient to sustain a focus on the same substantive conflicts indefinitely, no matter how solid such an order may appear at a given point in time. It is the interplay between these two grand background elements, between issues and structures, that generates a political dynamic, and shapes the course of politics.

Even then, idiosyncrasies abound, when a small set of political influences, both substantive and structural, are isolated for these individual cases. Yet at a higher level of abstraction, *contingent* interactions between eras and their orders are still inevitably half the product of any such enterprise. Even truly parallel policy problems and parallel social forces, when mixed with an array of differing issue conflicts and differing procedures for policymaking, could hardly conduce toward parallel political dynamics, much less identical outcomes. Nevertheless, many of the major aspects of postwar politics in the G-7 do fall into place—do fall into some larger and more general relationships—when a consistent framework is imposed upon them. These general relationships include:

1. Roughly similar contributions from similar public issues, albeit channeled individually by a national issue *sequence* and shaped individually by the particular operating coalitions which are, in practice, built around that sequence;
2. Powerful similarities (and also differences) emanating from such fa-

miliar and established structural influences as electoral systems and policymaking institutions, constrained, as ever in this analysis, by issue context and *societal* character;
3. The peculiar place of "divided governance," rightly understood— that is, dominant *and cross-cutting* issues *and alliances* —a place often obscured by the specifics of individual conflicts as well as by particular governmental arrangements, yet incipiently present in all these nations.

Despite gains of this sort, the resulting product must remain tentative, genuinely exploratory, in several senses. Neither these nations nor this time period are in any conceivable sense a "sample," not of any larger category of countries nor of any longer sweep of history. As a result, generalizations which they support—similarities or differences, patterns—must be treated principally as a goad to further testing, in other nations and/or other times. More tellingly, the framework of analysis—a loose framework, intended both to facilitate comparison and to allow dominant national characteristics to show through—is by definition both preliminary and only one among many such possibilities. It must thus *derive* its justification, from an ability to organize politics in a usefully comprehensible way and, especially, from an ability to produce additional, comparative insights.

On the other hand, the Group of Seven nations are arguably the major developed democracies, encompassing, as they do, the United States, Japan, Germany, France, Italy, Britain, and Canada. Moreover, their collective purpose—what caused them to be dubbed the "G-7"—is to reach (albeit sporadically) international economic decisions of the greatest potential consequence. To that end, they possess, as only seven among nearly two hundred nations, about 65 percent of the total gross domestic product on planet earth. Nevertheless, it is not just their collective prospect but their preformed collective character which is important here. In a self-consciously exploratory venture, the G-7 represent a way to select and focus upon major nations, without preselecting one or another individual characteristic of their politics as critical to their inclusion, and thus to the substantive findings which result.

Said differently, for a venture which requires comprehensive synthesis of the details of a small number of (national) cases, a focus on the G-7 yields arguably major nations, which have not been preselected with a specific finding in mind. They *are* all developed democracies, restricting comparison in some ways although simultaneously advancing it by way of this same constraint. Indeed, this particular preexisting set of cases has the additional compensating virtue of touching on each of the major developed regions of the world—Western Europe, North America, and East Asia—thereby avoiding the risk that "comparative politics in the developed nations" will implicitly equate to politics in Western Europe, leaving out, most noticeably, the United States and Japan.

The same sorts of things, perhaps with even more bite, can said about a focus on the postwar years. At the beginning, every one of these nations was involved—absorbed—with World War II, and this fact creates an obvious, comparative benchmark. At the end, the apparent demise of the Cold War was widely and instantly recognized as another truly international cut-point. Again, the advantage of these specific boundaries is that they are simultaneously grand and independent of this particular exercise in comparative analysis. Indeed, a focus on the domestic politics of the G-7 nations—Germany *may* yet prove the inescapable exception—would not necessarily yield these particular dates, or arguably even these general events, as internal benchmarks. So, the postwar period too appears to guarantee a substantial span of time, containing evidently major events, which nevertheless does not preselect its own findings. Both this choice of nations and this choice of period are in that sense intended to contribute to, and really to insure, the exploratory nature of the project.

Which is as good a place as any for some further cautionary notes, about the application of our chosen framework to these nations in this period. Most crucially, to say that a political era revolves around the same fundamental and continuing concerns is not the same as saying that the specific issues of daily politics are thereby the same. Surface conflicts obviously change from year to year, even sometimes month to month; the question is whether they reflect—embody—the same underlying concerns. Likewise, to say that a political order is created by a small set of structural factors which shape behavior in dominant (and recurrent) ways is not the same as saying that there is some single dominating influence on national politics, much less that the *same* small set of influences will shape politics across very different nations.

In other words, the fabric of politics remains infinitely rich even within these individual cases, infinitely varied across them. The critical question is whether it is possible to organize this richness into a hierarchy of influences, such that powerful—and again, recurrent—factors are isolated. The chapters which follow will contribute concrete detail and numerous highlighted examples to such a challenge. There are, however, three other implications from proceeding by way of political eras, political orders, and their consequent political dynamics, and these should probably just be underlined at the beginning.

First, this is an inherently (and consciously) synthesizing approach. Individual authors for individual nations are being forced to summarize the flow—the stream—of postwar politics in terms of a minimum of issues and a handful of structures, thereby drawing the product to a relatively high level of abstraction. Done successfully, this yields a single, comprehensive but comprehensible, political portrait. These national portraits, in turn, should have substantial value in their own right, quite apart from further comparisons.

On the other hand, and second, these authors are also being forced to *specify,* within the huge array of materials which must be synthesized for these nations, the particular substantive themes which contribute an ongoing era and the particular structural elements which shape and sustain their orders. Again, done successfully, this requirement should impart a pointed and concrete character to the same analysis, and to its analytic portraits. A succinct overview is not to be purchased at the price of vagueness and omission.

Third, and finally, proceeding in this way provides a conceptual handle on political change itself. What is required of each analysis, in essence, is a focus on: (a) continuities and their sustenance, (b) points at which one composite nevertheless gives way to another, and (c) key aspects of the difference (as well, of course, as some elements of constancy). Any framework is still only as good as its ultimate contribution, but this approach does at least encourage a further focus on change, while providing some designated touchstones through which to evaluate it.

Which proved to be a doubly good thing, given the course of political history while this project was unfolding. The time already seemed propitious, roughly four years ago, to look back across the postwar years. Yet none of the authors would have predicted the scale of surface change even among the G-7, just while this manuscript was moving toward publication:

1. When we began, for example, no Italian government in the postwar period had failed to feature the Christian Democratic party, as its numerical core.
2. When we began, several of our analysts had not been *born* when the Japanese government was last composed of something other than the Liberal Democratic party, by itself.
3. Shortly after we presented our first public drafts, the majority party in Canada, the Conservatives, moved from controlling the government to *possessing* exactly two members of the House of Commons.
4. In a softer echo, the Socialists, then dominant in the National Assembly in France, moved from having control of the government to having an internal debate about their own organizational destiny.
5. Had we begun only months previous to our actual start, we could in

fact have encompassed a fundamental change in the *boundaries* of one of our nations, Germany.

6. Had we waited a year or so longer, we could collectively have watched the United States take split partisan control of government to a new, a further and "higher," plateau.
7. And as we completed the manuscript, British politics tottered—or so all the polls said—on one or another of these analogies as the shape of its own immediate future.

For the political analyst, this constitutes a powerful reminder of the need for humility. More to the analytic point, it constitutes a powerful caution about assuming that any given event of the moment, no matter how large or noisy, reflects the character of a continuing era and its order. Politics in Italy and Japan remain remarkably in flux; politics in Canada, France, and Germany, the United States or Britain, fail to seem fluid only by comparison. On the other hand, these same warnings and reminders only emphasize the need for a carefully constructed, analytically sound interpretation of postwar politics in these nations, organized through a framework which can encompass both substance and structure, both continuity and change. *If we cannot know precisely where the politics of any (or all) of these nations is going, we also cannot hope to make sense of where it goes without some framework, highlighting potentially critical elements and, ideally, offering comparisons across nations and over time.*

With those aspirations, and with this particular framework as a means to work toward them, there did seem a logical sequence for the national chapters that follow. Or at least, informed by an earlier reading of these chapters in draft, an editor could take (a) the structural influence most proximate to politics, namely, the structure of national government itself, along with (b) the historical cut-point inaugurating the analysis, namely, the one which opened the first postwar era in each of these nations, to provide the rationale for a chapter sequence. Accordingly, the greater the institutional continuity and the earlier the date of the first era reaching into the postwar years, the earlier the national chapter falls in this volume.

The United States and Canada both featured continuity not only in the basic institutions of their governments but in the major organizing conflicts associated with them, a continuity stretching back before the Second World War, with the United States actually reaching a few years farther back. The United States and Canada can thus reasonably provide chapters 2 and 3. The United States is the direct responsibility of the editor, Byron Shafer of Oxford University, while Canada belongs, in all its complexity, to Richard Johnston of the University of British Columbia.

Britain offered a similar continuity in the structure of national government, coupled with a sharp break in the substance of politics in the immediate postwar years, while France offered initial continuity on both, *followed by* a fundamental change in the structure of government. Britain and France can therefore reasonably provide chapters 4 and 5. The study of postwar British politics is the responsibility of Andrew Adonis of the *Financial Times*, while France, in all its wondrous convolution, falls to Miriam Feldblum of the University of San Francisco.

The other three nations began the postwar period profoundly anew, each with an entirely new structure of government and a newly democratized practical politics within it. Germany came earliest to the most elementary sign of institutionalization within this democratized politics, the ability to change party control of government internally, so that Germany becomes chapter 6. Jens Hesse, founding director of the new European Center for Comparative Government and Public Policy Research in Berlin, takes on the task of aligning the postwar German story.

Japan actually crossed that same threshold next—full and formal change of party control—though the temporal gap with Germany was large, while the gap with Italy (not otherwise to be outdone in achieving its version of the same transition, again while we were at work) was small. Japan thus became chapter 7, and Stephen Anderson of the International University of Japan takes responsibility for its extended (and suddenly shifting) story, while Italy became chapter 8. Carol Mershon of the University of Virginia closes this string of national chapters by presenting the Italian case, and by re-raising some of the questions about framework and analysis that motivate the entire venture.

Chapter 9, a long synthesizing chapter, then looks at various similarities and differences—comparisons—within and across these nations in this period, though numerous such comparisons do characterize the individual-country chapters as well. The point of such a chapter, in any event, is to (re)align all those individual-country accounts in parallel (and highly condensed) fashion. This permits a wide range of partial comparisons across the G-7 nations; indeed, it almost *makes* some of these, through the simple process of parallel alignment. Along the way, numerous national factors prove to have a cross-national incarnation: the decline of brokerage politics, the rise of cross-cutting issue (and social) tensions, the "taming" of socialist parties, and the reconstitution of underlying coalitions, especially those involving corporate business and rural residents.

This synthesis also leads on, more or less automatically, to a concluding chapter (chap. 10) with two final tasks: to revisit the entire set of G-7 nations—all of them at once—through the vehicle of political eras and political orders, and to say a bit more about the grand relationship between eras and orders as they go about producing a diagnostic political dynamic. On one level, this is a chapter about issue *sequences,* structural *interactions,* and the way that those two grand forces are nearly always inseparable in practice. But on a deeper level, it is an argument that a focus on such alternative summary notions as "convergence" or "divergence" is almost always misplaced, and that the fundamental interaction between eras and orders actually puts limits—inherent limits—on the comparative enterprise.

The result—this volume—also benefited from an array of practical support which proved integral and crucial. Kent Calder at Princeton University and Nelson Polsby at the University of California, Berkeley, were truly generous in helping to assemble the team of G-7 scholars which appears here. The American Political Science Association not only provided a public forum for presenting early drafts of these chapters, but actually helped bring the non-American scholars to its annual meeting. The Andrew W. Mellon Fund at Nuffield College then allowed a subsequent collective session in Oxford, which the Warden, Fellows, and staff of Nuffield were reliably gracious in facilitating. And a small set of other scholars proved amazingly generous in their comments and contributions as the manuscript moved toward publication: Jens Bastian at the London School of Economics; Sudhir Hazareesingh at Balliol College, Oxford; Sidney Tarrow—several times—at Cornell University; and Vincent Wright at Nuffield.

Maureen Baker and Elaine Herman created the physical document itself, and only they share knowledge of its every tribulation. The referees for this ultimate document, Leon Epstein at the University of Wisconsin, Madison, and John Bibby at the University of Wisconsin, Milwaukee, then performed in a fashion which many believe no longer occurs; their comments (and corrections) were marvelously helpful. At the University of Wisconsin Press, the director, Allen Fitchen, was not just initially receptive when the project was broached—inevitably on little more than a prospectus and a prayer—but provided steadfast support throughout, which is also widely thought to have disappeared in the publishing world. Lydia Howarth handled the copyediting with a light but deft touch; Raphael Kadushin and Carol Olsen saw the entire manuscript through to production. The editor has taken the liberty of dedicating the result to the comparativists who first influenced his own thinking.

B. E. S.
October, 1995

2 *Byron E. Shafer*

The United States

To contemporaries, the end of the Second World War must—it certainly should—have seemed a moment of nearly limitless possibility in American politics, with all the promise and all the menace that such possibility implies. The war had been genuinely all-absorbing, so that its end represented a potential, natural break-point in the domestic politics of all the major participants. In any case, returning American soldiers and their families appeared to *want* nothing so much as a return to normalcy, which, in the context of the times, surely meant some condition of life which was neither armed combat nor economic depression.

On its own terms, this historical situation appeared to promise a different, a "postwar," political era. There was, of course, no reason to believe that such an era would be necessarily benign. Internationally, with the end of one major conflict, there were already signs—perhaps seeds—of one or more others, and this time the United States would find it harder to remain uninvolved. Domestically, and in more worrisome terms, there were many cautious analysts who feared (and believed) that the war would prove merely to have been an enforced interim, between the Great Depression which preceded it and a natural return to economic dislocations which had been suppressed but not corrected by worldwide armed conflict.

Despite all that, in the case of the United States, the immediate postwar years (and then a good many years thereafter) were actually to give further expression to a domestic political order called into being in the late 1920s and early 1930s, and institutionalized during the Great Depression and the Second World War. Admittedly, initial postwar politicking was to reinforce a sense of alternative possibilities for the United States, if not akin to those facing Germany, Japan, or Italy, then certainly equivalent to those facing Britain, France, or Canada. Yet within a few years, it would be clear to systematic observers that this was not to be. The opening postwar period was to be essentially of a piece with the prewar and interwar years instead.

Seen in one way, this fact does push the task of isolating the central issues and crucial structures of the postwar period farther back into American history. Seen in another, this same fact makes the second postwar era and order—our era—more impressive for its change, and more demanding in its explanation. New organizing issues and newly influential structures do characterize this second period, and differentiate it from the first. That difference, in turn, sets off a search for the further roots of this change. And the theme of change (or not) returns with particular force at the end of this investigation.

The Late New Deal Era

Whatever the promise of change or continuity inherent in the end of the Second World War and (fingers crossed) of the Great Depression, it was not unreasonable to expect that the reality of that promise would be registered quickly enough in domestic politics. And indeed, domestic politics appeared to offer preconditions for an immediate break. Franklin D. Roosevelt, president for both the New Deal and the Second World War, and the only four-term president in American history, was gone. Harry S. Truman, his successor, was hardly up to his standard in background, experience, or personal appeal. Accordingly, if both the depression and the war had been yet another interim, however dramatic, in the course of American history, the time was apparently ripe to affirm that fact, and to get on with some new political order.[1]

Then as now, the easiest way to test for continuity—or the most obvious way both to register a change and to suggest its emergent character—was by way of partisan electoral outcomes, distinctive patterns in the outcome of elections followed by distinctive patterns in the subsequent jockeying within government. By this measure, the first congressional elections of the genuine postwar period, in 1946, strongly suggested change, with the Republicans wresting control of both houses of Congress from the Democrats, their first such success since 1928. Two years later, Democrat Harry

Truman was to confound any simple and direct extrapolations from this incipient new Republicanism—the United States had surely not returned to the pre–New Deal partisan world—when he held the presidency and regained both houses of Congress. Yet a sense of political fluidity was just as surely sustained, only four years further on, with the victory of Republican Dwight D. Eisenhower for president and his reconquest of both houses of Congress.

On the surface and in its own time, all this might reasonably have betokened a major shift, a changed political era with different issue foci and different structural arrangements to sustain them. By hindsight, however, the immediate postwar period, for all its undeniable upheavals, still appears politically of a piece with what has come to be recognized as the "New Deal Era." From one side, its dominant issue concerns represent, in essence, two surface incarnations of the same underlying focus. From the other, its key political structures continue, attenuated a bit in their impact but otherwise undisturbed, across both domestic and international crises.

At bottom, the central organizing issues for the politics of this (entire) era were to remain the same, revolving principally around social welfare, secondarily around foreign affairs.[2] In the beginning, in the 1930s and into the 1940s, these general issue foci were embodied specifically in struggles over implementation of the welfare state and pursuit of a world war. Later, in the 1950s and into the 1960s, they were embodied instead in struggles over management of an aspiringly full-employment economy and prosecution of a "cold" war. Nevertheless, the central point is that all these struggles still represented particular and episodic embodiments of an underlying and continuing focus.

Moreover, lest this continuity seem dependent on simple substantive interpretation, it is worth noting that it was accompanied—reinforced, really—by an essential extension of the contribution of key political structures. For most of the nation, these key elements of a continuing political order—its diagnostic social cleavages, intermediary organizations, and institutional relationships—must also be traced back to the beginning of the New Deal era. Indeed, for part of the nation, the American South, key elements to a continuing order must actually be traced much farther back, to an earlier crisis which actively highlights continuities with prewar patterns.

Said differently, the period leading up to a true systemic change in American politics, in the 1960s, stretches back somewhere between forty and one hundred years, depending on the geographic region in question. In this stretch, the great event establishing the first of these benchmarks—perhaps still the great event of American history since the Revolution—was, of course, the Civil War. The central policy concern of its aftermath was how to respond to that national conflagration. And the central social division which resulted was regional, pitting South (the former Confederacy) against non-South (the former Union).

The non-south was to move on to other concerns, and a very different political order, within a few generations; the South was not. It is common to summarize the politics which resulted there as the emergence of a "solid South," solidly Democratic at every time and every level, but there was much more to the political order than that.[3] The Civil War did remain a formative experience, and then an explosive symbol, for all sorts of perceived differences from the rest of the nation. These experiences (and that symbol) did appear to counsel regional integrity—unity against a hostile outside world—above all else. And politics was to be organized around that central fact from the 1860s into the 1960s. Yet the classic further elements of a political order were all nevertheless present and operative.

Thus at the social base for politics, almost everyone considered themselves Democrats, with the notable exception of black southerners, who were quickly disfranchised. Among intermediary organizations, a Democratic party which was organized around courthouse rings and dominated by local notables transferred basically conservative demands to the institutions of government. And the conformation of public offices within that government did nothing to introduce differentiation: The South was Democratic presidentially, Democratic congressionally, Democratic gubernatorially, Democratic state-legislatively, and so on. Into the 1960s, it was also customary to assert that this was an additionally conservative democracy, courtesy of the disfranchisement of lower income *whites* which came simultaneously with the disfranchisement of blacks.

For the rest of the nation, the roots of the postwar political order run to a different, and more recent, great event. That event was the Great Depression, and the central policy question was, again inevitably, how to respond. The central social division which accompanied the alternatives was along lines of social class, pitting blue-collar America, the poor, and certain demographic minorities, along with the entire South, against white-collar America, as joined subsequently by (non-southern) farmers. Here too, the resulting divisions were powerfully formative, lasting well beyond direct memories of the critical event itself. Yet here too, there were further consequential distinctions within the accompanying political order.[4]

Thus the Democratic party which resulted was an amalgam of urban machines in the North, volunteer activist branches throughout the country, and the old courthouse rings in the South, joined principally by organized labor among the interest groups, and subsequently by the civil rights organizations. The role of labor was especially noteworthy. This was to be the high point of union membership; union *leadership* was an important secondary source of party finance; and union electoral organization became an increasingly important adjunct to (even substitute for) the official Democratic party.

The Republican party retained some rural rings of its own in the North, but actually moved earlier than the Democrats—albeit more from necessity than from choice—to become what would now be recognized as a contemporary, activist-based, political party, joined by big and little business, though less distinctively than with labor (and later racial minorities) for the Democrats. It was actually small business, rather than corporate business, which provided organized-group input to party officialdom. Yet corporate business remained a serious (and decidedly partisan) source of Republican party funding, and party officials tapped this link not just for finance but for "blue-ribbon" contenders for public office.

National institutions of government both responded to these other elements and helped to shape them, thereby contributing further to the composite political order. Again by hindsight, the critical characteristic of these institutions in the late New Deal era—highlighted by a comparison to the same institutions in the (subsequent) era of divided government— was the institutional power they reserved for formal officeholders, both electorally and operationally. In the case of the presidency, these crucial intermediary elites were the party officeholders who were still central to the nomination of presidents. In the case of Congress, they were instead its internal, organizational officeholders, most especially its committee chairmen.

Nominating arrangements were, in fact, part and parcel of the explanation for why presidential candidates concentrated on communicating modest differences around a national consensus, in social welfare and foreign affairs.[5] A successful Republican like Dwight Eisenhower did not mount an assault on the welfare state; he simply promised to manage it less expensively. A successful Democrat like John Kennedy did not mount an assault on the Cold War; he took pains to remind his audiences that Democrats were, in the main, equally committed. Indeed, while no Republican presidential candidate ever appeared to the left of his Democratic opponent on social welfare, Democratic candidates could appear to the right of their Republican opponents in foreign affairs, as with Harry Truman in 1948, or John Kennedy in 1960.

In private, party activists were already showing signs of displeasure with both sets of presidential responses—Republican moderation on social welfare, Democratic moderation on foreign affairs—which was a particular problem for the more activist-based Republican party. Yet nominating procedures remained sufficient to keep decisions in the hands of party officeholders, and these party officials normally preferred a cautious strategy premised on the demands of victory within an established order. Such a general description for the 1950s, in any case, remained consistent with its counterpart of the 1940s, rather than with some distinguishing postwar break.

Congress produced different but reinforcing incentives.[6] In truth, representatives and senators were already becoming comparatively immune to individual upsets at the polls by the 1950s, so that the greatest threat to their reelection had become an unsuccessful presidential candidate of their *own* party. This meant that congressmen needed to worry about the identity of "their" presidential nominee. Otherwise, what it implied was that the crucial political structures affecting their fortunes were internal, by-products of the formal procedures through which Congress transacted its official business.

In Congress, the key operative positions were its formal committee chairmanships, as they had been for decades. Throughout the 1950s and into the 1960s, however, those who ascended to these key positions, after a lengthy internal apprenticeship, were ordinarily individuals who had been actively schooled in the central concerns of the New Deal era. They were also disproportionately southern Democrats, whose collective factional fate was to serve as a nicely concentrated microcosm of the larger change which arrived in the 1960s. Yet regardless of regional origin, these committee chairmen, too, ordinarily preferred incremental tinkering with the policy core of the New Deal era.

The most consequential result of all this (and again, the simplest analytic handle on its continuity or change) was a recurring pattern of partisan outcomes.[7] In this, *Democrats* were the statistical preference to win the presidency, as they had been since 1932, and to bring both houses of Congress along with them. Indeed, the unity and vitality of the Democratic coalition was often the central story of electoral politics. Yet even in successful Democratic years, Republicans remained a majority in substantial geographic areas. As a result, they could potentially build upon these areas to secure the presidency whenever they had an especially attractive candidate, and he too could hope to drag Congress along to Republican partisan majorities.

On the other hand, these Republican presidencies—and even more these Republican Congresses—were individually based and short-lived. Republicans could not hope to *hold* the presidency beyond the tenure of a single successful incumbent, and their congressional reach, in such an environment, was all the more tenuous. Moreover, while the ability of Republicans to secure the presidency at all was obviously a postwar (or perhaps just "post-Roosevelt"?) gain, a continuing Democratic dominance emphasized continuity with the prewar years, as did the tendency of the presidency and Congress to move as a unit electorally—as, indeed, did everything from the dominant issues of partisan politics through the continuing character of the political parties and interest groups which (continued to) pursue those issues.

The Passing of an Old Order

The factors sustaining the late New Deal order were sufficient to maintain an essential continuity, then, with the years preceding the end of the Second World War. They were not, on the other hand, sufficient to sustain a New Deal era indefinitely. The 1960s were in fact to see the end of that era and the coming of one quite different. The forces producing this change were themselves sufficiently complex—and sufficiently open to argument—that they merit separate, subsequent sections. But the central elements of a new political order, at least with the benefit of hindsight, are easy to set out. Indeed, the point at which differences between the old order and the new crystallized is even easy to locate.

By hindsight, the electoral and institutional outcomes of 1964 still belonged, thematically and structurally, to the late New Deal era. By contrast, the outcomes of 1968 belonged to what would come to be known as the "era of divided government." At the time, there was no way of knowing that the composite outcome of the 1968 election was the key to the beginning of a new political pattern rather than evidence of simple deviation from the old, courtesy of a major split within the Democratic party, which allowed Republican Richard M. Nixon to succeed in wresting away the presidency but to fail in bringing a Republican Congress along with him. Precisely because this was the first time since before the American Civil War that an incoming president had failed to bring *either* house of Congress to a partisan majority with him, analysts could be forgiven for treating the result not as a diagnostic portent requiring fresh interpretation, but as a particularly dramatic blip.

A quarter-century later, none of that analysis remains tenable. For there is not just a new political order with different structural supports, nor even just an associated era with different substantive issues. There is also a different array of diagnostic outcomes within it, distinct from those following on from the New Deal order. The single simplest testimonial to the existence of the change remains, as ever, its characteristic pattern of partisan electoral results, different from its predecessor and stable in its own right. But the distinguishing feature of the change in an operational sense is a related set of key structural elements and dominant issue concerns. Seen in one way, these are the most immediate cause of altered partisan patterns. Seen in another, they are the product which frames a new political dynamic.

That change is present, at once, in the social base for politics, in the interaction of issue divisions and societal cleavages to be found there. It is probably present most dramatically in the character and role of what have come to be known as "cultural issues" in American politics. These are concerns with the basic—even the defining—character of American life. They touch on such matters as public order, the public role of religion, child-rearing practices, educational orientations, crime and punishment, abortion and euthanasia, public deportment, community prerogatives, and on and on.[8]

Two things, however, were especially noteworthy about the arrival of these concerns on the political stage. One was a simple extrapolation from their appearance. By definition, either a public consensus on appropriate values in these matters or an elite consensus on keeping them out of politics had disintegrated sufficiently to bring them—with a vengeance. But second, and more to the practical point, was the way that public positions on such cultural issues did not coincide, socially, with public positions on the old economic and social-welfare matters which had been central to the formation (and maintenance) of the New Deal order.

Which is to say: The progressive position on these matters did not coincide, socially, with the liberal position on economics, as the traditional side on cultural issues did not coincide with the conservative side on economics. Those favoring liberalism on social welfare were as likely to favor traditionalism on cultural values; those favoring progressivism on cultural values were as likely to favor conservatism on social welfare; and so on. It was not that these two great issue domains were inversely related. It was merely that cultural values now claimed a major role in American politics, and citizen positions on these matters were effectively *un*related to those on economic welfare.

Foreign affairs, in fact, was much the same.[9] The old, apparent, bipartisan consensus was also effectively gone. While there remained room for debate about whether this was principally a mass, principally an elite, or essentially a joint change, the same two crucial facts remained at its center. First, an operating consensus was again effectively missing. The extent and character of American involvements abroad, the degree and character of mobilization for such involvements at home, the proper orientation toward various categories of other nations—the role of the United States, and especially of American *values,* in the world outside—all these were now open to public debate.

And second, once more, the line dividing those emphasizing accommo-

dationism and international self-restraint from those emphasizing nationalism and active pursuit of American values did not coincide, socially,
with the line dividing those supporting extended social welfare and active
domestic government from those preferring limited social welfare and
limited government more generally. Said differently, the accommodationist side on foreign policy did not coincide with the liberal side on economic issues, just as the nationalist side on foreign policy did not coincide
with the conservative side on domestic economics.

The further result, inevitably, was that there were now *two* great issue-
areas to American politics: social welfare and economic benefit on the
one hand, versus cultural values and foreign affairs on the other. Moreover, there were now cross-cutting and inconsistent public majorities on
them. There was still room for debate about the roots of this situation.
Indeed, there were good grounds for arguing that public wishes were not
the critical force in creating it. But it *was* a social—and soon to be a
political—fact, the fact of two distinct majority coalitions. And that fact
was to be reflected nearly everywhere.[10]

Curiously, for a party system whose main members were often accused
of preferring to control government at the cost of programmatic concerns,
the two main American political parties neither hesitated nor fudged
when they came to address this newer and more complex world of policy
issues. What they did, in essence, was attempt to impose a *theoretical*
(rather than a social) consistency upon it: Democrats to the left on both of
these issue-areas, Republicans similarly to the right. Yet what this represented was not so much a conscious new electoral strategy, some new
means for winning control of government in a changed issue environment. Instead, it was a reflection of major structural changes: in the organizational character of the two main parties; in the composition of the
universe of interest groups around them; and in the values propelled to
(and held at) the center of politics, courtesy of the activists who increasingly operated both these parties and these groups.

In the analytic sense, these are the basic elements—parties, interest
groups, and activists—linking social cleavages to governmental arrangements, and partially transforming a composite order in the process. In a
much more practical sense, they are the organizations and individuals that
would have to *act upon* an initial deviation, like that of 1968, either to
return it to preceding patterns or to insure that this became, not a deviation, but the continuing shape of the political future. They are thus the
main landmarks in a geography of political intermediation for the United
States. They were likely, at the very least, to register any number of other
changes in this landscape. They were entitled to produce further direct
shifts of their own, when they themselves changed.

Among these basic elements, political parties remained closest to practical politics. Yet American political parties, in the newly emerging era, were no longer organizational "machinery" in any useful sense.[11] Instead, the two major political parties had both come to be built around—in effect, to be —networks of independent, issue-based activists. This trend actually began earlier on the Republican side. By the late 1950s, the Republican party was already an activist operation, featuring officeholders who were motivated principally by ideological positions or policy concerns, rather than by pecuniary goals or solidary attachments. Ideology and policy are hardly negligible incentives, and the Republican party had hardly withered. But it had become a different organizational creature than it was at the start of the New Deal era.

When the same tendencies then conquered the Democratic party within the following decade, the reconstruction of a party *system* was effectively complete. That system then had further consequences for a new political order, not just in what it contributed, but in what it failed to contribute. Into the 1950s, there was not only a societal consensus on economics and social welfare as the major dimensions of American politics. There was also serious party organization, especially in the dominant Democratic party, to see that politics remained centered on economic well-being. After the 1960s, it was not just that this underlying consensus had frayed. The sort of party organization associated with it, one dedicated to resisting a shift from social welfare and economic benefit to foreign affairs and cultural values, simply no longer existed.

This situation had, in truth, been evolving for a very long time. The late nineteenth century was actually the great period of assaults on organized political parties: by way of procedural reforms like the primary election, intended to remove control of elective office from internal party structures, and by way of substantive reforms like the civil service code, intended to remove control of administrative office from those same party structures. The impact of these reforms progressed gradually across the twentieth century, and parties as organizations were not without ways of fighting back. Yet by the 1960s, especially now that government itself had become the public protector and provider of last resort, the full structural impact had finally come home to roost. Parties as organizational machinery were nearly gone from American politics.

In practice, on the other hand, this disappearance may have mattered less than a single line of argument would suggest. For the possibility of organizational resistance—an elite insistence, by party officials, that politics remain focused on the central issues of the New Deal era—was by this time being undermined by much more than change in party organization. In fact, the newer and more vital *interest groups* had also arisen in exactly the new alternative policy areas, namely, cultural values and foreign affairs.[12] Which is to say: Organizationally changed or not, American political parties would presumably have found themselves increasingly surrounded by (and then inevitably allied with?) organized interests which were dedicated to moving in new directions, directions characterizing a new political era.

That the older, established, economic interest groups were in increasing disarray, most notably at the presidential level but really in their links to political parties generally, only magnified this effect. The old order, centered on social welfare and service provision, had been buttressed symbiotically by interest groups with an essentially economic focus: by organized labor on the Democratic side and by corporate business and farm organizations among Republicans. By the 1960s, this situation too was undergoing change.

The Democratic party had long been inclined to describe itself as a coalition of interests. Yet by the 1960s, this coalition was both expanding and shifting. The shift probably came first to public attention by way of various groups protesting the Vietnam War. Yet it became institutionalized, more effectively if less dramatically, in a veritable array of organizations centered on such matters as feminism, peace, environmentalism, homosexuality, and so on. At the same time, organized labor, the biggest of the interest-group players in the old universe, was simultaneously shrinking in the aggregate and showing new internal stresses, especially its own blue-collar/white-collar divisions.

Less widely recognized, however—and perhaps less extreme but surely moving in the same direction—was a counterpart shift within the Republican party. The great traditional Republican interest group, corporate business, was likewise in decline in internal party circles. Corporate Republicans had always operated indirectly, through simple deference buttressed by an ability to provide campaign financing and "blue ribbon" candidates. Such deference was inevitably in decline in an activist political party. Yet the detachment of corporations (and corporate leaders) from their localities, along with a concern for retaining bipartisan candidate "access," just as surely accelerated the trend.

The Republican party did continue to characterize itself as a party undivided by "special interests," and the declining profile of corporate Republicans was even, theoretically, consistent with this view. Regardless, such consistency was swamped by other changes, including most especially the fact that the really symbolic incarnations of the shift in interest groups associated with the era of divided government were at least as Republican as they were Democratic. The religiously fundamentalist Christian Coalition, for example, or the culturally traditionalist Eagle Forum, to take only two products of an equally fertile partisan soil, put a distinctly Republican stamp on the general shift away from economic or service organizations and toward those built around cultural divisions or foreign policy.

The roots of such a shift may ultimately run to the deepest of societal changes, only implicitly political in their nature. But the important point is that the newer groups were, ineluctably, pressing both parties *toward* the new political order. Finally, it must be noted that they no longer had to press very hard. For it was precisely cultural values and foreign affairs which were motivating the activists who did the work of modern political parties.[13] Said differently: As parties became increasingly dependent on such activists, and as activists were increasingly nurtured by the new universe of interest groups, they made their concerns, increasingly and ineluctably, integral to political party operations.

The Era of Divided Government

There was thus an insistent tension at the heart of a new political order: between two socially cross-cutting opinion majorities in the general public, of course, but further stressed by two political parties which put those underlying issue-areas together in yet a different fashion. Moreover, this was a world without some simple and inherent resolution. For it was a world where one of these parties continued to have a normal and presumptive majority on one of the two dominant issue-areas (the Democrats on issues of material redistribution—on economics and social welfare), while the other party *acquired* a normal and presumptive majority on the other (the Republicans on issues of national integration—on cultural values and foreign affairs).

As a result, it was the institutions of American national government, the third abstract element of any political order, which were to—which had to—provide a resolution. One aspect of this, the propensity to have split partisan control of governmental institutions as more than just a transitional outcome, was to give the new era its name: the era of divided government.[14] But it was really the interlocking combination of three key structural elements which would give it a lasting political character. The combination of cross-cutting social majorities at the bottom, theoretically parallel policy offerings in the middle, and nationally distinctive policy-making arrangements at the top was really the underpinning to a new political order. And this was destined not to go away even under unified partisan control.

The governmental institutions at the heart of this new order did not, of course, change in their basic conformation. Yet it quickly became clear that an existing constitutional arrangement had the potential to work very differently in the face of different cleavages, differentially transmitted. Indeed, it became clear, in the aftermath of new and cross-cutting issue divisions, that the individual institutions of American government already possessed a certain inherent and latent relevance to the grand issue-areas of an incipient new political order. They *permitted* all the possible partisan variants of governmental control, from unified Democratic to unified Republican with all the stops in-between. But they favored some over others, and in this institutional favoritism lay not just an explanation of the distribution of various partisan outcomes in the new political era. In this institutional favoritism lay also the continuing resolution of other structural tensions more generally.

Institutional predispositions for a changed contribution to the political order were actually a fact long recognized in other contexts. Thus the presidency had long been the logical focus for those most concerned with foreign policy.[15] The Constitution itself gave the president primacy, through his place as commander-in-chief and through his responsibility for negotiating international agreements. This primacy was powerfully reinforced by extraconstitutional developments in the modern era, that is, by World War II, the Cold War, the rise of a standing military establishment, and the coming of numerous multilateral defense agreements. Congress was subsequently to reassert itself somewhat, in the Vietnam years and after, but it was never to be more than an augmented influence on essentially presidential initiatives.

That said, there remained a crucial further distinction within Congress, where in matters of foreign relations, the Senate was surely more consequential than the House. It too had relevant constitutional powers, in the ability to approve most of the (presidential) personnel of foreign affairs and to pass upon any (presidentially negotiated) international agreements. By comparison with the House, it also possessed an established tradition of restraining presidents informally. It was the Senate Foreign Relations Committee, not the House Foreign Affairs Committee, which was intermittently the crucial site for assaults on executive power in the postwar period.

For cultural issues, roughly the same could be said. The institutional situation in this realm may seem less immediately obvious, but that has more to do with the disinclination of policy analysts to think of cultural issues in institutional terms than with anything intrinsic to these issues themselves.[16] Once again, the presidency was the logical focus for those concerned with cultural values, since it blended inherent formal and informal advantages over Congress. Because the *Supreme Court* was so often the ultimate custodian of policy outcomes in this realm, the constitutional powers of nomination to the Court and management of the Justice Department again made a president inherently better able to shape—or at least stand up to—this ultimate custodian. Even more to the political point, a single chief executive was just far better able to symbolize public values and moral leadership than was any given member of Congress, much less that multiheaded collectivity as a whole.

Congress, of course, did not have to abandon the field entirely, as occasional (and normally ineffective) insurrections over Court decisions on such matters as metropolitan busing could attest. But again, within Congress, there remained a crucial secondary distinction. Precisely because so many of the cultural issues of the modern era were initiated within, or critically propelled by, the Supreme Court, the constitutional powers of the Senate to advise and consent on Court nominations kept it inherently closer to these issues. So, probably, did the simple higher "public profile" of senators as opposed to House members, reflecting not just larger districts and a smaller cohort but, perhaps especially, much greater media attention and thus the prospect of sharing some of the same symbolic potential as the presidency.

For issues of social welfare and economic well-being, however, the situation was radically different. Here too, differing institutional predispositions had always been incipiently present, at least through the preceding political order. Yet here, these institutional attractions—for issues of welfare and service provision—produced the exact opposite result. In truth, at the inception of the New Deal, the presidency had been the premier institution in this realm as well. But by the 1960s, Congress had successfully reestablished itself.[17] It was congressmen who were now most deeply invested in the shaping of social-welfare policy, and they found they did not have to surrender this primacy. Moreover, this time, the *House* retained an advantage over the Senate within Congress.

Constitutionally, the very structure of Congress meant that its members were charged with the well-being of a specifically demarcated locale. Practically, the nature of congressional decision-making, premised on the notion of aggregating district wishes, surely reinforced that constitutional charge. In any case, the members of Congress collectively had long since built very practical links between welfare administration and congressional authorization, focusing their institution on the new social-welfare bureaucracy. And here again, the structure of the House, with greater substantive specialization by individual members and greater collective respect for the products of its committee system, added an extra House-based focus.

Seen from the other side, if an individual district relied heavily upon a particular program or needed a particular change in a given governmental formula, then Congress was likely to be a better target than the presidency, as the House was likely to be an even better target than the Senate. Said differently, if the coming of a standing military establishment had sealed the constitutional primacy of the executive in foreign policy, then the coming of an entrenched social-welfare bureaucracy had furthered the institutional primacy of the legislature in the same way.

Moreover, what was true of social welfare as a policy realm was even more true of the provision of direct—pecuniary and divisible—services and benefits.[18] Congress had always been a more plausible ombudsman and special pleader for these than the presidency, and again, the House more so than the Senate. Yet if formula-based legislation had constrained some aspects of the traditional "pork barrel," the burgeoning growth of government had facilitated others. Moreover, the last congressional generation, of individual senators but (again) especially individual representatives, had learned to place an operational premium on the personal rewards inherent in good "constituency service."

These institutional predispositions of Congress met a reinforcing, counterpart, citizen logic. For most citizens, when they needed a particular product from government, it made much more sense to contact their senator than their president, more still to contact their representative than their senator. This being the case, each great underlying (and cross-cutting) set of public policy issues appeared to have a (comparatively) appropriate home: foreign policy and cultural values with the presidency more than Congress, social welfare and service provision with Congress more than the presidency, and further distinctions along exactly the same lines between the two houses within Congress.

All this was still a "governing logic" somewhat removed from the experiences (and judgements?) of the average voter, and thus requiring substantial intermediation to make it a major influence on the structure of a continuing era of divided government. But in fact, there was a powerful "electoral logic" which linked these voters to those institutions directly, at least in the aggregate. And because it was precisely parallel to those same institutional predispositions—reinforced by, but especially reinforcing them—this *electoral* influence completed the order institutionalizing a larger era.

An electoral contribution began, abstractly, with the simple size of individual constituencies. The constituency for the presidency was, of course, the entire nation. In American politics, this was the only institution for which that was true, but in the era of divided government, the more important fact was that this was the one institution which could not, in principle, escape tensions from the two great (but cross-cutting) majorities in national public opinion. Democratic candidates could still emphasize their best issues; Republican candidates could even more easily emphasize theirs; but the specific components of many presidential campaigns would surely force both candidates to deal with both domains.

At the other end of the scale, the House of Representatives had the smallest districts, districts which, by virtue of being less than one-four-hundredth of the nation, were also far more homogeneous on average. As a result, House members could, quite reasonably, hope to escape the cross-pressures intrinsic to a presidential contest: many districts would present automatic—and obvious—majority preferences on both great issue-areas. Senate districts, finally, covered much of the intervening gamut, being identical with House districts in the smallest states, the equivalent of many independent nations in the largest.[19] In the aggregate, then, they belonged in-between.

That was still a fairly abstract electoral logic. The actual history of American politics since the New Deal era then gave it some very concrete implications, with a very genuine bite in an era of divided government. From the inception of the New Deal onward, there had always been more self-identified Democrats than Republicans in the general public, and while this gap narrowed across the last quarter-century, it never threatened to close. In the era of divided government, however, two further implications followed immediately from this fact. First, the majority party was disproportionately more likely to control those offices with a more homogenous—a less inherently competitive—electoral base, which meant the Democrats rather than the Republicans. And second, when there *was* unified partisan control of all major governmental offices, it was far more likely to be in Democratic than in Republican hands.

In an era of great but countervailing national majorities, it was presidential candidates, abstractly, who could not escape addressing those majorities and their concerns. By itself, this did not obviously shape *partisan* fortunes. Yet because Democrats were in fact the majority *party* in terms of mass partisan preferences, they could have expected to win the presidency in the absence of such cross-pressures. The presence of those cross-pressures was thus an automatic boon to Republicans for the presidency; this change alone contributed an obvious diminution in Democratic presidential prospects.

At the other end of the political system, it was House candidates, abstractly, who could best hope to escape these same pressures.[20] Yet because there were more Democrats than Republicans overall, but also because the present party system had been formed (in the New Deal era) around economic and welfare issues (where the Democrats retained their national majority), the House was especially likely to be Democratic. In this, congressmen from Democratic districts who found themselves with contrary (conservative) majorities on cultural and national issues were free—as presidential candidates were not—just to adopt the dominant (cultural/national) preference of their district, and thus insulate themselves from Republican challenges. In the process, these Democratic congressmen contributed a continuing (and heavy) Democratic anchor to the system. Senators, as ever, then found themselves largely arrayed between these two opposite environments.

Even then—an important, final, cautionary note—these were still only institutional and electoral *predispositions*. That is, they were contributory, not determinative. They suggested that split partisan control with Republican presidencies and Democratic congresses was the most likely outcome in an era with this structural character, and that unified Democratic control was the most likely alternative. Nevertheless, all four split or unified options remained possible in principle. Indeed, the logical response to general public disappointment with unified Democratic government at the time of a mid-term election was split partisan control in the other direction, with a Democratic president but a Republican congress.[21]

Substance and Structure

When all these elements came together—policy majorities, party programs, and institutional contributions—a change between orders had effectively appeared. In the narrowest sense, these congruent structural changes *constituted* the proximate explanation for the institutionalization of a new political era. Yet it is only when key structural changes are blended—rejoined—with what became critical shifts in the substantive content of public issues that it is possible to see how a new political dynamic arrived, more comprehensively and more permanently. Only then, when structural and substantive shifts are combined, do the immediate roots of a comprehensive change stand revealed.

Such a process might still have been disrupted, in principle, by the forceful imposition of other "great issues," so that the incipient organizing concerns for a new era were, in practice, overwhelmed from the outside. Just as it might have been disrupted by further structural shifts, not even initially rooted in matters explicitly political, which then caused a political order to work differently yet again. When the issue environment for American politics proved instead to reinforce these concerns, a basic change was on its way to effective institutionalization. When this environment met consistent and additionally reinforcing structural adaptations, that change was effectively complete.

Obvious and immediate issue candidates for stimulating a *deviation* from the political order of the late New Deal, by way of the election of 1968, were easy enough to identify. This was, after all, the high point of

Vietnam malaise in American life, and if public opinion on policy alternatives remained remarkably imperspicuous throughout the nomination and election campaigns of 1968, the simple fact of deep internal divisions over Vietnam was nevertheless sufficient to devastate the Democratic party.[22] Which is to say: appropriate pursuit of the war in Vietnam was surely the leading issue in foreign affairs; there was no reasonable way to cast it as a Democratic benefit.

The 1968 election was also the nearest subsequent presidential contest to serious and extended racial rioting in major American cities. There are analysts who believe that the civil rights movement itself, before any riotous degradation, had begun to cause a shift, an effectively cultural shift, between the two political parties. In any case, it would have been difficult to insulate a concern for the character of American life from a concern about American race riots at the time, and such concerns could hardly benefit the Democrats, the party in power and the party of racial minorities.[23] This was all the more true when public attitudes toward protest in general—civil rights protest, but antiwar protest even more— were added to the equation. Cultural issues, too, were playing powerfully Republican.

In such a (dramatic) context, on the other hand, it is all too easy to lose sight of the continuation of public preferences in economic and social-welfare matters, and of genuinely impressive testimonials to that continuation. This was, after all, the immediate aftermath of the second greatest increment to the welfare state in all of American history, under the banner of the Great Society. If many Democratic elites were determined to go farther, and if Republican elites were just recovering the courage to criticize these programs for going too far, the general public had actually supported most, and would continue (to this day) to support many programs.[24] Needless to say, there was nothing in evidence to suggest a sudden uptick in public desires that government not provide further, divisible and *personal* services and benefits.

A "Nixon deviation," then—a single election and perhaps even a single reelection in which Republicans captured the presidency but Democrats held (both houses of) Congress—seems entirely plausible, given the historical stimuli. The dramatic flash points for said deviation, however, in the Vietnam War, urban riots, and the Great Society, could hardly have continued to underpin the same general outcome for the next quarter-century, and indeed they did not. Accordingly, further plausible causes for a change of political era, by way of dominant issue-areas and key structural factors, remain essential to any explanation for the larger change, from the late New Deal *era* to the *era* of divided government.

Half of an explanation for the institutionalization of this change, albeit the more problematic half, does lie with the continuation of an expanded, newly dominant set of issue-areas. For there was in fact to be a succession of substantively related conflicts, in the realms of foreign affairs, cultural values, and social welfare. Yet these were unlikely, even in principle, to be a sufficient explanation for continuing change. Or at least, the preceding New Deal era had been sustained by an interlocking set of dominant issues and structural influences, so that there was an initial presumption that a successor would not be sustained—could not be institutionalized— unless differing issue concerns found differing (and sustaining) structural supports.

Nevertheless, there *were* critical elements of issue continuity, and these deserve emphasis. In foreign affairs, Vietnam as an issue actually lasted through the second Nixon administration. Each subsequent presidency then produced diagnostic foreign policy issues where nationalist Republicans could confront accommodationist Democrats, and where a nationalist public majority could express its convictions. The Iran hostage crisis for Jimmy Carter; mini-conflicts like Grenada and Libya for Ronald Reagan, plus his eight-year sparring match with the Soviet Union; mini-conflicts like Panama for George Bush, along with the far more serious Gulf War: these certainly contributed a string of consistent, reinforcing stimuli.[25]

The realm of cultural affairs was arguably as consistent, and more extreme. Vietnam protest and self-conscious "countercultural" initiatives also continued for some years after the 1968 election. Yet the cleavages associated with early divisions over progressive versus traditionalist cultural values were, throughout this period, constantly refreshed, gradually broadened, and probably in fact crystallized by a series of Supreme Court decisions. On criminal rights, on the public role of religion, on private morality, on community prerogatives, on questions literally of life and death, the Court enunciated a string of policies—and pursued a set of values— which were not shared by large portions of the American public.[26]

Yet in matters of public preference, what did not change was perhaps as consequential as what did. If cultural divisions, as a dominant and institutionalized concern, were effectively new to postwar politics, and if foreign policy divisions began to operate differently, the old economic divisions continued on, in easily recognizable form. Curiously, Richard Nixon appeared to understand this. The United States came as close as it has ever come to a guaranteed incomes policy under Nixon, through his Family Assistance Plan. In essence, this was the great Republican effort to accommodate public preferences on social welfare without augmenting the bureaucracy of the welfare state—and thus, just possibly, to create an institutionally comprehensive, new Republican majority.

Ronald Reagan, however, and then George Bush after him, showed no inclination to continue that effort.[27] Indeed, both produced evidence of continuity in economic and welfare attitudes. From one side, this was manifested in a continuing broad hostility to social welfare and service provision on the part of the active Republican party. From the other, it was registered in a continuing dedication by the general public to basic social programs—and hence to *Democratic* party positions here. Reagan actually took some tentative initiatives "against" social security, the ultimate bedrock of the American welfare state, in the course of trying to do something about budgetary entitlements; public reaction was fast—and furious. Bush, in his efforts to manage a budgetary deficit and avert a recession, flirted compulsively with tax reforms that threatened to reduce the progressivity of taxation, thereby risking reinforcement of public perceptions of the Republican party as the "party of the rich."

Nevertheless, these substantive continuities again provide only half an explanation for the entrenchment of a new political era. For in practical terms, day by day, these successor issues were inevitably joined by many others. At best, these others were dust in the eyes of the systematic observer. At worst, they ran in contrary directions, so that there was no inherent reason—no reason inherent solely to the sum total of individual issues of the day—why one or another should come to sustain a new political era. What that required, as in the preceding (New Deal) era, was a set of structural supports which helped to explain why certain issues were responsible for producing and reproducing the diagnostic pattern of partisan control of government, while other issues were structurally irrelevant, just "noise."

In fact, a search for the key structural supports of this new and diagnostic outcome, and thus for the further elements of change propelling them, can be focused very quickly. Public positions on the dominant issue-areas of the era of divided government probably did become more polarized in the new era. Yet there is no compelling reason to believe that public majorities on these issues actually shifted. In the same way, countervailing majorities now battened onto different institutions within the (same) national government: usually, foreign affairs and cultural values onto the presidency, social welfare and service provision onto Congress; sometimes, the reverse. Yet there was even less reason to believe that these institutions had shifted, at least recently, in their comparative receptivity to such issues.

What had shifted, instead, was the *partisan linkage* among issue-areas, public majorities, and governmental institutions, such that the phenomenon of countervailing partisan majorities both came into being and found an available institutional focus. And at the core of this changed linkage, of course, lay a congruent shift in political parties, interest groups, and activist preferences within parties and groups. In the era of divided government, then:

1. There was not just a steady stream of individual issues in the realms of national integration and material (re)distribution, a stream which might in principle have served to extract split partisan control of national institutions of government from countervailing public majorities.
2. There was also—and essentially—a powerful predisposition on the part of those who were most active in partisan politics to select out precisely these issue concerns and to place them at the center of party affairs, while *recombining them in a fashion inconsistent with mass public preferences.*

Said differently, there was no inherent need for a stable constitutional structure to convert the Republicans into the party of cultural traditionalism or the Democrats into the party of cultural progressivism. Just as there was no self-evident need for social cleavages to do so: there appeared to be as many (if not more) cultural traditionalists among the Democratic, as opposed to the Republican, rank and file. Yet once the two parties *had* reoriented themselves along these additional lines, previously incipient institutional incentives and previously irrelevant social cleavages could join these new partisan connections—and forge a new and continuing order.

Indeed, the simultaneous arrival of party organizations as networks of issue activists, along with this recombination of activist issue preferences, was perhaps the only way to explain such otherwise anomalous phenomena as the role of, for example, abortion attitudes in national party affairs. How else explain the fact that in the era of divided government, one could find almost no anti-abortion delegates at a Democratic National Convention, while the pro-abortion minority at a Republican Convention felt constrained to hide its preferences, despite the fact that this issue split the mass base of each party almost identically? Yet if, in the era of divided government, cultural values (along with foreign affairs) generated activism, the situation ceased instantly to be anomalous.[28]

In the process, the institutionalization of cultural and national cross-pressures became assured. With one recurring caveat: these remained *cross*-pressures because the public did not surrender its (fundamentally liberal) preferences on social welfare and service provision. It is the cross-cutting partisan character of these dominant issue-areas, then, along with their differential social bases and differential attachment to major institutions of national government, which effectively sustained a new political era, and converted the putative "Nixon deviation" into the first incarnation of a new and soon-to-be institutionalized political era. Yet the underlying cross-pressures continued even when there was unified partisan control of government, and it is this fact which explains the crucial difference between unified Democratic administrations in the late New Deal era and "unified" Democratic government in the era of divided government.

Deeper Roots?

There is, in principle, no limit to the search for further causes—deeper roots—to major political change. Indeed, having isolated a set of apparent driving elements for the break between political eras, the analyst is implicitly encouraged to go on and ask about further stimuli producing change in these key elements themselves. Moreover, an all-purpose list of available candidates instantly presents itself. Economic restructuring, international relations, technological discovery, media evolution, even demographic shifts—all these grand possibilities are reliably present in the developed nations, and specific applications from one or another could in principle be decisive.

On the other hand, the great risk in all such "further explanations" lies in their very generality—their all-encompassing character, its simultaneous omnipresence and vagueness, and a consequent ability to "cause" whatever happens, in whichever direction it transpires. Indeed, the case of the postwar United States will provide a particularly apt example. Better, then, to constrain such an examination from the start, with a focus on the next-most-proximate causal steps and, here, on a more explicitly political chain of explanation as well. In this way, any putative next causal links should still be capable of precise specification. At the same time, genuinely grand background influences should not fail to enter, when they have pointed and specific roles to play.

By these standards, two leading candidates for a deeper influence on the break between political eras in the postwar United States come immediately to attention. Both sit at the boundary between social and political change. Both run consistently across the postwar period. Both are capable of highly specific treatment. And both, in practice, operate in an empirically clear direction, despite theoretical possibilities of much greater variety. One is a national trend in partisan affiliation, a trend with powerful implications both for partisan homogeneity and for issue preferences within both parties. The other is a regional trend in economic growth, a trend compressing two grand political shifts, explosively, while converting its region into the stereotypical home of split partisan preferences.

The first of these, the national trend, began with partisan attachments in the general public. The Great Depression and then the New
Deal, conjoint events which launched an extended "New Deal era,"
had been accompanied critically by a sharp shift in the balance of partisan identifications at the social base for American politics. From a
world with an effective Republican majority, there was, in short order,
a world with a demonstrated Democratic majority instead. More surprisingly, despite some resurgence in the fortunes of Republican *candidates,* this trend toward Democratic identifiers actually continued into
the postwar period.[29]

In other words, as older (and more Republican) cohorts passed out of
the electorate, and as new voters entered a political era with a Democratic
majority and a general tendency for Democrats to control government—
where being a Democrat meant being "where the action is"—the drift in
partisan preferences within the general public continued. Note, however,
the peculiar (and implicitly countervailing) character of this trend, when
linked with economic development more generally. For the late New Deal
era was also a period of sweeping economic change in the United States,
including a shift from a blue-collar toward a white-collar occupational
base along with a sharp move upward in the median level of education.

If mass partisan attachments had remained in the mold of the early New
Deal period, then—Blue-collar Americans Democratic, white-collar
Americans Republican—economic development should have produced a
gradual but ineluctable *decline* in the share of Democrats, and rise in the
share of Republicans. Instead, throughout the late New Deal era, the
opposite was occurring. Yet apart from any superficial ironies, and apart
from a very concrete warning against applying grand causal factors uncriti-
cally, this growing partisan majority was eventually to contribute a major
indirect push toward the subsequent era of divided government.

More specifically, what this growing partisan imbalance implied was
exaggeration of the issue tensions—or at least, of the preconditions for
tensions—within the overall Democratic coalition. If the share of Democrats in the general public was increasing, while the share of white-collar
Americans was increasing as well, the white-collar share of the Democratic party—its better-educated, wealthier, and higher-status identifiers—should almost inevitably have been increasing even faster, as in
fact it was. Yet these individuals were precisely those Democrats who
were most attracted to the progressive position on cultural issues and to
the accommodationist position on foreign affairs, the positions which
were to cause cross-pressures within the dominant party coalition.

That was not nearly the end of the indirect impacts from this continuing
partisan shift, however. For in truth, by comparison with socially similar

individuals in the Republican party, these white-collar Democrats were even more liberal on the new issue-areas—even more culturally progressive and internationally accommodationist—and thus presumably even more likely to open issue-based cleavages within the social base of the Democratic party. Moreover, they were more likely to *participate* in matters political, in general elections but especially in nominating contests, than were their blue-collar, older-line, Democratic brethren. By extension, they were far more likely to become activists within the Democratic party, giving the active party a more culturally progressive and internationally accommodationist tilt,[30] and giving the party a widened elite-mass cleavage too.

Accordingly, this larger sociopolitical development is probably the one which interacted most strongly with the gradual shift in the character of political parties as organizations, from patronage-based hierarchies of party regulars to issue-based networks of participatory activists. Patronage-based organizations had at least blue-collar roots; issue-based activists were reliably white-collar. Augmented tensions among all Democratic identifiers, and especially, augmented tensions between party activists and their less active rank and file, followed inexorably from all of this.

The Republican party had its own, different but complementary, echo of the same developments. The overall "story" of the late New Deal era remained one of a gradual but ineluctable shift toward the Democrats, so that internal Republican impacts from this larger shift had to be seen principally as reverberations. Nevertheless, the Republican response not only completed the story. It also contributed the rest of the coordinate change among political intermediaries, which was to prove so essential in the shift to an *era* of divided government. Indeed, every aspect of Democratic party developments had its counterpart, opposite, Republican result.

Seen from the other partisan side, then, those better-educated, white-collar individuals who became Democrats in the late New Deal era were precisely the individuals who might have kept the active Republican party more progressive on cultural values and more accommodationist on foreign affairs, had the original class lines of the New Deal order held. It is thus their absence, coupled with the shift to activist-based political parties, which explains the complementary polarizing character of the Republican party too on these crucial concerns.[31] A culturally progressive and internationally accommodationist, active Democratic party was joined, naturally and in some sense automatically, by a culturally traditionalist and externally nationalist, active Republican party.

The deeper roots of a tension between cultural/national concerns on

the one hand and welfare/service concerns on the other were thus imma-
nent in this great, postwar, partisan shift. That tension crystallized in the
election of 1968. It was institutionalized in the years thereafter. And it
came to constitute the crucial sustaining element for the new era of divided government. Yet this tension, with its national impact, was to be
joined by a major subnational trend, more temporally and geographically
concentrated but also deeper and more intense in its impact. This
subnational trend was economic development, pure and simple. Its region was the American South. And it became the other great background
influence of the postwar period, lying behind—or rather, wrapping
around—the shift to an era of divided government.

In this, if American politics as a whole was to move from one great era
to another in the postwar years, from the late New Deal era to the era of
divided government, then the South was actually to undergo two such
transformations, simultaneously. This was because the political changes
associated with the Great Depression and the New Deal nationwide had
only been grafted onto, rather than transformed, the structure of politics
in the American South. So that it was only in the postwar years that the
thoroughgoing changes associated with the New Deal era finally penetrated there.[32]

By then, however, the further changes associated with the era of divided government were already roiling politics in the rest of the nation. In
the United States of the 1960s, these could hardly have failed to reach into
the South as well, even if some, like the civil rights revolution, had not
begun there. In any case, what were effectively New Deal implications for
politics were to acquire their impact in the South in a distinctive—and
subsequently distinguishing—temporal sequence. That is, they were to
acquire their impact in conjunction with the shifts which were leading on
to the era of divided government in the rest of the nation.

To be more specific: economic development, and thus the arrival of an
industrial economic order, and thus the normal partisan alignments accompanying such an order in the United States, proceeded apace in the
American South during the postwar years. While the rest of the nation
was becoming more Democratic, then, the South was actually acquiring
Republicans and, along with them, a Republican party. Inevitably, some
of this growing Republicanism was due to migration and some of it to
conversion. Yet both aspects seemed (again finally) to be about to bring
the South, too, into the national order.

In this nascent integration, as the South became the last great area to
"catch up" with industrialization, outside entrepreneurs—more likely
than the natives to be Republican—moved South. Yet as regional industrialization proceeded, the South also acquired the kind of economic base,

and with it the kind of class structure, which had produced the New Deal coalition in the rest of the nation. Which is to say: it acquired the social base for an indigenous Republican party, and in short order, it acquired the party as an operating organization as well. Had these developments been occurring while the non-South was standing still politically, that is, had the New Deal era merely continued ever onward, southern politics would presumably have become a less stereotypical embodiment of national arrangements.[33]

That was, of course, not to be. For while all of this was occurring in the South, the same shifts which were to move the nation as a whole *out* of the late New Deal era (and into the era of divided government) were also, incipiently and then more forcefully, invading the South as well. As a result, by the time there was a serious, organized, Republican presence in the American South, thereby "nationalizing" the region in one sense, there was also a national political drift toward partisan divisions on cultural/national as well as economic/welfare matters, one offering consistently liberal or consistently conservative options on them all.

The challenge of this national drift, in turn, was especially intense in this particular (subnational) region. For if there was no evident popular majority nationwide for uniformly liberal or uniformly conservative policy combinations, those combinations were actually most discordant with—really, anathema to—popular preferences in the South. Or at least, if the South had previously been the most Democratic region of the nation, it was also the most traditionalist and nationalist of Democratic regions. Accordingly, when its residents too did not give up a general supportiveness of New Deal economics, and when they remained highly supportive of concrete governmental services, the result was a particularly concentrated version of the new national pattern.

In response, the South remained the most heavily Democratic region in congressional elections for most of this period, despite the birth of a real, congressional, Republican party. Yet the South simultaneously became *the most Republican region* in presidential elections, at the same time and year after year. As a further consequence, the South became the archetypal home of divided government, reliably and by large margins. Rather than becoming an attenuated version of the national pattern, it thus became a caricature. In so doing, of course, it completed—and locked in—the national trend. By extension but not surprisingly, when deviations from the dominant partisan patterns appeared, as with Democratic presidencies plus Republican Congresses, it was the South that led the way.

Further Change?

Does such an investigation, of factors shaping change from the preceding to the current political eras, suggest *further* change, to a new successor era?·Which is to say: having addressed, retrospectively, the dominant issue dimensions and key structural influences associated with the break from the New Deal era to the era of divided government, can the same analysis be applied prospectively as well? In this, can the analyst look upon the evolution of contemporary issue concerns and contemporary structural factors and suggest possibilities for the period following the era of divided government?

As ever, careful analysis provides mainly cautions. In the case of political eras which begin with a central cataclysmic event, as the New Deal era began with the Great Depression, there is no good and sensible way, by definition, to project such an event before it happens. And in the case of political eras which arise from the interaction (and culmination) of several long-running trends, such as the era of divided government, there are rarely good prospective reasons for selecting one collection of trends rather than another as the critical shape of a future which has not yet happened. The possibility of additionally winnowing them out, specifying them, *and* producing (in advance) their interactive threshold seems even more remote.

Concretely, in turn, there are no inescapable reasons for assuming that American politics is posed to undergo one of these era shifts, certainly not on the scale of the portents in several of the other G-7 nations. Germany, the nation, has changed its fundamental boundaries, and thereby its size, composition, wealth, and even collective internal history. Canada may (or of course, may not) be about to go in the opposite direction. Japan has broken the mold of its postwar politics, though the shape of its future remains unclear. Italy, the same. The United States promises nothing self-evident on this scale.

Nevertheless, the obvious and orthodox way to assess a potential change in political eras has always been, initially, by way of partisan outcomes. And here, the elections of 1992 and 1994, in their substance and especially in their proximity, raise the conditional character of political change in a particularly intense way. Individually, each is not just a plausible reflection, in its specifics, of a general era of divided government; each elaborates the structural logic of that era in useful ways. Yet coming as close upon each other as they did, their conjunction serves as an implicit warning that no era—and no order—can usefully be elaborated forever, before an alternative conceptualization acquires far more analytic power.

The election of 1992 did, of course, restore the Democrats, by virtue of the triumph of Bill Clinton for president, to formally unified control of the elective institutions of national government. Superficially, then, divided government came to an end. On the other hand, an "era of divided government," as defined by a particular grand issue focus and supportive key political structures, could hardly go out of existence merely because one individual captured one office. Indeed, not only does the operative structure of this era continue to provide the best means for interpreting that (individual) outcome. The Clinton election of 1992 provides another means of seeing the intrinsic continuity in its era.

Thus the main contours of candidate strategy were in fact utterly unchanged in 1992. The Republican ticket hammered away at foreign affairs and cultural values, specifically embodied, this time, by victory in the Gulf War and by questions about the character of their opponent. In return, the Democratic ticket harped upon social welfare and service needs, embodied, again for this particular contest, by health care and physical infrastructure. Such emphases would have been familiar—and predictable—at any point within the preceding quarter-century.

Yet there was, quintessentially, one more thing.[34] Ever since the coming of the era of divided government, the basic Republican strategy within this framework had been clear enough: push cultural/national issues down from the presidency and into Congress. From the other side, the Democratic counterimperative had been equally clear: push economic/welfare issues up from Congress and into the presidency. The election of 1992, then, represented the great Democratic success at this strategic maneuver. For the first time in a quarter-century, economic issues dominated the presidential campaign sufficiently to produce their ineluctable result, and a Democratic president got to join with solid majorities in both houses of Congress to govern the country, if they could.

By itself, this represented merely the less common of the two most likely outcomes within the issue context and structural contours of modern American politics. In that sense, the issues and structures of an era of divided government seemed sufficient to explain this outcome, without any change in eras. What makes this judgment more intricate and interesting but less ultimately definitive, however, was the outcome of the midterm elections of 1994. For if 1992 represented the great Democratic success at the strategic maneuvers demanded by an era of divided government, then 1994—coming in dizzying succession, for most analysts—was to represent the great Republican success at these same maneuvers.

Republicans across the nation managed in 1994 to capitalize upon cumulating concerns about the character of American life.[35] Crime was the lead issue in many national polls, but the theme of unpredictability in normal social life—unpredictability in response to hard work under traditional values—penetrated everywhere. The cumulative impact, in turn, allowed Republicans to accomplish something which had eluded them for forty years, the recapture of both houses of Congress, without even the assistance of a Republican presidential candidate. In passing, the same result invigorated another abstract possibility for the era of divided government: a Democratic presidency facing a (fully) Republican Congress.

Such an outcome gained emotional impact in its immediate aftermath from the fact that it came so close upon the superficially opposite outcome of 1992. On the one hand, the most parsimonious interpretation even of that dramatic shift—to 1992, and then from 1992 to 1994—was still as a logical extension of the political order associated with the era of divided government, an interpretation which gains force from the way it provides underlying continuity to superficially distinctive results. On the other hand, *possibilities* for more fundamental change were also raised by each of these outcomes individually, much less by both in quick succession.

And at that point, the sane analyst probably stops. There have, in the years leading up to that point, been two great periods to postwar American politics, each with its own dominant issue-areas and key structural supports. The first actually extends all the way back to the depression, to the 1930s. Elements from this period—leftovers—remain today, but it was actually being undermined by changes in party organization, in interest group composition, and in activist values for a long time, as reinforced by creeping national shifts in partisan attachment and by differential regional trends in economic development.

All these changes came together suddenly in the 1960s, producing a second postwar political era, which has been with us ever since. The component elements of this new era of divided government have been central to understanding American politics in all the intervening years, and they shed new light on—they give a further consistency to—the most recent incarnations as well. A third era may well be implicit in the details of current American politics, but it has not yet revealed itself in a definitive way. When it does, it will come with an integral combination of newly dominant issue concerns and newly consequential structural supports. Or so the entire postwar period suggests.

Notes

1. John Morton Blum, *V Was for Victory: Politics and American Culture During World War II* (New York: Harcourt Brace Jovanovich, 1976); John Gunther, *Inside U.S.A.* (New York: Harper & Brothers, 1947); Samuel Lubell, *The Future of American Politics* (New York: Harper & Brothers, 1951); Hugh Thomas,

Armed Truce: The Beginnings of the Cold War, 1945–46 (London: Hamish Hamilton, 1986); and Kenneth T. Jackson, *Crabgrass Frontier: The Suburbanization of the United States* (New York: Oxford University, 1985).

2. Eric F. Goldman, *The Crucial Decade—And After: America, 1945–1960* (New York: Vintage, 1960); Alonzo L. Hamby, *Beyond the New Deal: Harry S. Truman and American Liberalism* (New York: Columbia University, 1973); James L. Sundquist, *Politics and Policy: The Eisenhower, Kennedy, and Johnson Years* (Washington, D. C.: Brookings, 1968); Michael Barone, *Our Country: The Shaping of America from Roosevelt to Reagan* (New York: Free Press, 1990).

3. The classic analysis of the southern political order in the immediate postwar years remains V. O. Key, Jr., *Southern Politics in State and Nation* (New York: Knopf, 1949). For the roots of this order, see J. Morgan Kousser, *The Shaping of Southern Politics: Suffrage Restriction and the Establishment of the One-Party South, 1880–1910* (New Haven: Yale University, 1974). See also Dewey Grantham, *The Life and Death of the Solid South* (Lexington: University of Kentucky, 1988).

4. Most crucial to consider are James L. Sundquist, *Dynamics of the Party System: Alignment and Realignment of Political Parties in the United States*, rev. ed. (Washington, D. C.: Brookings, 1983), chaps. 10–12, and Everett Carll Ladd, Jr., with Charles D. Hadley, *Transformations of the American Party System*, 2d ed. (New York: Norton, 1978), chaps. 1 and 2. See also Ladd, *American Political Parties: Social Change and Political Response* (New York: Norton, 1970).

5. The most comprehensive examination within this period is Paul T. David, Malcolm Moos, and Ralph M. Goldman, eds., *Presidential Nominating Politics in 1952*, 5 vols. (Baltimore: Johns Hopkins, 1954). An operational summary can be found in the very first edition of what would become the leading text on the topic, Aaron B. Wildavsky and Nelson W. Polsby, *Presidential Elections: Strategies of American Electoral Politics* (New York: Scribner's, 1964).

6. A key source for Congress in this period is the work of Ralph K. Huitt, collected as Huitt, *Working Within the System* (Berkeley: IGS Press, 1990). Also crucial are David B. Truman, *The Congressional Party: A Case Study* (New York: Wiley, 1959), and Stephen K. Bailey, *Congress Makes a Law* (New York: Vintage, 1964).

7. Most useful is Angus Campbell, "Surge and Decline: A Study of Electoral Change," *Public Opinion Quarterly* 24 (Fall 1960): 397–418. But see also those classic examinations, Angus Campbell et al., *The American Voter* (New York: Wiley, 1960), and Angus Campbell et al., *Elections and the Political Order* (New York: Wiley, 1966).

8. Intimations of the rise and potential impact of these concerns are clear enough, by hindsight, in Philip E. Converse et al., "Continuity and Change in American Politics: Parties and Issues in the 1968 Election," *American Political Science Review* 63 (December 1969): 1083–1105, and John P. Robinson, "Public Reaction to Protest: Chicago, 1968," *Public Opinion Quarterly* 34 (Spring 1970): 1–9. A first self-conscious attempt to collect these matters is Richard M. Scammon and Ben J. Wattenberg, *The Real Majority* (New York: Coward-

McCann, 1970). See also William E. Leuchtenberg, *A Troubled Feast: American Society Since 1945* (Glenview, Ill.: Scott, Foresman, 1982).

9. The contemporary result can be found in John E. Reilly, ed., *American Public Opinion and U.S. Foreign Policy* (Chicago: Chicago Council on Foreign Relations, 1987). Views along the way, emphasizing the cross-cutting nature of mass opinion here, include Everett Carll Ladd, Jr., and Charles D. Hadley, *Political Parties and Political Issues: Patterns in Differentiation Since the New Deal* (Beverly Hills: Sage, 1973), and Richard Jensen, "The Last Party System: Decay of Consensus, 1932–1980," in Paul Kleppner et al., *The Evolution of American Electoral Systems* (Westport, Conn.: Greenwood, 1981), chap. 6. A view of the elite counterpart is Ole R. Holsti and James N. Rosenau, *American Leadership in World Affairs: Vietnam and the Breakdown of Consensus* (Boston: Allen & Unwin, 1984). See also John Morton Blum, *Years of Discord: American Politics and Society, 1961–1974* (New York: Norton, 1991).

10. Systematic pursuit of these two great issue-areas, and their relationship, is Byron E. Shafer and William J. M. Claggett, *The Two Majorities: The Issue Context of Modern American Politics* (Baltimore: Johns Hopkins, 1995). An impressionistic predecessor is Byron E. Shafer, "The Election of 1988 and the Structure of American Politics: Thoughts on Interpreting an Electoral Order," *Electoral Studies* 8 (April 1989): 5–21.

11. The situation by the 1960s is carefully surveyed in David R. Mayhew, *Placing Parties in American Politics* (Princeton: Princeton University, 1986). The more dramatic side of its evolution is Alan J. Ware, *The Breakdown of Democratic Party Organization, 1940–1980* (Oxford: Oxford University, 1985). Conversion of all this into a general American model, finally, is Leon Epstein, *Political Parties in the American Mold* (Madison: University of Wisconsin, 1986).

12. Kay L. Schlozman and John T. Tierney, *Organized Interests and American Democracy* (New York: Harper & Row, 1985); Allan J. Cigler and Burdett A. Loomis, eds., *Interest Group Politics*, 2d ed. (Washington, D.C.: CQ Press, 1986); and Jack L. Walker, *Mobilizing Interest Groups in America: Patrons, Professions, and Social Movements* (Ann Arbor: University of Michigan, 1991). Lest this seem purely a modern phenomenon, see Peter H. Odegard, *Pressure Politics: The Story of the Anti-Saloon League* (New York: Columbia University, 1928). For business and labor in an earlier day, see Raymond A. Bauer, Ithiel de Sola Poole, and Lewis Anthony Dexter, *American Business and Public Policy: The Politics of Foreign Trade* (New York: Atherton, 1968), and Derek C. Bok and John T. Dunlop, *Labor and the American Community* (New York: Simon & Schuster, 1970).

13. An investigation of this process is at the heart of Byron E. Shafer, *Quiet Revolution: The Struggle for the Democratic Party and the Shaping of Post-Reform Politics* (New York: Russell Sage, 1983). One survey of its product, some years later, is David S. Broder, *Changing of the Guard: Power and Leadership in America* (New York: Simon & Schuster, 1980).

14. Recognized in such titles as: Gary C. Jacobson, *The Electoral Origins of Divided Government: Competition in U.S. House Elections, 1946–1988* (Boulder, Colo.: Westview, 1990); Gary W. Cox and Samuel Kernell, eds., *The Politics of*

Divided Government (Boulder, Colo: Westview, 1991); David R. Mayhew, *Divided We Govern: Party Control, Lawmaking, and Investigations, 1946–1990* (New Haven: Yale University, 1991); and James A. Thurber, ed., *Divided Democracy: Cooperation and Conflict Between the President and Congress* (Washington, D.C.: CQ Press, 1991).

15. Aaron Wildavsky, "The Two Presidencies," *Trans-Action* 4 (December 1966): 7–14; Paula Stern, *Water's Edge: Domestic Politics and the Making of American Foreign Policy* (Washington, D.C.: CQ Press, 1979); Cecil V. Crabb, Jr., and Pat M. Holt, *Invitation to Struggle: Congress, the President, and Foreign Policy*, 4th ed. (Washington, D.C.: CQ Press, 1992); John Rourke, *Congress and the Presidency in U.S. Foreign Policymaking: A Study of Interaction and Influence, 1945–1982* (Boulder, Colo.: Westview, 1983); Thomas M. Franck and Edward Weisband, *Foreign Policy by Congress* (New York: Oxford University, 1979); Barry M. Blechman, *The Politics of National Security: Congress and U.S. Defense Policy* (New York: Oxford University, 1990).

16. Indeed, the presidency is the focus of most research in this general area, as with Barbara Hinckley, *The Symbolic Presidency: How Presidents Portray Themselves* (New York: Routledge, 1990), and Mary E. Stuckey, *The President as Interpreter-in-Chief* (Chatham, N.J.: Chatham House, 1991). For the place of one cultural issue (abortion) in Senate campaigns, see Marjorie Randon Hershey, *Running for Office: The Political Education of Campaigners* (Chatham, N.J.: Chatham House, 1984). See also Stephen Hess, *Live from Capitol Hill!: Studies of Congress and the Media* (Washington, D.C.: Brookings, 1991), and Stephen Bates, ed., *The Media and the Congress* (Columbus, Ohio: Publishing Horizons, 1987).

17. For evolution of the programs themselves, Edward D. Berkowitz, *America's Welfare State: From Roosevelt to Reagan* (Baltimore: Johns Hopkins, 1991). General links include Morris P. Fiorina, *Congress: Keystone of the Washington Establishment* (New Haven: Yale University, 1977), and Randall B. Ripley and Grace A. Franklin, *Congress, the Bureaucracy, and Public Policy* (Homewood, Ill.: Dorsey, 1976). For direct interventions, see Joel D. Aberbach, *Keeping a Watchful Eye: The Politics of Congressional Oversight* (Washington, D.C.: Brookings, 1990).

18. There are numerous aspects to this enterprise. Most generally, John A. Ferejohn, *Pork Barrel Politics: Rivers and Harbors Legislation, 1947–1968* (Stanford: Stanford University, 1991). For the more personalized response, John R. Johannes, *To Serve the People: Congress and Constituency Service* (Lincoln: University of Nebraska, 1984). For institutionalization of this pursuit, Harrison W. Fox, Jr., and Susan Webb Hammond, *Congressional Staffs: The Invisible Force in American Lawmaking* (New York: Free Press, 1977). Finally, for explicit attention-gathering, Timothy E. Cook, *Making Laws and Making News: Media Strategies in the U.S. House of Representatives* (Washington, D.C.: Brookings, 1989).

19. Suggestive works include Nelson W. Polsby and Aaron Wildavsky, *Presidential Election: Contemporary Strategies of American Electoral Politics*, 8th ed.

(New York: Free Press, 1991), especially chap. 1, "The Strategic Environment: Participants"; Alan I. Abramowitz and Jeffrey A. Segal, *Senate Elections* (Ann Arbor: University of Michigan, 1992); Richard F. Fenno, Jr., *Home Style: House Members in Their Districts* (Boston: Little, Brown, 1978); and Ross K. Baker, *House and Senate* (New York: Norton, 1989).

20. Sundquist, *Dynamics of the Party System*, especially chap. 17, "Years of Disruption: Cross-Cutting Issues Nationwide"; Jensen, "The Last Party System"; Mark C. Westlye, *Senate Elections and Campaign Intensity* (Baltimore: Johns Hopkins, 1991); Gary C. Jacobson and Samuel Kernell, *Strategy and Choice in Congressional Elections*, 2d ed. (New Haven: Yale University, 1983); and Alan Ehrenhalt, *The United States of Ambition: Politicians, Power, and the Pursuit of Office* (New York: Times Books, 1991).

21. Just as one logical response to that same split control, for those unhappy with its product, was unified Republican—not just unified Democratic—control at the next election. And round and round again.

22. For the long view on Vietnam, see George C. Herring, *America's Longest War*, 2d ed. (New York: Wiley, 1988). Different slices of its impact in 1968 include Converse et al., "Continuity and Change in American Politics," and Lewis Chester, Godfrey Hodgson, and Bruce Page, *An American Melodrama: The Presidential Campaign of 1968* (New York: Dell, 1969). See also Eric F. Goldman, *The Tragedy of Lyndon Johnson* (New York: Dell, 1968), and Doris Kearns, *Lyndon Johnson and the American Dream* (New York: Harper & Row, 1976).

23. The central summary document of the period is *Report of the National Advisory Commission on Civil Disorders* (New York: Dutton, 1968), known informally as the "Kerner Commission Report." For a careful look at the impact on public opinion, see Edward G. Carmines and James A. Stimson, *Issue Evolution: Race and the Transformation of American Politics* (Princeton: Princeton University, 1989). For the corrosive effect of both Vietnam and racial disorders on the national Democratic coalition, see Gareth Davies, *From Opportunity to Entitlement: The Transformation and Decline of Great Society Liberalism* (Lawrence: University of Kansas, 1996), along with Allen J. Matusow, *The Unraveling of America: Liberalism in the 1960s* (New York: Harper & Row, 1984).

24. Besides Sundquist, *Politics and Policy*, and Davies, *From Opportunity to Entitlement,* see Gilbert Y. Steiner, *The State of Welfare* (Washington, D.C.: Brookings, 1971); Daniel P. Moynihan, *Maximum Feasible Misunderstanding: Community Action in the War on Poverty* (New York: Free Press, 1969); Sar A. Levitan and Robert Taggert, *The Promise of Greatness: The Social Programs of the Last Decade and Their Major Achievements* (Cambridge: Harvard University, 1976); and, more generally, James T. Patterson, *America's Struggle Against Poverty, 1900–1980* (Cambridge: Harvard University, 1981).

25. These events contribute some of the data for, among others, Rourke, *Congress and the Presidency in U.S. Foreign Policymaking,* and Blechman, *The Politics of National Security*. More generally, see Robert D. Schulzinger, *American Diplomacy in the Twentieth Century*, 2d ed. (New York: Oxford University,

1990), especially chaps. 13–15, and John Spanier, *American Foreign Policy since World War II*, 12th ed. (Washington, D.C.: CQ Press, 1991), especially chaps. 9–13.

26. An operational overview is David M. O'Brien, *Storm Center: The Supreme Court in American Politics* (New York: Norton, 1986). One slice of the complaint about the result is Raoul Berger, *Goverment by Judiciary: The Transformation of the Fourteenth Amendment* (Cambridge: Harvard University, 1977). The cases themselves (plus many others) can be consulted in David M. O'Brien, ed., *Civil Rights and Civil Liberties*, vol. 2 of his *Constitutional Law and Politics* (New York: Norton, 1991.

27. For the Nixon effort, see Daniel P. Moynihan, *The Politics of a Guaranteed Income: The Nixon Administration and the Family Assistance Plan* (New York: Random House, 1973). Various misadventures with social welfare during the Reagan years are threaded throughout Richard F. Fenno, Jr., *The Emergence of a Senate Leader: Pete Domenici and the Reagan Budget* (Washington, D.C.: CQ Press, 1991). Finally, for the continuities of public opinion in the general realm, see Fay Lomax Cook et al., *Convergent Perspectives on Social Welfare Policy: The Views from the General Public, Members of Congress, and AFDC Recipients* (Evanston, Ill.: Center for Public Affairs and Policy Research, 1988).

28. For abortion politics generally, see Barbara Craig and David M. O'Brien, *Abortion and American Politics* (Chatham: Chatham House, 1992), and Kristin Luker, *Abortion and the Politics of Motherhood* (Berkeley: University of California, 1984). See especially the articles and citations in the special issue of *American Politics Quarterly* on "The Politics of Abortion," 21 (January 1993).

29. Careful, sophisticated, *and opposite* conclusions about the mechanics of the initial change are represented by Kristi Andersen, *The Creation of a Democratic Majority, 1928–1936* (Chicago: University of Chicago, 1979), and Robert S. Erickson and Kent L. Tedin, "The 1928–1936 Partisan Realignment: The Case for the Conversion Hypothesis," *American Political Science Review* 75 (December 1981): 951–62. More generally, see James L. Sundquist, "Aftershocks of the New Deal Earthquake—in the North," chap. 10 of Sundquist, *Dynamics of the Party System*. The aggregate numbers for the postwar years are usefully collected in Warren E. Miller and Santa A. Traugott, comps., *American National Election Studies Data Sourcebook, 1952–1986* (Cambridge: Harvard University, 1989). Aggregate implications are squeezed from them in Robert Axelrod, "Where the Vote Comes From: An Analysis of Electoral Coalitions, 1952–1968," *American Political Science Review* 66 (March 1972): 11–20.

30. Most generally, see Lester W. Milbrath and M. L. Goel, *Political Participation*, 2d ed. (Chicago: Rand McNally, 1977), and M. Margaret Conway, *Political Participation in the United States*, 2d ed. (Washington, D.C.: CQ Press, 1991). More pointedly, see James I. Lengle, *Representation in Presidential Primaries: The Democratic Party in the Post-Reform Era* (Westport, Conn.: Greenwood, 1981), and Shafer, *Quiet Revolution*. Attitudinal implications are elicited in Everett Carll Ladd, Jr., "Liberalism Upside Down: The Inversion of the New Deal Order," *Political Science Quarterly* 91 (Winter 1976–77): 577–600.

31. See, most especially, Nicol C. Rae, *The Decline and Fall of the Liberal Republicans: From 1952 to the Present* (Oxford: Oxford University, 1989). For the first serious portents, see Robert D. Novak, *The Agony of the G.O.P. 1964* (New York: Macmillan, 1965). A systematic elaboration is Everett Carll Ladd, Jr., *Where Have All the Voters Gone? The Fracturing of America's Political Parties*, 2d ed. (New York: Norton, 1982). For the underlying logic, see Peter B. Clark and James Q. Wilson, "Incentive Systems: A Theory of Organizations," *Administrative Science Quarterly* 6 (September 1961): 219–66.

32. For example, James L. Sundquist, "Aftershocks of the New Deal Earthquake—in the South," chap. 11 of Sundquist, *Dynamics of the Party System*, and Everett Carll Ladd, Jr., with Charles D. Hadley, "First Rendings: The Case of the South," chap. 3 in Ladd, *Transformations of the American Party System*. Earl Black and Merle Black, *Politics and Society in the South* (Cambridge: Harvard University, 1987), especially chaps. 1–3; James C. Cobb, *Industrialization and Southern Society, 1877–1984* (Lexington: University of Kentucky, 1984).

33. Robert J. Newman, *Growth in the American South: Changing Regional Employment and Wage Patterns in the 1960s and 1970s* (New York: New York University, 1984); Dudley Poston, Jr., and Robert H. Weller, eds., *The Population of the South* (Austin: University of Texas, 1982); Thad A. Brown, *Migration and Politics: The Impact of Population Mobility on American Voting Behavior* (Chapel Hill: University of North Carolina, 1988); and especially, Alexander P. Lamis, *The Two-Party South*, 2d exp. ed. (Oxford: Oxford University, 1990).

34. The familiar, and always initially authoritative, series are: Michael Nelson, ed., *The Elections of 1992* (Washington, D.C.: CQ Press, 1993); Gerald M. Pomper, ed., *The Election of 1992* (Chatham, N.J.: Chatham House, 1993); and Paul R. Abramson, John H. Aldrich, and David W. Rohde, *Change and Continuity in the 1992 Elections* (Washington, D.C.: CQ Press, 1994).

35. Stephen Gettinger, "'94 Elections: Real Revolution or Blip on Political Radar," *Congressional Quarterly Weekly Report* 52 (November 5, 1994): 3127–32, plus the full issues of "New Speaker, New Order," *CQ Weekly Report* 52 (November 12, 1994), and "New Kings of the Hill," *National Journal* (November 12, 1994). The victors' own semi-official prospect and retrospect are Ed Gillespie and Bob Schellhas, *Contract with America* (New York: Times Books, 1994), and James W. Robinson with Russ Colliau, comps., *After the Revolution: A Citizen's Guide to the First Republican Congress in 40 Years* (Rocklin, Cal.: Prima, 1995).

3 *Richard C. G. Johnston*

Canada

In the postwar period, Canada emerged from the British Empire only to become a reluctant adjunct of the American one. As the country sought to redefine itself in terms at once cosmopolitan and North American, it risked coming apart at the seams. Change so profound was bound to have an impact on Canadian politics. But the country's political orders were not merely passive: their embodiment of prewar issues and commitments shaped many of the particulars of Canada's postwar response to itself and to the world.

As in the United States, at least two postwar periods are clearly identifiable and the first extends back to the 1930s. Also as in the United States, critical postwar shifts involved, among other things, reversals in longstanding sectional patterns. In both countries, amateurs became more important in politics. This altered more than just the tone of politics. The more parties came to be driven by policy commitments, the less effective they became as brokers; the shift in style helps explain shifts in the system's social base and increases in its overall polarization. Unlike the United States, Canada saw a third postwar order emerge in the 1980s, only to explode in 1993. If 1993 ended one order, the next one has yet to congeal. If its future is in doubt, so is the future of the very country, and for the same reasons.

Building Blocks

For national politics, Canada inherited the United Kingdom's simple, majoritarian institutional arrangements: disciplined parties use a plurality
electoral system to seek single-party majority governments; governments, once formed, dominate parliaments; this permits centralization,
even within the executive, and a culture of secrecy. But in contrast to the
United Kingdom, the society to which these arrangements have been
adapted is a federation: sprawling, thinly populated, ethnically complex,
intensely localistic, and free of the Great Power aspirations which commonly justify executive dominance. The very appropriateness of key elements in the political order is thus a matter of debate.

Canada is, first of all, a binational state. One nation, French Canada,
is located overwhelmingly in Quebec, which is, concomitantly, the one
jurisdiction on the continent with a francophone majority. Quebec is big
and complex and so can readily be imagined as sovereign in its own
right. Because removing it from the federation would cut the Atlantic
provinces off from the other English-speaking ones, forming a government which includes both French and English is essential to the polity's
very survival. As it happens, binational brokerage is also a necessity for
assembling a winning coalition. Quebec seats constitute roughly one-
fourth of the national parliament and, equally importantly, tend to come
en bloc: controlling Quebec puts a party halfway to an outright majority.
Only once (1917) did a single-party majority form without significant
Quebec representation; every other government formed with little or no
Quebec support was a short-lived minority.

But if the system has encouraged parties to do the right thing for the
nation's survival, it has done so at the price of compromising the simple
majoritarianism of the Westminster model. For extended periods, the
playing field has been tilted against all parties but one, the Liberals. And
the system's major beneficiary, Quebec, has also been the country's most
permanently disaffected region. To many observers, Quebec wins twice
over: it dominates national governments, yet benefits from threatening to
leave the game entirely. Meanwhile, apprehension of Quebec's departure
constrains large areas of what in other countries is open policy debate.

The other nation is commonly referred to as English Canada. But En-
glish Canada hardly sees itself as a nation; its country is Canada, full stop.
And the "English" in English Canada is a linguistic reference only; ethni-
cally, Canada outside Quebec is complex and becoming even more so.
The traditional self-definition of English-speaking Canada as somehow
British made it difficult from the beginning to insist that citizens of non-
British origin must become just "Canadian," a difficulty only com-

pounded by the presence of French Canada. Now, of course, the Britishness of English Canada lacks credible overseas backing.

And overseas backing used to matter. By G-7 standards, Canada is poorly positioned to be master of its fate. It has always sought security through association with a great power. When Britain was the power in question, Canadians had to ask how much they owed the Empire. Not surprisingly, the answer depended on how British one was or felt oneself to be. Because sentiment played so large a role in reinforcing the older connection, the power shift from Britain to the United States occasioned much political grief within Canada. All along, many Canadians resisted association with any great power.

If Canada is exposed strategically, so is it economically. Throughout the postwar period, Canada exported roughly 30 percent of its gross national product. Canada tends to run surpluses on trade but to run deficits everywhere else in the current account. The country thus regularly imports capital to balance its payments. Traditionally, Canada exported raw materials and primary manufactures and continues to do so for many commodities. As a result, conflict between primary and secondary industry is a critical element of the party battle. As in other countries, this conflict became even more acute as the primary sector shrank.

The shrinkage of the primary sector accompanied a geographical reorientation of Canadian trade: the country has become steadily more integrated into the U.S. economy. Down to the 1940s, Canadian trade was as much overseas, mainly with Britain, as north-south, with the United States. Observers used to speak of the "North Atlantic Triangle,"[1] which described, among other things, the fact that Canada used raw-material exports to Britain to pay for manufactured imports from the United States. Now, the overwhelming bulk of Canadian exports go directly to the United States, and increasingly exports consist of finished goods. Canada now needs the American market in ways it just did not at the beginning of the postwar period.

The conflicts just enumerated—over Canadian identity and over commercial policy—were the constitutive forces for the two old parties, the Liberals and the Conservatives. Rapid postwar change in the country's ethnic makeup and in its economic and strategic context thus account for much of the change in the party system's base and in the organization of power. All the traditional divisions have a sectional aspect, and change in the traditional cleavages inevitably changed the sectional foundations of the system. Within each political order, electoral law—specifically, the plurality electoral formula—compounded sectional differences in the vote as they were translated into seats, the basic currency of power. Between orders, the electoral system also compounded shifts, in Canada as a whole and in the sectional base.

If economic change upset relations between the two old parties, so also did it threaten to displace one or the other of them entirely. Expansion and reorientation of the country's secondary industry, as it exacerbated preexisting cleavages on commercial policy, also created the preconditions for conflict within the industrial sector, for unionization. Circumstances that favored unionization also created demands for macroeconomic management and for expansion of the welfare state. One test of the political strength of these demands has been support for a party with links to the union movement. Before 1961, this was the Cooperative Commonwealth Federation (CCF). After 1961, the CCF became the New Democratic Party (NDP) and as it did so, the social-democratic presence in the electorate grew.

The emergence of the NDP as a serious force is another defining element in the shift between the first and second postwar orders. Thanks to the NDP, single-party majorities became harder to achieve after 1960. All along, the strength of the CCF and NDP was also critical to the politics of social insurance and welfare. Two periods of intense attention to the welfare state can be distinguished and each was associated with real or apprehended CCF/NDP strength. Innovations in welfare policy neutralized the CCF/NDP threat and, with the neutralization of the threat, social policy innovation effectively ceased.

Liberal Party Hegemony, 1935–1957

In 1945, the government formed by the Liberal party was ten years old. It was already one of the most successful in the country's history, yet its run was to last twelve more years. No alternative to the Liberals seemed credible as a party in government. If the Liberals often had to carry on a delicate balancing act, especially during the war, all the elements in the balance could be found inside their own caucus. Once the party had resolved on a course, it swept all in federal politics before it. C. D. Howe, a long-serving Liberal cabinet minister summed up the attitude: "Who's gonna stop us?"

It helped that the government was very broadly based. It also helped that the party was as careful as circumstances permitted not to force any question that threatened the country's integrity, that seriously jostled any key group's sense of identity. Similarly, even though the government presided over a massive wartime centralization, it was usually careful not to tread on the prerogatives of provincial governments. Its prudence reflected its structure: just as the country was federal, so was the party.

The electorate that kept returning Liberals to power was cleaved along lines predating the war, although the war may have reinforced some cleavages. One fissure was sectional, east versus west. The other major cleavage—between Catholics and Protestants—was invisible even to many who lived it and was as ill understood then as it is today; in part, this is an essay in recovery of the bases of that division. Finally, the electorate was divided by the union movement, a division which may have started in the 1930s but which became consequential only in the run up to the 1945 election.

The Liberal government's popular base was marked by sharp geographic discontinuities. As table 3.1 indicates, the Liberal party tended to get outright majorities of the vote only in Quebec and the Atlantic provinces. Liberals returned wide pluralities in Ontario and Manitoba and very thin ones, if any, in Saskatchewan, Alberta, and British Columbia. Liberal support was deepest in Quebec and otherwise exhibited a marked east-west gradient. Conservatives were even more confined than Liberals to an eastern base. Only in Ontario and the Maritime provinces did they receive more than about a quarter of the popular vote, and in Alberta and Saskatchewan their average share was barely 15 percent. The party was also weak in Quebec, although, strikingly, no weaker than in the western provinces. And it was a measure of Conservative haplessness that where they were relatively strong (in Ontario, for instance), the Liberals were even stronger.

Western Canada was remarkable for its rejection of both old parties. Only in Manitoba did both Liberals and Conservatives stake respectable claims, and even there over one-third of the vote went to third parties. In the other western provinces the total share of third parties was over 40 percent. Most of this third-party vote went to the CCF, which formed the provincial opposition in British Columbia in 1933 and the government in Saskatchewan in 1944. These two provinces, in turn, dominated the CCF's modest parliamentary presence in Ottawa. Outside the west, the CCF was hardly a factor: its Ontario share typically was smaller even than its Alberta one, and its shares in Quebec and the Atlantic provinces were weaker still. The other party of the west was Social Credit, which emerged in historically peculiar circumstances in Alberta in 1935 and which never gained much ground in federal elections outside that province.[2]

The character of party competition thus differed fundamentally between east and west. In Ontario and the provinces to its east the battle was between the Liberal and Conservative parties, with the Liberals always on top. In the west the Liberals survived but did not flourish as they faced off against an autonomous rival, sometimes the CCF, sometimes Social

Table 3.1.   The Geography of Votes

Region	Period (1) 1935–57[a]	(2) 1963–84[a]	(3) 1984–93[a]	Shift (2)–(1)	(3)–(2)
		Liberals			
BC	32.9	29.8	19	−3.1	−10.9
Alta	30.1	24.2	13	−5.9	−9.0
Sask	39.5	25.0	18	−14.5	−6.8
Man	42.2	30.9	29	−11.3	−1.7
Ont	45.4	42.4	34	−3.0	−8.0
Que	58.0	51.9	32	−6.1	−19.6
NB	53.7	46.0	39	−7.7	−7.3
NS	50.8	39.8	40	−11.0	+0.3
PEI	52.4	44.1	46	−8.3	+1.4
Nfld[b]	69.6	51.1	40.7	−18.5	−10.4
Canada	47.0	42.0	30.0	−5.0	−12.0
		Conservatives			
BC	23.4	31.2	40.5	+7.8	+9.3
Alta	16.0	54.3	60.3	+38.3	+6.0
Sask	15.6	42.8	39.1	+27.2	−3.7
Man	25.4	40.8	40.1	−15.4	−0.7
Ont	39.5	36.5	42.9	−3.0	+6.3
Que	22.1	19.5	51.5	−2.6	+32.5
NB	39	41.1	47.0	+2.1	+6.9
NS	37.3	47.8	45.8	+10.5	−2.0
PEI	45.4	51.1	46.7	+5.7	−4.4
Nfld[b]	28.0	38.7	49.9	+10.7	+11.2
Canada	28	38.7	46.5	+4.3	+12.5
		CCF-NDP			
BC	29.9	31.5	36.0	+1.6	+4.6
Alta	12.1	9.3	16.0	−2.8	+6.5
Sask	35.9	30.3	41.0	−5.6	+11.3
Man	24.0	25.2	24.0	+1.2	−0.9
Ont	10.5	9.9	21.0	+9.4	+0.6
Que	1.2	7.3	11.0	+6.1	+4.1
NB	3.0	8.7	12.0	+5.7	+4.0
NS	7.9	11.8	13.0	+3.9	+1.5
PEI	1.5	4.7	7.0	+3.2	+2.3
Nfld[b]	0.4	9.4	9.1	+9.0	−0.3
Canada	11.8	17	17	+5.1	−0.2

(*table continued on following page*)

Table 3.1. *(continued)*

| Region | Period | | | Shift | |
	(1) 1935–57[a]	(2) 1963–84[a]	(3) 1984–93[a]	(2)–(1)	(3)–(2)
			Others		
BC	13.8	7.5	3.8	−6.3	−3.7
Alta	41.8	12.2	11	−29.6	−1.4
Sask	9.0	1.9	1.5	−7.1	−0.4
Man	8.4	3.1	6.6	−5.3	+3.5
Ont	4.6	1.2	2.3	−3.4	+1.1
Que	18.7	21.3	4.3	+2.6	−17
NB	0.8	4.2	2.7	+4.2	−1.5
NS	4.0	0.6	0.9	−3.4	−0.3
PEI	0.2	0.1	0.8	−0.1	+0.7
Nfld[b]	2.0	0.8	0.3	−1.2	−0.5
Canada	11.5	7	6.8	−4.5	−0.2

[a]Period averages do not include the election in the last year of the period.
[b]Elections of 1949 and 1953 only in first period.

Credit. Manitoba, as befitted its transitional location had the country's only true three-party system.

Table 3.2 outlines the nongeographic bases of party choice outside Quebec. It gives group differences estimated from a merged file of Gallup polls, divided into periods corresponding to this paper's narrative. Although only three nongeographic factors appear in the table, the estimation from which the reported coefficients emerged also included dummy variables for each province of residence, with Ontario as the reference category. Quebec dwellers were excluded from estimations for two reasons. First, Quebec is bound to be a huge outlier in any estimation which includes linguistic and religious variables: the province is over 80 percent francophone and about 90 percent Catholic. Inclusion of Quebec respondents is bound to make any religious or linguistic coefficient look big, even if the groups in question are politically indistinct outside Quebec. Second, group differences within Quebec tend to be small but *sui generis;* although it is the pivot for Canadian elections, Quebec is an electorate apart.[3]

The implication of the 1953–57 estimation in table 3.2 is that Catholics outside Quebec were about as likely as—indeed for much of the period, more likely than—their co-religionists in Quebec to vote Liberal. About two Catholics in three voted Liberal, where for non-Catholics the proportion was closer to two in five. Only about one Catholic in three voted Conservative; among non-Catholics the Conservative share was closer to one in two. These differences were not artifacts of the association be-

Table 3.2.   Non-Geographic Bases of Party Choice Outside Quebec

Base	1953–57	1957–63	1963–73	1974–83
		Liberal		
Catholic	.23	.25	.22	.18
French	.07	.03	.12	.16
Union	−.08	−.04	.08	−.03
Constant	.43	.38	.43	.34
		Conservative		
Catholic	−.17	−.21	−.20	−.17
French	−.05	−.05	−.09	−.14
Union	−.09	−.09	−.07	−.10
Constant	.46	.49	.39	.47
		CCF-NDP		
Catholic	−.02	−.02	−.20	.003
French	−.02	−.004	−.06	−.02
Union	.16	.12	.16	.13
Constant	.09	.10	.17	.18

NOTE: Entries are unstandardized regression coefficients from OLS; for details on data and estimation see n. 3.

tween religion and language. Although francophones outside Quebec were more likely than other Catholics to vote Liberal and less likely to vote Conservative, the linguistic difference within the religious community was dwarfed by the contrast between the whole Catholic community and the rest of the population.

In part, the system's east-west tilt reflected conflict over commercial policy. Canada's economic development was channeled by: protective *tariffs* to promote secondary manufacturing, mainly in Ontario and Quebec; a *homestead* policy along U.S. lines to hasten settlement of the prairie west; and subsidized construction of *railways* to expand the market for Canadian manufactures, to preempt American designs on the western provinces, and to control the export of Canadian grain.[4]

Once a transcontinental economy with complementary metropolitan and hinterland elements came into being, the very policies which shaped it became a focus of political conflict. Western settlers saw themselves as more colonized than colonizing; tariffs raised the price of their inputs, and railways behaved like monopolists. These central elements in prairie demonology were associated with the Conservatives, and the party continued to defend its policies well into the 1960s. Although Liberals opposed the policies only sporadically and with diminishing intensity as years passed, masterly inactivity combined with occasional Conservative reaffirmation of its tariff and railway commitments kept the Liberal party acceptable to many western voters.

Conflict over commercial policy does not account for all the geography in Table 3.1, particularly for differences among the eastern provinces. Differences that remain to be explained were to a great extent just the geographic reflection of the primary nongeographic division, between Catholics and Protestants: the more Catholic the province, the larger the Liberal share. Nevertheless, the association of Catholic religion and Liberal party preference arose not from party and denominational divisions over faith and morals but from conflict over external policy. Starting in 1899, the most regularly recurring ethnoreligious division in Canadian political life was over how much Canada and Canadians owed the Empire.

The issue first emerged in rough outline with controversy over a Canadian contingent in the South African War; was sharpened by debate over Canada's role, if there was to be any, in the naval arms race of the pre–World War I years; and peaked in 1917, when Canadians were forced to weigh the moral claims of the Empire in the most immediate way conceivable, over conscription of manpower for overseas service. The issue continued through the 1920s and 1930s, as Empire fitfully yielded to Commonwealth and as the dominions were forced to anticipate the Second World War. The 1939–45 war brought back all the questions that had been so divisive in 1914–18.

Canada's association with the Empire mixed considerations of sentiment, trade, and security. Britain was always an important source of immigrants, even after the migrant flow became ethnically diverse at the turn of the twentieth century, and immigration reinforced ties of sentiment. As mentioned above, trade relations down to the postwar period continued to be triangular; most critically, Canada's exports still went mainly overseas. Many Canadians could recall a period in which Canada-U.S. relations were actively hostile, and tensions certainly persisted. So long as Britain remained credible as a Great Power, then, the British connection was Canada's necessary counterweight; only by calling on it could Canada meet the United States on roughly equal terms.[5]

Overseas connections were still important to Canadian policymakers as late as 1950. It seems fairly clear, for instance, that Canadian enthusiasm for NATO reflected a calculation that alliance with the United States would be much easier in a multilateral context than in a bilateral one. When Canadian soldiers went overseas in Korean or NATO service, they did so as part of British or Commonwealth formations.[6] But there was never anything approaching a consensus on the proper course of external policy. If Canada could assert itself only through British channels, groups which could not live with this implication advocated perforce a quietist external policy, accommodationist toward the United States and isolationist overseas.

French Canadians generally preferred the quietist view, as has been widely remarked. But their co-religionists outside French Canada also tended to this view, and the Catholic community, French and English together, was then —as it is now—a formidable political force, close to half the total electorate.[7] One of the keys to political longevity was the ability to maintain a delicate balance between ethnoreligious blocs. Conservatives, however, routinely overplayed the imperial hand. Whatever the geopolitical merits of their position, it was electoral suicide, as long as Liberals trod carefully, which they usually did. The Second World War did bring Mackenzie King's government to the brink of collapse: it was forced in the end to conscript manpower for overseas service, but before it got to that point it suffered losses on both its pro- and anticonscription wings. It was set back in the 1945 election and, as table 3.2 indicates, ethnoreligious divisions continued into the early 1950s.

But the Liberals managed postwar foreign policy challenges well. Where after World War I, Liberal governments were isolationist, after World War II, they were cautiously internationalist. As long as Mackenzie King was prime minister, the internationalism was diffident indeed, as he led a rearguard action within his own cabinet. After his retirement in 1948, the party became more decisively internationalist. His successor, Louis St. Laurent, happened to believe in a higher international profile for Canada and could argue for it with special authority; as a French Canadian, he could not be accused of pursuing imperialistic notions in internationalist disguise. It helped the Liberals that Canadian internationalism had by this time been largely drained of its British content. Now the Great Power sun around which the Canadian moon orbitted was the United States. This galled Conservatives—and many Liberals too—but at that point there was no issue which decisively divided Britain from the United States and thus forced Canadians to choose between the old hegemony and the new.

In domestic politics, the most important development was a modest elaboration of the welfare state. In this domain, Canada was a late starter even by North American standards. The 1935–57 Liberal hegemony began with no obvious social policy mandate. Indeed, the nearest thing to a comprehensive program was enacted in the death throes of the Conservative government that Mackenzie King and the Liberals displaced. Much of the program was struck down by the Judicial Committee of the British

Privy Council, but the Liberals could hardly interpret their own victory as a rebuke to the judiciary. The welfare state the Liberals actually implemented was precipitated by World War II and by apprehension of a CCF surge.

The first major scheme, unemployment insurance, predated the rise of the CCF,[8] but that party's spectacular growth between 1943 and 1945 impelled all other social policy innovations in the period. By 1943, the CCF formed the opposition in three provinces, including the largest one, Ontario. In some of the earliest Canadian Gallup polls, the CCF returned shares rivaling those for the Liberals, and, as mentioned above, in 1944 the CCF took power in Saskatchewan. In 1944, the Liberal government established the Family Allowance program, passed the National Housing Act, and created the framework for labor relations that has lasted to this day. In 1945, the government committed itself in a White Paper on Employment and Income to countercyclical macroeconomic management and fleshed out this commitment, together with proposals for further extension of the welfare state, at a Dominion-Provincial Conference on Reconstruction.

But there matters largely stopped. Ontario and Quebec, the two largest provinces, resisted the centralization implicit in these proposals, and the Mackenzie King government lacked the will to insist. Moreover, the Liberals paid no price for their diffidence: the CCF stalled in postwar polls, and the Liberals surged in 1949, partly at the CCF's expense. Two universal, noncontributory elements in the 1945 White Paper, an old-age pension scheme and hospitalization insurance, eventually became law, but grudgingly and with only modest funding.

The politics of the welfare state thus did not, in the end, disturb the major party balance. Advocacy tended to come from offstage, with occasional appearances on stage by the CCF. Liberal hesitations in 1943 may have helped the CCF grow, but by 1945 further hesitation had no such effect. The Conservative party in the period seemed a little slower than the Liberals to enter into the welfare state consensus, but as a rule, once Liberals acted, Conservatives supported them. The country hardly seemed seized with controversy over the issue.

Parliamentary life mirrored the complacency of the period. The government dominated parliament, numerically and morally. Evidence for the numerical part of this claim is in table 3.3. In 1935, the Liberals returned the largest seat majority to that date in Canadian history, a majority which only grew in 1940. The 1945 election cut the majority sharply, yet this seemed only to concentrate the government's mind. In 1949, its parliamentary share surged again, and it remained very comfortable in the 1953 election. In four of five parliaments, the government controlled over 70

Table 3.3.   The Geography of Seats

	Period			Shift	
Region	(1) 1935–57[a]	(2) 1963–84[a]	(3) 1984–93[a]	(2)–(1)	(3)–(2)
			Liberals		
BC	45.8	27.0	3.4	−18.8	−23.6
Alta	22.4	3.9	0.0	−18.5	−3.9
Sask	48.4	6.6	0.0	−41.8	−6.6
Man	72.3	18.7	21.0	−53.6	+2.7
Ont	61.4	55.9	29.0	−5.5	−26.8
Que	88.2	79.9	19.0	−8.3	−60.5
NB	72.0	55.9	30.0	−16.1	−25.9
NS	83.7	25.0	36.0	−58.7	+11.4
PEI	85.0	14.3	63.0	−70.7	+48.2
Nfld[b]	85.7	63.3	57.0	−22.4	−6.1
Canada	66.7	49.2	21.0	−16.9	−28.0
			Conservatives		
BC	23.6	35.4	53.0	+11.8	+17.3
Alta	8.3	92.8	98.0	+84.5	+5.9
Sask	6.0	67.9	47.0	−61.9	−23.4
Man	10.3	58.5	57.0	−48.2	−1.3
Ont	37.7	36.5	59.0	−1.2	+22.0
Que	4.1	5.4	81.0	+1.3	+75.3
NB	28.0	37.3	70.0	+9.3	+32.7
NS	9.7	72.4	64.0	−62.7	−8.7
PEI	15.0	85.7	38.0	+60.7	−48.2
Nfld[b]	4.3	34.7	43.0	· +20.4	+8.2
Canada	18.9	37.3	66.0	+18.4	28.8
			CCF-NDP		
BC	19.7	34.3	44	+14.6	+9.7
Alta	0.0	0.0	1.9	0.0	1.9
Sask	33.5	25.5	54.0	−8.0	+28.1
Man	17.5	28.2	22.0	+10.7	−6.7
Ont	0.5	13.4	12.0	+12.9	−1.5
Que	0.0	0.0	0.0	0.0	0.0
NB	0.0	0.0	0.0	0.0	0.0
NS	6.5	1.3	0.0	−5.2	−1.3
PEI	0.0	0.0	0.0	0.0	0.0
Nfld[b]	0.0	0.0	0.0	0.0	0.0
Canada	6.3	8.7	13.0	+2.4	+3.9

(*table continued on following page*)

Table 3.3.   (*continued*)

Region	Period			Shift	
	(1) 1935–57[a]	(2) 1963–84[a]	(3) 1984–93[a]	(2)–(1)	(3)–(2)
			Others		
BC	10.9	3.2	0.0	−7.7	−3.2
Alta	69.4	3.4	0.0	−66.0	3.4
Sask	12.1	0.0	0.0	−12.1	0.0
Man	0.0	0.0	0.0	0.0	0.0
Ont	0.5	0.0	0.6	−0.5	+0.6
Que	7.7	14.7	0.0	+7.0	14.7
NB	0.0	6.8	0.0	+6.8	−6.8
NS	0.0	1.3	0.0	+1.3	−1.3
PEI	0.0	0.0	0.0	0.0	0.0
Nfld[b]	0.0	0.0	0.0	0.0	0.0
Canada	8.1	4.8	0.2	−3.2	−4.6

[a]Period averages do not include the election in the last year of the period.
[b]Elections of 1949 and 1953 only in first period.

percent of the seats and outnumbered the Conservatives, the official opposition, about five to one.

Notwithstanding the east-west electoral gradient described above, the parliamentary Liberal party came as close as any party can to representing, if not all the people, at least all the provinces. In the typical election, Liberals controlled a plurality of seats in every province but one (Alberta) and an outright majority of seats in over half. The Liberal cabinet was a collection of regional chieftains, each able to speak authoritatively for his province. Such a chieftain was authoritative in two senses: able to get his cabinet colleagues to take him seriously and unrivaled back home. The cabinet was acutely conscious of the regional impact of its policies, even as the prime minister sought pan-regional consensus. Meanwhile, the prime minister respected the autonomy of each provincial leader within his sphere. There simply was no such thing as a national party; there was only a federation of provincial parties. In its structure as in its behavior, the Liberal party did not challenge the identification of Canadians with their provinces. Yet it was able, by indirection, to mobilize Canadians for total war and to begin creating a national welfare state.[9]

The Liberal party took on a national appearance only when it gathered in convention.[10] The most important conventions were for choosing a leader, and only two such gatherings occurred before 1957. Until recently, Canadian parties were the only ones in the Westminster tradition to go outside parliament in this way. Each party felt forced to do so at a critical juncture. For the Liberals this came in 1919, when their representation outside Quebec was feeble; the convention's strategic value seemed confirmed by the party's success at the next election. The 1948 convention reinforced the 1919 lesson: it followed the 1945 setback and led, seemingly, to the smashing 1949 victory.

Whatever its electoral uses, leadership selection by extraparliamentary convention has subtly affected the constitution. Party leaders can appeal to a (somewhat specious) extraparliamentary mandate to overawe their backbench and cabinet colleagues. This encourages a centralization within parties altogether at odds with—and which may even encourage— other, centrifugal forces in Canadian politics. Also, the intraparty tendency the leader represents may be in conflict with the tendency that dominates parliamentary ranks. In government, the result may be sullen backbench submission and the artificial bottling-up of potential threats to the party. In opposition, sporadic rebellion—all the more frequent for being pointless—has not been uncommon.[11]

For Liberals in this period, though, these concerns seem beside the point. It is fairly clear that the 1948 convention—and perhaps the 1919 one as well—ratified what almost certainly would have been the parliamentary party's own choice. Sitting M.P.s dominated selection of delegates from their own constituencies, and, notwithstanding the 1945 reverse, over half the constituencies had a Liberal M.P. Whatever the mechanics of selection, Liberals have embodied the strategic logic of the electoral system in their choice of leaders: since 1887, strict alternation between French and English has been the rule. Once the party moved to conventions in 1919, enforcement of the rule required great subtlety. Never was this rule written down, and may Liberal activists never accepted it. But it was widely enough supported to be effective.

Accordingly, when it was the English turn, no francophone offered himself as a leadership candidate. When it was the French turn, only one francophone came forward; virtually all francophone delegates supported him, and a significant fraction of the rest rallied to him, many of them specifically to maintain the alternation. This has not been tokenism: the three Liberal leaders from Quebec before 1984 became long-serving prime ministers, heads of government for well over half the total Liberal time in power between 1896 and 1984. The Liberal share of the Quebec vote has typically been higher when the leader is from that province than otherwise. Even when the leader was not from Quebec, the Liberal share remained high enough to win almost all of the province's seats. The alternation rule worked well as long as Conservatives remained indifferent or hostile to Quebec.

All this said, the geographic inclusiveness and the lopsidedness of Liberal parliamentary majorities were artifacts of the plurality electoral system. Only in 1940 did the Liberals win an outright popular majority. The key to Liberal success in and after 1935 was the fragmentation of the rest of the vote. The largest single opposition party, the Conservatives, received an average share in this period of only 29.7 percent. The largest share for any other single party in any election, for the CCF in 1945, was 15.7 percent.

The Diefenbaker Interlude

By the mid-1950s, the old party system was living on borrowed time. The commercial-policy divisions which the Liberal party had finessed so successfully were waiting to explode as the western wheat economy experienced intense pressure, pressure which reflected a general reorientation of the Canadian economy. The postwar alignment of international forces no longer corresponded to the one around which the primary Catholic/ Protestant cleavage was organized: obligations to the Empire were ceasing to be a pivotal question as the Empire evaporated and its metropolitan center declined. Meanwhile, the Liberal government seemed to be rotting from within. Regional ministers lost touch with their bases; those still attuned to their bases lost influence at the center. The government turned more and more to its advisors in the civil service; indeed, the boundary between politics and administration seemed to erode.

On the economy, the Liberals sinned as much by omission as commission. The government seemed oblivious to the decline of the western wheat economy. Some of the agrarian decline was a structural shift common to many crops and countries, but it also reflected a global shift in the terms of trade, partly as the United States began to dump New Deal surpluses on the market. Western Canadian farm incomes dropped dramatically between 1953 and 1957, and the crisis breathed life into demands first articulated before World War II. As the agrarian program outgrew its first-generation critique of tariffs and railways, grain producers began to shift away from demanding an implicit reduction in Ottawa's role and toward advocacy of direct national intervention in markets for capital and, most critically, for the commodities themselves.

The new demands reflected Canadian experience with centralized marketing during the wars and were reinforced by awareness of the very New Deal programs that created U.S. surpluses. But neither major party was prepared to come out and advocate what amounted to protection for primary producers. The protection they continued to defend, if only tacitly, was for secondary producers, and this stance was starting to seem archaic. Their premise, that Canada-U.S. trade was asymmetric, was undermined as this period accelerated a trend already visible before World War II, which saw the United States displace the United Kingdom as the primary export destination for Canada. In the 1950s, these exports still tended to be primary products, and a very large percentage of export-oriented firms were American-owned. Foreign, mainly U.S., investment began to surface as an opposition issue.

Canadians also awakened to the reality of U.S. power in the Suez crisis. In later years, the crisis was remembered in Canada for the Nobel Peace Prize that Liberal foreign minister (later leader and prime minister) Lester Pearson won for his efforts to resolve it. In electoral terms, however, Suez may have cost the Liberals dearly. Whatever the realities in the Middle East and in UN diplomacy, the government's position on the crisis violated a basic rule of the old external-policy regime: never choose the United States over Britain. The argument that the government could hardly do otherwise, if it was to save its honor, was undoubtedly lost on many English Canadians in 1956. The Conservatives could even make an argument that would soon become commonplace: America as hypocrite. Why, the Conservatives asked, could Britain and France not defend the canal they had built and financed when the United States rested secure in control of its canal in Panama? For his part, the Liberal prime minister was reduced to characterizing Britain (and France, but this mattered less politically) as "the Supermen of Europe." Never before had a Canadian prime minister used such pejorative language about what was still routinely referred to as the Mother Country.[12]

Underlying these mistakes was a hardening of the government's arteries. Much has been made of two events which symbolize a party grown arrogant. In 1955, the government sought to extend its postwar defense production powers to legislate by fiat, but could supply no rationale for doing so, and met such a storm in the House that the bill had to be withdrawn. In 1956 came the "pipeline debate": the government sought rapid approval of a bill granting right-of-way and securing loans for an American-controlled gas pipeline venture; the opposition resisted but debate was cut off unilaterally by the government, the first time this had been done since 1913. The event left the government vulnerable to attack both for having abused parliament and for having sold out to American interests.[13]

That is not to say the Liberal government was doomed, come what may. Poll evidence on satisfaction with the Liberals in power is striking. In Gallup polls the Liberals *never* lost ground between elections; questions about the prime minister's handling of his job produced astonishing levels of approval; and neither the 1955 nor the 1956 events mentioned in the preceding paragraphs made any impression on vote intentions.[14] What the lack of effect illustrates is, however, that dissatisfaction with the status quo does not automatically produce rejection of it; there must also be a credible alternative. Activation of dissatisfaction requires an individual at the head of the opposition party able to articulate the strategically correct subtext.

The Conservative party had conspicuously failed to find such a leader, in order to articulate an alternative to the Liberals' centrist agenda. This was not for lack of trying. Conservatives chose four leaders in convention (twice as many as the Liberals) before 1956; in 1942, a fifth leader was chosen by an extraordinary meeting of party notables, and two other individuals served as acting leaders for nontrivial periods. Although the party was comatose in the western provinces throughout this period, two of its four conventions chose leaders actively identified with the region; the Liberal party never did so. The Conservatives in convention also made a gesture across the ethnoreligious divide: in 1938, they chose R. J. Manion, a Roman Catholic with a francophone wife. Twice a convention chose an individual with an impressive record in provincial politics.

But of all these conventions, only the first one, in 1927, rejuvenated the party. And the cup of victory which followed was of course poisoned, for the party's victory in 1930 made it the scapegoat for the depression and set it up for the fall in 1935. Finally, in December of 1956, the Conservatives found the key to the Liberal safe: almost in spite of themselves,[15] they made John Diefenbaker from Saskatchewan leader. Diefenbaker did not merely articulate resentment against Liberal hegemony; his whole being—his lower jaw, especially—seemed to resonate with it. And in this spirit was the Diefenbaker interlude inaugurated.[16]

The Liberal collapse began in 1957. Polls suggested an easy Liberal victory until some point in the last two weeks of the campaign, whereupon a comfortable Liberal lead became a standoff. Although the Liberals actually won a narrow plurality in the popular vote, the Conservatives returned a narrow plurality of seats. The Liberals declined to test their luck in the new hung parliament, and so was formed the first Conservative government in twenty-two years and the first minority government since 1926. The parliament which followed served mainly as a stage for the new government to smite the old one for its sins. Parliament was dissolved again in 1958, and this time the Conservatives won a majority even larger than the Liberal ones secured by Mackenzie King and St. Laurent.

Over the 1957 and 1958 elections, the Conservative vote share grew most where the party had formerly been weakest. Growth was most dramatic in the west, especially in 1958. Even Quebec shifted significantly toward the Conservatives. Simultaneously, the old religious cleavage in English Canada widened, according to table 3.2. On the other hand, no sooner had the Conservatives swept the field than their rot began. Polls suggested that the government was in serious trouble by mid-1960. Virtually all gains of 1958 over 1957 were dissipated in the election of 1962, and, once again, the Conservatives were a minority government with a smaller popular vote than the Liberal opposition.

This government was racked by dissension and fell in early 1963. In that year's election, most 1957 gains over 1953 were dissipated, and the party was once again consigned to opposition. Nevertheless, the symmetry of Conservative rise and fall was more apparent than real, according to table 3.1. Where the party had gained most, it remained strong, in the prairie west and, to a lesser extent, the Atlantic provinces. Its only losses came in Ontario, its pre-1957 bastion, and in Quebec. The Conservatives' geographic base, so to speak, rotated. The same could not be said of the party's nongeographic foundations, as table 3.2 indicates only a subtle reshaping.

The size of the Liberal collapse and the fact that the party's 1953–58 losses were directly proportional to its 1953 strength suggests that the biggest single story was about generalized retribution on a government grown old. But it took the electorate two stages to punish the Liberals fully. The first stage, the 1957 election, featured modest swings and a rather accidental parliamentary result. At this point, anti-Liberal reaction appears to have been fairly focused: Conservative gains between 1956 and 1957, according to Gallup evidence, came almost entirely among Protestant English Canadians; this points to Suez as a critical factor in the initial shifts.[17] Generalized retribution followed only when a wider circle of the electorate saw that the Liberals were truly vulnerable.

If agrarian distress fails to account for the 1953–58 Conservative surge, it was critical to the pattern of 1958–63 decline. The fact that all regions supported the Conservatives to about the same degree in 1958 suggests that the huge 1953–57–58 swing in the prairie provinces was an artifact of the starting point, a token of the region's earlier aversion to the Conservatives rather than of any specifically regional focus to John Diefenbaker's early appeal. *After* 1958, Diefenbaker's appeal took on its regional cast: the region which resisted the anti-Conservative tide in the 1960s was the one which had suffered most in the 1950s. This fit the Diefenbaker government's advocacy of a greater federal role in promoting resource extraction. Rhetoric outran reality, but the symbolic shift was huge. Never before had the Conservative party argued that resource extraction was the key to Canada's future; the party's traditional role had been to argue the opposite.

In defiance of their civil servants and of received opinion, the Diefenbaker government set out both to subsidize wheat and to seek new markets. They lightened the effective carrying charges for producers;

they built a massive irrigation complex in southwestern Saskatchewan; they sold wheat in volumes never seen before and in markets (such as communist-bloc countries) that took political courage to enter. When the Liberals returned to power, this effort slackened. For the oil industry, the Conservative government turned the old commercial policy on its head. By world standards, Canada is a small, high-cost, oil and gas producer and enjoyed, before 1973, no serious prospect of comparative advantage in any market. In 1961, the Ontario market was reserved for Alberta production, and for the first time, consumers in the east were forced to pay above the world price for a western resource.

If the commercial-policy reorientation secured the new Conservative base, it could not contain the party's losses elsewhere. As with the Liberals in 1957–58, some of the Conservative retreat in 1962–63 was across the board and bespeaks generalized retribution on a government that was just not very good. National resources policy aside, the government lacked an agenda. At least it lacked one that fit the realities of postwar diplomacy and of Canada's own sociocultural evolution.

On the diplomatic front, John Diefenbaker was the last Canadian prime minister to seek influence over British foreign policy, symptomatically in a failed attempt to stop Britain from seeking admission to the European Community. Diefenbaker took the Commonwealth very seriously, but was forced to admit that doing so involved concessions to a third-world agenda that Conservatives had earlier abhorred. To his credit, he made a virtue of this necessity. In any case, the Britain that Diefenbaker sought to influence was a shadow of its former self, part of Europe yet wedded as closely as Canada to American global strategy. Diefenbaker himself hesitated to accept Canada's strategic position, and his hesitations contributed to the government's ultimate collapse.

Diefenbaker's fall was occasioned by debate over whether or not to yield to U.S. pressure to accept nuclear weapons and was lamented as the defeat not just of a party but of Canadian nationalism.[18] If it *was* a defeat for Canadian nationalism, it was for a variant less and less widely shared, not least within John Diefenbaker's own party. The American pressure the Diefenbaker government resisted was to deliver on a commitment the government itself had made, and the advice Diefenbaker rejected came from his own ministers. Intentionally or not, the ministers anticipated later trends: after 1963, recruits to the Conservative party tended to be quite pro–United States, partly as a consequence of the sectional realignment engineered, ironically, by Diefenbaker himself.

Nostalgia also played a role in John Diefenbaker's attitude to the symbolic aspects of Canadian nationhood, although here the story is complex. As the bearer of a German surname, Diefenbaker was strategically placed. He had experienced xenophobia directly; as late as 1956, anti-German sentiment was a subtext in the resistance of Conservative notables to his rise. Under the circumstances, it was natural for him to advocate an unhyphenated Canadianism. But such an emphasis was double-edged. On one hand, it helped bind some non-British groups to the Conservative party. On the other, it could readily be interpreted as code for ethnic exclusion and, most particularly, as resistance to any variant of francophone and minority-ethnic assertion.

Inadvertently or otherwise, Diefenbaker encouraged the second interpretation by his abiding emphasis on specifically British themes. Even if his successors as Conservative leader found Diefenbaker's own views distasteful, they nonetheless benefitted from—and had to work with—coalitional materials he assembled. When the dust settled in 1963, the Conservative coalition was larger than before. It may have been so because of John Diefenbaker's equivocal ethnic appeal and legacy, but serious questions remained about the party's potential to grow.

Government on Sufferance, 1963–1984

Superficially, the 1963 election restored the natural order of things: Liberals in government, Conservatives in opposition. For the next twenty-one years, the Liberals were out of power for less than a year. The CCF disappeared, but its offspring, the NDP, abided. Social Credit dwindled quickly outside Quebec, but its Quebec variant surged in 1962 and 1963 and did not entirely disappear until 1980. Underneath, however, a profound realignment of the electorate occurred, and from this followed a redefinition of the political order. Although the Liberal party remained the only party with any pretensions to dominance, its pretensions were a pale shadow of earlier ones. Governments could no longer absolutely dominate parliament, nor could they claim to represent all parts of the country.

Now, the governing Liberals almost never won a plurality of seats outside Quebec. And the country's various sectional, jurisdictional, class, and ethnic parts became more conscious of their separateness—and assertive in their claims. The weakened standing of parties in government matched and probably contributed to a weakening in the position of the whole central government apparatus. At the same time, the national parties became more truly national in how they were organized. Yet this nationalization made it harder for them to accommodate all groups and sections and only exacerbated tensions between Ottawa and the provinces.

First of all, popular-vote shares of key players converged modestly.

Roughly speaking, the Liberal share dropped about five points, while Conservative and NDP shares grew about five points. The accounting does not balance because other parties, notably Social Credit, also shrank. The party best placed to govern was thus significantly weakened. The principal opposition party was stronger, but still far from the zone of single-party seat majorities. The third player was still well back but was now seemingly poised to move up to major-party status.

The Liberal share shrank everywhere, but shrinkage was greatest in the peripheries, the prairie west and the Atlantic provinces, where the Conservatives held on to their 1953–58 gains. Now, Liberals could squeeze popular-vote majorities out of only two provinces, Quebec and Newfoundland. The party held on to pluralities in only two other provinces, Ontario and New Brunswick. Elsewhere the party was a distant second, and in two provinces, British Columbia and Saskatchewan, typically finished third. Conservatives now usually won popular-vote majorities in two provinces and pluralities in four others. In no province did the Conservatives finish worse than second, although in Quebec the second-place finish was even more derisory than it had been before 1958. The NDP gained where the CCF had been weak. Most consequential was the party's growth in Ontario, which now gave the NDP its fourth-largest share of a provincial percentage and, because of its size, almost half the party's total vote. Otherwise little changed in the social-democratic coalition, apart from a modest slide in the old homeland, Saskatchewan.

If change in the geography of the system reflected a first-round reorientation of commercial policy, the new geography produced further commercial-policy shifts. Now the Liberals were dominated by the nationalist heartland. By the late 1960s, Liberals began to worry about the foreign investment that in the 1950s they had welcomed. The new tendency was reinforced by the oil crisis of the 1970s. As the world oil price rose, Canadian production became competitive in North American markets. The question became: who would capture rents from higher prices? The Liberal government under Pierre Trudeau answered: the same Ontario consumers whom John Diefenbaker had forced to subsidize the western industry. To them were added consumers in Quebec and the Atlantic provinces whose imported oil was subsidized by revenues from a tax on exports of Alberta oil to the United States.

In the early 1980s, the Liberal government upped the ante by introducing the National Energy Policy (NEP), at whose heart were sector-specific taxes designed to capture any remaining rent. Revenues were used to subsidize various "Canadianization" moves: creation of a national oil corporation and production subsidies for firms meeting Canadian ownership requirements, especially if they were willing to look for oil in the very high-cost Arctic fields that, not incidentally, lay under federal control. This attack on the Alberta oil industry drove the Conservative party in an increasingly *anti*-nationalist direction.

The ethnoreligious foundations of the system became, if anything, more important than before, according to table 3.2. The religious cleavage widened in the 1957–63 transition and then narrowed. In Liberal vote intentions, the religious cleavage eventually shrank, relative to the pre-1957 pattern; for the Conservatives, the cleavage simply returned to its pre-1957 width. All the while, the linguistic cleavage was widening, such that by the 1970s the linguistic gap within the Catholic community was almost as wide as the religious gap within the anglophone community.[19] If we had other ethnic indicators, we would find a parallel shift: ethnicity, independent of religion, became generally more important in Canadian elections. The Liberal party thus became ethnoreligously more specialized and the Conservative party modestly less so. In Protestant English Canada, the Liberal share shrank dramatically, such that the party's coalition centered even more around the traditional Catholic and francophone core, supplemented by non-Europeans.

The Conservative party, conversely, made gains in three groups. It reinforced its preexisting base among Protestant English Canadians; it added significant support from the non-British groups most like the British, namely, voters with origins in the Protestant monarchies of Northern Europe; and it gained the support of anti-Communist voters of Central and Eastern European origin. This sharpening of ethnic differences reflected an intensification of symbolic politics. If the Empire had retreated from the world at large by 1963, its skirmishers inside Canada held on longer. Coalitions built around the foreign policy questions of 1900 conditioned responses by the parties to the ethnic challenges of the 1960s.

The pivotal group in the ethnic drama was still French Canada. Although the agenda soon expanded beyond francophone questions, it is difficult to believe that other ethnic issues would have gained so much force but for the primary challenge posed by French Canada. The francophone agenda has two parts, one for Quebec, another for the rest of the country. Before 1960, governments in Quebec were mainly on the defensive. Although they resisted central government initiatives, they had no program of their own. Indeed, the public philosophy of the province was anti-statist; effective control of social policy and education, two critical elements in provincial jurisdiction, lay with the Catholic Church. By the later 1950s, the disjunction between the rural and clerical ethos of the provincial government and the urban reality of the province was extreme.

The election in 1960 of a provincial Liberal government, whose agenda went beyond bringing Quebec in line with other provinces, changed all that. Henceforth governments in Quebec sought to expand the scope for action by the one jurisdiction francophones dominate, to the point that some have advocated eliminating virtually all direct links between Ottawa and individual citizens in the province. For the rest of Canada, the francophone agenda arises from the federal government's natural desire to create a countervailing pole for francophone loyalty, to make francophones feel secure in the country as a whole. To this end, Ottawa has bilingualized its own operations, used its spending power to promote bilingualism among anglophones and to shore up francophone minorities outside Quebec, and imposed bilingual usages on the market. These measures tended to get nominal support from all parties, but were clearly most congenial for a Liberal party which in 1963 found itself forced back on its traditional francophone base in central Canada.

Accommodating French Canada could not be done in isolation; coalition partners had to be found, and out of this necessity arose the broadening of the ethnic agenda. The symbolism of the polity was the place to start, for by the 1960s, the pretence that Canada (apart from Quebec) was a British place could no longer be sustained. Many non-British groups were happy to see the specifically British public visage of government effaced. Beyond this, the culturally specific claims of francophones encouraged other groups to stake similar ones, to demand symbolic recognition of their contributions to Canadian life. Again, although legislation responding to these claims tended to get all-party support, the policy fitted the Liberal party's coalition best.

Left out of all of this were Canadians of British and Northern European origin, whose traditional definition of the country was now under threat. John Diefenbaker captured this widely felt sense of dispossession, and Conservatives benefitted from a politics of nostalgia even after he lost control of the party. The groups that indulged in the nostalgia tended to believe that they were the natural majority. So long as they were out of power, Conservatives could claim that brokerage, building a coalition of minorities, was a peculiarly Liberal sin.

The rise of the NDP again forced the system to pay more attention to welfare and labor policy. Recall the pre-1960 pattern: the CCF threatens to gain electorally; Liberals find the median voter with unerring precision and do no more and no less than that voter wants; Conservatives converge on the median almost instantly; and the CCF threat recedes. The difference after 1960 is that the NDP was much stronger than the CCF had been. Not only was the electoral threat from the NDP greater in an anticipatory sense, but the party actually controlled more seats. Equally critically, from 1963 to 1968 and again from 1972 to 1974, Liberal governments controlled only a minority of seats and felt pressed to move toward the NDP position.

Thanks to all this, the 1960s and 1970s saw the last major extension of the country's social insurance and welfare system: the Canada Pension Plan, a universal but earnings-based contributory scheme; "medicare," a publicly run, cost-shared, universal, compulsory insurance system for virtually all physician services; and the Canada Assistance Plan, under which Ottawa pays about half of all outlays on social assistance, "welfare" in the traditional sense. The unemployment insurance system was expanded significantly. Once these programs were in place, no groundswell could be detected for further elaboration of the welfare state. After 1974, the NDP was never again in a position to extract concessions from a minority Liberal government. Welfare politics shifted to defending or paring back what had been accomplished.

Labor politics in Ottawa followed roughly the same trajectory. Liberal minority governments, pushed by the NDP, opened the federal civil service to collective bargaining and strike action. Postal strikes, in particular, became part of the regular background noise of Canadian life. Persistent inflation sharpened the class dimension in Canadian politics. As a majority government from 1968 to 1972, the Liberals sought to curb price increases. Forced to court NDP support between 1972 and 1974, Liberals made fighting unemployment a priority. With their majority restored in 1974, Liberals gave the country a dose of comprehensive price and (mainly) wage controls in 1975–78 that was bitterly opposed by organized labor. In the 1980s, a recurring anti-inflationary move was public-sector wage restraint.

The parliamentary situation that ensued from all this seemed to bring out the best and the worst in the political class. The 1960s were extraordinarily creative, in that Liberal governments undertook numerous policy initiatives and confronted the country's ethnic complexity directly. But these governments never seemed entirely legitimate. Four of the seven elections from 1963 to 1980 yielded hung parliaments. Governments were in a minority for almost eight of the twenty-one years from 1963 to 1984.

Table 3.3 shows how narrow the parliamentary foundations of Liberal government became. Where before 1957 the electoral system made Liberal governments seem *more* broadly based than they, in a sense, deserved to, after 1963 the reverse was true. The fact that over one western voter in four supported the Liberal party (as compared with one in three in the earlier period) found almost no reflection in parliament. Almost all of the government's sitting members were from central and Atlantic Canada; almost all western M.P.'s sat on the opposition benches. The last Liberal government of the era, formed in 1980, had no M.P. from west of Winnipeg, only one from west of Ontario.

Governments thus lacked legitimacy in the country's fastest growing region, a region responsible, moreover, for a disproportionate share of Canada's exports. Given the strictly partisan logic of cabinet government, westerners felt the burden of taxation without representation. The high point was the National Energy Policy. Where John Diefenbaker's preoccupation with resource policy signaled a gut appreciation of the western sensibility, Liberal governments focused on natural resources not so much to support the industries as to bleed them. And most of the time, Liberals seemed preoccupied with the linguistic and ethnic questions that preoccupied Quebec and metropolitan Toronto but alternately bored and infuriated many in the west.

Life in the House of Commons became very bitter. Although Conservative M.P.s were now twice as numerous as they had been before 1957, they hardly seemed closer to power. It was as if their numbers empowered them only to act out their frustrations, not sublimate them. If Diefenbaker increased his party's parliamentary share precisely by keeping the pot of resentment against those in power on the boil, his successors often found themselves struggling to keep their own backbenchers' aggression in check. At various points, parliament ground to a halt, most notably over the new Canadian flag in 1965 and over the NEP in 1982. The Conservative opposition regularly invoked the imagery of the 1956 pipeline debate, but now it was they who held the procedural initiative. Governments, though weak, were forced to arm themselves with majoritarian devices, yet actual use of the devices created the appearance of authoritarian insensitivity.

On both substance and procedure, Liberal governments were often forced to seek help, and the NDP was usually the logical place to look. Given the NDP's western base, its support helped mitigate some of the Liberals' legitimacy problem. But the NDP was not in the mainstream itself, and the Liberal governments had to be wary of seeming subservient to a minority interest. The NDP too had to be very careful: they could not afford to appear to be just the Liberal party in disguise. Both parties face a predicament arising out of the logic of the plurality electoral formula in a multiparty context. The NDP is, after all, interested in policy, as most parties are,[20] and thus has a stake in influencing the government. But the plurality formula militates against the NDP's actually entering a coalition.

In the constituencies, NDP and Liberal candidates must periodically go against each other head to head, lest their respective organizations atrophy. They cannot plausibly do so, however, if their parties are formally linked in government. All parties thus face incentives to acquiesce in single-party minority government and must contend with all the difficulties that go with it.[21]

Some of Liberal governments' creativity, then, came out of the difficult parliamentary situation; certainly, the most creative—at least the most active—governments were the minority ones. But the party's creativity also reflected its own organizational transformation, accomplished in the 1957–63 interregnum. Toward the end of the old order, the Liberal machine ran on self-sustaining momentum: it employed the levers of power to perpetuate itself even as its grass roots withered. Once swept from power, the party was forced to renew itself or die. A handful of reformers, mainly from urban centers, staged two remarkable conferences which outlined party policy for the decade to come. Reformers proved willing to tackle politically hard questions, to push the party to make choices, and to seek office themselves when 1962 arrived.

Making choices makes enemies, and the very policy commitments that reformers urged on the Liberal party narrowed the party's appeal. The new urban focus of the party alienated erstwhile supporters in the west; Liberals could no longer hope to compete with the highly western-focused appeal of the Conservatives. And the Liberals could no longer count on regional chieftains to check the zeal of amateurs. Connections were now much more directly between the national office and the local constituency. In many provinces, provincial and federal organizations split from each other, with the deepest division in Quebec. Entirely different types of political animals could be attracted to each wing. The federal Liberal party became, in fact, a *national* organization. But it did so at the price of restricting the party's appeal in the nation at large.[22]

Similar stories can be told about the other parties. John Diefenbaker attracted a personal following and was beholden to no regional strongmen. As discontent with his leadership spread after 1963, it had to be expressed through national organs. Although Diefenbaker himself was an ideological chameleon, recruits to his party in its new places of strength tended to be consistently conservative, to champion small-business and small-town values. And to the extent that they were attracted by the Diefenbaker style, new Conservatives placed a low value on compromise.

The NDP simply carried forward the amateur style that the CCF had pioneered. Its founding convention in 1961 was supposed to signal a formal link to organized labor, and this promised to make the NDP a brokerage party in its own right.[23] In fact, the link to labor was only modestly tighter than it had been under the CCF. It proved politically impossible to strike a formal partnership with an entire labor federation or even with the national office of an individual union. Instead, affiliation was a matter for union locals, and union representation was diluted.[24] In the end, the most important thing about the NDP was just that it was *bigger* than the CCF. With the party's growth came a growth in the overall importance of the amateur style.

A New Political Order?

Where in 1957 Liberal collapse came as a surprise, in 1984 it was widely expected. Still, the scale of the collapse was startling. The swing against the Liberals in 1984 alone was almost as large as the swing over the two elections of 1957–58. The shift was greatest in areas of erstwhile strength and was absolutely stunning in Quebec, the traditional bastion. Conservative gains were virtually the mirror image of Liberal losses. Under Brian Mulroney, the Conservative party returned as geographically homogeneous a popular vote as John Diefenbaker received in 1958 and about as large a parliamentary majority.

As in 1957, much of the 1984 story must be a simple one of cumulative grievance. This time the Liberal run had lasted twenty-one years. Liberal survival was testimony less to the unerring ability of that party to find the median than to the unfeasibility of the Conservative alternative. Once again when a plausible alternative appeared, retribution was severe. The retrospective nature of the 1984 result is strongly suggested by the restoration of virtually all the *status quo ante* in English Canada in 1988. Absolved of further responsibility for the sins of government, Liberals recovered virtually all their erstwhile turf outside Quebec, and the Conservative majority was drastically reduced.

But a majority it remained. No government had returned successive majorities since 1953, and no Conservative government had done so since 1891. The key to the new Conservative dominance was Quebec: the one-sided Liberal share became a one-sided Conservative one, and now it was the Conservative party that started the race halfway to a parliamentary majority. The Conservatives continued to perform respectably outside Quebec; indeed, the alignment of forces outside Quebec largely reproduced the pre-1984 pattern. Liberal support still followed a steep east-west gradient, with the NDP share as the geographic complement to the Liberal one. Conservatives enjoyed significant support everywhere and maintained their base in the prairie west. Nongeographic differences also continued as before.

In Quebec, in contrast to other provinces, the 1984 result was not just retribution on an old Liberal government. The consolidation of Conservative gains in 1988 confirmed that the new version of the party differed radically from the old. For the first time ever, Conservatives offered Quebec a leader from that province.[25] Although Brian Mulroney was not a native French-speaker, he was thoroughly and colloquially bilingual and completely identified with his province. He did for the Conservatives in Quebec what John Diefenbaker did for them in the west. Moreover, the Conservatives trapped the Liberals in the alternation logic that had served them well. In 1984 they had to choose a successor for Pierre Trudeau, and this time it was a non-Quebecker's turn. To make matters worse, a francophone aspirant, Jean Chretien, broke the unspoken rule and mounted a serious campaign to succeed Pierre Trudeau.

Chretien did not in the end seriously threaten John Turner's march to leadership, but his mere presence as the second strongest candidate (with Trudeau's apparent approval) forced the Liberal party to do something it had never done before: choose an anglophone over a francophone. This created little turmoil among party elites; Quebec notables tended to disapprove of Chretien personally, and they understood the logic of alternation profoundly. But there was considerable disappointment among rank-and-file francophone delegates and in the party at large. And if the choice was correct for the long run, it was precisely wrong for 1984. Quebeckers now faced an unprecedented menu: a Conservative party led by a Quebecker and a Liberal party led by a non-Quebecker.

Conservatives continued to be strong outside Quebec. Although they continued to draw on the ethnoreligious coalition John Diefenbaker built, the geography of the coalition resembled that for the Liberals, 1935–57. This was no accident: the Conservatives reverted in many ways to the old Mackenzie King formula of minimal interference with provincial prerogatives. It still seemed true that the way to hold a national coalition together was by avoiding the question of what the nationality was. By constructing a pan-Canadian coalition, Conservatives were stronger in parliament than any government had been for some time. Parliament was not overawed in the way that it had been from 1935 to 1957, but neither did the Mulroney government exist on sufferance. The Liberals were weak especially from 1984 to 1988; they were hardly recognizable as a government in waiting.

On the other hand, in the very breadth of the Conservative electoral coalition lay the seeds of its undoing.[26] The party gained and kept power by assembling a radically incoherent coalition: francophones and francophobes. Incoherence may be the inevitable concomitant of brokerage, but the problems of the Conservatives were special. As the cultural nostalgia so important to his party's appeal outside Quebec did not include an expansive vision of French Canada or of the powers of the francophone heartland, Quebec, Brian Mulroney's difficulties would have been great enough had he merely embraced the Liberal party's approach to French-English relations. In 1984 this indeed seemed to be his position. But his difficulties were compounded by the fact that his post-1984 coalition included many Quebeckers deeply opposed to the Liberal view, who advocated a policy that was even harder to sell to the Conservative heartland than the Liberal one had been.

Recall that Liberal policy was designed not to accommodate Quebec nationalist demands but to deflect them. The Liberal model of language policy was *personal*. Language rights are presented as a kind of civil right, quasi-universalistic and highly portable: francophones should be able to receive services from government and to school their children in French regardless of place of residence.[27] This is a definition of the problem suited to a minority sensibility, and such a sensibility fits well in a party which, like the Liberals, defines itself as a coalition of minorities. This kind of appeal also works among liberal-minded members of the dominant group: the language of rights carries far more weight in Anglo-American culture than the language of power.

But the language of power is what moves the francophone elite in Quebec, as it also moves, when carefully crafted, popular majorities in that province. For Quebec policymakers, the Liberal party's personalistic theory of language is at best noble but unrealistic. At worst, it is a cover for the interests of the linguistic minority with the greatest survival prospects, anglophones in Quebec. The challenge as Quebec elites see it is not to save francophone communities outside the province; the latter tend to get written off as unsalvageable. Rather the challenge has been to secure the dominance of French inside the province, in face of the anglophone minority's traditional (now waning) economic power and of the overwhelming tendency of immigrants in Quebec to prefer English to French. Out of this concern grows a desire to constrain immigration and to regulate the public use of language. Quebec's chosen policy is designed not so much to secure francophone rights as to secure—and express—francophone power.

Federal Liberals may regret the orientation of Quebec, but before 1982 they could not do much about it. Almost all of what Quebec elites set out to do lay squarely within the province's jurisdiction. Language policy in the country as a whole thus proceeded on two tracks: Quebec governments pursued a territorial strategy; Ottawa pursued a personal strategy. So long as each government stayed within its sphere, voters in Quebec approved of both strategies. Quebec voters could in perfect rationality support nationalist policies and governments in the province, where the nation in question is Quebec, and antinationalist ones in Ottawa, where the nation in question is Canada as a whole. Moreover, Pierre Trudeau's own assertion of a personalistic language policy made him the most effective champion of any definition of French Canadian interests in the entire history of federal politics. And as long as the Conservatives seemed indifferent to Quebec, Trudeau's game was the only one in town.

Two choices—one by Liberals, the other by Conservatives—compromised the Liberal formula for success in Quebec. Liberals may have overplayed the personalistic hand. The *Constitution Act, 1982* markedly expanded the entrenched and justiciable part of Canada's constitution. Before 1982, only the federal-provincial division of powers came before the courts. The rest of the constitution was unwritten and conventional, in the best British style, and Canadian courts abided by the strict Diceyan rule that conventions are unenforceable at law. After 1982, an elaborate Charter of Rights and Freedoms, applicable to both levels of government, was entrenched, and Canada embarked on U.S.-style rights litigation.

Most of the rights at issue codify centuries of Anglo-American usage and assumptions. But these rights are arguably just the penumbra: the heart of the charter is an entrenchment—opposed resolutely but unsuccessfully by virtually the entire provincial elite in Quebec—of the personal model of language rights. Where before, federal language policy was a compound of statute law, benignly exercised administrative discretion, and the spending power, now it became a set of justiciable rights. Some of these rights were designed precisely to trump language policies which all major provincial parties in Quebec supported. Where the Liberal party under Trudeau profited politically from the fact that Quebec voters were not forced to choose between alternative linguistic conceptions, the charter ensured that the choice would, sooner or later, be thrust upon them.

One avenue for forcing the choice was the courts, and over the 1980s litigation began to eat away at Quebec language policy. In the short run, this vindicated minority rights; in the long run, it may have refueled separatist sentiment. This is where the Conservative party's choice comes in. Having cashed in his authenticity as a Quebecker on electoral victory, Brian Mulroney then chose Quebec cabinet ministers deeply committed to the territorial view of language policy. Where the Liberals sought alternately to deflect or confront Quebec's linguistic nationalism, the new Conservatives from that province wanted to accommodate it. By making this choice, Conservatives offered Quebec voters something closer to their first preference in language policy than Liberals did.

But the new position of the Conservatives in turn compromised the apparent structure of the very political order which fell into place in 1984. Accommodating Quebec nationalism offends the populist supporters who were John Diefenbaker's legacy to his party. For the first four years, Brian Mulroney was able to keep the western end of the coalition happy by yielding to its commercial-policy demands. The National Energy Policy was swept away early on. In 1985, the government announced its intention to seek a free trade agreement with the United States; the agreement initialed in October of 1987 satisfied a broad range of western demands. Most pointedly, it promised to create a continental energy market, something Alberta exporters had been seeking for years. Not only had the NEP been killed, but thanks to the Canada-U.S. agreement, the corpse could never be resurrected.

Quebec voters had also become ardent free traders, although for reasons that remain mysterious. The province runs a mercantilist economic strategy and remains relatively dependent on labor-intensive industry. Some lay the conversion of Quebeckers at the feet of a new cultural security, but this claim is difficult to square with the ample evidence of *in*security elsewhere in the policy landscape. An ominous possibility is that nationalists in Quebec see Canada-U.S. free trade as fulfilling the preconditions for a relatively costless move to outright political independence. Be that as it may, an emphasis on Canada-U.S. relations was the strategically perfect choice in 1988. Had the emphasis been elsewhere, the Conservative majority might not have survived,[28] and once the trade question was settled, the Conservative electoral coalition exploded.

Or Breakdown?

The language pot boiled over less than a month after the 1988 election, as the Supreme Court, acting under the charter, struck down a centerpiece of Quebec language law. Quebec replied by reenacting the essentials of its language policy and sheltered it from further judicial review under a little-used provision of the 1982 constitution. The ensuing controversy convinced many Quebeckers of the iniquity of the charter and many outside Quebec of the iniquity of that province's government. The controversy put at risk what the Conservative government had hoped would be the centerpiece of its strategy of reconciling opposites: the Meech Lake Accord, an all-province constitutional agreement whose core was legal recognition of Quebec as a "distinct society" within Canada. Controversy raged over what the clause really meant, but it was clearly reviled outside Quebec.[29]

The accord's death in June of 1990 only deepened the sense of crisis. Over the next two years, Quebec and the rest of Canada, in entirely separate processes, went through extended constitutional self-analysis. Quebec set 26 October 1992 as the deadline for offers from the rest of the country; if no offer was made, Quebeckers would vote on whether the province should become fully sovereign. As none of the central players in the drama wanted this to be the question for Quebeckers, yet another constitutional package was negotiated, the Charlottetown Accord. This agreement was much broader than the Meech Lake Accord, reflecting the wider range of interests invited to the negotiating table. The new agreement received support from the entire elected political class and from a remarkably diverse set of interest groups. Notwithstanding the breadth of its backing, the Charlottetown Accord also failed, rejected in an all-Canada referendum on 26 October, Quebec's deadline.

The failure of both constitutional initiatives highlighted the Conservatives' brokerage dilemma. Neither accord rallied English Canadians normally sympathetic to francophone interests, in part because each bargain at best finessed, at worst offended, universalistic moral claims now backed by the Canadian Charter of Rights and Freedoms; both accords were preoccupied mainly with questions of power. Whatever the charter will come to mean in law, it is clear that it has become the symbolic focus for groups hitherto on the margins of Canadian politics; it is *their* piece of the constitution, and they do not want it tampered with.[30] Each accord posed at least a symbolic threat to the social programs of the 1960s and almost certainly made further federal initiatives on social welfare unlikely. Both accords sought to constitutionalize the accommodationist style the Conservatives brought back to federal-provincial relations.

One implication of the recent constitutional impasse may be that a major strategic premise of the Mackenzie King era is no longer valid. Recall that King kept his national party going by being very reluctant to challenge provincial sensibilities. It was in precisely this accommodationist, decentralizing ethos that Brian Mulroney saw his strategic advantage. Now, however, there exist national—strictly speaking, pan-regional—groups and interests that would strive to block decentralizing initiatives, groups called into being by postwar shared-cost programs as well as by the charter. Moreover, *any* attempt to placate French Canada, even by Liberal-style policies, offended the Conservative core. For a significant fraction of the Conservative base in the electorate, accommodating French Canada/Quebec was the only thing the constitutional accords were about. Nice distinctions between personal and territorial language policies, for instance, were of no importance, what they knew was that this was just another concession to French power. Stopping French power—and the power of other minorities—had been the point in voting Conservative.

The Conservative-dominated political order thus came in question virtually the moment writs were returned in 1988. Outside Quebec, a new entity called the Reform Party surged, most sharply in old Social Credit strongholds, places John Diefenbaker had brought into the Conservative camp. Reform expresses discontent with party politics as such, but behind the antiparty rhetoric is the same aversion to strategically placed minorities that Conservatives had earlier courted. The Conservatives' Quebec base also fractured, starting in 1990. As the Meech Lake Accord collapsed, several Conservative M.P.s from Quebec followed Lucien Bouchard, a just-resigned cabinet minister, to cross the floor and sit as a new party, the Bloc Québécois. Although two Liberals joined their parliamentary ranks, most Bloc popular support came at Conservative expense.

Perhaps, then, Brian Mulroney's attempt to build a coalition with francophones and francophobes was doomed from the outset. The task required brokerage skills of the highest order, and Mulroney could lay a powerful claim to possessing them. But he employed them in a context increasingly hostile to the very idea of brokerage.

If Conservative ranks were splintering, the center-left was consolidating. Polls indicated that by 1993, NDP support had dropped to levels not seen since the early days of the CCF. In part, this was the bitter fruit of the NDP's unprecedented success only two years earlier. In 1990–91, the NDP formed governments in Ontario, Saskatchewan, and British Columbia, provinces comprising over half the country's population.

The Ontario and British Columbia governments ran aground quickly. In British Columbia, the problem was the NDP's own version of coalitional incoherence, in the form of conflict between unionized workers and environmentalists. In Ontario, the party inherited, then exacerbated, a fiscal mess which ultimately forced it to attack unionized public sector workers, its own electoral core, with draconian layoffs and wage rollbacks. New Democrats had always argued that the Liberal party was not an acceptable second choice for left voters, as it could not be trusted to safeguard labor or environmental interests. That claim was now undercut: if Liberals still could not be trusted, neither could the NDP after 1992. By turning on its own, the NDP facilitated strategically motivated defection to the Liberals, the party best placed to defeat the Conservatives.

The center-left imperative to consolidate against the Conservatives was a compound of economic dislocation, higher taxes, and the personal unpopularity of Prime Minister Mulroney. In this period, Canada ran one of the tightest monetary regimes in the world, which virtually eradicated inflation but at an enormous price in jobs and output. Tight money coincided with rapid post-1988 adjustment to commercial union with the United States. Although Canada gained a disproportionate share of new North American investment and Canada's trade balance with the United States improved, certain firms and industries retrenched drastically, leaving many displaced workers with no hope of comparable employment.

As this was happening, tax rates climbed, on personal incomes and, perhaps most critically, on consumption. The Conservative government's single most unpopular move seems to have been its imposition of a point-of-sale value-added tax, the Goods and Services Tax (GST). This tax replaced an older sales tax, imposed on goods at the manufacturer's gate. The new tax made the federal presence visible where before it had been invisible; it fell upon a broader range of goods than any earlier sales tax; it covered services, never taxed before; and it was not, despite claims to the contrary, revenue neutral—it increased the overall incidence of taxation. It was passed in the face of adamant opposition, expressed by public opinion polls and by an unusual game of parliamentary chicken in the normally dormant Senate.

Senators are appointed by the Crown on the advice of the prime minister and may sit until age seventy-five. This serves the governing party's patronage interests but usually neuters the chamber politically, even when it has an opposition majority. Liberals still had such a majority in 1991, and decided that their credibility required them to use it against the GST. If this opposition was extraordinary—an appointive body rejecting a major bill, indeed a money bill, from a popularly elected government— so was the government's response. It gave itself a Senate majority under an appointment procedure designed for just such a deadlock, but never before used. Although the government had constitutional propriety on its side, the symbolism was dreadful: last-minute patronage appointments to a widely reviled body to ram through a highly unpopular tax.

Liberals opposed the tax, but were unlikely to repeal it. The GST, or its equivalent by another name, will be central to any attempt to cut Canada's public sector deficit and debt, among the largest proportionally in the industrialized world. And the deficit problem may have been, ironically, one of the few cards left for Conservatives to play. It is true that they had handled the deficit badly; even if the annual deficit shrank as a percentage of GDP, its current-dollar magnitudes did not, and debt continued to cumulate. But Conservatives were still more credible on the deficit than Liberals and New Democrats. Their only real rivals were Reform, ideologically hostile to the public sector as such and thus relatively believable as deficit cutters.

Reform represented two poles of attraction for disgruntled Conservatives: an ethnolinguistic stance reminiscent of John Diefenbaker, and credibility on the deficit. This twofold pull created a delicate structure of preference on the right. The ethnic and fiscal agendas were separable; opinion on one could not be predicted from opinion on the other. By implication, Reform could attract vast numbers of Conservatives if it could activate both agendas. By 1993, Reform had made itself the clear opponent of mainstream ethnic politics. But its distinctiveness on the deficit remained to be established. If Conservatives could keep Reform's deficit positions out of the news, or if they could enhance their own credibility on the question, they might also neutralize Reform's undoubted anti-ethnic appeal. Even if they could not staunch defection to the Liberals, they might at least secure their right flank.

They still had one other problem to solve: Brian Mulroney, the most unpopular prime minister in living memory. Even though the Charlottetown Accord was not really his creation, his advocacy of the deal was clearly a major millstone that helped sink it.[31] Some of his unpopularity stemmed from policy choices and from the post-1990 recession, but some of it was clearly personal. Mulroney recognized this himself and stepped aside in early 1993.

The ensuing succession seemed to bring the history of leadership conventions full circle. Recall that before the 1960s, all parties tried to stage-manage successions, and governing parties usually succeeded. In the 1960s, however, conventions became harder to manage, thanks to the increased role of amateurs and the consequent invigoration of constituency associations. The Conservatives actually delivered three conventions (1967, 1976, and 1983) that featured political drama of the highest order. Pierre Trudeau's convention victory in 1968 was very narrow, but by the 1980s the Liberal process was getting back under control. In 1983, three Conservative candidates still needed the convention to settle their own struggle, but among them, these three reached the convention with all but a handful of delegates locked up. In 1984, John Turner was the anointed Liberal successor and had a fairly easy time of it; 1990 was Jean Chretien's turn, and his victory was easier still.

Although Turner and Chretien won handily, each faced a serious opponent who represented a counter-tendency within the party, who was not just positioning himself for the next time. And each won not because sitting M.P.s used control of their constituency organizations to deliver the convention, but because each was able to secure the organizational and financial wherewithal to win trench warfare, constituency by constituency. In 1993, the Conservative party eliminated the serious competition, or so it seemed at first. The party did not lack credible, ambitious figures, but only one, Kim Campbell, became an official candidate. She was clearly favored in early polls; virtually all the party's financial and organizational resources gravitated to her; all senior rivals simply decided not to run.[32]

But this presented problems in its own right. Some degree of contestation is necessary for conventions to serve their other purposes: regeneration of policy debate, identification of potential financial support, recruitment of new constituency activists, testing of campaign machinery. To this end, Jean Charest, a relatively junior cabinet minister, became first the designated foil and later the magnet for growing disgruntlement with Kim Campbell.

Campbell had been a highly regarded minister of justice, had a style quite unlike the Canadian political norm, and seemed to carry much less baggage than any of her potential competitors. As the campaign progressed, however, what seemed like assets started to look like liabilities. She did win, but the convention proved more divisive than expected. The final ballot forced Conservatives to do what Liberals did in 1984: choose an English-speaking non-Quebecker over a francophone Quebecker. To save the party outside Quebec, this may have been absolutely necessary. But it compromised hopes of recovering votes lost to the Bloc Québécois and left bitterness in the organization.

For all that, the party recovered over the summer, as Campbell dominated political news coverage. At the dissolution of Parliament in early September, her party level-pegged the Liberals. Thanks to geography, this level-pegging still favored those Liberals (in contrast to earlier years), but at least the Conservatives were back in the game. Most importantly, Reform's preemption of the Conservative base outside Quebec seemed to have stalled. Reform had done enough damage to make a Conservative victory difficult, but not enough for Reform itself to displace the Conservatives. In time, the logic of the plurality electoral formula would ordinarily work against Reform, and Conservatives might hope that that time would arrive before campaign's end.

Instead, it was the Conservatives who collapsed. One plausible reading is that they entered the campaign poised on a knife edge, vulnerable to small mistakes, and that at a critical moment, Kim Campbell discredited herself, lost "ownership" of the deficit issue, and allowed Reform back into the game, even as she reminded hesitant Liberals why they were leaning Liberal in the first place. In a matter of days, the Conservative coalition unraveled. As it did so, losses occurred not just on the antideficit flank but on the anti-French, anti–ethnic-accommodation flank as well.

In the end, the Conservative vote share was slightly smaller than Reform's, slightly larger than the Bloc's. But where the Bloc returned fifty-four seats (and formed the official opposition) and Reform won fifty-two seats, the Conservatives won only two, neither belonging to Kim Campbell. The NDP received less than 10 percent of the vote and, like the Conservatives, received too few seats for official parliamentary party status. The Liberal party won a comfortable majority.

The political order apparently inaugurated in 1984 was unrecognizable in this outcome. It may be too strong to say that the marriage of francophones and francophobes could not have lasted in principle. But once shattered, it will be very hard to reassemble. What will replace the 1984–92 alignments remains to be seen. The current Parliament can prefigure the future only weakly. Neither the Quebec nor the non-Quebec components of current arrangements can be in anything like a sustainable equilibrium.

Although the superficially spectacular event of 1993 was the surge by Reform, for our purposes the more profound change was the rise of the Bloc Québécois. On the Bloc—more generally, on the Quebec electorate—hinges the next political order, whatever its shape. For the first time ever, Quebec voters declined to be the pivot for governments. They gave the Liberal party a respectable minority of Quebec seats, but Liberals commanded an overall majority even without these seats—the first time this could *ever* be said of a Liberal government—and the majority of Quebec seats went to a party which could not possibly be in government.

The Bloc's *raison d'être* is to help take Quebec out of Canada; whether the party succeeds or fails, that *raison d'être* will soon cease. If Quebec leaves, then the very foundations of Canadian political orders will shift irrevocably; a wholly new logic of power must emerge. If Quebec stays, the Bloc must either find a new *raison d'être* or retire from the field. Even if the Bloc persists, Quebec voters may well consign it to oblivion, and revert to their historic role in making and breaking governments. If they do, then one basic element of all earlier orders will be restored.

The non-Quebec components of any future order also depend on what Quebeckers do. If Quebec leaves, the general salience of ethnic accommodation must diminish. It will not disappear, for "new Canadians," persons of neither British nor French (and increasingly of non-European) background, carry great electoral weight. But they will not have the original non-British group, French Canada in Quebec, with which to ally. The ethnic agenda may be forced to attach itself to class politics, a subarctic analogue to Australian party politics; this has already happened in provincial politics in those provinces where the

NDP is strong. Which party—Liberals or NDP—inherits the left and which party—Conservatives or Reform—inherits the right cannot be forecast. Both the number of parties and the specific identity of parties strategically privileged on each side would depend on the relative weight of the class and ethnic agendas.

If Quebec stays in Canada, the next order is likely to resemble an earlier one. Most importantly, the party best able to stake a binational bargain should be poised to dominate the order. At this juncture, that party seems to be the Liberals. Although they do not depend on Quebec in this Parliament, they remain the only party with serious representation both inside and outside that province. If Jean Chretien does not conform to the ideal-type Quebec politician, he is nonetheless from Quebec, and his very presence testifies to the Liberal party's continuing commitment to French-English alternation. The Liberal party is as much as ever the party of ethnic accommodation, even if on language policy that means Pierre Trudeau's version.

Other parties seem even less able than before to span the binational divide and to build multiethnic coalitions. The Conservative party has some potential in this respect, but in the short run, surviving Conservatives outside Quebec see Reform as the primary threat, best countered by mimicking the insurgent. From one side, this might enable them to outlast Reform; but from the other, it would deprive them of their traditional opportunity to be the consensual option to a faltering Liberal government. Reform itself is no vehicle for ethnic accommodation. Now that Reform is in the game, its strategists may dream of reaching out. If they do so, however, they risk facing the same dilemma—and repeating the same experience—of the Conservative party.

It is entirely possible, then, that the next Canadian political order will resemble the one of 1963–84. Only the Liberal party will be able to form a single-party government. Its chances of securing regular majorities will depend on the degree of vote consolidation in three places: Quebec, the non-Quebec right, and the non-Quebec left. If the Bloc disappears, the Liberals may well reconstitute their old Quebec base. If Reform and the Conservatives both persist, vote splitting will turn many seats over to the Liberals in Ontario and Atlantic Canada and a few seats in the west; this should ensure Liberal majorities. If either Reform or the Conservatives yields to the other, Liberal prospects will be correspondingly diminished.

Finally, what will happen to the NDP? If its current low estate reflects only punishment of certain provincial governments or some other short-term factor, then the party should reemerge as an intermittently important actor on the national stage. Indeed, it could be vital again in propping up Liberal minority governments. If instead NDP weakness reflects underlying forces working against the left worldwide, then Liberals should be in a commanding position, even if non-Quebec parties of the right get their collective act together. Sir Wilfrid Laurier once said that the twentieth century would belong to Canada. He was wrong, but it did belong to his Liberal party. Will the same be true of the twenty-first century?

Notes

I have benefited greatly from advice and comments by the G-7 group, from Byron Shafer especially. Timely suggestions also came from Keith Banting, Les Pal, and Elaine Bernard. My colleagues in two Canadian election studies, André Blais, Henry Brady, Neil Nevitte, Elisabeth Gidengil, and Jean Crête, have been a continuing source of stimulus and advice; some ideas in this chapter may properly belong to one or more of them. Gallup survey data presented in this chapter were first compiled under the auspices of J. A. Laponce, using files acquired by the UBC Data Library through the International Survey Library Association. The file was extended and refined with the assistance of Neil Sutherland, under a grant from the Social Sciences and Humanities Research Council of Canada. Support for analysis and writing also came from the University of British Columbia, Queen's University, and Harvard University. Errors of fact or interpretation remain solely the responsibility of the author.

1. John Bartlet Brebner, *North Atlantic Triangle: The Interplay of Canada, the United States, and Great Britain* (New York: Columbia University; Toronto: Ryerson, 1945) is the definitive statement of the logic of the old relationship.

2. Social Credit enjoyed modest success in British Columbia and went on to dominate provincial politics there into the 1990s.

3. The Gallup file contains 286,879 respondents. Estimations in table 3.2 were confined to data sets with a full set of regional, linguistic, religious, and union-membership items and, as mentioned in the text, exclude Quebec respondents. The numbers of cases for the four time periods in the table are, respectively, 15,504; 10,862; 23,769; and 63, 459. Entries in the table are unstandardized coefficients from ordinary least squares (OLS) estimation, where the factors are represented by dummy variables. OLS is not strictly appropriate for dichotomous dependent variables, but alternative estimation strategies are prohibitively expensive for such large samples and yield less readily interpretable results. To avoid clutter, I have not reported standard errors or t-statistics. Standard errors are very small for these estimations. The largest was around 0.04; most were around 0.01. Almost all coefficients were significantly different from zero, but that result matters little here. As point estimates, all reported coefficients are highly stable and, thus, probably close to the mark.

4. The standard source on Canadian commercial policy is still W. A. Mackin-

tosh, *The Economic Background of Dominion-Provincial Relations* (Toronto: University of Toronto, 1964). See also V. C. Fowke, *The National Policy and the Wheat Economy* (Toronto: University of Toronto, 1957).

5. The best statement of this logic is Norman Penlington, *Canada and Imperialism, 1896–1899* (Toronto: University of Toronto, 1965).

6. James Eayrs, *In Defence of Canada: Peacemaking and Deterrence* (Toronto: University of Toronto, 1980); Denis Stairs, *The Diplomacy of Constraint: Canada, the Korean War, and the United States* (Toronto: University of Toronto, 1974).

7. In this period and for most of the twentieth century, Catholics have constituted around 45 percent of the electorate. Before 1960, francophones made up 30 percent of the electorate and, thus, about two-thirds of the Catholic total. Now, Catholics are closer to 50 percent of the electorate, whilst francophone Catholics make up only 25 percent.

8. Leslie Pal, *State, Class, and Bureaucracy: Canadian Unemployment Insurance and Public Policy* (Montreal: McGill-Queen's, 1988).

9. This account of the operating style of the King and St. Laurent governments is indebted to David E. Smith, "Party Government, Representation, and National Integration in Canada," in Peter Aucoin, ed., *Party Government and Regional Representation in Canada* (Toronto: University of Toronto, 1985), 20–25.

10. The standard source on leadership choice in Canada is John C. Courtney, *The Selection of National Party Leaders in Canada* (Toronto: Macmillan, 1973). For evidence and arguments about conventions since 1973, see George C. Perlin, ed., *Party Democracy: The Politics of National Conventions* (Scarborough: Prentice-Hall, 1987).

11. The strongest statement to this effect is Thomas A. Hockin, "Canada's 'Mass Legitimate' Parties and Their Implications for Party Leaders," in Thomas A. Hockin, ed., *Apex of Power: The Prime Minister and Political Leadership in Canada* (Scarborough: Prentice-Hall, 1977), 70–85.

12. For the prime minister's outburst and the surrounding debate, see James Eayrs, *The Commonwealth and Suez* (Oxford: Oxford University, 1964), 416–21.

13. The best account of the breakdown of the government's intelligence network is Reginald Whitaker, *The Government Party: Organizing and Financing the Liberal Party of Canada 1930–58* (Toronto: University of Toronto, 1977). For a pointed example of the waning of one regional minister's influence, see Norman Ward and David E. Smith, *Jimmy Gardiner, Relentless Liberal* (Toronto: University of Toronto, 1990). Gardiner was acutely aware of the agricultural trends mentioned above.

14. Evidence for the course of vote intentions is from yet-to-be-reported research by myself with the merged Gallup file. On prime ministerial approval levels, see Richard Johnston, *Public Opinion and Public Policy in Canada: Questions of Confidence* (Toronto: University of Toronto, 1986), chap. 2.

15. Although Diefenbaker won on the convention's first ballot, his success reflected the weakness of his opponents. For an account of failed elite maneuver-

ing to find a strong blocking candidacy, see Peter Stursberg, *Diefenbaker: Leadership Gained 1956–62* (Toronto: University of Toronto, 1975), chap. 1.

16. This expression originated with Peter Regenstrief, *The Diefenbaker Interlude: Parties and Voting in Canada* (Toronto: Longman, 1965).

17. The account of Gallup evidence is based on my own analyses with the Gallup merged file. James Eayrs, *Canada in World Affairs, October 1955 to June 1957* (Toronto: Oxford University, 1959), pp. 182–93, has a striking firsthand account of the elite-mass difference of opinion on Suez.

18. George Grant, *Lament for a Nation: The Defeat of Canadian Nationalism* (Toronto: McClelland & Stewart, 1965).

19. This is a generalization about voters outside Quebec. Quebec was slow to come all the way back to its pre–1957 level of Liberal support. Within Quebec, throughout the 1963–84 period, francophones were less likely than anglophones to vote Liberal.

20. A point made with special force by Michael Laver and Norman Schofield, *Multiparty Government: The Politics of Coalition in Europe* (Oxford: Oxford University, 1991).

21. The Canadian system exemplifies Strom's notions about minority government and majority rule perfectly. See Kaare Strom, *Minority Government and Majority Rule* (Cambridge: Cambridge University, 1990).

22. This paragraph draws heavily on Smith, "Party Government, Representations, and National Integration in Canada," and on his *The Regional Decline of a National Party* (Toronto: University of Toronto, 1981). Also important are Joseph Wearing, *The L-Shaped Party: The Liberal Party of Canada 1958–80* (Toronto: McGraw-Hill Ryerson, 1981); Tom Kent, *A Public Purpose: An Experience of Liberal Opposition and Canadian Government* (Montreal: McGill-Queen's, 1988); and Denis Smith, *Gentle Patriot: A Political Biography of Walter Gordon* (Edmonton: Hurtig, 1973).

23. Precisely this has happened in provinces where the party is a serious contender to form the government.

24. The best account of the difficulties facing the CCF and NDP link to labor is Gad Horowitz, *Canadian Labour in Politics* (Toronto: University of Toronto, 1968).

25. The party had chosen a Quebec leader once before, in 1891, but the man in question, Sir John Abbott, was from the province's English-speaking commercial elite and was only a caretaker.

26. Some text in the following paragraphs is adapted from Richard Johnston, Andre Blais, Elisabeth Gidengil, Henry E. Brady, and Neil Nevitte, "Collapse of a Party System: The 1993 Canadian Election" (Paper presented to the 1994 Annual Meeting of the American Political Science Association).

27. The personal emphasis should not be pushed too far in describing Liberal policy. As the exercise of minority language rights requires the presence of colinguals, language regulations typically specify minimum numbers for activation of a right and countenance circumstances in which individual and collective interests conflict.

28. For an account of the parties' strategic options, couched in the language of spatial theory and with spatial evidence on attitudes and perceived party locations, see Richard Johnston et al., *Letting the People Decide: Dynamics of a Canadian Election* (Montreal: McGill-Queen's; Stanford: Stanford University, 1992), chap. 3.

29. Again see ibid, chap. 3.

30. The place to start on this controversy is the brilliant collection of essays by Alan C. Cairns, *Disruptions: Constitutional Struggles from the Charter to Meech Lake* (Toronto: McClelland and Stewart, 1991). Although it is not clear that the patterns Cairns identifies hold in the mass public, his characterization of the chattering classes seems incontestable, and that is what matters here.

31. Richard Johnston et al., *The Challenge of Direct Democracy: The 1992 Canadian Referendum* (Montreal: McGill-Queen's, 1995).

32. The ideas in these paragraphs are an unabashed crib from R. Kenneth Carty, "Transforming the Politics of Party Leadership" (Unpublished manuscript, University of British Columbia, 1994).

4 *Andrew Adonis*

Britain

"The mistake we made was to think we won the war."
—*James Callaghan, 1976*

Alone of the G-7 states, Britain faced the postwar world with its regime undisturbed but its prewar political order in tatters. Fifty years on, the regime remains not just virtually unaltered but still central to practical politics, despite a further transformation of eras and orders. Compared with the rest of the G-7, it is a remarkable picture of change within continuity: partisan alterations yielding shifts in public policy within a stable constitutional and institutional framework, undisturbed by violent internal or external shocks.

Britain has nevertheless experienced two electoral watersheds since the Second World War. First was the Labour landslide in the election immediately after the defeat of Germany, which installed, under Clement Attlee, an administration intent on recasting economy and society on socialist principles (as it saw them). And second was the Conservative victory in 1979, which brought Margaret Thatcher to power, intent on undoing or recasting Attlee's legacy.

On the one hand, then, neither great electoral shift has followed or heralded a change of regime. On the other hand, the United Kingdom's postwar eras have not been devoid of constitutional change. Decolonization, along with accession to the European Community in 1973 and the continuing process of European integration culminating in the 1991 Maastricht Treaty, have had a significant impact on Britain's international sway and on the autonomy of its policymaking. Yet they have made little impact on the regime itself, insofar as it affects the allocation of power within the United Kingdom, and even less on the character of the two postwar political orders.

These two postwar orders reflected radically different social dynamics, as did the legislative and distributional programs pursued by governments under the respective orders. The second and third sections of this chapter highlight the social shifts and the policy agendas that went with them, seeking to apply Byron Shafer's illuminating notion of eras and orders. For Britain as for the United States, "the periodization of . . . electoral politics is a useful intellectual device—and the ability to say something about current electoral outcomes in relation to those extended electoral periods even more so."[1] Two such extended periods are described below, divided by the two watersheds mentioned above: the "social-democratic" order inaugurated by Attlee's 1945 victory, which endured until 1979, and the subsequent Thatcherite order, which still prevails.

The social-democratic order was characterized by a largely working-class electorate, highly unionized and leaning toward a Labour party preaching social welfare, nationalization, redistribution, and government intervention to maintain demand and employment. To keep itself in electoral competition, the Conservative party sang much the same tune in this period, though carefully cultivating a constituency—embracing most of the "salariat" and a fair proportion of the more affluent and more independent "workers"—hostile to much of it. After 1979, however, the tables were turned: those hostile elements, grown in size and dwarfing the manual working class by the mid-1980s, were mobilized into a winning electoral coalition by Thatcher's Conservatives, preaching individualism, small government, low taxes, and a free economy, though still obliged to maintain the welfare-state legacy of the previous era for fear of ceding a critical section of its coalition to opposition parties giving greater emphasis—within, increasingly, a Thatcherite frame—to social welfare.

To British observers, this periodization and characterization is unlikely to be controversial, suitably garnished with ecological and survey data. From a G-7 perspective, however, it has to be remarked at the outset that it is extraordinary. Contrary to the experience of France, Canada, and Italy, at no stage since the war have the major parties in Britain been aligned by fundamental attitudes to the regime. Unlike Japan and Italy until nearly yesterday, and despite the Conservatives' electoral sway in the postwar era, the country's dominant social and ideological forces have never—as yet—found sufficient expression wholly within one party to give that party unshakable control over the executive. And in contrast to every other member of the G-7, at no time since 1945 has dissensus on the fundamentals of foreign policy been a party-aligning issue, despite the Great Power and colonial status of Great Britain for twenty years after the Second World War.

Above all, therefore, this chapter seeks to explain the character of Britain's postwar politics. It finds a large part of the explanation in the links between the strands of change and continuity noted at the outset. Two interrelated themes are explored. First is an electoral or mass-politics theme. This involves the impact which the plurality electoral system and the almost unlimited concentration of executive and legislative power on one institution, the national executive, have had on the character of the political order and on the electoral positioning of the major parties.

While the electoral system has undoubtedly helped pressurize both mainstream and minority interests into a two-party system, operating in classic Downsian compete-for-the-center fashion, that alone is insufficient to account for the extraordinary continuity of policy in most areas. Also critical is a powerful political and constitutional tradition guaranteeing a wide degree of executive autonomy, serving to keep large spheres of public policy out of the party-political arena, and molding popular attitudes to (and expectations of) the political process, which have themselves shaped dominant electoral opinion.

This leads on to a second major theme. In whole policy fields, notably imperial, foreign, social, and European policy, the nature of this first dynamic has actually rendered shifts in elite (not electoral) opinion, the formative influence on the political order, with the electorate intruding only on rare occasions—such as during the United Kingdom's entry into the European Community in 1972–75—when the elite was divided. It is in the area of elite preoccupations, and their impact, that the comparative perspective yields an approach foreign to most British commentators—who, taking as given the sphere of electoral competition and rarely questioning why its scope is as it is, have failed to see the role and autonomy of Britain's elite as a formative influence on its electoral order.

Accordingly, the chapter is divided into four sections. The first surveys the regime, examining the key institutions and traditions of the British state in the postwar period and their impact on the character of its elite and electoral politics. The second and third sections describe and explain the two political orders, both in their social base and in their policy focus. The fourth is then an analysis of elite values and preconceptions in these respective periods. Taking the long postwar view, Britain's political culture has been more homogeneous, and effective political authority more centered on a single national political class, than in any other of the G-7 states. An understanding of the evolution of that elite mentality is thus vital to understanding Britain's postwar political order in its broadest sense.

Continuity

In Britain, though much changes, more abides. The United Kingdom's constitutional and political development is littered with revolutions that never quite materialized. Monarchs were executed or fled in 1649 and 1688, but near relatives picked up the institution of the monarchy and made it work. The aristocracy was expected to flee when the Great Reform Act of 1832 began the process of enlarging the electorate, but the aristocrats adapted too, continuing to dominate the culture and personnel of government until well into the twentieth century. In the present generation, the "radical center" was widely expected to rewrite—write, some would say—Britain's constitution, but the project never got off the electoral ground. While Thatcherism, the avowedly revolutionary force which swept the electorate before it for a decade, left behind only a modest constitutional imprint.

Decolonization apart, Britain has made only two clean constitutional breaks this century: its decision to join the European Community in 1972 and its separation with southern Ireland in 1922. Yet even those appear jagged and incomplete in retrospect. For all the assertions that Edward Heath's treaty would "take Britain into Europe," signing the Treaty of Rome was for the United Kingdom but the first installment in a painful process of integration, with which most of the British political class has still to come to terms. As for the separation with the Republic of Ireland (as it now is) in 1922, the settlement which gave the south independence but left the six northeasterly counties within the United Kingdom, intending to resolve the "Irish question" by offering enough to pacify the dominant political groups on each side of the divide, served instead to perpetuate it.

Even withdrawal from Empire was far from swift or surgical. As the Union Jack lowered over the Indian Raj for the last time in 1947, who would have thought that thirty-five year later, Britain would be devoting its undivided energies to a colonial war in the Falkland Islands, and that forty years later, political scientists would be arguing about its importance to the outcome of a recent British general election?[2] Much the same might be said of Northern Ireland in the 1990s.

Which is not to argue that changes in Britain's political and constitutional fabric since the Second World War have been insignificant. On the contrary, the end of Empire and the process of European integration have had an impact on the British polity comparable to that wrought by the creation of the mass electorate in the later decades of the last century. "Things that have been secure for centuries are secure no longer": Lord Salisbury's fears for the "disintegration" of the British state in the early 1880s could be neatly paraphrased in the early 1990s, replacing "democracy" and "the working class" with "Brussels" and "the European Union." In relative terms, the changes since 1945 in its external relations and international standing have been incomparably greater than those experienced by France, Canada, Italy, and the United States; arguably greater even than those experienced by Germany and Japan, both of which have undergone one, not (as for Britain) two, major postwar reorientations in their world roles.

Britain won the war and lost the peace. In the 1950s, variations on that quip were neat debating points. "Of course," Harold Macmillan told Bob Boothby in 1960, "if we succeeded in losing two wars, wrote off all our debts—instead of having nearly £30,000 millions in debt—got rid of all our foreign obligations, and kept no force overseas, then we might be as rich as the Germans."[3] By Callaghan's day, Britain's economic and political predicament was not dismissed so flippantly: its elite was gripped by apocalyptic visions of decline, and the tale of Britain's relationship with the European Community is the story of its attempts to reverse that decline.[4] We are still in the early chapters.

We need, therefore, to get to the roots of Britain's enduring constitution. Since the United Kingdom has neither revered founding fathers nor a central written document, that is not easy. It can, however, be confidently asserted that its modern constitution is substantially the handiwork of reformers of the mid- to late-Victorian era. Foremost among them was William Ewart Gladstone, four times Liberal prime minister between 1868 and 1894, a committed and charismatic reformer with a deep reverence for traditional forms and influences, who successfully married England's predemocratic constitution to a mass franchise. In the following generation, David Lloyd George, successively chancellor of the exchequer and prime minister in the "New Liberal" and coalition governments between 1908 and 1922, did more than any other to ensure that the Gladstonian fabric weathered the twin twentieth-century perils of total war and of growing demands for social welfare, emanating from the newly enfranchised working classes. In the late 1940s, Attlee's labor government injected a further dose of collectivism, welfare, and state control, while leaving the constitutional edifice unreformed.[5]

It was the same with the next radical government, the Conservative administration led by Margaret Thatcher from 1979 to 1990. It is commonly supposed that Thatcher transformed Britain's constitution, politicizing the civil service, undermining cabinet dominance and local government, while converting the premiership into a veritable presidency.[6] None of those charges stands up to dispassionate scrutiny. Save for the reorganization of parts of the central bureaucracy into executive agencies (with cross-party support), Thatcher left the civil service in the condition she found it. Local government, ever the weak creature of statute in Britain, has been hacked about by governments in every decade since the 1830s. As for the cabinet and prime minister, A. V. Dicey's Law of the Constitution said it all back in 1885:

The sovereignty of Parliament is still the fundamental doctrine of English constitutionalists. . . . [This] sovereignty can be effectively exercised only by the Cabinet which holds in its hands the guidance of the party machine. And of the party which the party majority supports, the Premier has become at once the legal head and, if he is a man of ability, the real leader.[7]

The constitution today would have been familiar in all essentials to Gladstone. Its central institutions—Crown, Lords, Commons, Cabinet—are the same. So are its fundamental doctrines—the unitary state, the legal sovereignty of the Queen-in-Parliament, the supremacy of the House of Commons within Parliament, cabinet responsibility to a Commons majority. Those doctrines have not gone unchallenged: strong Nationalist demands for some form of self-government for Scotland, for instance, have surfaced periodically since the 1960s. But then, equivalent demands from both Scots and Irish Nationalists were evident a century ago and made equally little headway, despite Gladstone's own support for them. The United Kingdom's one experiment with quasi-federal notions in the intervening century, the Stormont parliament established in Northern Ireland in 1922, was terminated in 1972 in the face of terrorist and sectarian violence, and even when in existence was viewed as an exceptional remedy for an exceptional situation.

It would, of course, be naive to assert that the constitution is in all respects the same as it was a century ago. Until the First World War, the House of Lords was far more powerful than it is today. A large proportion of senior ministers—even prime ministers—were based in the Lords not the Commons, drawing their strength from a landed aristocracy which acted as a significant social and constitutional check on "democracy." The significant point, however, is that the main impact of the weakening of the Lords, and of other intermediary political institutions, has been to reinforce the traditional doctrines above. As Ferdinand Mount puts it, Britain's constitutional development this century has seen a "thinning of the system"[8]—a weakening of fetters on the executive, a more pronounced centralization, a fiercer antipathy to derogations of parliamentary sovereignty, even where (as with the European Community) these have been unavoidable.

This brief historical essay is necessary to emphasize how deeply entrenched, and predemocratic, are the constitutional exigencies shaping Britain's political order. There has never been a coherent division of powers at the center. Indeed, since the demise of the House of Lords, there has been no institution with the constitutional capacity to "divide" executive power in the first place.[9] The state has always dealt with pressure groups and corporate interests almost exclusively through Whitehall. And there is no territorial division of power, but only one tier of government worth the name—central government in London.[10] In no part of Britain (excluding Ireland) has significant legislative power been devolved since the union with Scotland in 1707: the creation of the separate Scottish and Welsh offices, in the 1880s and 1960s respectively, was purely an exercise in executive reorganization.

England constitutes almost 85 percent of the population of the United Kingdom, and since the establishment of the Tudor dynasty in the fifteenth century it has been governed by a single parliament and a single executive. Separate national identities persist, and in some respects are strengthening, but all postwar efforts to enact devolution for Scotland and Wales have come to nought. Only one attempt, the 1978 Scotland and Wales Acts, even got as far as the statute book, and that under the aegis of a Labour government congenitally skeptical about the enterprise from the outset.[11] Proposals for devolution to the regions of England have never been treated seriously: even the elected councils established for Greater London and the other metropolitan districts in the 1960s, as an upper tier of local government, were abolished in 1986 when the pretensions of their leaders were perceived as threatening by ministers in London.

The "power" for which parties contest is accordingly located at the center and capable of being secured through only one election: a general election for the House of Commons, held about once every four years. (I say "about" because the prime minister, exercising the royal prerogative, decides the date of the election, subject to a statutory requirement that an election be held at least once every five years—an arrangement itself typical of the "top down" nature of Britain's constitutional evolution). Britain has the oldest democracy in the G-7, but it has fewer vital elections than any of the other six: a general election is the only electoral instrument capable of shaping its political order.

Moreover, general elections, though formally held to elect members of the legislature, are invariably treated as elections of the executive; and party leaders, formally only parliamentary candidates standing in individ-

ual constituencies, assume presidential stature in the process. There are
no primaries: the electorate as a whole plays no part in the selection of
candidates, a power in the hands of party activists and—whatever party
rules and textbooks say—the party leaderships in London.[12] Indeed, it is
not just subnational government that is absent: so are subnational regional groupings of any consequence within parties.

One telling anecdote underlines the point. On becoming leader of the
Conservative party in 1975, Margaret Thatcher's knowledge of other European political systems was exiguous. Briefing her on the federal nature
of Italy's Christian Democrats before a visit to that country, John Davies,
the party's then foreign affairs spokesman, drew an analogy:

> "It's rather as if I were the party potentate in north-west England," he said,
> "and you had to bargain for my favour."
> "You mean the party leader isn't really the party leader?" she asked.
> Those present nodded slowly.
> "How simply terrible," came the reply.[13]

Two further aspects of the constitutional inheritance shaping Britain's
political system need to be stressed. First, the electoral system, first-past-
the-post (FPP) in single-member constituencies (again essentially unchanged since Gladstone), poses a high entry barrier for new parties and
constitutes a strong force for cohesion and centrism within the two major
parties. A two-party system is not, of course, the necessary result of FPP.
But in a country with the social and political homogeneity of Britain, it
tends to be so. And in terms of seats in the House of Commons, where it
matters, it has in fact been the result for most of the past century—and the
entire postwar era (see table 4.1).

Second is the rule that all ministers must sit in Parliament, and virtually
all senior ministers in the House of Commons. The effect of this rule has
been to weld the governing party to the national executive—as securely as
"responsible government" has fused together the legislature and the executive. In Britain, government is not only responsible to, but actually
located in, the House of Commons, physically dominating it. Typically,
about a third of the M.P.s supporting the governing party are ministers or
their parliamentary secretaries. Ministerial office is virtually the sole ambition of most M.P.s, and its monopoly of ministerial office makes Parliament the sole avenue into office. Necessarily, therefore, members of the
House of Commons are the political class in Britain. Virtually all executive politicians are first and foremost career parliamentarians, nurtured
by their party elites and almost wholly dependent upon them for their
political base.

These constitutional facets form the contours of Britain's postwar po-

Table 4.1.Electoral Change, 1945–1992

Election	Conservative	Labour	Liberal[a]
The Social-Democratic Era			
1945	40 (213)	46 (393)	9(12)
1950	43 (298)	46 (315)	9(9)
1951	48 (321)	49 (295)	3(6)
1955	50 (345)	46 (277)	3(6)
1959	49 (365)	55 (258)	6(6)
1964	43 (303)	44 (317)	11(9)
1966	42 (253)	48 (363)	9(12)
1970	46 (330)	43 (287)	8(6)
1974 (Feb.)	38 (296)	37 (301)	19(14)
1974 (Oct.)	36 (276)	39 (319)	18(13)
The Thatcherite Era			
1979	44 (339)	37 (268)	14(11)
1983	42 (397)	28 (209)	25(3)
1987	42 (375)	31 (229)	23(22)
1992	42 (336)	34 (271)	18(20)

NOTE: Perentages of the U.K. vote, rounded; minor parties omitted; House of Commons seats in parentheses.

[a]Liberal 1945–79; SDP/Liberal Alliance 1983–87; Liberal Democrat 1992.

litical system. The potential for split-level alignments of the kind Byron Shafer has identified in the United States[14] is extremely weak: the only electoral tier that matters (to impose an analogy) is "the presidency." The extraordinary electoral success of the Conservatives, preeminently the party of government, is bound up with that fact to an extent unappreciated by British political scientists who take their system for granted. In Britain, as in the United States, the national administration is expected by the electorate to embody national values and to exhibit qualities of unity, strength, and resolution at home and abroad— qualities the Tories have almost invariably been better at commanding than have their opponents.

Moreover, the electoral system, by giving no quarter to small national (as opposed to Nationalist) parties, has insured that when one of the two major parties fractures badly, the process of reconstitution has to take place largely within the bounds of that party, while the other (united) party governs. In the past century, there have been six such ruptures: five of them—including the two which occurred since 1945—have fractured the main non-Tory party. The Bevanite assault of the early 1950s created virtual civil war inside the Labour party for most of the 1950s. The rupture following Labour's 1979 defeat was more bitter still, leading to formal secession by an influential section of the party leadership which formed a new party (the Social Democratic Party [SDP]) and heralding three (at least) Tory election victories—in 1983, 1987, and 1992—won by relative majorities over an enfeebled Labour alternative.

The jury is still out on whether Labour's chronic electoral weakness will ultimately oblige it to coalesce with the center-left Liberal Democrats (the successor to the 1980s SDP/Liberal Alliance). But the election to the Labour leadership in 1994 of Tony Blair—young, well-spoken, sub-Tory in his language, predilections, and style, yet in unfettered control of his party—makes it abundantly clear that any realignment must now embrace the existing Labour party as its dominant component. The exigencies imposed thereby have made change a painfully slow process.

External forces—notably decolonization and membership of the European Union—have not featured so far in Britain's postwar political order. The omission is deliberate. For despite the significant consequences of both for the international sway of the U.K. government, neither has had anything more than a marginal effect on the constitutional doctrines and practices that regulate the structure of government within the United Kingdom itself. Indeed, for all that E.U. membership has served to reduce the autonomy of the British executive vis-à-vis its developing European counterpart, the only domestic redistribution of power wrought by the European Union has been a still greater increase in the authority of the executive vis-à-vis Parliament, and a modest decrease in the discretion of the judiciary, now bound to give supremacy to European over U.K. law.[15] Since the United Kingdom is neither a federation nor is it ruled by coalitions, the need to reorganize the executive to adapt to Brussels has not (as in Germany) necessitated significant changes either to relations with subnational government or to relations between parties.

A glaring instance of the insulation of British constitutional practice from the European Community norm is the pre- and post-Maastricht debate over the principle of subsidiarity, a doctrine enjoining the devolution of executive authority. John Major's government championed the principle at the European level, securing its inclusion in the Maastricht Treaty, while at the same time resisting loud domestic demands for a Scottish Parliament and for a strengthening of local government within the United Kingdom. In time, the influence of European constitutionalism might be expected to make an impact on Britain. There is evidence that it is already doing so in the Labour and Liberal Democrat parties.[16] But that is for the future, not the past or present.

It is against that background of a broadly fixed set of constitutional precepts that Britain's postwar political orders have to be viewed. Under them, its indirectly elected executive occupies the supreme position in the state. Simple notions of the location of power and of the purpose of parties and politics reign, imbuing the political class with a strong "executive mentality" and (generally) endowing the major political parties with an all-or-nothing approach to electoral politics, as well as obliging them to integrate broad ideological and social coalitions in order to win elections. The exigencies imposed thereby are explored in the following sections.

The Social Democratic Era, 1945–1979

The 1945 election gave Attlee's Labour party a huge majority—394 seats to the Conservatives' 210, with more than 200 Labour gains. In terms of votes cast, the victory was less emphatic, but Labour's 48 percent of the poll nonetheless represented a 10 percent swing on the previous (1935) election, the largest in this century. The Conservatives had been dominant for most of the previous sixty years, since the extension of the franchise to the majority of working-class males in 1884. Labour was to have the upper hand for the next thirty-four years.

Measured by years in government, the two parties actually divided the honors fairly evenly over the period, holding office for a little over seventeen years apiece. Their share of the electoral spoils was also fairly even, Labour outpolling the Tories in six of the ten elections between 1945 and 1974,[17] but securing an average vote less than one percentage point higher than the Tories across the ten.[18] However, the critical election of the period was that of 1945, and the Tories' capacity to remain in effective competition thereafter depended upon their accommodation with the social-democratic principles acted upon by the Attlee government.

The extent of the consequent realignment was dramatic. In the interwar decades, a dominant Tory party had been challenged intermittently by loose, shaky alliances of the Labour and Liberal parties. With Labour acutely divided and deeply ambivalent about the very idea of governing in a minority, and with many Liberal M.P.s far more anti-Labour than anti-Tory—Churchill himself was a Liberal until 1923—they offered little more than breathing spaces for the Tories to regather their strength.

By contrast, after the 1945 landslide it was Labour that set the agenda, undistracted by the need for pacts and alliances with other parties. The Liberals, relegated to the sidelines, barely escaped parliamentary extinction over the next thirty years. Within three years of taking office, Labour had nationalized most of the utilities, the coal mines, the railways, and a number of other "strategic" industries. A universal unemployment and sickness insurance system had been established, enhanced state pensions granted, and a National Health Service (NHS) set up, socializing medical care to a degree unparalleled anywhere else in the world. National and local government officials were vested with powers to plan, organize, and direct unmatched in peacetime.

Under financial and factional pressures, Labor's progress shuddered to a halt in 1948.[19] Yet the line drawn then, deeper and more permanent than anything conceivable five years before, was the line to be defended by both parties for the next thirty years. By 1950, under the guidance of pragmatic, executive-minded leaders like R. A. Butler, Anthony Eden, and Harold Macmillan, the Conservatives had accepted the essentials of the Attlee settlement.

The party battle remained strident. Yet its components were variously just: (a) rhetoric ("freedom" against "socialism"); (b) storms over short-term crises (Suez in 1956, devaluation in 1967, and the miners' strikes of 1973–74); (c) arguments around the theme of executive competence (as the Tories degenerated into scandal and lethargy in the early 1960s and as economic management failed to sustain growth and full employment in the late 1960s and 1970s); and (d) programs for incremental change. Piecemeal nationalizations and denationalizations, tinkering with taxes either to manipulate supply or manipulate an election, the "management" of industrial relations, incremental changes—mainly new user charges—to the NHS: that was the substance of the difference between the two parties.[20]

Increasingly in the period following the Second World War, the curbing of "illegitimate" trade-union power led to bitter party-political controversy. But beneath the partisan fury, the reality was an increasing desperation by governments of both parties to exert their autonomy in industrial and macromanagement against an overweening trade-union leadership. Failure to tame the unions destroyed both the Tory Heath and the socialist Callaghan. Reasserting executive autonomy was the most urgent priority of Thatcher, and her reputation for "governing competence" largely depended upon it.[21]

If the Tory elite acquiesced in "social democracy at home" as the price of power, it did so in no small part because of its overriding concern with imperial and foreign policy, and its belief—broadly justified—that in office it could shape a consensus for sustaining Britain's international role. Given their class, training, and experience, it was natural for Tory leaders to take that view. Nor, given their education and careers (notably as senior members of the wartime coalition), is it surprising that Labour leaders of the postwar period should have deferred to this view so readily. As nationalist pressures mounted in the colonies and imperial withdrawal became a matter of when and how, not if, controversy over Britain's world role wracked both parties.

But the divisions were similar, and in both parties the majority came out on the same side on most issues. The Tories never so much as contemplated Algerian-style resistance to preserve imperialism, and throughout the "approach to Europe" phase (1960–75), the great majority of Tory M.P.s supported membership of the European Community. In both cases, the executive mentality of the Tory leadership was critical, keeping most issues out of the party-political (and therefore electoral) arena. The 1956 Suez crisis and 1975 referendum on European Community membership were distinct aberrations.

The social base of the social-democratic order had three pillars: the wartime realignment of the manual, unionized, working class behind the Labour party; the persistence of the Tories as the natural party of "the rest"; and the rallying of an unprecedentedly large section of the political intelligentsia behind Labour, notably the self-consciously "progressive" element, much of which—including its ideal type (Keynes, Beveridge)—had remained fervent Liberals until the 1940s. In the latter case, the following thirty years saw Labour dominated by an Oxford elite which a generation before would almost certainly have been Liberal.

Harold Wilson, Labour prime minister from 1964 to 1970 and 1974 to 1976, had been an officer of the university Liberal Club at Oxford. Roy Jenkins, variously chancellor of the exchequer and home secretary in Wilson's governments, was to become first leader of the SDP and end his career combining the posts of chancellor of Oxford University and leader of the Liberal Democrats in the House of Lords. Tony Crosland, the guru of social democracy in the 1950s and 1960s, was the son of a Liberal and served as an Oxford don before entering Parliament. Michael Foot (Labour leader from 1980 to 1983 and a pivotal figure in the 1970s) and Tony Benn (de facto leader of the left's parliamentary faction in the 1970s and early 1980s) were both Oxford-educated, and both sons of Liberal M.P.s. All five were first elected to the Commons between 1945 and 1950.

The wartime realignment gave Labour a decisive swing in the manual working class, which had divided its support in the prewar years. For the next thirty years, the bedrock of Labour's electoral position was the support of a solid two-thirds of this manual sector, most of it socialized by trade unions which formed an integral part of the Labour party. Though its level of manual working-class support fluctuated, elections were essentially won and lost among the skilled workers, who identified—or, at least, were perceived by the political class to identify—their social and political demands with the broader working class.[22]

Why the sudden shift in 1945? In reality, the shift was not particularly sudden. The 1945 election was the first to be held since 1935 because the election due in 1940 had been delayed for the duration of the war—the longest interval between two elections in Britain since the Glorious Revolution of 1688. In any case, four key developments took place between the two elections: the war; the rise to voting age of a second generation of the working-class electors enfranchised in 1918, increasingly socialized in pro-Labour families or trade unions; dissolution of the cross-party coalition, which had embraced a significant part of Labour's interwar leadership and which had "artificially" bolstered the Tories in the 1931 and 1935 elections; and the acquisition by Labour of a reputation for "governing competence," through its high-profile participation in Churchill's 1940 coalition.

There is no space to elaborate on these four themes. Suffice it to note that while two of the factors (the war and the rise of a new electoral generation) were essentially social facets, the other two (partisan realignment and Labour's governing competence) were explicitly political and systemic. It was the four factors combined which gave Labour its strength. In a complete turning of the tables on the prewar position, in 1945 it was Labour that was generally felt to be the "safer" and more competent party of government.

From then until 1979, Labour never entirely lost that aura. In 1951, Attlee and his colleagues appeared (and were) exhausted; but they were not discredited. And once seven years of internal ideological wrangling had been more or less resolved, by 1960, Labour again assumed the "governing mantle," outclassing the scandal-ridden Macmillan and the aristocratic Home. Finally, a Labour party already exhibiting symptoms of the implosion that was to occur after 1979 was rescued once more by Edward Heath, through his crass mismanagement of the miners' strikes of 1973–74. It was stressed at the outset that British general elections are about government first and last; the party best able to exude governing competence—in this period, Labour—has a clear, often decisive, advantage.

However, the very nature of the 1945 realignment was to have a significant bearing on the evolution of the social-democratic order. It was, as Ross McKibbin argues persuasively, predominantly a realignment within the manual and skilled working class. Between the 1935 and 1945 elections, support for the Conservatives within the working class fell from about 50 percent to 30 percent—the "normal" level at which it remained for the next generation.[23] Why? McKibbin broadly accepts the factors outlined above, adding an ideological one: a radical shift in "official" (that is, state) attitudes to the unionized working class, rendering its aspirations legitimate and therefore undermining the capacity of the Conservatives to divide and rule on the interwar model.[24]

Glib sentimental writing about the "mood of national unity" during the war years has led to the supposition that a surge of national enthusiasm for collectivist and socialist policies swept Britain in 1944–45. In fact, the war did little to change political alignments within the middle class: "the great majority of those who were middle-class or continued to think of themselves as middle-class had to remain Conservative: the party could not have got 40 percent of the vote otherwise."[25] Indeed, McKibbin believes the war may actually have reinforced negative stereotypes of the working class among the "not-working-class."

In the longer view, however, the war worked decisively to the Conservatives' advantage in a different respect: it removed from electoral contention a nonsocialist Liberal party which, prior to 1931 and after 1974, was the Tories' most lethal opponent in provincial England. This fact is critical to explaining why the Tories' bedrock vote remained so high in the post-1945 period. It also makes greater sense of Labour's progressive electoral decline post-1966, as the social order favorable to the Tories assembled—and in 1979 took Margaret Thatcher's Conservatives into government.

The Thatcherite Era, 1979–

The British Conservative party has the distinction of being both the oldest and the most consistently successful political party, not merely in the G-7 but across the democratic world. The Conservative party which rules today is lineally the same party, not merely one with the same name, that governed Britain under Lord Liverpool fifty years before the unification of Germany. Indeed, it was parliamentary politicians widely dubbed as Tories—including Liverpool's father—who, a generation before that, resisted the French Revolution and fought and lost the American War of Independence.

Tories live with and in their history. David Willetts, a Conservative M.P. who has written an incisive study of modern Conservatism, entitles his first chapter "The Tory Tradition," harking back to Pitt the Younger and to Burke to describe the party's contemporary identity.[26] In reality, the party of Neville Chamberlain and Baldwin, let alone the parliamentary grouping consolidated by William Pitt in the 1790s, would be largely foreign to the modern Tory. Largely but not completely: the rhetoric of national unity, order, discipline, strong-executive government, and free markets reverberates across the Tory ages.

Many a Tory would add to that list the eschewing of ideology and a supple and adaptable approach to politics. In practice, the Tories have been as ideological as the next party wanting to impose its will on the political order. But their success in trimming that will to the politically possible has been one of the party's most abiding traits. Trimming, of course, can often lead to transformation: a century ago, Lord Salisbury's aristocratic landowning Tories nervously embraced "democracy" and the rising industrial and professional middle classes as allies. By the time of Baldwin twenty-five years later, those classes had fairly taken over the party, and its appeal was verging on the populist.

In the decades between the New Liberalism of the pre–First World War Liberal governments and the high noon of the social-democratic order in the mid-1960s, the conscious Tory trimming was vis-á-vis "collectivism." At first, the party tried simply to resist the tide. In the process, it lost three elections in a row (one in 1906 and two in 1910) and was expelled from government for a decade, its longest period of opposition since its foundation.

That searing experience dictated future strategy. For all its partisan rhetoric, from the Lloyd George coalition (1916–22) until Margaret Thatcher's election as party leader in 1975, the Tory leadership appeased at almost the first sign of serious electoral or institutional trouble. The Unionist party surrendered the Union; the imperial party sacrificed the Empire; the party of the aristocracy bonded to the rising middle class, thereby hastening its political demise; the free-market party accepted, and sometimes pioneered, greater state intervention and welfare provision; the party of Pitt and Disraeli even wobbled dangerously on the necessity for strength abroad in the face of European fascism rampant.

In the same way, many of the Tories' most dynamic leaders of the period—Chamberlain in the 1920s and 1930s, Butler in the 1940s, Macmillan in the 1950s, and Macleod in the 1960s—positively gloried in beating Labour at their own game. Public housing in the 1950s? The Tories would build more and faster than Labour. Nationalization from the 1940s to the 1970s? Attlee's legacy untouched, save for a few token reversals. Taxes across the whole period? No cuts, save just before elections.

The 1945 landslide was treated in the same way. By 1950, safeguarding the achievements of the previous five years was Labour's cry, while Churchill's reinvigorated Conservatives were proposing to tamper with little of it. On that basis—contemporaries called it "Butskellism," a marriage of the leading Tory and Labor ministers, R. A. Butler and Hugh Gaitskell— the Tories won three elections in the 1950s and governed from 1951 until 1964.

To appreciate the position of the Conservatives in the social-democratic order and to be able to relate it to the second, post-1979 order, it is critical, however, that statements of official ideology are separated from underlying beliefs and commitments. Because in the 1950s successive Tory ministries pursued prowelfare policies, withdrew from the Empire, and held back from all but token privatization, it does not follow that the Tory outlook had become essentially collectivist, "little England," and pro-state management of industry. In fact, Tory language, and the underlying convictions it expressed, remained remarkably unchanged throughout. "Conservative Freedom Works" was the party's election slogan at the height of Butskellism in 1955.

True, for some, accommodation was turning into conviction. But even the most ardent accommodators saw it as that—accommodation, the necessary price for the party to win elections and maintain social peace once in government. Even Macmillan, the arch accommodator, who entitled his program for the 1950s "The Middle Way," was careful to differentiate his vision of the welfare state from Labour's. "We believe that unless we give opportunity to the strong and able, we shall never have the means to provide real protection for the old and weak," he told the party meeting that confirmed him as leader in 1957.[27] Setting out The Conservative Case in 1959, Lord Hailsham was far blunter: "In fighting socialism in the twentieth, as they fought liberalism in the nineteenth century, Conservatives will be found to have changed their front to meet a new danger, but not the ground they are defending."[28] Ian Macleod, the hero of "liberal" Tories until his untimely death in 1970, believed that the essence of modern Conservatism was "to see that men had an equal chance to make themselves unequal."[29]

For most Conservatives, the Thatcher decade was largely a change of ground, not of front. It was not in fact a straightforward return to the *status quo ante* socialism. In some areas, notably the discarding of some traditional attitudes to social hierarchy, a shift had taken place. Even in social policy, the Thatcherite emphasis on Victorian self-help and Christian individualism did not signal an assault on the welfare state, much though the ardent Thatcherites wished to launch one. Electoral exigencies had not relaxed to that extent.

For the rest, though, the values of Thatcher were essentially the values of Lord Salisbury a century before, once he had come to terms with political democracy in the 1880s and discounting at least partially his notions of imperial and racial ascendancy. Small but strong government, low taxes, free markets, the defense of property large and small, self-reliance, Christian charity, a hostility to "welfare"—the same principles applied to different circumstances. They were, moreover, principles endorsed by most Tories in the intervening decades. What changed over the period was not so much the underlying principles as Tory perceptions of their ability to marry them with programs marketable within successive electoral orders.

In comparative European (though not U.S.) terms, the Labour party was a moderate social-democratic force. Moreover, as we have seen, in foreign and imperial policy it was the right, not the left, which defined the political center. Both aspects made accommodation more palatable than it might otherwise have been. But they did nothing to mitigate the necessity for it. Under Macmillan, the imperative was acknowledged with flourish, under Edward Heath (leader 1965–75), it was done with rather more evident distaste. Either way, it was done with an inner conviction which, for most Tories, rarely extended much beyond an appreciation of the exigencies of "modern politics."

The essential change between the social-democratic and the Thatcherite orders was that the Tory leadership—the leader, in particular— discovered that it needed to accommodate significantly less than before. Underpinning the transition was a marked shift in the social base of electoral politics. The 1970s and 1980s saw the composition of the English electorate, and the electoral geography of England, shift dramatically in the Conservatives' favor. In this, it is important to stress "English" and "England." In Scotland and Wales, ostensibly similar changes did not work to the Tories' advantage. Yet in 1987, those regions together comprised only 14 percent of the U.K. electorate (Northern Ireland, with its idiosyncratic party system, accounted for a further 2 percent), and the party proved more than able to compensate through strength in the union's "predominant partner."

By the 1960s, McKibbin's 1945 Labour vote was crumbling fast. In 1964, the salariat comprised 18 percent of the electorate and the manual working class 47 percent; by 1983, the proportions were 27 percent and 34 percent, respectively.[30] Owner-occupiers accounted for 39 percent of the residential housing stock in 1961, 63 percent in 1986.[31] The litany could continue, with educational qualifications or real disposable income—all telling a similar story. In no case is there a simple correlation between the growth of the salariat, the decline of the manual working class, more affluence/ownership/education, and Conservative electoral success. In Scotland, the correlations are weak or even negative.

Throughout the 1980s, students of electoral behavior were reluctant to admit the existence of correlations in England either. Writing after the 1983 election, Anthony Heath and colleagues saw "trendless fluctuation" in the movement of votes between elections since 1964.[32] Ivor Crewe, focusing on the rising number of voters declaring themselves uncommitted plus the failure (according to opinion surveys) of Thatcherism to refashion public attitudes to the role of the state, merely concluded that the "committed electorate" had given way to the "hesitant electorate."[33]

If opinion polls are the gauge, volatility there certainly was—enough to convince one and all by the end of the 1992 election campaign that the

English electorate, depressed by recession and alienated from the Tories by a succession of extraordinary public-policy debacles, was about to fluctuate decisively in Labour's direction. But when the real votes were counted, this fluctuation evaporated, and Labour recorded a significantly lower percentage of the vote than that with which it had lost office in 1979. Surveying English electoral politics in the last thirty years, the fluctuations appear anything but trendless, and the most significant hesitation in the electorate was the consistent refusal of at least 45 percent of it to vote anything but Conservative.

The Tories' post-1979 parliamentary strength was built on a virtually hegemonic grip over the constituencies of southern England. Of the 260 seats south of the midlands, constituting 41 percent of the mainland total, the Conservatives won 227 (or 87 percent) of them in 1987, polling an average of 52 percent of the popular vote across them. Taking England, which now accounts for four-fifths of the United Kingdom's constituencies, the Tories in 1987 won 358 of the region's 523 seats (67 percent) with an average poll of 46 percent, in spite of three-party contests throughout. The proportions of the vote were similar in 1992, although higher-than-average swings in marginal seats gave the Tories thirty-eight seats fewer than in 1987. The party nonetheless secured 61 percent of England's seats with 45.5 percent of the vote across the region.

This regional dimension to the Tories' electoral strength was not new to the 1980s. Long before class politics clearly asserted itself, in the early part of this century, the Tories' electoral base was firmly located in the home counties and the suburbs of the major cities. Nor is there anything new in dubbing the Tory party the English National Party: they have been doing it themselves for three centuries and more. "My politics are described by one word, and that word is ENGLAND ," Disraeli declared to his electors in 1832.[34]

Yet in no run of four successive elections between 1830 and 1974 was the Tories' strength in its heartland so absolute,[35] nor previously was Tory strength, especially in terms of parliamentary seats, so disproportionately concentrated on its heartland as it was between 1979 and 1992. Indeed, had it not been so, the electoral consequences would have been dire, given the party's concomitant decline in Scotland, Wales, and northern England. Taking the period from 1955 to 1987 as a whole, the two-party (that is, Labour-Tory) swing to the Tories was 8.9 percent in the south and 5.9 percent in the Midlands, ample compensation for swings to Labour of 8.6 percent in the north and 19.1 percent in Scotland. (Wales saw a meager swing of 0.6 percent to the Tories).[36]

Statistical analysis of the 1987 and 1992 elections reinforces this by revealing a strong correlation in Scotland and northern and western England between the social composition of constituencies and their voting behavior, but at best only weak correlations between those variables in southern and eastern England. In the first three areas, the higher the proportion of unemployed, manual, and skilled nonprofessional workers, the better Labour performed at the expense of both the SDP/Liberal Alliance (Liberal Democrats in 1992) and the Tories. In the south and west, however, it was location, distance from London and direct lines of communication with the metropolis, which appear to account for much of the variation in voting behavior. Put crudely (and conceding exceptions), the more integrated a seat with the dynamic parts of the metropolitan economy, the more Tory.

Thus under Thatcher the electoral base of Conservatism was not only secure, but more and more socially homogeneous and geographically concentrated. In the 1970s and 1980s, Tory England was expanding England. By the mid-1980s, half of Britain's population lived south of Birmingham. In 1935, southern English counties outside the inner London area elected 165 M.P.s; in 1987, the region returned 235; after the next boundary revision, due in 1994, it will be around 250, an increase of just over 50 percent in sixty years.

Elites in Mass Politics

It was not, however, simply a question of the vitality of Tory support in southern England: the *perception* of that vitality counted just as much in the shift from the first to the second postwar political orders. Between 1982 and 1989, Tory support, as recorded in opinion polls, remained consistently higher and less volatile than that for any other party, not only at but also between elections. For thirty-three of the forty-seven months of the 1983 to 1987 Parliament, the party led the polls, a remarkable record. And for the entire 1983–87 Parliament, its registered support rarely dipped below 35 percent and was usually nearer 40 percent, a figure neither Labor nor the SDP/Liberal Alliance proved able to reach—or at least, in Labor's case, to sustain.

It was a different story in the first two years of the 1979–83 Parliament and the last two of the 1987–92 Parliament; and we may now—it remains too soon to be sure—be on the threshold of a third electoral order, in which the Tories are once again in close competition with Labour or a loose Labour/Liberal alliance of some sort. Yet the eight years from 1981 to 1989 was a period when the Tories were not merely dominant but seemed invincible. And their invincibility appeared—not least to the party's leadership—to be almost entirely due to national factors and efforts.

In their own perception of the forces significant to their holding power nationally, local government became decreasingly important to the Tories. Even local constituency parties came to be seen as less important than hitherto, although they continued to play a crucial role in the selection of candidates. Ironically perhaps, the Tories first impressive result in local elections across the country after Mrs. Thatcher entered Downing Street came in May, 1992, a month after the party's surprise fourth parliamentary victory.

One final factor must be noted. The electoral collapse of the Labour party in the early 1980s, and the failure of the SDP/Liberal Alliance to concentrate its support sufficiently to pose a serious electoral challenge to the Tories in more than a few dozen seats, gave Tory M.P.s elected in 1983 and 1987 extraordinarily large majorities in their own constituencies, even though the party's national percentage of the vote was unimpressive in historical terms. At 42.2 percent, the Tories' 1987 percentage was the lowest won by any Conservative government since 1922. But in their own constituencies, 300 of the 376 Tory M.P.s returned in 1987 had leads of more than 10 percent over their nearest rivals. And for the seventy-six M.P.s with majorities of less than 10 percent, defeat would have required a swing of a size equal to the largest recorded in any post-1945 election— and that was the 1979 swing *to* the Tories.

To be sure, such a swing seemed entirely plausible in the depth of the Tories' poll-tax trauma of 1990–91. It even appeared possible during the 1992 election campaign, although in the event, barely half of the seventy-six seats fell. But until 1990, only a very small proportion of Tory M.P.s elected in 1987 actually believed themselves vulnerable to defeat at the next election, even allowing for a comparatively respectable Labour performance at the polls. The Conservatives were therefore not merely in a far healthier electoral position in the 1980s than previously: for most of the decade they believed themselves to be well nigh electorally invulnerable. This helped to give Tory leaders— Mrs. Thatcher first and foremost—the courage of their private convictions, and it rendered the parliamentary party fairly malleable in their hands. To appreciate the strength of this argument, compare 1959 and 1987, two elections yielding Tory Commons majorities of around 100. Yet in 1987, the Conservative lead over Labour in the popular vote, 11.5 percent, was more than twice the 1959 margin.

The comparison is different but equally stark if one looks back to the 1920s, the previous period when the Tories were the largest (and usually governing) party in an essentially three-party electoral contest. Both the 1922 and 1924 elections resulted in decisive Conservative victories, on a scale to match 1983 and 1987 in terms of seats won. However, taking the two sets of elections together, a study of the results

indicates that around 28 percent of Tory M.P.s in the 1920s had majorities in their constituencies of less than 10 percent of the votes cast,
whereas for the 1980s the figure was around 19 percent—a third fewer
marginal seats in the 1980s.

The comparison with the 1920s can fruitfully be taken further by applying to the Conservative vote in the 1980s an analytical technique employed by Ross McKibbin in his study of interwar Conservatism[37]—
namely the "two-party preferred vote," ascertained by supposing that all
voters who did not vote for the two largest parties were required to choose
between them. There are obvious problems calculating this vote, and it
can only be done crudely from the broad pattern of polls and surveys of
the "center party" vote. There are also clear limitations in the usefulness
of the preferred vote, since electoral outcomes depend upon first preferences alone. Even so, the preferred vote helps illuminate the dynamics of
electoral change and the realignments to which they give rise.

If we apply the McKibbin model to elections since 1964, then, assuming
a roughly equal division of Liberal second preferences between the two
major parties, for the five elections between 1964 and 1974 the mean
Conservative preferred vote was 47.5 percent. On the same assumption,
the mean Conservative preferred vote for the four elections between 1979
and 1992 was 52.5 percent. And that may in fact underestimate the Tory
preferred vote: a survey of the 1987 vote[38] suggests that SDP/Liberal Alliance voters divided Tory/Labour in their second preferences in the ratio
3:2. Returning to the 1920s and 1930s, the Conservatives' preferred vote
in elections between 1922 and 1935 was between 55 and 59 percent, apart
from the highly exceptional 1931 election when it rose to 67 percent.[39]

On a "preferred" basis, the interwar Tory vote was thus similar to
(though actually larger than) the vote of the 1980s, but with two significant differences. First, its distribution in the earlier period was less consistently favorable to the Conservatives in terms of seats gained. Second,
interwar Tory leaders regarded their position as critically dependent not
only on the divisions of their opponents (as in the 1980s) but on their
ability to accommodate the moderates among the leaders of their
opponents—just as forty years before, Lord Salisbury's strategy had depended critically upon drawing over the Whig leaders to break the
Gladstonian majority.

The 1931 election returned 473 Tories in a House of Commons of 615,
yet the postelection reconstruction of the "national" government saw the
former Labour prime minister, Ramsay MacDonald, retain his post, with
the foreign and home secretaryships going to Liberals. Imagine Margaret
Thatcher after the 1987 election yielding her post to Denis Healey, and the
Tories accepting David Owen and David Steel as, respectively, home secre-

tary and foreign secretary in the same government, and one appreciates in a flash the difference in the Tories' underlying confidence and strength.

The ideological flip side to the coin is equally striking, graphically exhibited by the progressive shift of both the center parties and Labour to "Thatcherism" over the course of the 1980s and 1990s. After its 1979 defeat, the Labour party veered to the autarkic left, while the Social Democratic Party which broke away from its right wing in 1981 professed fealty to Croslandite "social democracy." One defeat later, the SDP, under the leadership of David Owen, shifted decisively to accept the Conservatives' market policies and critique. As Owen puts it in his memoirs:

The SDP had to break the stranglehold of the 1960s. An understanding of the market economy was the first essential step towards the radical libertarian force I wanted to create. . . . To align myself with Margaret Thatcher in condemning all these initiatives ["failed" past initiatives in state intervention and direction] had its political advantages, and the label of "sub-Thatcherite" did not worry me. . . . It was a small price to pay to rid the SDP of being stuck in the 1970s, promising a better yesterday.[40]

Labour moved more slowly. But after its second defeat at Thatcher's hands, it moved in precisely the same direction, repudiating nationalization, state economic dirigisme, and further redistribution through the tax system, while defending the existing level of state welfare provision and liberalism in the social sphere—both of which, significantly, Thatcher did nothing to jeopardize, despite her personal predilections. For Nigel Lawson, a key architect of Tory economic strategy as a junior finance minister from 1979 and chancellor of the exchequer from 1983 to 1989, this was a conscious attempt to redefine the center ground. "The pursuit of moderation necessarily becomes self-defeating," he argued in an influential 1980 lecture, because "if Conservatives are always to split the difference between their former position and that of the Socialists, not only will they be dragged along by the Socialists, but they will actually provide them with an incentive to become more extreme."[41]

It is important, then, to distinguish between the objective electoral strength of the Tories and the party's subjective belief in its electoral vulnerability. The Conservatives have governed for seventy of the past one hundred years. They won outright, with or without allies entirely dependent upon them, four of the ten elections held between 1867 and 1914, four of the six between the wars, and eight of the fourteen since 1945. Yet in all periods previous to the 1980s, the Tories believed their position to be highly vulnerable. Until then, most Tory leaders conceived their party to be a minority force, able to secure power not only by working largely within the programmatic constraints of their opponents, but by seducing as many of those opponents as they could with self-respect and without splitting their own party.

That was emphatically not the case after 1979. Both the language and the sentiments changed. Not that the art of compromise was foreign to Margaret Thatcher. Until her final debacles over the European Community and the poll tax, she was politically adroit, sensitive to broad elite sentiment on social issues, especially where her reactionary instincts were confined to rhetoric, and in all spheres ready to make strategic withdrawals as circumstances demanded. But circumstances demanded it far less of her than of her Tory predecessors.

Hand-in-hand with the transformation in the electoral position of the Conservative party between the first and the second electoral orders went a pronounced change in its elite, a change of significance in explaining the character of the Thatcherite order. Between the early 1920s and 1974, the social background of the Tory elite changed remarkably little. Even the postwar Maxwell-Fyfe reforms, a deliberate attempt to broaden the social basis of the parliamentary party, had in practice more impact on party organization, in particular on the role and funding of constituency parties, than on the candidates and M.P.s they selected.

True, the period saw the retreat of the landed aristocracy proper from the Tory benches in the Commons. Yet in other respects, little altered: the dominance of the solid upper-middle class over the party's ranks in the Commons remained unimpaired, and even the Tory aristocracy, with its parliamentary base in the Lords, continued to feature prominently in Conservative governments. As late as 1951, Churchill could include five peers in his cabinet of sixteen; in 1962, a substantial proportion of Macmillan's government was related to the duke of Devonshire, the prime minister's brother-in-law; a year later, the party leadership itself went to a fourteenth earl (Lord Home).

By contrast, the twenty years after the war saw the mainstream professional classes advance steadily within Labour's parliamentary ranks. Reinforcing its still-significant working-class contingent, this made Labour's parliamentary party far more socially representative than its Conservative counterpart. Of the Tory M.P.s elected in 1923,[42] 79 percent were educated at the most elite private schools; in 1974, the figure had declined only to 74 percent, with the proportion of Etonians falling only from a quarter to 17 percent. The occupational balance within the party also remained broadly constant over that period: the proportion drawn from the higher reaches of the civil service, the professions (mostly the Bar), and the armed forces was 56 percent in 1923, 57 percent in 1939, and 49 percent in 1974, with businessmen constituting about one-third throughout.

On the face of it, the social composition of the Conservative elite changed additionally little between 1974 and 1987. Of those elected in 1987, two-thirds were private-school educated, 42 percent were professionals, and 37 percent hailed from a business background—proportions similar to those of sixty years before. But below the surface, a significant shift had occurred. The businessmen elected in 1987—37 percent of the party's M.P.s—represented a far broader spectrum of business and financial interests than their 1974 (let alone their 1923) forebears. Of the 1987 contingent, only 11 percent were Etonians (down from 17 percent in 1974), typical of the general shift away from the more expensive and elitist private boarding schools toward "minor" boarding schools, independent day schools, and, increasingly, state grammar schools.

A comparable broadening was evident in the university background of Tory M.P.s: over the same thirteen-year period, the proportion from Oxbridge declined, from 56 percent to 44 percent, while the proportion educated at provincial universities doubled, from 13 to 26 percent—rising to 28 percent among the 1992 contingent. Even the still-large Oxbridge contingent was more meritocratic, less "private school," and markedly less elitist in manner than cohorts of previous generations. Increasingly, Tory M.P.s hailed from the lower middle class and skilled working class. The sons and daughters of teachers, doctors, even small tradesmen, increasingly replaced the sons of landowners, business leaders, and wealthy professionals—though the latter remained in a majority.

By 1990, the Tories were hailing John Major, son of an itinerant trapeze artist and grammar-school boy who never made it to university, as their "ideal type." In all three respects, Major was evidently still atypical of most of his M.P.s. But the social groups they typified—the broad spectrum of middle-class professionals with a fair sprinkling of sons of skilled workers and the petite bourgeoisie—made the Conservative parliamentary party more representative of its electorate than at any time in the past century. In 1939, one critic remarked, apropos of the fact that out of four hundred Tory M.P.s there were but ten solicitors, eight accountants, and four teachers: "The Conservative Party is indeed exclusive, excluding entirely members of nearly all the main occupations from becoming Conservative members of Parliament."[43] By 1969, the solicitors and accountants were not quite so rare. By 1989, they and their kin were running the party.

Under Thatcher, therefore, the Tory side of the House was as representative of its voters as was the Labour side. Moreover, the social groups it represented were expanding, while Labour's were contracting fast. It was not, however, just a question of numbers and electoral appeal. The transformation brought to the fore a Tory elite more self-confident of its rapport with the electorate, and more self-assured in its ability to sustain its support, than any in the party's modern history. This was true of Thatcher herself, par excellence. As she once put it: "Deep in their instincts, people find what I am saying and doing right. And I know it is because it is the way I was brought up. I'm eternally grateful for the way I was brought up in a small town. We knew everyone, we knew what people thought. I sort of regard myself as a very normal, ordinary person with all the right instinctive antennae."[44] But it extended well beyond Thatcher to her parliamentary party as a whole: a broader-based leadership, far more confident than its forebears—particularly in the 1950s and 1960s—of its ability to turn the social-democratic tide.

For a time in 1990, and again in the run up to the 1992 election, it appeared that the second order might be about to give way to a third, in which not merely the Conservatives' hegemony but much of the constitutional fabric outlined in the opening section would be dismantled. It did not happen. A more confident grasp of Britain's postwar political order should perhaps have warned that it was not going to give way, at least once Margaret Thatcher had been ousted and her extraordinary poll-tax folly reversed. That done, the dynamics of the Thatcherite order were likely to keep the Tories' electoral coalition intact so long as the alternative government remained a Labour party indelibly associated in the public mind with the pre-1979 era. Indeed, even if the latter should come to power in the 1990s, the *order* under which it arrives seems likely to manifest more of continuity than of change.

Notes

James Callaghan made the remark quoted in the epigraph to this chapter at a private dinner in Bonn given by Chancellor Schmidt. Alan Bullock, *Ernest Bevin, Foreign Secretary* (New York: Norton, 1983), 51.

1. Byron E. Shafer, "The Notion of an Electoral Order," in Byron E. Shafer, ed., *The End of Realignment? Interpreting American Electoral Eras* (Madison: University of Wisconsin, 1991).

2. Helmut Norpoth, "The Falklands War and Government Popularity in Britain," *Electoral Studies* 6 (April 1987): 3–16; A. F. Heath, Roger Jowell, and John Curtice, *How Britain Votes* (Oxford: Pergamon, 1985), 162.

3. Alistair Horne, *Macmillan, 1957–86* (London: Macmillan, 1989), 239.

4. Anthony S. King, *Is Britain Becoming Harder to Govern?* (London: BBC, 1976), encapsulates the massive 1970s literature on "decline"; Stephen George, *An Awkward Partner: Britain in the European Community* (Oxford: Oxford University, 1990), is a sound chronological account of the "tale."

5. Cf. H. C. G. Matthew, *Gladstone, 1809–74* (Oxford: Clarendon, 1986), and his introduction to vols. 10 and 11 of *The Gladstone Diaries* (Oxford: Clarendon, 1990); Andrew Adonis, *Making Aristocracy Work: The Peerage and the Political System in Britain, 1885–1914* (Oxford: Clarendon, 1993), chaps. 7 and 9; J. Scully, *The Origins of the Lloyd George Coalition: The Politics of Social Imperialism, 1900–1918* (Princeton: Princeton University, 1975); Kenneth O. Morgan, *Consensus and Disunity: The Lloyd George Coalition, 1918–22* (Oxford: Clarendon, 1979); Kenneth O. Morgan, *Labour in Power, 1945–51* (Oxford: Clarendon, 1988).

6. Cosmo Graham and Tony Prosser, *Waiving the Rules: The Constitution under Thatcherism* (Milton Keynes: Open University, 1988), and Michael Foley, *The Rise of the British Presidency* (Manchester: Manchester, 1993), are par for the more analytic course.

7. A. V. Dicey, *Introduction to the Study of the Law of the Constitution*, 1885, 8th ed. (London: Macmillan, 1915), cii.

8. Ferdinand Mount, *The British Constitution Now: Recovery or Decline?* (London: Mandarin, 1992), 21.

9. Except for governments lacking a majority in the House of Commons, which have to share power, to a small degree, with minor parties. Since 1945, there have been only two such governments, lasting less than three years between them.

10. There is a growing division of powers between the United Kingdom and European executives (viewing the European Commission and the E.C.'s Council of Ministers together as such), a comparatively recent development dealt with below.

11. James G. Kellas, *The Scottish Political System*, 3d ed. (Cambridge: Cambridge University, 1984) 151–57.

12. For the "cadre" nature of British parties, see Samuel H. Beer, *Modern British Politics*, 3d ed. (London: Faber & Faber, 1982).

13. Hugo Young, *One of Us: A Biography of Margaret Thatcher* (London: Macmillan, 1991), 169.

14. Shafer, "The Notion of an Electoral Order."

15. See Dawn Oliver, *Government in the United Kingdom* (Milton Keynes: Open University, 1991).

16. See the Institute for Public Policy Research's proposed *Constitution for the United Kingdom* (London: IPPR, 1991).

17. Labour outpolled the Tories in 1951, but the Tories won twenty-six more Commons seats than Labour, and Winston Churchill took office for the second time, nursing a small overall majority for four years. The Conservatives outpolled Labour in February of 1974, but Labour won four more seats than the Tories, and Harold Wilson headed a minority government until the second election of the year. Such are the vagaries of Britain's electoral system.

18. Labour's total was 44.5 percent to the Tories' 43.6 percent. The third-party Liberal vote never rose above 11.2 percent, and was generally well under 10 percent until the 1974 elections, when it leapt to nearly 20 percent.

19. Kenneth O. Morgan, *The People's Peace: British History, 1945–1990* (Oxford: Oxford University, 1992), 71–111, for the "collectivist retreat."

20. See Paul Addison, *The Road to 1945* (London: Quartet, 1975); Kathleen Burk, *The First Privatisation: The Politicians, the City, and the Denationalization of Steel* (London: Historians' Press, 1988); Samuel Brittan, *The Treasury under the Tories* (Harmondsworth: Penguin, 1969); Eric Butterworth and Robert Holman, eds., *Social Welfare in Modern Britain* (London: Fontana, 1975).

21. See Jim Bulpitt, "The Disipline of the New Democracy: Mrs. Thatcher's Domestic Statecraft," *Political Studies* 34 (March 1986): 19–39.

22. In one simplified paragraph, this is the thesis of the most systematic analysis of electoral behavior in the period: David Butler and Donald E. Stokes, *Political Change in Britain* (London: Macmillan, 1969).

23. Ross McKibbin, *Ideologies of Class: Social Relations in Britain, 1880–1950* (Oxford: Clarendon, 1990), 288.

24. Ibid., 290–93.

25. Ibid., 287.

26. David Willetts, *Modern Conservatism* (London: Penguin, 1992). Significantly, the last chapter is entitled "Europe."

27. Horne, *Macmillan,* 17.

28. Viscount Hailsham, *The Conservative Case* (West Drayton: Penguin, 1959).

29. Nigel Fisher, *Ian Macleod* (London: Deutsch, 1973), 73.

30. Heath, Jowell, and Curtice, *How Britain Votes,* 36.

31. A. F. Heath, *Understanding Political Change: The British Voter 1964–1987* (Oxford: Pergamon, 1991).

32. Heath, Jowell, and Curtice, *How Britain Votes,* 35.

33. Ivor Crewe, "The Electorate," in Hugh Berrington, ed., *Change in British Politics* (London: Cass, 1984), 204.

34. John Vincent, *Disraeli* (Oxford: Oxford University, 1990), 68.

35. In terms of seats, that is.

36. John Curtice and Michael Steed, App. 2 to David Butler and Dennis Kavanagh, *The British General Election of 1987* (New York: St. Martin's, 1988), 330–31.

37. McKibbin, *Ideologies of Class,* 259–84.

38. Heath, *Understanding Political Change,* 58.

39. McKibbin, *Ideologies of Class,* 260.

40. David Owen, *Time to Declare* (London: Michael Joseph, 1992), 598–99.

41. Nigel Lawson, *The View from No. 11: Memoirs of a Tory Radical* (London: Bantam, 1992), 1053.

42. The statistics in this and the following paragraphs are drawn from David Butler and Michael Pinto-Duschinsky, "The Conservative Elite, 1918–78," in Zig Layton-Henry, ed., *Conservative Party Politics* (London: Macmillan, 1980), and from Byron Criddle's analysis of candidates in the 1987 and 1992 elections in Butler and Kavanagh, *British General Election of 1987,* and their *The British General Election of 1992* (Basingstoke: Macmillan, 1992).

43. Simon Haxey, *Tory MP* (London: Gollancz, 1939), 190–91.

44. Young, *One of Us,* 208.

Miriam Feldblum

France

Among the G-7 countries, France has experienced perhaps the greatest variety of postwar formal and practical transformations. After World War II, France did not completely overhaul its past constitutional arrangements, as Germany, Italy, and Japan did. Instead, French political elites repudiated the wartime Vichy regime and replaced the prewar (Third Republic) constitution with a new one to inaugurate the Fourth Republic. Twelve years later, a national crisis over Algerian independence prompted the return of General Charles de Gaulle to power and the establishment of yet another constitutional regime. This Fifth Republic led to practical changes in France that have no parallel in postwar Britain, the United States, or Canada. At the social base for politics, a new order overturned the existing balance of forces; in government, it altered basic institutional arrangements; among key intermediaries, it led to the transformation of the French party system.[1]

Today, after more than thirty-five years of life under the Fifth Republic, the traditional French instability appears to have ended.[2] France has now witnessed successive alternations in power between conservative and socialist governments. This includes the most recent electoral ascension by the Gaullist leader, Jacques Chirac, to the French presidency, an office occupied since 1981 by the Socialist François Mitterrand. Yet French political life can be considered to be in a period of flux as well. Or at least, contemporary French politics has featured substantial further shifts in both structural influences and substantive issues. Since the early eighties, in the party system where these two factors meet, the extreme right, the National Front party (FN), has risen to prominence, while the far left, the Communist Party (PCF), has dramatically declined. Among major parties, the Socialists (PS), the Gaullist Rally for the Republic (RPR), and the centrist Union for French Democracy (UDF) have all stumbled into disarray at various points in only the past decade.

Socialist reforms, aimed at decentralization, have shifted some authority from centralized state structures to regional and local institutions. The advent of "cohabitation" in France, that is, the coexistence of a president and prime minister from opposing political parties, appearing first in 1986 (until 1988) and again in 1993 (to 1995), broadened the repertoire of partisan possibilities. New issues, including questions of immigration and European integration, have arrived forcefully in French political life, affecting the stakes of national and local politics. Amidst all these changes, an increasing number of voters in France have begun to doubt the relevancy of traditional Left-Right distinctions for understanding contemporary politics.[3]

To what extent do the different constitutional arrangements in postwar France constitute distinctive "political orders"? Are the practical transformations witnessed in France this past decade indicative of a new political order as well? Or are these merely variations on a continuing dominant political pattern? My purpose in this chapter is to identify postwar political orders and their eras in France, as distinguished by their structural influences and issue differences.[4] My central argument is that postwar France has been characterized by three such successive orders. I call the first the era of *fragmented governance* (till 1958), and the second the era of *majoritarian governance* (1959–1983). In the past decade, I argue, the contours of a new political order have become visible; this latest, I have dubbed the era of *divided governance* (1983–).

This chapter is divided into three parts. In the first part, I discuss the immediate postwar political order in France, one of "fragmented governance," which lasted until the demise of the Fourth Republic in 1958. This political order was not a new one, but extended back to—and resonated with—the political order of the prewar Third Republic. Despite the seeming break of the Vichy Regime and of a new constitution, it was continuities from prewar to postwar periods in France's multiplistic party system, in its fragmented governing structures, and in its localized political focus which were more concrete.[5] "Fragmented governance" thus refers to political structures and institutions as well as to the multiple nature of societal cleavages and issue themes during this period.

The establishment of the Fifth Republic in 1958 inaugurated a new political order, one of *"majoritarian governance."* In the second part of this chapter, I analyze how Fifth Republic institutions and political structures modified the mode of governance and representation. I examine the creation of majoritarian blocs, the coming of presidentialist governance, and the reduction of social cleavages into broader-based divisions. "Majoritarian governance" refers to the transformation of political structures and to the nationalization of political conflict and issue themes. In the analysis, I underscore how the dominant political order of majoritarian governance endured through the 1970s, albeit in a revised pattern and under strain.

A new political order of "divided governance" does emerge in the 1980s in France. In the third part of this chapter, I discuss why the transformations taking place since the 1980s are more than just variations of the majoritarian order.[6] The term "divided governance" is not simply a substitute for divided *government,* which has been used in the American context mainly to characterize split partisan control of governmental institutions. In the era of divided *governance* in France, "cohabitation"—the French analogue to split partisan control, the "presidential-premier" model—has been an important outcome of new divisions, but not the defining feature.[7]

"Divided governance" refers instead to the emergence of new divisions in French political life, whose impact has extended to transforming French modes of representation and politicking, which, in turn, have further shaped the character of the new order. The new divisions represent cross-cutting pressures along the lines of cultural and national issues on the one hand, and economic and welfare issues on the other. They have altered even the old cleavages between the Left and Right, "the two large families of French political life."[8] In a conclusion, I discuss the significance and possible ramifications of these political orders.

The Era of "Fragmented Governance"

France's era of "fragmented governance" can be understood best by examining its structural influences and issue conflicts, especially at opposite ends of the political system, in governmental institutions and at the social base. In the period immediately following World War II, the possibilities for an entirely new political order in France appeared great, especially as "there existed a serious chance for a thorough overhauling of the party system."[9] The Vichy regime was delegitimized because of its collaborationist role during the war. The Third Republic (and its party system) were likewise discredited because of the stalemates and fragmentation that marked French politics before the war.

Under the provisional postwar government (1944–46) headed by General Charles de Gaulle, the leader of French forces outside France during the war, existing political bodies heatedly debated the contours of a new constitution. De Gaulle, a fierce opponent of the multiparty system of the Third Republic, advocated the creation of a strong presidential executive and the reduction of parliamentary power. On the other side, left-wing politicians and parties favored maintaining the supremacy of the parliament and coalition politics. This debate over competing styles of governance was not a new one in France. Since its Revolution in 1789, France has witnessed the succession of sixteen different constitutions, which have included monarchist regimes, revolutionary governments, plebiscitarian empires, and republican orders. Throughout the different eras, "representative" governance has been pitted against "plebiscitarian" or populist governance. Regime instability was in part a product of this conflict.[10]

In 1945, echoing this legacy of division, de Gaulle called for a "Republican monarch" and for direct appeal to the general will of the people. In response, the Left called for legislative autonomy, more along the lines of a British-style parliamentary government.[11] This latter vision (of parliamentary governance) prevailed, and the Fourth Republic came into existence. De Gaulle's propositions lost both through divisions within the Right and through the postwar strength of the Left. De Gaulle was not supported by the Vichy Right, whose past associations, in any case, placed them in a weak position to wage constitutional battles. By contrast, the Communists (PCF), the Socialists (SFIO), and the Christian Democrats (Mouvement Républicain Populaire, MRP), all of whom had played dominant roles in the wartime resistance movements, were well positioned.

These latter three parties carried nearly 75 percent of the popular vote in 1946. The Communists, in particular, emerged as a more popular force after the war than they had been before. The party was even included for the first time as a partner in a tripartite governing coalition (until 1947). The aspirations of the new governmental coalition included the desire to see the new Republic overcome the instability of the Third Republic, which in its seventy-year existence went through 108 governments. To that end, the constitution of the Fourth Republic called for a reduction in presidential power, allowed for a more autonomous National Assembly, and set up the possibility of a strong prime minister.

Intentions aside, the Fourth Republic was not to be successful in consolidating power or maintaining governments. Within its constitutional framework, the new order still encouraged "the traditional forms of atomistic representation and rule by shifting coalitions of the center."[12] It led to a regime of continuous coalition governments with no real autonomous power. The confluence of political factors, including an intensifying Cold War and the exclusion of Communists from governing coalitions after 1947, contributed additionally to a period of fragmented governments. During the twelve-year tenure of the Fourth Republic, there were twenty-five of these.

Stalemated executive leadership did not translate into administrative paralysis, however, due in large part to the French state bureaucracy. The French administrative model, dating back to the Napoleonic period, was designed to be "statist, powerful, centralized, hierarchically-structured, ubiquitous, uniform, depoliticized, instrumental, expert, and tightly controlled."[13] Though the model may never have been fully in place, France has been shaped by its statist orientations. During the Fourth Republic, it was actually the more stable and centralized, technocratic state bureaucracy that forced the rapid pace of economic and social reconstruction. Civil servants were the main agents generating postwar French economic "plans," and in fact, provided for important continuity in the bureaucracy from the prewar, through the Vichy, to postwar administrations.[14]

While bureaucratic dominance in the policy process during this period does find parallels in postwar Japan, national politics in France was still not fundamentally defined by the state bureaucracy.[15] At bottom, national governance was defined instead by fragmentation—regional and social, electoral and institutional. There were several reasons for this. Called a "regime of parties," the Fourth Republic actually perpetuated a "nonparty" or ineffective party system. John Frears has remarked that parties in the Fourth Republic "failed to govern."[16] Electoral victory did not confer the power or resources to determine policy. Institutional fragmentation was accompanied by the "undisciplined, fragmented, multiparty system" of the Third Republic.[17] Politics was localized and not national. Many leaders were local notables; most parties were not "national" entities. These weaknesses were not new. As early as 1917, Socialist leader Leon Blum moaned, "If only we had in France political parties, and if these parties had an organization and a doctrine."[18]

The use of proportional representation as the electoral system during most of this period further encouraged smaller parties and fractured electoral results. Electoral rules thus complemented the "regional fragmentation of electoral competition," which was a key feature in French political life.[19] Territory, religion, social life, and class operated as deep cleavages in society. For example, Catholicism and the western regions in France have traditionally been correlated with support for the Right. The Midi, on the other hand, was known as "secular, republican . . . anti-clerical, and anti-militaristic."[20]

At the same time, postwar economic reconstruction was bringing about irreversible changes for the traditional French social classes. At the beginning of World War II, France was the most peasant of all the industrialized countries; 45 percent of the French population lived in rural communes, while 37 percent of the active population worked in agriculture. These figures were to decline so sharply that by the eighties only 5 or 6 percent of the active population worked in agriculture.[21] Parallel developments could be observed in other sectors as well. Traditional patterns of social class were simply breaking up in the process of economic modernization, urbanization, and reconstruction.

The mixed and fluid electoral fortunes of political parties in subsequent years reflected in part the consequences of these social and economic transformations. There were six major political forces in the Fourth Republic: the Communists (PCF), Socialists (SFIO), Radicals (with UDSR), Christian Democrats or the Popular Republican Movement (MRP), the moderate and liberal Right (CNI—National Center of Independents), and the Gaullists (RPR). After 1954, the extreme Right Poujadists also emerged. The Communists maintained the strongest organization and a mostly stable proportion of the vote during this period; their share of the vote in parliamentary elections was 28.2 percent in 1946, 26.9 percent in 1951, and 25.9 percent in 1956. The success of the Communists was sustained by dedicated activists, capitalizing on salient class cleavages during this period.[22] The Socialists (SFIO), on the other hand, declined from a high of 23.4 percent in 1945 to 15.2 percent in 1956.

Among the moderate and Right forces, the Christian Democrats experienced a sharp drop in popular support, from which they never really recovered. The Gaullist forces were extremely successful on the local level in the late forties. In 1951, the RPF obtained a little over 20 percent of the vote in the national legislative elections, before falling apart again in 1956. Other parties on the Right intermittently obtained over 10 percent of the vote in the legislative elections of the period. Within this volatile electoral scene, the nationalist Poujade movement emerged as a "sleeper" party, capturing 11.6 percent of the vote in 1956. More than other parties, the Poujadists were able to benefit from the acute domestic discontent of the petite bourgeoisie in flux.[23]

The volatility of the vote underscored the fragmented nature of representation during this period. Besides social cleavages, other domestic and international factors began to dominate French political life. Specifically, the Cold War and growing problems of decolonialization in Indochina and Algeria placed great pressures on the political forces in the Fourth Republic.

To summarize the analysis thus far, the political order of the Fourth Republic was an era of *"fragmented governance,"* whose roots were in the social and institutional context of the prewar Third Republic. Regardless of new constitutional arrangements, old partisan alignments prevailed; with the exception of the place of the Communists, the Third and Fourth Republics were of a similar partisan cast. Though the postwar years marked the beginning of fundamental social and economic transformations in France, the older, multiple, social and regional cleavages still defined political life. That said, it was this fragmented character, when confronted by the break-up of old patterns, as overlaid by the entry of new issue foci, which established the groundwork for a shift in political orders.

The growing crisis over decolonialization in Algeria finally brought down the Fourth Republic, whose institutional and political framework could not cope with this grand national issue. On 13 May 1958, the French government was threatened with a military coup d'état in Algiers. In response, Charles de Gaulle was called back into government by the parties in power to resolve the crisis and protect the republic. Once more in charge, de Gaulle obtained support for proposing a new constitution, to be voted on by the public in a referendum. The Gaullist vision of a powerful executive and much-weakened parliament carried an absolute majority of the votes on 28 September 1958. The Fifth Republic was established. Following the vote by an electoral college, de Gaulle assumed the powers of the new presidency on 8 January 1959. The referendum gave dc Gaulle a clear mandate to govern, not least because of the high rate of voter participation and the decisive defeat of the "no" campaign.[24]

The referendum signified not only victory for the Gaullist forces, but also a shift in the larger balance of social forces in France. The Fifth Republic was "born out of the death" of the Fourth Republic, and it was born to the Right. The referendum was strongly opposed by the Communists and other segments of the non-Communist Left. These Left forces decried the loss of democratic accountability and parliamentary sovereignty. François Mitterrand, for example, then one of the leaders of the new Left, called the Fifth Republic a "permanent coup d'état." Other Left forces only resigned themselves to the new constitution because of the Algerian crisis. From the very beginning, Left forces were thus "outsiders" in the Fifth Republic.[25]

The 5th Republic and "Majoritarian Governance"

From 1958, a shift to a new order was in evidence. The arrival of a newly dominant issue focus, Algeria, followed by overwhelming popular support for the new constitution; the associated realignment of the electorate from Left to Right; along with real changes in institutional arrangements: all these events signaled the shift. The legislative elections of 1958, held under the new electoral regime of majoritarian two-ballot voting, confirmed the electoral realignment: the Right parties won 54.3 percent of the vote.[26] Moreover, they won decisive control of the National Assembly, although the Gaullist party itself did not obtain an absolute majority.

The Fifth Republic meant the beginning of a new political order in France from numerous perspectives. John Frears has asserted, "France needed to be equipped with a new and more effective political order, and it was. The next few years saw the solution of France's colonial crises, the building of a new legitimacy for political institutions . . . and the transformation of the party system."[27] Colette Ysmal has argued that "the 5th Republic overturned the parties and the system of traditional parties in France, those which had instructed political life under the 3rd and 4th Republics."[28] The Fifth Republic constitution shifted the balance of power away from parliament to the executive, consisting of both prime minister *and* president.

The Fifth Republic brought a new order of "majoritarian governance." Why *majoritarian*? After 1958, French institutions were increasingly governed by majoritarian blocs rather than shifting coalitions. Politics became nationalized, the party system reorganized, and multiple social cleavages at least reduced. Majoritarian governance was defined in part by practical political shifts, in part by social transformations and new national issues. In the following sections, I analyze the institutionalization of majoritarian governance within a variety of contexts—governmental, electoral, partisan, and social.

The policymaking ramifications of the new constitution were ultimately great. "The Fifth Republic signified precisely the end of parliamentary sovereignty."[29] The formal constitution established a strong executive, and de Gaulle's subsequent reading of it established presidential (and not prime-ministerial) dominance.[30] The foundations for de Gaulle's "presidentialization" were laid in the constitution, which set up the strong dual executive of prime minister and president. According to the constitution, the president was to be elected separately and indirectly, and given an array of executive powers, most of which were to be used in consultation with the prime minister. These included the right to assume total emergency powers, to dissolve the National Assembly and call for new elections, to call public referendums on certain issues, and to appoint the prime minister. The running of the government was accorded to the prime minister, but the new constitution distinguished vaguely between the tasks of the two offices, enabling de Gaulle's later expansionist reading.[31]

Transformation of the electoral system accompanied these institutional changes. With the intent of diminishing the proliferation of parties, the new constitution instituted a two-ballot system of elections, which provided for the top two or three candidates on the first ballot to compete in a second, run-off election. The system, in practice, favored the leading parties because of the necessity to engage in electoral agreements on the second ballot. A new political order then developed gradually. Until 1963, the problems of Algerian decolonialization dominated domestic French politics, and the personal dominance of de Gaulle largely defined the French order. With the exception of the Communist Party, most forces on the Left and Right tacitly supported de Gaulle through 1962, when Algeria finally won its independence from France.

The year 1962 is often considered a watershed year for the Fifth Republic. It was the year that the Algerian "crisis" ended. It was also the year that de Gaulle won a referendum on direct election of the president, enacting a critical modification of the 1958 Constitution. The referendum was highly controversial. Opposed from the start by the parliament and parties, including segments of de Gaulle's own supporters, with its very constitutionality assailed, it nevertheless passed with a solid majority of the popular vote (62.2 percent). Because his government had been censured, de Gaulle then dissolved the National Assembly and called for new elections to take place in less than a month, in November, 1962.

De Gaulle assembled most of his supporters to run under a united party alliance, the UNR-UDT. The elections then solidified the Gaullist hold on the electorate, confirming this electorate's shift to the Right, a trend that would continue through the 1960s.[32] Nevertheless, in 1962, the Communists and the other leftist parties managed to retain their electoral base. As a result, the most important losers were the centrist parties, whose proportion of the vote fell considerably from the 1958 legislative elections. The Gaullists and their allies simultaneously became the dominant force on the Right.[33] Benefiting from the two-ballot majoritarian regime, the Gaullist coalition obtained for the first time an absolute majority in the National Assembly.

In light of the referendum and these elections, 1962 surely marked the confrontation of French political parties with the "majoritarian fact" of the Fifth Republic.[34] Courtesy of the direct election of the president and the two-ballot electoral system, parties were being forced to form blocs in order to compete more effectively. At the same time, they were propelled to reshape themselves into more disciplined, mass organizations. The centrist coalitions of the Third and Fourth Republics did badly. For this reason, François Borella has asserted that a new regime with a modern majority-party system "was really born in 1962."[35] Jean Charlot has also described the new imperatives as part of the "Gaullist phenomenon."[36]

The transformation of the party system was striking. For the 1965 presidential election, several forces on the Left, including the Communists and Socialists, jointly supported the new Left leader, François Mitterrand, as their candidate, though Mitterrand himself was not a member of either the SFIO or PCF. Such a strategy would have been unthinkable just years earlier. In turn, many of the older parties, and even the newer parties of the Third and Fourth Republics, began to disappear. Today, for example, only the Communists (PCF), the Radical party, and the CNIP (National Center of Independents and Farmers) extend beyond the beginnings of the Fifth Republic. In the 1967 legislative elections, the Gaullist party regrouped under the name the Union of Democrats for the Fifth Republic (UDR), in part to incorporate other Right and centrist forces under its wing. For its part, the noncommunist Left organized the Federation of the Democratic Socialist Left (FGDS), and arranged for second-ballot agreements with the Communists.[37] The full Left panoply included the extreme left, the Communists, the Socialists (SFIO), and the Movement of Left Radicals (MRG).

Three related trends were notable in this evolving party system. First, the system and the electoral process became "clarified" and "simplified."[38] While multiple parties remained (and remain) in France, the central cleavage between Left and Right became more defined. Second, the party system became "presidentialized"; in other words, the emergence of these majoritarian blocs was related to their aspirations to win the presidency.[39] Third, and in response, the shifting centrist coalitions, which had been a central feature of the political system, began to disappear.[40] These trends helped institutionalize majoritarian governance. According to Ezra Suleiman, "What distinguishes the Fifth Republic from the Fourth is not so much the altered institutional arrangements in favor of the executive, nor the relative ministerial stability, as the existence of a majority party which dominates the executive, the legislative, and probably the bureaucracy."[41]

Yet the character of this era was not simply defined by a changed policy-making or electoral context. The increasing nationalization of politics was a key development as well. This meant a shift from the localized character of political (and social) life of the Third and Fourth Republics. It meant the diminution of regional, class, and ideological fragmentation. The resulting nationalization of politics was rooted in several factors. One was the presidential focus of the new political order along with its majoritarian electoral system. These trends alone reduced fragmentation. Another factor was the continuing transformation of the social base and of the social *classes*. This development reduced the multiple underlying cleavages and led to the entry of new national issue foci.

By the mid-1960s, postwar demographic and economic changes were having an even greater impact. The farming population was in dramatic decline. A new middle class of professional and white-collar workers ("cadres") had emerged. The proportion of women in the workplace rose. The postwar baby-boom generation came of age. The saliency of class identifications diminished. The cultural bases for politics, such as religion, remained important but also showed signs of change.[42] Religious practice itself declined, as the secularization of French society grew. Cultural liberalism, defined as attitudes that are antiauthoritarian and opposed to traditional morality, spread.[43]

Taken together, these social and cultural changes produced what Henri Mendras has called, "the second French revolution."[44] The revolution received a superficial symbolic incarnation in the 1968 May uprising in Paris, which almost brought down the French government. Yet even as they caused political turmoil, these social and cultural transformations were actually contributing, more consequentially, to the nationalization of political life. And this nationalization of politics, in turn, contributed to a general congruence of political and social cleavages with national themes.

It was in this period that consensus over national institutions began to emerge. Again, according to Henri Mendras, a national consensus over "the church, the army, the school, the republic" began to form by the end of the 1960s. Unlike the situation in the earlier period of fragmented governance, these institutions no longer operated as "instruments of identification and differentiation amongst the French people." Since that period, Mendras has argued, these institutions "have lost their old divisive character and all form part of the profound consensus which underpins modern French society."[45] By the 1970s, younger members of the electorate, both liberal and conservative, expressed support for culturally liberal views.[46] National issues, such as the international security environment, also reinforced feelings of national consensus and helped define the political temper of majoritarian governance.

Majoritarian Governance after De Gaulle

The aftermath of 1968 did, however, prove a critical milestone in the further development of majoritarian governance. In 1968, the May riots rocked Paris; French politics was obviously in great flux. Some segments of the electorate began to shift from the Right back to the Left, at least on the local levels. At the same time, student revolts, strikes, and the threat of chaos provoked waves of anticommunism and greater support for the established Right. The centrist-Right parties thus benefited, simultaneously, from public concerns. In specially called elections to the National Assembly after the May riots, centrist-Right parties won 58.9 percent of the vote; the Left, forced to deal with calls to boycott the elections, received only 40.5 percent. De Gaulle himself, however, weakened by the riots and confronted with the defeat of a presidential referendum, resigned in 1969.

His departure, in the most extreme sense, called into question the survival of the Fifth Republic. For many contemporary observers, Gaullism was the linchpin of the new order. But the departure of de Gaulle did not bring down the political order. Instead, de Gaulle's former prime minister, Georges Pompidou, won the 1969 presidential election, in the process proving the viability of the Fifth Republic without de Gaulle. Pompidou also contributed to the institutionalization of majoritarian governance.[47] As president, Pompidou followed de Gaulle's presidentialist practices. As partisan leader, he widened the conservative majority by incorporating the non-Gaullist parties of the Right, including Giscard d'Estaing and the Independent Republicans.

Into the 1970s, then, the Right solidified its formation as an electoral bloc. There was a temporary consolidation of the center (UDF), which was subsequently incorporated into the rightist bloc as well, simultaneously weakening the leverage of the Gaullist party within that bloc. In the 1974 presidential election, called after Pompidou's death, Valéry Giscard d'Estaing, the leader of a moderate-Right fraction, successfully stood as the rightist candidate in the second round. His campaign split the rightist coalition but effectively broke the Gaullist hold on the Right.[48]

In contrast to the Right's electoral successes, the Left faced another period of disarray and renewal after 1968. The 1968 and 1969 elections signaled the demise of several Left parties that had survived from the Third and Fourth Republics, including the Socialist party, the SFIO.[49] At the same time, the riots had revealed the emergence of potential new Left constituencies. In 1969, the non-Communist Left reshaped the former SFIO into a new party, called simply the Socialist Party (PS). That move reinvigorated the Left. More than the other parties, the new PS proved able to unite diverse currents and attract cross-class electorates. PS appealed, for example, to the so-called "sociologically left," the emergent professional ("cadre") classes that included white-collar workers and management, along with the secular, culturally liberal groups.[50]

During the 1970s, the Socialists became the dominant force on the Left, displacing the Communists. That shift turned out to be critical for French politics. According to Jérôme Jaffré, the rise of the Socialist party was "a capital change that open(ed) the way for the alternation of power."[51] In 1972, a "Common Program of Government" was negotiated between the Socialists under the leadership of François Mitterrand, the Communists, and the Left Radicals (MRG). Subsequently, in the 1973 legislative elections, the Socialists presented more or less unified Left slates during the national elections to match those of the Right majority. Not surprisingly, the Left attained its highest proportion of the vote since 1956. Oliver Duhamel called the 1973 elections a turning point for the Left because it marked the return of a more balanced electorate: the Right won 53 percent of the vote, while the Left won 46 percent.[52]

By the presidential elections of 1974, a further, more refined realignment of Left and Right was visible. First, the contest featured a Socialist-Right confrontation. The era of the Communist-Gaullist confrontation, which had dominated Fifth Republic politics to that point, was over. Second, the electorate continued its shift toward the Left. Left candidates received 46 percent of the vote in the first ballot in 1974, a marked change from their previous showings of 31 percent in 1969 and 32 percent in 1965. In the final round of the election, Giscard d'Estaing beat François Mitterrand by the narrowest of margins, 50.51 percent to 49.49 percent of the popular vote.[53] Polls, too, continued to confirm the progress of the Left, so that by the *mid*-1970s, the Socialists appeared to be, in fact, the dominant party in French public opinion.

The rise of the Socialists was then further aided by conflict on the Right. In 1976, the friction between Valéry Giscard d'Estaing and his prime minister, Jacques Chirac, the leader of the Gaullist party (RPR), finally led to Chirac's resignation amidst the uneasy maintenance of the Right coalition. At the same time, the Socialists continued to expand their electorate, becoming an acknowledged contender for governmental power. By the 1978 legislative elections, the Left represented a practical majority of the electorate; Left candidates as a whole won 50.2 percent of the vote. The conditions for "cohabitation," however, were not fulfilled:[54] because of their own growing internal divisions, the parties of the Left did not obtain a majority in the National Assembly. The Gaullist party, now called Rally for the Republic (RPR), and Giscard d'Estaing's party, Union for French Democracy (UDF), retained their majority standing, although the president's party was in a minority position within its bloc.

The consolidation of the center into the rightist bloc, along with the organization of Right and Left political forces into competing blocs, constituted two crucial developments of the Fifth Republic, adding up to the bipolarization of the party system. If we consider again the 1974 presidential election, it is noteworthy that the contest featured a clear choice between Left and Right: the centrists were no longer an independent pole in French electoral politics. Yet at the same time, Giscard d'Estaing could benefit as the presidential candidate for the majority Right even as his own party was in the minority in that bloc.[55]

This bipolarization of the party system was the product of both a revised electoral system and the "presidentialized" mode of governance of the Fifth Republic.[56] Traditionally, French republics featured a multiparty system and were governed by coalitions of a shifting center. That pattern made sense when no party had the possibility of achieving a parliamentary majority on its own.[57] But under the Fifth Republic, the gradual dominance of presidential governance meant a Left or Right bloc had the capacity—and possibility—to govern. The institutional and electoral system thus encouraged parties to create "presidential majorities."[58]

Bipolarized electoral politics represented a significant shift in the political history of the French party system. Multiple parties remained, of course. But the most important stage of the electoral process, namely the second ballot, usually featured only two candidates who most often represented the competing Left and Right blocs. Voting studies of the French electorate demonstrated that French voters were "gradually coming to think of partisan competition in bipolar terms."[59] By the mid-1970s, four major parties could be identified in a bipolar schema: the Socialists (PS) and Communists (PCF) on the Left and the Gaullists (RPR) and centrist-right wing (UDF) on the Right. Given the Gaullist domination of the Right for many years, and the Socialist domination of the Left after the 1970s, the party system has also been described as "multipartyism with a dominant party."[60]

Bipolarization was not without its ironies. De Gaulle, in establishing the Fifth Republic, had denounced the "régime de partis" of the Fourth Republic. But it was the Fifth Republic that created a modern party system, a real "regime of parties," where disciplined mass parties possessed the vocation and capacity to govern.[61] The trend of bipolarization did not mark, however, the beginnings of a new political order. The bipolarized pattern of party competition was a response to the "majoritarian fact." It accentuated the central ideological cleavage between Left and Right that buttressed majoritarian governance.

To summarize the analysis of majoritarian governance thus far, this order characterized French national politics after 1958. The order was the product of a series of institutional and practical changes. First, the 1958 constitution, de Gaulle's personal leadership, and evolving presidential dominance of the policy process brought out the institutional context for majoritarian governance. Second, the revision of the electoral system, simplification of party competition, and the political confrontation between the Gaullists and Communists brought forward the structural context. Later, the evolving bipolarization of the party system, and the central cleavage between the Right and the Socialists accentuated the parameters of majoritarian governance. Beyond that, the reduction of social cleavages and the related nationalization of political life set up a new social and political context more generally. Finally, the national issue foci and areas of national consensus that emerged after 1958 contributed to the implantation of majoritarian governance.

The Socialists and Majoritarian Governance

By the 1970s, however, strains on this majoritarian governance were also visible. Economic and social issues became increasingly divisive on the national agenda. The effects of the European and international economic environment were becoming more difficult to manage politically. Indeed, the economic crisis of 1973–74 signaled the closure of the "thirty glorious years" of economic reconstruction and fast-paced industrialization. For France, as for other industrialized countries, government was confronted with the task of containing economic damage and formulating new policies within the constraints of an increasingly international environment. In the face of all this, class tensions seemed resurgent, and class-based voting patterns were again on the increase.

There were explicitly partisan strains on majoritarian governance as well. Like Pompidou, Giscard d'Estaing sought to lead a majoritarian, "presidentialized" government during his tenure as president from 1974 to 1981. But Giscard's efforts were often stymied by lack of support from the Gaullists, who were still the majority in the Right bloc, and by their leader, Jacques Chirac. Meanwhile, dissension in the Left was also visible. Overall, then, despite the endurance of two majoritarian blocs, each one seemed increasingly fraught with frictions.

Finally, Giscardian institutional practices at times strengthened and at times limited the presidential bias of the executive. In their analysis of presidential governance in the Fifth Republic, John Keeler and Martin Schain distinguish d'Estaing's tenure as president as being moderated or "tempered," in part by an assertive prime minister when Chirac held that office, and in part by new governmental reforms, which gave the parliamentary opposition more power.[62] In order to bypass the opposition in his own "presidential majority," Giscard d'Estaing relied heavily on executive tools and on a presidentialist reading of the constitution; for example, he "increased the number and scope of presidential interministerial councils."[63] On the other hand, his constitutional amendment to increase the authority of the Constitutional Council in effect diminished presidential dominance.

In 1981, François Mitterrand finally won election to the presidency of France. He won with the support of "the Union of the Left," and his election brought a Left government to power for the first time in the Fifth Republic. His election also appeared, initially, to constitute a potential turning point in postwar French political eras. Or at least, the Left's longstanding opposition to the institutions and organizing principles of the Fifth Republic appeared to be the ultimate test for the continuity of the constitution. Mitterrand's own political trajectory only reinforced that challenge.

For in fact, the Socialist government, from Mitterrand's campaign platform onward, self-consciously understood itself to be inaugurating a new political order: "*110 Propositions pour la France* was one of the most radical documents" to be issued by a major candidate in Western politics.[64] The new government promised to reorganize French economic and social life, through nationalizations, decentralizations, industrial-relations reforms, and civil and social reforms, too. Moreover, from 1981, the Socialists enacted legislation and executive decrees in all these areas .

Yet a new political order was not inevitable after 1981. Why? First, the Socialists did not reject the political institutions and structures of the Fifth Republic. In fact, Mitterrand quickly adapted a "presidentialist" reading of constitutional arrangements. As a result, the Left appeared simply to fashion majoritarian governance to their purposes. According to Jean Charlot, the two 1981 elections and subsequent Socialist dominance gave Mitterrand the same power of "absolute monarch" that had characterized de Gaulle's rule. Other observers, too, have remarked on the ironic similarities between de Gaulle and Mitterrand.[65]

Beyond that, and within two years, a major part of the grand program of economic reform and social transformation proved unworkable. By 1983, and especially after the exchange rate crisis of 1983 March, the Socialist government began the famous U-turn on much of its own economic program. Besides domestic discontent, the influence of Germany and the constraints of the international economic environment were decisive in this period.[66] At the same time, the electoral outcomes of 1981 had actually reflected the continuing centrality both of majoritarian politics and of the Left-Right cleavage. The presidential ballot featured two somewhat cohesive majoritarian blocs by the second round. In the first ballot, Right candidates obtained slightly more votes (48.9 percent) than those on the Left (47.2 percent). By the second ballot, Mitterrand defeated Giscard d'Estaing by a slight margin, 51.7 percent over 48.2 percent.

The new legislative elections called by Mitterrand immediately after his election brought the Left its best score since 1946. This election gave the Socialists an absolute majority in parliament, the first such occurrence since the UDR had won an absolute majority in the 1968 legislative elections. At the same time, the Communists did poorly, and their showing marked the beginning of their electoral decline.[67] Nevertheless, the elections arguably demonstrated the stability of the bipolar system rather than its dissolution. The balance of power within each of the blocs shifted—significantly on the Left—but the capacity to form majoritarian blocs remained in place.

While the Left's arrival in power did not transform the political order, then, electoral and institutional trends in the early eighties suggested that the structural conditions for majoritarian governance were changing. Indeed, the municipal elections of 1983 marked another turning point in the French electoral order. The far-Right politician, Jean-Marie Le Pen, and his party, the National Front, achieved electoral prominence in those elections. Just as the low share of the Communists' vote confirmed their decline, the National Front's showing signaled their arrival. The majoritarian blocs showed signs almost of collapse.

In response, after 1983, the Left revamped important parts of its electoral programs. The Right continued to struggle with divisions among its parties, as well as with the presence of the National Front. Accompanying these changes, new national debates arose, centering on immigration, security, and law and order. Largely as part of their original political program, the Socialists passed a series of electoral reforms during this period. These reforms revised the electoral rules so that different kinds of proportional representation would be in place for local and regional elections, as well as for the legislative elections of 1986. Even as the establishment of proportional representation aided in a more accurate reflection of party constituencies, the reforms also enabled the proliferation of issue-themed, nonpresidentialist parties. Likewise, they accentuated differences between national and local politics by displaying the different voter logics operative in national, regional, and European elections.

At the same time, a confluence of Socialist institutional practices diminished the "presidentialist bias" of the mode of governance.[68] The government's decentralization reforms shifted authority away from centralized state structures to regional political, economic, and social structures.[69] An increase in the authority of the Constitutional Council translated into a further reduction of executive bias within the central state. Though there is no doubt that Mitterrand, once in power, accepted the Gaullist presidential framework, he also altered the functional division of power within the executive. After 1983, Mitterrand gave more authority to the prime minister in order to detach himself from the day-to-day politics of government. Mitterrand referred to this development when he claimed that Chirac "often thought he was snatching from me powers that I had already reallocated."[70]

The Era of Divided Governance

These electoral and institutional transformations suggest that in the period following 1983, an era of "divided governance" was rapidly displacing the era of majoritarian governance. Why *divided*? The emergent order featured new divisions of power in the French mode of governance, a depolarized party system with divisions between presidentialist and nonpresidentialist parties, new (and dual) national issue foci, and dualistic political and social cleavages that cut across traditional Left-Right lines. In the following sections, I analyze the emergence of the new order of divided governance within the electoral and institutional, the structural and substantive, contexts.

Observers of recent French politics initially may wonder about this line of argument. Certainly, in the 1993 legislative elections, a renewed Center-Right alliance had won more seats and more of an absolute majority than at any point since 1958. For the new presidential campaign in 1995, the Left continued their decline, when the Socialist Party was nearly unable even to find a viable presidential candidate while the Communists remained a negligible force.[71] At one point, in early 1995, it appeared that the Left might be absent from the second round of the 1995 presidential elections, something that had not happened since 1969. The eventual scenario was less extreme, but with the presidential victory of Jacques Chirac, the Right regained complete control of both the National Assembly and the presidency.

One interpretation is that events in the nineties reaffirm the continuation of majoritarian governance, with a simple hesitation in the 1980s. But in this analysis, I argue that these events actually reflect a different political order. Transformations in the French party system, for example, have been dramatic. According to George Ross, the decline of the Communist Party "is arguably the single most important dynamic" experienced by the modern party system.[72] From its status as one of the four major parties in France, the PCF has become a marginalized, smaller party.[73] Moreover, its electoral decline was swift. Already in 1981, the PCF received only 16.1 percent of the vote in the legislative elections; this dropped to 9.7 percent in the 1986 legislative elections, and stabilized at 11.2 percent of the vote by the 1988 legislative elections. That the Communists largely retained their representation in the National Assembly in the legislative elections of 1993 March reaffirms their status as a minor party based on compact and loyal constituencies.[74]

The decline of the PCF contributed additionally to the collapse of the majoritarian order. Or at least, the Communist Party's decline ended the quadripartite character of the bipolarized majoritarian party system in France. There is no longer a possibility of balance between the Socialists and Communists. This same development, however, opened up electoral space for new sources of political protest, and so contributed to the rise of issue-themed parties. The absence of the PCF as a serious contender "removed the major institutional source of certain forms of left radicalism from the French partisan scene."[75] Indeed, the marginalization of the PCF after 1983 took place at the same time as the dilution of the Socialist political and economic programs. Taken together, the two trends signaled for some the burial of "the traditional idea of revolution and socialism" with its accompanying tensions for French political regimes; in some ways, it signaled nothing less than "the end of French exceptionalism."[76]

The era of majoritarian governance had been effective in part because it furnished a response to the traditional political instability and ideological tensions in France. Further transformations on the Left, then, reopened questions about the continuity of the structural preconditions for majoritarian governance. And indeed, a primary beneficiary of the shifts in the traditional Left vote and of discontent within the Right electorate was the far-Right National Front (FN) party. The National Front had been created in 1972 by Jean-Marie Le Pen. The party made its political breakthrough in French politics in the 1983 municipal elections. Since then, this nationalist, anti-immigrant party has become a well-implanted presence in the party system. Indeed, it has expanded and nationalized its electorate, making it a much more durable party than observers first thought.[77]

The National Front benefited from several factors. One was the introduction of proportional representation. In the 1984 European elections, the National Front obtained 11 percent of the vote; because of the proportional representation system in place for European elections, it received ten representatives. In the 1986 legislative elections, the party polled 9.65 percent of the vote; it received thirty-five seats in the National Assembly, because the Socialists at that time had reinstituted a system of proportional representation.[78] In the 1992 regional elections, the National Front obtained 13.9 percent of the vote; because of the modified proportional representation in place for regional elections, the party claimed 239 elected officials. By contrast, during the 1993 legislative elections, without proportional representation, the party received 12.52 percent of the vote in the first ballot but only 5.66 percent in the second round: they were left without representation in the National Assembly. During the 1990s, the National Front has thus experienced a decline in actual candidate wins. Nevertheless, the Front has continued to demonstrate that it is an electoral and substantive force even when none of its candidates are winning.[79]

Another factor benefiting the National Front was a growing protest vote among alienated constituencies. According to Nonna Mayer and Pascal Perrineau, this protest vote is directed against the established parties, both on the Right and Left, against both their view of politics and their policies: Le Pen and the National Front have consistently attracted this segment of the French electorate.[80] Moreover, even if an increasing proportion of the French find Le Pen and the National Front dangerous, there also exist an increasing number who say that they are in agreement with his views.[81] In the 1988 presidential election, Jean Marie Le Pen received an unprecedented 14.39 percent in first-ballot voting.[82] And in the 1995 presidential campaign, Le Pen received 15 percent of the votes in the first round, underscoring the national visibility and continuing draw of the National Front.

Le Pen and the National Front have played an important role in the shift from majoritarian to divided governance. First, the National Front exacerbated fragmentation on the Right. Since the early 1980s, conservative parties have been placed in the position of competition with the National Front. Even when they have successfully contained it, the majoritarian Right parties contributed to the legitimation of the Front. Yet the consequences for them have often not been politically profitable.[83] Moreover, the success of the National Front has eroded the character of a previously defined, bipolarized party competition. In this, its success has contributed to the depolarization of the party system and to the new phenomena of "presidential" versus "nonpresidential" parties and elections.[84] Finally, and regardless of partisan impacts, the National Front has placed its anti–immigrant, nativist issue platforms at the center of many electoral battles. The rise of the National Front has been part of the more general emergence of a new set of dominating national debates over immigration, national identity, and European integration. Conflict over immigration and related issues in the 1980s has helped set the contemporary political temper in France.

The electoral emergence of the Greens in 1988 and 1989 then attested further to the depolarization of the French party system: "Neither Right nor Left" has actually been a slogan of the French Greens.[85] Like National Front constituents, Green voters represent a protest by an increasing proportion of the electorate dissatisfied with the established parties.[86] These newly prominent (though not "new") environmentalist parties have been a more marginal presence than the National Front, their electoral outcomes more mixed.[87] Overall, however, the environmentalist and far-Right electorates have contributed to volatile voting behavior in France over recent years.

By contrast, the major parties have experienced disarray, occasionally verging on collapse, in the new electoral context. Throughout the 1980s, the majoritarian bloc of the RPR and UDF was fragile; at times, its existence was in question. Even during periods of Left unpopularity, popular support for these Right parties did not increase substantially. Finally, in 1992, the majoritarian Right reinvigorated its alliance and renewed a common program. That year, the RPR and UDF won important victories in local (cantonal) elections. As the Socialist party, in turn, collapsed amidst internal party and government scandals, the Right went on to score an overwhelming victory in the legislative elections of 1993 March.[88] Nevertheless, for all parties, contests have become more personalized, and presidential and legislative elections, along with national and local elections, increasingly decoupled.[89]

Do the trends in the party system provide evidence for an emergent new order? Some observers think not. After listing the array of electoral, institutional, and practical changes that took place in the 1980s, Howard Machin contends, "As a consequence of all these changes, an inconsistent institutional and electoral environment for party competition had been created by the late 1980s."[90] A critical factor in this inconsistency for Machin was the disappearance of the "single dominant political cleavage in the party system," in other words, the cleavage between Left and Right political blocs that was central during the period of majoritarian governance. Yet, another interpretation is possible. Indeed, what appears inconsistent from the perspective of majoritarian governance becomes more coherent when the shift toward divided governance is taken into account.

Thus, changing structural influences and ideological cleavages have set up a new context for French politics. Without discounting the myriad causes leading to its defeat, the collapse of the Socialists in 1993 was also a reflection of social and ideological change. Even before the election outcome in 1993, Michel Rocard, the leader of the moderate Socialists, called for a "rupture" of the old Socialist party and a "re-birth" of the Left. In a move to attract a wider constituency of social-ists, centrists, communist reformers, ecologists, and human-rights activ-ists, Rocard acknowledged the saliency of new social cleavages and ideological parameters. For Rocard, the Greens epitomized the social transformation: "When the French can no longer find the wellsprings of their identity in a social class nor in a religion nor in a professional category nor in a generation, not even in an economic level, what is left for them to identify with? What remains for them is what immedi-ately surrounds them: their environment . . ."[91]

The effort was apparently to little avail. In preparation for the 1994 European elections, Rocard led the Socialists' continuing efforts at "So-cial Transformation," with the aim of attracting cross-cutting segments of the Left, but the Socialists obtained only 14.5 percent of the vote in the elections in June. For the 1995 presidential elections, the Socialists ulti-mately chose Lionel Jospin, a respected figure of the traditional Socialist Left, whose electoral platform nevertheless featured an explicitly new Left agenda, the apparent strategy being to capture both old Socialist constituencies and new cultural progressives.

New Concerns for a New Era

The central cleavage between the Left and Right has disappeared, or at the least changed character, as new divisions emerged. On the one hand, there is an evident convergence among the parties in many key policy areas. On the other hand, there are new ideological cleavages that do not coincide with the traditional Left-Right cleavage but cross-cut it. The di-minishing relevancy of the Left-Right cleavage for *voters* has become a prominent feature of French politics. Public opinion polls have shown that the majority of the respondents continue to self-situate themselves on a Left-Right continuum. At the same time, a majority and increasing proportion of voters do not find the distinction useful in helping them understand the differences between the parties.[92]

This new "paradoxical" attitude has been correlated to both increas-ing convergence among the parties and the advent of cohabitation. Not surprisingly, the electorates of the National Front and of the environ-mentalist parties are the most resistant to a simple Left-Right contin-uum. The National Front electorate includes former leftist voters, while the ecologist electorate includes centrists and others. These con-stituencies must be the most skeptical about the relevancy of the Left-Right divide for understanding the parties, since both are outside this convergence and cohabitation.[93] New kinds of national debates have coincided with these distortions of the Left-Right cleavage. One of the most salient issue-areas to arise in the 1980s is immigration. Until the 1980s, immigration policy was largely defined as a technocratic issue for bureaucrats. Since then, debates over immigration and its corollaries, national identity and citizenship, have dominated French elections and politics.

Debates over immigration reflect the changed ideological and structural context of French politics. There is an increasing national convergence between the Left and Right over basic policies and principles. At the same time, however, debates on immigration issues are highly divisive and strongly contested; they have flourished in the new context of issue-themed, nonpresidentialist politics. Neither the convergence nor the conflict fall neatly into the previously defined partisan lines. Nor have they translated into an increase in centrist politics; in the area of immigration and citizenship, French politics as a whole moved to the Right by the end of the 1980s.

The debates over immigration also reveal new divisions in France's mode of governance. Immigration policy is no longer defined by a bureaucratic or executive-dominated policy process. Existing institutions such as the Council of State and the Constitutional Council, as well as new official bodies such as the Commission on Nationality and the High Council for Integration, have played more visible and consequential roles than would have been possible during the height of majoritarian governance.[94]

The era of divided governance is rooted, too, in the new cleavages that arose in the wake of postwar social and cultural transformations. In France as in other industrialized countries, new issue themes of cultural liberalism versus cultural conservativism and of economic deregulation versus social protectionism emerged following World War II. By the 1980s, the growing significance of these themes began to have an impact as well on France's basic Left-Right cleavage. In general, economic liberalization has been adopted by parties on the Right, while cultural liberalism is associated with parties on the Left. Yet divisions within the *public* on these themes do not necessarily follow partisan lines: "A segment of the left electorate has been converted to economic liberalism, and a slice of right electorate defends the left's social attainments."[95]

Gérard Grunberg and Etienne Schweisguth have shown that a growing proportion of the French electorate are supportive of both economic and cultural liberalism. Moreover, they argue that the economically and politically liberal segments of the electorate have supported both the Left and the Right. Thus, voters supporting economic and cultural liberalism contributed to the Socialists' successes in the 1980s. Just as they played an important role in the Right's victory in the 1986 legislative elections. Later, their votes helped reelect Mitterrand as president in 1988.[96]

This cross-cutting cleavage of cultural and economic liberalism has influenced all levels of politics. Take the highly divisive referendum over the Maastricht Treaty, held in France in September of 1992. In a 1992 *Eurobarometer* survey about the Maastricht Treaty, 49 percent of the French respondents said they feared European integration; these figures are up dramatically since the previous decades, when the question of European integration was not a politicized issue. The top three reasons given were fear of unemployment, loss of national identity, and concern over immigration.[97]

One (official) interpretation of such surveys has been that a "serious information gap" exists about the realities of European integration.[98] Another interpretation is that the dissensus over European integration is much more substantive and long-term because it reflects the dualist issue foci and cross-cutting pressures of a new era. According to Nonna Mayer, traditional cleavages, such as "social class, religion, and property, seem to have little influence" on pro-European attitudes. Rather, the new cleavages along the lines of cultural and economic liberalism and conservativism appear more decisive.[99] Indeed, the saliency of Europe and European integration as a national issue coincides with the cross-cutting combinations of cultural liberalism or social traditionalism, and social protectionism or economic liberalism, characteristic of the new political temper.

These cross-cutting cleavages have translated into patterns of differential voting by the French electorate. Traditional voting patterns along the lines of region, religion, and social class have undeniably, if cyclically, diminished, as French voters exhibit different voting strategies in legislative and presidential elections, in national and local elections. In the 1988 presidential election, for example, the geographic distribution did not follow traditional regional divisions. Thus, François Mitterrand made inroads in traditionally conservative areas. Electors were willing to "vote for a solidly implanted right deputy and for a left president; for a left deputy, known and appreciated for a long time, and for a conservative president."[100] Taken together, cross-cutting cultural and economic pressures, along with a divided but not bipolar party system, in the face of a changing French electorate, laid the groundwork for "cohabition" and the institutionalization of divided governance.

Institutions, Cohabition, and Divided Governance

The advent of "cohabitation" in 1986 took place in this context of voter discontent and electoral flux. The term itself describes a split partisan executive, that is, the coexistence of a president from one party with a prime minister (plus parliamentary majority) from another party or partisan bloc. Before the national legislative elections of 1986, the Socialists had instituted a system of proportional representation, partly in an attempt to salvage a major presence in the National Assembly. Despite this change, the Right won a clear majority of votes (54.7 percent) in the 1986 elections. Counting the seats won by the RPR–UDF alliance, the FN, and other conservative parties, the Right regained control of the legislature. Mitterrand, however, disregarded calls to resign. Instead, he appointed Jacques Chirac, the Gaullist leader of the opposition, as his prime minister.[101]

The advent of cohabitation in 1986 clearly was an instance of divided government. On the other hand, as noted in this chapter's introduction, divided government should not be conflated with divided *governance*. The era of divided governance was not an outgrowth of the institutional phenomena of cohabitation; the shift occurred earlier in terms of a changing political context and cross-cutting pressures in the electorate. Nor is divided governance dependent on the electoral occurrence of cohabition. Divided governance was still an accurate description of French politics, I argue, when the Socialists regained control of the government from 1988 to 1993, as it remained in 1995, when the Right regained the presidency and maintained control of the National Assembly.

While the voting patterns that produce cohabition parallel trends in the United States, where the electorate has often voted for a Democratic Congress and a Republican president, the trend has appeared contradictory to French observers. A French study of elections under the Fifth Republic suggested that the voting patterns of the 1980s marked "a fundamental and totally new separation in the Fifth Republic between the perception of a president, of whom much is asked, and those of the . . . political parties, whose image evokes too little."[102] Once more, another formulation is possible. Voting trends point to an evolving division between the president, whose office holds great cultural and national symbolism, and the prime minister, whose office is based on the majority in the National Assembly.

The Right's evident success in 1986, President Mitterrand's very successful reelection in 1988, the Right's return to parliamentary control in 1993, and, still subsequently, the public-opinion support for a 1995 presidential bid by (Socialist) Jacques Delors, former European Commission president, all bear witness to the increasingly differentiated strategies of the electorate in presidential and (national) legislative elections. These voter strategies have extended to rising public support for cohabitation. In 1987, a SOFRES survey found that a clear majority of respondents (53 percent) thought cohabition should be a "parenthesis" in Fifth Republic institutional operations; only 33 percent thought cohabition should signal a more "durable change." By 1993, 40 percent of respondents believed that cohabitation should have more durable effects on the functioning of governing institutions, and only 46 percent believed it should be a "parenthesis."[103]

As shown in studies by Grunberg and Schweisguth, the voting patterns producing cohabition can be related to cross-cutting social pressures in the French electorate, supporting cultural liberalism or social traditionalism and economic liberalization or social protectionism.[104] It is noteworthy that centrist and environmentalist voters appear most likely to view cohabitation as a long-term phenomenon. Despite his work on cross-cutting voter attitudes, SOFRES analyst Gérard Grunberg—like many other French commentators—still appeared somewhat bemused by voters' increasing support of cohabition in 1994. He was led to wonder if the "cohabitionist fervour" was not explained "by the satisfaction (by voters) of seeing such an evolution?"[105]

Beyond its reconfiguration of the electoral order, the institutional advent of cohabition has shaped and deepened the era of divided governance in significant ways. Thus cohabitation further developed the practical and institutional divisions associated with divided government. In this, cohabitation refined the divisions between president and prime minister. More exactly, it contributed to a decrease in presidential dominance and undercut the possibility for majoritarian governance. In the Fifth Republic, the functional divisions of power between president and prime minister had always been ill-defined. It is not surprising, then, that cohabition accentuated the ambiguities in the collaboration and opened up possible competing interpretations of the constitution.[106]

During the period of cohabition, Mitterrand and Chirac developed an explicit style of divided government. It was not divided government in the American sense, because Mitterrand and Chirac more or less carved out distinctive areas of jurisdiction. In several important policy arenas, Chirac and Mitterrand did clash, and the Chirac government produced no more than a stalemate. But in general, Chirac and his government operated more in the style of a European prime minister than of a Republican Congress facing a Democratic president. Mitterrand acted as an arbitrator rather than a policymaker in the domestic policy process and confined his initiatives to the international arena. His development of a detached presidential style, begun already after 1983, continued even when the Socialists regained control of the government in 1988.

Public-opinion polls during his first period of cohabition showed that Mitterrand benefited from the capacity to distance himself from day-to-day governmental policymaking. Chirac, in contrast, suffered, due to his reduced maneuvering capabilities. This role of president as "arbitrator" was anticipated in the 1958 Constitution, even though De Gaulle personally concentrated more on presidential dominance. While Mitterrand stressed presidentialism in his first years in office, he strengthened the role of arbitrator during the period of cohabition. Chirac, for his part, stressed a more prime-ministerial and parliamentarian reading of the Constitution than had prevailed during the period of presidential dominance. But as Jean Massot has argued, this parliamentarian reading was "much more limited" than announced;[107] Mitterrand was never reduced to figurehead status.

In return, according to public-opinion surveys, the French public has refined its views of the offices of president and prime minister. A comparison of surveys taken during the first and second periods of cohabition shows that respondents increasingly delineated the constitutional duties of the two offices. In the 1993 SOFRES survey, respondents more clearly placed control over "economic policy" and daily administrative responsibilities in the hands of the prime minister. "National defense decisions" and the task of representing France abroad, on the other hand, were perceived as being more in the president's domain. Foreign policy remained the most contested policy arena.[108]

Within the context of the 1993 legislative elections, heated debates over the contours of the new cohabition recurred. The overwhelming conservative majority in the National Assembly led some rightist politicians, including Chirac, to assert that the new Right government would present a stronger, "more firm" face to Mitterrand's attempts at governance. Some argued for an increase in parliamentary power as well. Others, including Valéry Giscard d'Estaing and Charles Pasqua, were more reticent to revoke the Gaullist state system.[109] Mitterrand himself reiterated his plan to follow through on his constitutional prerogatives: he would not relinquish his dominant role in the areas of defense and international politics, including European integration. At the same time, perhaps with an eye to the future, he advocated a reduction in the president's prerogatives.

Despite this campaign rhetoric, the new cohabitation of 1993 between President Mitterrand and Prime Minister Edouard Balladur was markedly less conflictual than the earlier one. Balladur, a centrist and strong Europeanist, appealed to several different kind of constituencies; his popularity remained high during most of his tenure.[110] The cohabitation of 1993 demonstrated that salient cleavages were no longer simply a matter of partisan lines. Questions of immigration and European integration continued to be politically divisive. However, the divisions were often cross-cutting, and not only between the majoritarian bloc and minority opposition. Partisan lines were blurred in the debates over European integration, national identity and national community, and economic liberalization and social protectionism.

Political elites clearly have played a critical role in institutionalizing divided governance. The second cohabitation was indicative of the adaptability of French political institutions and their elites. The weakness (and parliamentary absence) of the National Front on the national legislative scene also contributed to the relative ease of cohabition in 1993. Yet the refinement of constitutional divisions and the continuing interrelations between President Mitterrand and Prime Minister Balladur were as important. Today, the phenomenon of cohabition is arguably a coherent outcome in contemporary French politics.

Yet its significance is still not self-evident. When Jacques Delors announced his decision not to run as the Socialist presidential candidate in 1995, among the reasons he gave was cohabitation; he did not want "to be obligated to cohabitate with a government, not sharing (his) orientation."[111] Beyond the discomfort of explicitly political elites, French commentators too have been quick to call cohabition an "aberration" or a "parenthesis."[112] Poll data and electoral analyses underscore the ambiguities in interpreting public attitudes toward cohabitation. Before the 1993 legislative elections, polls seemingly indicated that voters did not like cohabition. After the elections, there appeared to be an upsurge in support, such as documented in the SOFRES poll cited above.[113]

Electoral outcomes that produce the conditions for cohabition have been interpreted to show that voters do like cohabition, while those that reproduce quasi-majoritarian outcomes have been proof of cohabitation as aberration.[114] The elections since 1986 demonstrate that divided governance is not simply about cohabitation. In the 1988 elections, voters were responding to the experience of cohabition.[115] When Mitterrand was reelected president at that time, he first tried to assemble a multipartisan government. When that failed, he once again dissolved the National Assembly. Mitterrand had won reelection against Chirac handily, 54 to 46 percent. But the Socialists achieved only a "working minority" in the National Assembly as the result of the legislative elections.

From the perspective of a bipolarized, majoritarian political system, the presidential and legislative elections of 1988 appeared contradictory.[116] Reflecting on the 1988 presidential and legislative elections, François Fûret exclaimed that voters "vote(d) successively according to two different logics, as if to correct one by the other."[117] The contradictions disappear when an understanding based on majoritarian governance is replaced by one based on divided governance. In contrast to 1981, when Mitterrand asked the voters for a Socialist parliamentary majority, for "the capacity to govern," in the aftermath of the 1988 election Mitterrand asked for a much more modest showing. Chirac, on the other hand, lost the 1988 election in part because "he tried to fight it as a left-right duel while Mitterrand—more in tune with the times—was able to transcend the traditional dichotomy."[118]

Mitterrand sought to operate in what can be called a post-majoritarian world by making an "opening" toward the center. Since his prime minister, Michel Rocard, was a strong advocate of this new opening, the newly reelected Socialist government invited centrists and other politicians to join their government. Though not successful, the orientation of an "opening," or what Jean-Luc Parodi has called a "half-opening," continued under the new Socialist government.[119] Despite the apparent emergence of a dominant majoritarian bloc in the victory of the conservative parties, the 1993 elections affirmed the new order of divided governance. That is, the elections reflected the willingness of voters to follow different logics in presidential and legislative elections. Only 17 percent of the respondents in a poll taken during the 1993 March elections said that a rejection of Mitterrand was their reason for voting against the Socialists.[120]

Early polls on voter intentions for the presidential election of 1995 April, taken during the 1993 electoral period, still showed respondents split more or less evenly between the Right candidate and the Left candidate.[121] Yet the 1993 elections demonstrated the decreasing importance of this Left-Right cleavage as a determinant in voter's actual judgments of political parties. Thus the periods of cohabitation and the periods of "post-majoritarian" governance have complemented and not contradicted the electoral context and social pressures. Both Mitterrand's second tenure and, later, the second period of cohabitation continued a "depresidentialized" mode of governance. Both periods reflected the changed priorities of the electorate in the new order of divided governance.

Cohabitation in an extreme sense can be considered to be simply a random electoral occurrence. From the perspective of divided governance, however, cohabitation is not an aberrant episode in French politics. It is, in fact, a fundamental though not necessarily constant characteristic of the current domestic order. While the legislative elections of 1988 ended a period of *divided government,* as reinforced by the presidential elections of 1995, the features of *divided governance* remain. The support shown for Jacques Delors before this decision not to run, and more recently, the contest between centrist Edouard Balladur and rightist Jacques Chirac, both members of the RPR, confirm the dualistic ideological cleavages that now cross-cut traditional partisan lines. Even without cohabitation, split majoritarian or non-majoritarian governments—what might be labeled post-majoritarian governments—have become characteristic outcomes in the era of divided governance.

Conclusion

In this chapter, I have argued that three political orders emerged successively in postwar France. In brief, the period of fragmented governance was defined by its multiple and rigid social cleavages, its highly polarized ideological politics, and its antagonistic governing modes. By contrast, the period of majoritarian governance expressed the character of transformed and more fluid social cleavages, of the elaboration of a national culture, and of the institutionalization of a dominant governing mode. The new order of divided governance, finally, appears to be characterized neither by fragmentation nor by a set of dominant arrangements.

Instead, the era of divided governance is defined by a series of growing dualisms in modes of governing, in social cleavages, and in political representation. These divisions are not marked by bipolar politics but by cross-cutting politicking and alliances. In place of the majoritarian mode of governance and of bipolar electoral outcomes, the French political order is characterized by differentiated voter logics in presidential and legislative elections, and in European, national, and local elections; by the advent of divided government and the institutionalization of tempered presidentialism; and by the strong emergence of broad, cross-cutting, social pressures.

According to the analysis presented here, these shifts were rooted in changes in governmental institutions, political intermediaries, and social cleavages, along with ideological concerns and even the international environment. Important to consider is that each era has not simply been the product of political elites as they adapted to these changes. Each era also reflects the changing responses of the electorate. What do these shifts in the French domestic order signify? The foundational shifts sketched in this chapter point to the changing pressures, circumstances, and resources shaping a domestic order. Within each order, electoral outcomes provided part of the narrative, but did not necessarily coincide with the critical moments. Instead, the postwar period experienced a series of domestic and international changes—structural and substantive changes—which informed the interplay of political elites and set the parameters for possible reform. Finally, the disappearance of traditional ideological and social cleavages and the emergence of new dualistic divisions have proven to be as consequential for the postwar political orders.

Notes

I would like to thank Byron Shafer for his insightful comments and suggestions, the other contributors to this volume for their commentary, and Martin Schain and Kay Lawson for their constructive suggestions and close reading of earlier drafts of the chapter. Research assistance was provided by Claire Van Zevern and financial assistance by the University of San Francisco Faculty Development Fund.

1. On the transformation wrought by the Fifth Republic, see Jean Charlot, *The Gaullist Phenomenon* (London: George, Allen, Unwin, 1971); Colette Ysmal, *Les Partis Politiques sous la Ve République* (Paris: Grasset, 1987); Alain Lancelot, *Les Élections sous la Ve République* (Paris: PUF, coll. Que sais-je, 1988).

2. Of course, the apparent stability of the Fifth Republic has not precluded many throughout the years from predicting the arrival of a Sixth Republic or return to the Fourth Republic. Nevertheless, except for the Third Republic (1875–1940), none of the other constitutional frameworks lasted longer than eighteen years, and the Third Republic constitution is regarded as a much more minimalist framework than the current one. Henry Ehrmann and Martin Schain, *Politics in France,* 5th ed. (New York: Harper-Collins, 1992), 20. For a perspective on the end of French exceptionalism, see François Fûret, Jacques Julliard, and Pierre Rosanvallon, *La République de Centre: La Fin de l'Exception Française* (Paris: Calmann-Lévy, 1988).

3. For recent findings on changing attitudes of French voters, see Daniel Boy and Nonna Mayer, eds., *The French Voter Decides* (Ann Arbor: University of Michigan, 1993).

4. See Byron E. Shafer, "The Structure of Electoral Politics at the Accession of George Bush," in Byron E. Shafer, ed., *The End of Realignment? Interpreting American Electoral Eras* (Madison: University of Wisconsin, 1991), and his introduction to this volume for a fuller discussion of "political orders" and "political eras."

5. It has been commonplace for scholars to place the Vichy Regime in parentheses when analyzing the evolution of French political orders. See, for example, André Hauriou, Jean Gicquel, and Patrice Gelard, *Droit Constitutionnel et Institutions Politiques* (Paris: Montchrestien, 1975), who totally omit the Vichy regime in their cyclical analysis of French political orders. That is not the intention here. Rather, it is to acknowledge—as Robert Paxton, *Vichy France: Old Guard and New Order, 1940–1944* (New York: Columbia University, 1972), has well documented—the continuities that existed from the prewar to the postwar era despite French protestations that the Vichy regime was an aberration and an imposition in French politics, and that after the war, there was a complete rejection of the Vichy regime.

6. For the view that contemporary party politics is a variation of the dominant majoritarian order, see Ysmal, *Les Partis Politiques;* Jean-Luc Parodi, "De la Cohabitation à l'Entrouverture: Profil de l'Année Politique" *Pouvoirs* 48 (1988): 165–76; Boy and Mayer, "The Changing French Voter," in Boy and Mayer,

French Voter Decides, 167–72; J. R. Frears, *Parties and Voters in France* (London: St. Martin's, 1991); Alistair Cole, "The Presidential Party and the Fifth Republic," *West European Politics* 16 (April, 1993): 49–66. For the view that the French party system has shifted away from the bipolarized pattern, see Howard Machin, "The President, the Parties, and the Parliament," in Jack Hayward, ed., *De Gaulle to Mitterrand* (New York: New York University, 1993), 120–49.

7. John Keeler and Martin Schain label cohabitation a "presidential-premier" model. See their "evolutionary" analysis of French governmental phases in the Fifth Republic, in their article, "Models of Democracy in Fifth Republic France: Institutions, Actors, and Regime Evolution," in Kurt von Bettenheim, ed., *Presidential Institutions and Democratic Politics: Comparative and Regional Perspectives* (Pittsburgh: University of Pittsburgh, 1995).

8. Frédéric Bon and Jean-Paul Cheylan, *La France Qui Vote* (Paris: Hachette, 1988), 25.

9. Henry Ehrmann, *Politics in France* (New York: Harper-Collins, 1958), 198.

10. See Ehrmann and Schain, *Politics in France,* 11–15; and Jack Hayward, "From Republican Sovereign to Partisan Statesman," in Hayward, *De Gaulle to Mitterrand,* 1–35.

11. For a succinct discussion of the events of 1945–46, see Hayward, "Republican Sovereign to Partisan Statesman," 13–16. This representative tradition is not fully parallel to representative traditions in other countries, in part because of the enduring coexistence of the highly competing traditions of executive and parliamentary power.

12. Cited in John R. Frears, *Political Parties and Elections in the French Fifth Republic* (New York: St. Martin's, 1977), 272.

13. Vincent Wright, "The Administrative Machine: Old Problems and New Dilemmas," in Peter Hall, Jack Hayward, and Howard Machin, eds., *Developments in French Politics* (New York: St. Martin's, 1990), 116 and passim. For a sampling of the large literature on the French state and bureaucracy, see Ezra Suleiman, *Politics, Power, and Bureaucracy in France: The Administrative Elite* (Princeton: Princeton University, 1974); Pierre Birnbaum, *The Heights of Power* (Chicago: University of Chicago, 1982); and Michel Crozier, *État Modeste, État Moderne* (Paris: Fayard, 1987). Also useful is the discussion of the policy process in Ehrmann and Schain, *Politics in France.*

14. See Paxton, *Vichy France.* On the French "plans," see also Peter Hall, *Governing the Economy* (New York: Oxford University, 1986).

15. On the era of "bureaucratic dominance" in postwar Japan, see Stephen Anderson's chapter in this volume.

16. Frears, *Parties and Voters in France,* 6.

17. Machin, "The President, the Parties, and the Parliament," 120.

18. Cited in Ehrmann and Schain, *Politics in France,* 132. Also see François Borella, *Les Partis Politiques dans La France d'Aujourd'hui* (Paris: du Seuil, 1973), 8.

19. Henri Mendras and Alistair Cole, *Social Change in Modern France: To-*

wards a Cultural Anthropology of the Fifth Republic (Cambridge: Cambridge University, 1991), 113.

20. Bon and Cheylan, *La France Qui Vote,* 15. For a recent analysis of the geographical distribution of votes, see François Goguel, "Géographie électorale de l'élection présidentielle," in Le Figaro, *L'Élection Présidentielle 1988.*

21. Mendras and Cole, *Social Change in Modern France,* 15–17; "Il faut sauver les derniers paysans," *Le Point,* September 28, 1991, 14.

22. These figures are from Frears, *Political Parties and Elections,* 272; also see Mendras and Cole, *Social Change in Modern France,* 25–30, 82–83.

23. Lancelot, *Les Élections,* 14.

24. The rate of participation among the electorate was very high, nearly 85 percent in metropolitan France. See Lancelot, *Les Élections,* 17; Pierre Avril, *La Ve République: Histoire Politique et Constitutionnelle* (Paris: PUF, 1987), 13–27.

25. Olivier Duhamel describes the role of the Left in the Fifth Republic in these terms. See his book, *La Gauche et la Ve République* (Paris: Presses Universitaires, 1980).

26. Colette Ysmal, *Le Comportement Électoral Des Français* (Paris: La Découverte, 1990), 13.

27. Frears, *Political Parties and Elections,* 15.

28. Ysmal, *Les Partis Politiques,* 19.

29. Avril, *La Ve République,* 31.

30. The Constitution itself set up a strong executive, but with significantly more power and functions invested in the prime minister than in the president. See Keeler and Schain "Models of Democracy"; Jean Massot, "La Pratique Présidentielle sous la Ve République," *Regards sur l'Actualité* (1988): 27–37; Machin, "The President, the Parties, and the Parliament," 120–49; and William Andrews, *Presidential Government in Gaullist France* (Albany: SUNY, 1982).

31. For more extended discussion about the Constitution and the powers of the president and prime minister, see Hayward, *De Gaulle to Mitterrand;* Keeler and Schain, "Models of Democracy"; Avril, *La Ve République;* Jean Massot, *L'Arbitre et le Capitaine: La Responsabilité Présidentielle* (Paris: Flammarion, 1988).

32. The Right obtained 56.2 percent in the 1962 November legislative elections; 56.4 percent in the 1967 May legislative elections; and 58 percent in the 1969 legislative elections. Ysmal *Le Comportement Électoral,* 13.

33. For the results of the 1958 and 1962 elections, see Lancelot, *Les Élections,* 18–23, 31–37.

34. The expression is taken from Ysmal, *Les Partis Politiques.*

35. Borella, *Les Partis Politiques,* 9.

36. See Charlot, *The Gaullist Phenomenon.*

37. On the electoral results, also see Lancelot, *Les Élections,* 44–45.

38. These are Colette Ysmal's expressions. See Ysmal, *Les Partis Politiques,* 56, 95.

39. The term is Howard Machin's. He has documented how parties in the Fifth Republic increasingly aimed to form "presidential majorities" that would consist

of a "strong coalition of parties, led by the president's own party." See his article "The President, the Parties, and the Parliament," 120–21.

40. The erosion of a center situating itself between Left and Right can be seen in the declining votes for such centrist parties: 31 percent in 1958, 20 percent in 1962, 18 percent in 1967 and 1973. From 1974, the centrist alliances were reclassified as part of the conservative majority. See Ysmal, *Le Comportement Électoral*, 81.

41. Suleiman, *Politics, Power, and Bureaucracy*, 164.

42. On religion as a determinative factor in French politics, see Jacques Capdevielle et al., "Tableau des Électorats en Mars 1978" in Jacques Capdeville, ed., *France de Gauche, Vote à Droite* (Paris: FNSP, 1981), 43–45; Bon and Cheylan, *La France Qui Vote;* Boy and Mayer, *French Voter Decides.*

43. See Gérard Grunberg and Etienne Schweisguth, "Profession et Vote: La Pousseé de la Gauche" in Capdeville, *France de Gauche.*

44. See Henri Mendras, *La Seconde Révolution Française* (Paris: Gallimard, 1988), and Mendras and Cole, *Social Change in Modern France;* see also Jérôme Jaffré, "Trente Années de Changement Électoral," *Pouvoirs 49* (1989): 15–25. There are many ways to categorize social classes in France; all studies, however, underscore the decline in the agricultural populations and rise of the "cadres"-style class (e.g., white-collar workers, middle management, professionals); see, for example, Grunberg and Schweisguth, "Profession et Vote." On the decline of religious practice, see G. Michelat and M. Simon, *Classe, Religion, et Comportement Politique* (Paris: FNSP, 1977).

45. Mendras and Cole, *Social Change in Modern France*, 120.

46. See Ysmal, *Le Comportement Électoral*, 52.

47. The continuation of De Gaulle's interpretation of the constitution was not clear at the time. Commenting on the contest between Pompidou and his rival, also from the Right, Maurice Duverger wrote, "What are really at stake in the battle between M. Pompidou and M. Poher are the institutions [of the 5th Republic]. Both would carry out almost the same policy but would exercise the presidential function in different ways, almost leading to two opposed regimes." Cited in Hayward, "Republican Sovereign to Partisan Statesman," 36. For analyses on the "presidentialization" of the French political system, see Massot "La Pratique Présidentielle" and Hayward, *De Gaulle to Mitterrand.*

48. See, for example, Ysmal, *Les Partis Politiques;* Alistair Cole and Peter Campbell, *French Electoral Systems and Elections since 1989* (Aldershot: Gower, 1989).

49. Lancelot, *Les Elections*, 48–50.

50. See Grunberg and Schweisguth, "Profession et Vote," 165–67. Studies have shown that those who profess no religion overwhelmingly favor Left parties; the trend toward secularization continues, with religious practice declining from 21 percent in 1974 to 13 percent in 1988 (Jaffré, "Trente Années").

51. Jaffré, "Trente Années," 18.

52. On the evolution of the Socialist Party, see John Gaffney, *The French Left and the Fifth Republic: The Discourses of Communism and Socialism in Contempo-*

rary France (Basingstoke: Macmillan, 1989); Ysmal, *Les Partis Politiques* and *Le Comportement Électoral;* more generally on the left, see Duhamel, *La Gauche et la Ve République;* for a breakdown and analysis of the electoral results, see Lancelot, *Les Élections,* 64–67.

53. The geographic distribution of the second-round votes matched the traditional cleavage between the Left and Right in the country. Lancelot, *Les Élections,* 74.

54. Accordingly, much was written about "When the Left Can Win" (Jean Charlot, *Quand la Gauche Peut Gagner* [Paris: Morean, 1973]) and the electoral phenomena of "France of the left, vote to the Right," as the Left failed to live up to its electoral potential in the 1970s (Capdevielle et al., "Tableau des Électorats").

55. On the 1974 election, see Frears, *Political Parties and Elections,* 26–27; Ysmal, *Les Partis Politiques;* Alistair Cole, *French Political Parties in Transition* (Aldershot: Dartmouth, 1990).

56. Massot (1988) has analyzed the "presidentialization" of the executive in "La Pratique Présidentielle," and Machin has analyzed the "presidentialization" of the party system in "The President, the Parties, and the Parliament."

57. When the trend toward a bipolar system began in the 1960s, many contemporary commentators did not think it was a durable trend.

58. The revised electoral system itself did not produce the formation of more or less unified Left and Right blocs. See, for example, Philip Cerny, "The New Rules of the Game in France," in *French Politics and Public Policy,* ed. Philip Cerny and Martin Schain (New York: St. Martin's, 1980).

59. Frank L. Wilson, *French Political Parties under the Fifth Republic* (New York: Praeger, 1982).

60. Jean Charlot was using the typology of party systems developed by Maurice Duverger. Jean Charlot, "Les Mutations du Système de Partis Français," *Pouvoirs* 48 (1989): 27–35.

61. Ysmal, *Les Partis Politiques;* Wilson, *French Political Parties;* Frears, *Political Parties and Elections;* Borella, *Les Partis Politiques.*

62. Keeler and Schain, "Models of Democracy." They characterize d'Estaing's tenure as a "tempered presidential model."

63. See Hayward, "Republican Sovereign to Partisan Statesman," 63.

64. George Ross, "Introduction," in George Ross, Stanley Hoffmann, and Sylvia Malzacher, eds., *The Mitterrand Experiment* (New York: Oxford University, 1987), 11.

65. See Charlot, "Les Mutations du Système," 32; Jean Charlot, *Le Gaullisme d'Opposition, 1946–1958: Histoire, Politique du Gaullisme* (Paris: Fayard, 1983). See also Stanley Hoffmann, "Mitterrand's Foreign Policy, or Gaullism by Any Other Name," in Ross, Hoffmann, and Malzacher, *The Mitterrand Experiment.*

66. For an analysis of the Socialist economic programs and U-turn, see Howard Machin and Vincent Wright, eds., *Economic Policy and Policy-Making under the Mitterrand Presidency 1981–1984* (London: Francis Pinter, 1985); for an over-

view of the various reforms enacted by the Socialist government, see Ross, Hoffmann, and Malzacher, *The Mitterrand Experiment.*

67. The PCF decline was rooted in earlier causes; for example, see George Ross, "Party Decline and Changing Party Systems," *Comparative Politics* 25, no. 1 (1992): 43–56.

68. Part of the analysis in this section is drawn from Machin, "The President, the Parties, and Parliament."

69. See Vivien A. Schmidt, *Democratizing France: The Political and Administrative History of Decentralization* (Cambridge: Cambridge University, 1991).

70. Quoted in Jack Hayward, "Republican Sovereign to Partisan Statesman," 34. For a contrasting view, see Keeler and Schain, "Models of Democracy," who argue that Mitterrand's first tenure as president from 1981 to 1986 was characterized by a "hyperpresidential" model of governance. For an overview of the evolution of presidential and prime ministerial powers in the Fifth Republic, see Keeler and Schain's article, and the articles in Hayward, *De Gaulle to Mitterrand.*

71. The unexpected withdrawal of Jacques Delors, former president of the European Commission, as a presidential candidate in December 1994 left the Socialists without a self-evident contender.

72. George Ross, "Party Decline and Changing Party Systems," in Ross, Hoffmann, and Malzacher, *The Mitterrand Experiment,* 43. This section does not treat the causes of the Communist decline, which were rooted in "environmental" factors, such as the transformation of the French social base, and "internal" factors, such as the organizational strategies of the party. For an analysis of these factors, see George Ross's article. See also Martin Schain, "The Electoral Decline of the French Communist Party," Paper prepared for the International Conference of Europeanists, March 23–25, 1990, Washington, D.C.

73. George Ross, "Party Decline and Changing Party Systems"; Schain, "Electoral Decline."

74 For the results of the 1993 election, see *Le Monde,* March 30, 1993. As Schain ("Electoral Decline") argues, declining electoral support is only one aspect of the decline of the PCF; organizational and strategic factors have been part of the more general decline of the PCF; on the decline of the Communists and the Left, also see Ysmal, *Le Comportement Électoral.*

75. Ross, "Party Decline," 44.

76. Fûret, Julliard, and Rosanvallon (*La République de Centre*) identify both the decline of the Communists and the dilution of the Socialist agenda as contributing to the burial of traditional socialism in France; for this reason, he interprets the 1988 elections, when Mitterrand won reelection on a national consensus–style platform, as part of the "end of French exceptionalism."

77. Numerous studies have now been written on the National Front. For a sampling, see Guy Birenbaum, *Le Front National en Politique* (Paris: Balland, 1992); Nonna Mayer and Pascal Perrineau, "Why Do They Vote for Le Pen?" *European Journal of Political Research* 22 (1992): 123–41; Nonna Mayer and Pascal Perrineau, eds., *Le Front National à Découvert* (Paris: Foundation Nationale de la Science Politique, 1989); Subrata Mitra, "The National Front in

France—a Single-Issue Movement?" in Klaus von Beyme, ed., *Right-Wing Extremism in Western Europe* (London: Frank Cass, 1988), 47–64; Monica Charlot, "L'Émergence du Front National," *Revue Française de Science Politique* 36, no. 1 (1986): 30–45; and Shields (1990). As James Shields points out, in the 1970s many commentators predicted the disappearance of viable extreme rightism in France, and even in the later 1980s, commentators would understate the durability of the National Front. James G. Shields, "A New Chapter in the History of the French Extreme Right: The National Front," in Cole, *French Political Parties in Transition*.

78. Contrast these results with the 1988 legislation elections, when the party again polled 9.65 percent of the vote, but obtained only one representative because the majoritarian two-ballot system was back in place. The 1986 electoral outcome certainly informed the Socialists' decision in 1993 *not* to reintroduce proportional representation in order to salvage themselves again.

79. On the 1993 election results, see *Le Monde,* March 23 and 30, 1993.

80. Mayer and Perrineau, *Le Front National*; Nonna Mayer and Pascal Perrineau, *Les Comportements Politiques* (Paris: Armand Colin, 1992); Annick Percheron, "Les Mutations Politiques de la France," in CEVIPOF, *L'Électeur Français En Question* (Paris: Foundation Nationale des Sciences Politiques, 1990).

81. Mayer and Perrineau, *Les Comportements Politiques*.

82. In contrast, Le Pen polled 0.4 percent of the vote in the 1974 presidential election. On the Le Pen vote in the 1988 presidential election, see Nonna Mayer, "Explaining Electoral Right-Wing Extremism: The Case of the Le Pen Vote in the 1988 French Presidential Election," Paper delivered at the American Political Science Association meeting, September 2–5, 1993, Washington, D.C.

83. Martin Schain, "The National Front and the Construction of Political Legitimacy," *West European Politics* 10 (April, 1987): 229–52.

84. See Jean Charlot's argument on how the FN "depolarized" the French system ("Les Mutations du Système," 33); see also Machin, "The President, The Parties, and The Parliament," on the FN and the rise of "non-presidential" parties.

85. Cited in Paul Hainsworth, "The Greens in the French Party System," in Cole, *French Political Parties in Transition,* 91.

86. Percheron, "Les Mutations Politiques," 11.

87. The Green party's candidate received 3.8 percent of the vote in the presidential election of 1988. In the 1989 European elections, the Green parties received 10.59 percent of the vote. But in the 1993 March legislative election, the environmentalist parties, now splintered into three groups, obtained 10.7 percent of the vote in the first round and only 0.18 percent in the second.

88. Jean Marie Colombani, "M. Michel Rocard Veut Accélérer la Rénovation de la Gauche," *Le Monde,* February 23, 1993.

89. Daniel Boy and Nonna Mayer, "L'Électeur, Est-Il Stratège?" in CEVIPOF, *L'Électeur Français.*

90. Machin, "The President, The Parties, and the Parliament," 133.

91. Michel Rocard cited in Colombani, "M. Michel Rocard." Since the elections, calls to create a new party have fizzled.

92. See Guy Michelat, "À la Recherche de la Gauche et de la Droite," in CEVIPOF, *L'Électeur Français en Question* (Paris: Foundation Nationale des Sciences Politiques, 1990), 101–3;

93. Ibid., 95–99. Also see SOFRES, *Opinion Publique* 7 (1990) and SOFRES, *Opinion Publique* 8 (1991). But note that the activists in the two parties, unlike their constituents, do place themselves on the Left-Right continuum.

94. It should be noted that already in the 1970s, the Council of State issued important opinions affecting governmental immigration policies. See Patrick Weil, *La France et ses Étrangers* (Paris: Calmann-Lévy, 1990) on the evolution of governmental policy.

95. Daniel Boy and Nonna Mayer, "The Changing French Voter," in Boy and Mayer, *French Voter Decides,* 169–70.

96. See Gérard Grunberg and Etienne Schweisguth, "Social Libertarianism and Economic Liberalism," ibid., 45–64.

97. *Eurobarometer* 38, no. 2 (1992): 57.

98. Ibid., p. 57; See also Elisabeth Guigou, "Les Françaises et l'Europe, Regard d'Une Pro-Maastricht," in SOFRES, *L'État de L'Opinion 1993* (Paris: Seuil, 1993), 87–91.

99. Nonna Mayer, "Attitudes towards the Region, Europe, and Politics in 1992 France." Paper prepared for American Political Science Association, Washington, D.C., 1993, 7.

100. Colette Ysmal, *La Comportement Électoral,* 76; see also A. Laurent, C.-M. Wallon, and Y. Leduc, "La Distribution des Électorats," in Le Figaro, *L'Election Présidentielle 1988.*

101. Some analysts argue that Mitterrand's stance actually encouraged discontented Socialist voters to register their protest and vote against the Socialists because they knew that Mitterrand would be there to act as a buttress against the right (Jean Gicquel, "De la Cohabitation," *Pouvoirs* 48 [1988]: 69–79).

102. Bon and Cheylan, *La France Qui Vote,* 488.

103. Gérard Grunberg, "La Deuxième Cohabitation," in Olivier Duhamel and Jérôme Jaffré, eds., *SOFRES. L'État de l'Opinion, 1994* (Paris: Seuil, 1994), 47–52.

104. Grunberg and Schweisguth, "Profession et Vote."

105. Grunberg, "La Deuxième Cohabitation," 52–53.

106. The Fifth Republic Constitution is vague on the division of tasks of the president and prime minister. The debates over cohabitation often have invoked the parts in the constitution which indicate that the prime minister would be responsible for the daily tasks of the government, and that the president would be predominant in foreign and military affairs. See Hayward, "Republican Sovereign to Partisan Statesman," 34, 43–44. For an overview of the relationship between the president and prime minister in the Fifth Republic, see the informative articles in Hayward, *De Gaulle to Mitterrand.*

107. Massot, "La Pratique Présidentielle," 27.

108. Grunberg, "La Deuxième Cohabitation," 46–48.

109. Thomas Ferenczi, "Quels Pouvoir pour le Chef de l'État?" *Le Monde,* March 9, 1993.

110. See Alain Duhamel, "Edouard Balladur, ou le Retour de l'Autorité," in Duhamel and Jaffré, *SOFRES 1994,* 14–16.

111. Jacques Delors, on the program "7 sur 7," TF1, cited in *Le Monde,* December 13, 1994, 1.

112. See Frears, *Parties and Voters in France,* and Parodi, "Cohabitation à l'Entrouverture."

113. See, for example, Philippe Habert, "Les Français contre Une Nouvelle Cohabitation," *Le Figaro,* June 17, 1992, 1.

114. Roger Eatwell, "Plus ça change? The French Presidential and National Assembly Elections, April–June, 1988," *Political Quarterly* 59 (Oct.–Dec., 1988): 462–70.

115. Alain Guyomarch and Howard Machin, "François Mitterand and the French Presidential and Parliamentary Elections of 1988: Mr. Norris Changes Trains?" *West European Politics* 12 (January, 1989): 199–210.

116. See Eatwell, "Plus ça Change"; cf. Guyomarch and Machin, "François Mitterand and the Elections of 1988"; Howard Machin, "The President, The Parties, and Parliament," 16.

117. Fûret, Julliard, and Rosanvallon, *La République du Centre,* 16.

118. Hayward (1990), 32.

119. Parodi, "Cohabitation à l'Entrouverture."

120. Ferenczi, "Quels Pouvoirs."

121. See Eric Dupin, "La Gauche peut-elle encore Gagner la Présidentielle?" *Libération,* April 16, 1993, 8.

6 *J. Jens Hesse*

Germany

For some members of what was to become the Group of Seven—not least Germany—the end of the Second World War meant the beginning of a new political era and order, by definition.[1] Externally induced and internally accepted, new political structures were created that were intended to foster democratic behavior, allow for responsive and accountable government, and facilitate policies based on the rule of law and what was later to be termed *soziale Marktwirtschaft* ("social market economy"). To describe this process in its international and domestic contexts borders on the impossible, thanks to the complex interaction of prevailing traditions, pressing needs, external influences, institutional prerequisites, economic imperatives, cultural characteristics, and various (often divergent) public policies. Within the framework of political eras and political orders, then, a number of key categories—that might also be of use for comparative purposes—must therefore be applied to organize both these complex proceedings and the vast available literature on them.

First among these, and central to explaining (West) German governmental stability over forty years of its existence, it is the notion of *institutional adaptability.* This term is meant to refer to the polity at large, embracing: its legal environment; its basic political or quasi-political institutions, ranging from governmental authorities and intermediary organizations to formally autonomous but highly political institutions such as the Federal Central Bank (*Bundesbank*) and the Federal Constitutional Court (*Bundesverfassungsgericht*); and a number of public/private bodies, created to overcome special cleavages and disparities. This further emphasis on institutional adaptability seems especially warranted in the German case, not just because the institutional arrangements for postwar German politics did have such a clear and comprehensive beginning, but because adaptability was a constant focus of postwar German political actors as well.

Actors do, of course, matter within the confines of this institutional adaptability, and public policies even more so, but actors are perceived here predominantly within a focus on adaptation—influencing government, shaping it even, but never as decisive and long-standing in influence as some elements of, for example, the Basic Law (the *Grundgesetz*). What might appear at first glance as another variant of "the new institutionalism," however, is intended to go much further. A concentration on institutional adaptability should allow for a different but (hopefully) innovative longitudinal analysis of Germany's postwar history. This would put emphasis on the crucial stages of its development—the political eras—without excessively isolating or personalizing them. It ought to be possible in this way to shed light on the crucial interdependence of macro-and micropolitical developments, contributing at the same time to our knowledge about structural change and the impact of public policies.

This implies that governmental arrangements themselves will not be regarded as a constant, as an element of inertia in a dynamically changing environment. On the contrary, specific public policies react upon the political, economic, and social conditions out of which they themselves arise; they shape and modify governmental arrangements and adapt them to novel economic and social conditions. For this reason, political institutions are not perceived as fixed settings in the sense of a regulatory framework. Rather, they should be seen as part of the complex interrelationship between organizational structures, routines, and patterns of interaction, and, eventually, policy contents, a relationship that is itself influenced by societal developments.[2]

But such adaptation involves more than the ability of organizations and political actors to adjust to a changing environment. The ability to respond to external challenges almost surely involves *incentives toward compromise* and a certain degree of *partisan convergence*. So one ought to distinguish between the institutional elements of the adjustment process, that is, the formal impetus toward adaptation, and actual processes of political convergence, in effect the associated informal guarantee. Social cleavages, partisan organizations, and their institutional reflections, along with, especially, the growth of social coalitions and their shifts, have to be included here; they shape the substantive issues and governing arrangements which are characteristic of postwar German politics. So the *social bases* of political life will, of course, play a significant role, not in an isolated way but linked to the development of the institutional setting.

Two further analytic decisions should be mentioned in advance. When speaking about Germany, I will concentrate on the former Federal Republic. This does not imply a "winner-take-all" attitude, just the need to keep the evidence manageable, as reinforced by the fact that the West German political framework has indeed been transplanted into (or at least onto) East German society. Its workings thus form the basis of Germany's future political order—and have anyhow always been crucial to the German Democratic Republic, either as something to look up to or to contrast with, in a class-conscious attempt to create a socialist state. Nevertheless, the principal characteristics of the former East German regime will be mentioned briefly, no longer as a challenge but now as a historically bypassed approach, an experiment, to create a totally different polity and society on German territory.

A second decision concerns the interchange between the international and the domestic political order. Though it is obvious that neither the birth of the Federal or the German Democratic Republic, nor the demise of the latter, ought to be addressed without reference to international developments, prime emphasis here will be on domestic issues. This again is in the nature of a hypothesis: political stability and adaptability developed despite (or even because of) the significant turbulences posed by the international environment, not least the Cold War.[3]

In the analysis that follows, as with the chapter on Britain, I begin by briefly describing the institutional setting in which the German polity operates. In subsequent sections I then try to explain its development since 1945. Three periods are singled out as crucial "political eras":[4] (a) an *era of reconstruction and growth,* encompassing the immediate postwar years, the very different attempts to rebuild basic governmental institutions within the two Germanies, and the range of policies that allowed for a process of stabilization and normalization during the Cold War; (b) a subsequent *era of adaptation and consolidation,* starting with the election of 1969, that proved to be decisive in passing the ultimate test of a successful democratization process, an alternation in government; and (c) an upcoming *new era,* as yet unnamed, induced by the double challenge of German unification and European integration. This periodization follows the traditional way of distinguishing the succession of governments and political leaders only to a very limited extent, concentrating instead on a number of economic, social, and even cultural developments that seem to be crucial in the German case.[5]

Basic Characteristics of the German Institutional Setting

In legal, organization, and procedural terms, the years between 1949—or when the constitutions in both German states were adopted—and 1990 were characterized by an unusual degree of stability in the (West) German political system. Perhaps paradoxically, this stability largely resulted from a functional and territorial dispersion of power, which has characterized the postwar (West) German polity. The political-constitutional framework which developed after 1945 emphasized functional deconcentration and, perhaps even more importantly, territorial decentralization in the form of a federal system. This federal element in the constitutional makeup of the new Germany could be explained in part as a conscious reaction to the experience of highly centralized totalitarian government under the National Socialist regime. In part, it also reflected the more or less explicit preferences of the Allied Powers, for whom the reemergence of strong central government was unacceptable.

Most importantly, however, the establishment of a federal system through the Basic Law of 1949 also signaled a *return* to Germany's constitutional traditions. The key characteristics of the system as it developed on the basis of the 1949 constitution included the following:

1. The separation of legislative, political, and administrative powers between central, regional (*Länder*), and local levels;
2. The procedural integration of the three levels in decision-making, program development, and implementation ("cooperative federalism");
3. A high degree of functional deconcentration of state power at the central level, with not only a considerable degree of departmental autonomy, but also the establishment of functionally and politically autonomous bodies, such as the Federal Central Bank and Federal Constitutional Court. Such functional differentiation complements territorial decentralization;
4. An economic system in which free-market elements clearly dominated, but were combined with a strong emphasis on cooperation, collaboration, and consensual decision-making between employers, employees, and the state ("liberal corporatism");
5. A high degree of centralization and integration in the area of *social* organization, which contrasts with a functionally and territorially dispersed statehood. This applies both to the party system and to the sphere of interest groups, where centralization is particularly marked for employers' associations and trade unions;
6. The absence of large-scale regional disparities, social conflicts, and ethnic cleavages, implying a social homogeneity which facilitated insti-

tutional stability, though, as we shall see, more reliably in the first two eras than in the third;

7. Gradual institutional change and adaptation, supported by a low turn-over in governments at both the federal and state levels. Although coalition government was more or less the norm, this nevertheless produced stable administrations; and

8. An emphasis on legality, a well-established civil service, and bureaucratic processes, which tended to constrain the scope of action but rarely led to long-term blockages.[6]

While the political system of the Federal Republic could thus be characterized as a stable system of checks and balances, the institutional setting of the German Democratic Republic took a very different course.[7] Following the principle of "democratic centralism," state power was both functionally and territorially centralized. Whereas the formal framework for the exercise of state functions was differentiated, actual power was concentrated in a small number of central state and party organs. In legal terms, a sphere of local government did exist, but local authorities operated under the dual subordination of central state organs and the centralized party bureaucracy. Economic activity was comprehensively state-guided and controlled. Likewise, independent social organizations were virtually nonexistent, with the partial exception of the established churches.

The Adenauer Era: Reconstruction and Growth

The Immediate Postwar Years: Occupation, Continuity, and Change (1945–1949)

When the Basic Law and the Constitution of the German Democratic Republic were adopted in 1949, thus concluding the division of Germany, some essential steps to establish a democratic political system and to rebuild the foundations of statehood had already been taken.[8] Despite the fundamental character of the breakdown of the National Socialist state and the unconditional surrender of 1945, Germany did not experience a "Stunde null" (zero hour). Following specifically German traditions based on an established understanding of the role of the public sector, pressing needs were addressed immediately, including initial steps to provide necessary shelter and housing, to secure the physical survival of the population, and to establish minimal administrative services.

Uncompromised politicians also started to stabilize local government, to provide additional services, and to create interpersonal networks that turned into nascent roots for a domestic political order. Backed by the occupational powers, this soon led to the first constitutional acts, such as the licensing of political parties, the creation of a public broadcasting system, and the founding of a free press. The formal setup of administrative units followed, complemented by a gradual reestablishment of schools and universities. The Parliamentary Council (*Parlamentarischer Rat*) did not therefore start from scratch: *Länder* and local governments had been established in all occupied zones; an administration had developed initial routines; and parties were trying to extend their influence beyond the zones initially permitted to them.

On the one hand, all this followed an indigenous tradition of thinking about the state, about its theoretical nature and actual characteristics, in both philosophical and legal terms. On the other hand, in more directly operational terms, it also followed from an established historical division—a scattering—of political authority amongst states, principalities, and provinces. Both these factors have had an important influence on the development of German methods of government and on the manner in which the problems of government were conceptualized. Since institutional arrangements and procedures evolve slowly, it is worth noting that the emergent political order was rooted in previous experiences and traditions. The inheritance of ideas about constitutional principles and about the structure of governmental institutions thus derived from the experience of the nineteenth century, an experience that has proved to be enduring.[9]

Rebuilding the State (1949–1961)

It should not come as a surprise therefore that the Basic Law of 1949 was strongly influenced by an evolving concept of the *Rechtsstaat,* leaning in particular toward a specific form of constitutional government. In this, the Basic Law guaranteed the rights and powers of parliament, at the same time protecting the executive against divisions of opinion *within* parliament. The powers of the federal government were carefully defined. Parliamentary responsibility was concentrated on the federal chancellor, and there were elaborate provisions to ensure that the *Bundestag* could not withdraw its confidence from the chancellor without first agreeing on a successor. In turn, Parliament was predominantly viewed as a law-making machine.

The operationalization of these governmental arrangements was inevitably a major focus of the first postwar era. But so was the creation of informal political arrangements to support them. And so was a matrix of public policies aimed, especially, at rejuvenating the larger society around them, and particularly its economy. Together, these three major foci were responsible for the key structural elements of the first postwar order. Together, they were so collectively demanding as to militate against—really to squeeze out—any other major matters during the extended (Adenauer) era of reconstruction and growth.

In a critical initiative in this Adenauer era, the new Parliament, operating under the *Rechtsstaat* concept, moved to provide a framework for the protection of human rights and dignity, setting out a long catalogue of what might be described as the ethical content of statehood. In order to make these rights enforceable, it then created provisions for judicial review of the constitutionality of a wide range of public acts and decisions, and the scope for appeal to the courts against administrative actions was extended by a clause stating that in no circumstances could the citizen be denied access to the courts. Law as a basis for public action, law approved by Parliament, became therefore a crucial characteristic of the West German political order. Indeed, the emphasis on legal norms, and on institutional devices for ensuring that public actions conformed to them, expressed a continued preference for the resolution of political disputes through authoritative judicial decisions rather than by resorting to the more informal methods of political accommodation.

The establishment of the Federal Constitutional Court was intended to guarantee this crucial understanding of *Rechtsstaat;* the Court has to interpret the constitution and must, therefore, base many of its decisions on explicitly political judgments. Besides upholding the personal freedoms set out in the Basic Law, the Court arbitrates on disputes between the major organs of the state, protects the federal-*Länder* balance, rules on the constitutionality of political parties, and exercises a controlling function on federal legislation.[10] All this has made the Court an important and authoritative force, or alternatively, in the eyes of critics, has led to a "judicialization of politics," enhanced by the growing tendency of politicians to externalize contentious issues. It could also be argued that the ever-growing importance of the Court not only judicialized politics but politicized the judiciary, too.

It has rightly been observed that the institutional structures provided by the Basic Law amounted in this way to a set of consensus-inducing mechanisms, creating a process that helps *fashion* the consensus, rather than the latter being present beforehand.[11] Nevertheless, constitutional devices would not have been good enough if the political and party system had developed in a different way. A fragmented and polarized party system, reminiscent of the Weimar Republic, might well have led the checks and balances of the Basic Law to become a recipe for deadlock and immobility. With this possibility in mind, the Basic Law attempted to ensure that the party system would form a stable element by discouraging the emergence or survival of small parties and factions. Proportional representation, but a provision that parties gaining less than 5 percent of the votes were excluded from parliamentary representation, were intended to guarantee that the system could not experience the instability encountered during the Weimar Republic. The concentration of political power in three moderate parties, CDU/CSU, SPD, and FDP, thus became essential to the successful operation of the Basic Law.

Based on this emerging framework, the new political order also surfaced within a wider economic and social context. Framed by Adenauer's policy of *"Westintegration"*[12] (counterpoised by a parallel policy of integrating the GDR into the Eastern bloc through the Soviet Union), the years between 1949 and 1961 were dominated by a publicly induced reconstruction, based upon a socially controlled market economy—this being perceived as the appropriate means to secure the rebuilding of the economic (and social) foundations of society. Though there had certainly not been a social revolution after 1945, the emerging society did differ sharply from the previous one: urbanization and industrial development were at the forefront of these differences, leading to what was conventionally called the *Wirtschaftswunder*.

This total commitment to economic reconstruction really did not allow other issues to be brought to the fore in public debate. The Social Democrats did try to question basic decisions of the Adenauer governments, but they lacked the opportunity of gaining a majority. With the demise of the aristocracy, a formally "classless," socially homogenized society emerged, devoted to economic success, preoccupied with the restoration (or creation) of economic and social well-being, and eager to avoid ideological confrontations. State planning, control, and ownership were rejected, not only in response to the obvious success of the "economic miracle" but also because of the obvious difficulties that the other Germany, the German Democratic Republic, experienced during these years.

As a result, entrepreneurial initiative and the pursuit of profit were encouraged; trade was liberalized, and exposure to market competition was preached as the best way to achieve rising output; the government rejected any active role in steering the economy and pursued, in the interests of price stability, orthodox financial policies. This did not imply a dogmatic rejection of state intervention or of public subsidies in ownership. For historical reasons, the federal and *Länd* governments inherited extensive public industrial holdings, and heavy public investment in infrastructure along with public financial support for several branches of industry have been common.

Even allowing for special factors, in particular Marshall Aid and the absence of a defense budget for some years, these economic policies produced a rate of recovery that no one foresaw in the immediate postwar years. Such a social and economic climate supported the growth of pragmatic and nonideological policies; active pluralism thus took root. At the same time, the political parties accepted clear identities within a surprisingly short period. Networks of organized interests also quickly came to be viewed as legitimate in influencing the course of public policy at all levels.

Stabilization and Normalization During the Peak of the Cold War (1961–1969)

During the 1960s, the stimulant of reconstruction came to a halt, without really threatening economic growth, thanks to a great increase in exports. This development could be described as a process of "normalization," insofar as public policies were no longer dictated by the pressing needs of the postwar years but rather by tasks that were equally crucial in other industrialized West European countries. Inevitably, the population started to compare achievements, and public criticism gained weight. The latter focused primarily on problems associated with uncontrolled economic growth. It asked, effectively, for codetermination. And it raised questions about the democratic potential of the Republic's institutions.

A gradually growing disenchantment with the ruling CDU/CSU, along with the first signs of an economic recession, coupled with unrest especially among the young, led in 1966 to a Grand Coalition between the Christian Democratic Party and the Social Democrats. This coalition did secure a number of important policy decisions, but it could not reach agreement on a cohesive core of common policies. It was therefore not surprising that the 1969 elections led to a more profound political change, in the establishment of a "social-liberal coalition," formed by the Social Democratic Party and the Free Democrats, under the chancellorship of Willy Brandt.[13] Although not as neat or linear as during the 1960s, developments during this period can still be characterized as stable, leading in particular to the normal democratic procedure of an alteration in government.

The domestic political order thus withstood its first substantial test. The transition of power came to be perceived as part of normal democratic development; the agenda shifted to issues raised by the broader population; and domestic policies did not polarize society. The constant threat imposed by the continuing Cold War probably helped in securing a high degree of stability and consensual identity within West German society, aided by the great economic boom that increased the prosperity of all social strata until at least 1966, and the gradual parallel development of the welfare state.

When the postwar boom ground to a halt with the recession of 1966–67, new problems—macroeconomic management, the harmonization of social conflicts, the equalization of horizontal/vertical and social/regional disparities, the first ecological dilemmas—appeared to require increased governmental intervention. On the other hand, initial policy responses, in these last years of the first postwar era, were still a logical extension of earlier responses. There were, for example, important changes to the relationship between federal, *Länder*, and local governments. The need for intergovernmental coordination grew; as a result, horizontal cooperation was extended and increasingly supplemented by processes of vertical coordination and control between the public authorities of the different levels.

In the same way, the 1967 Act for the Promotion of Stability and Economic Growth not only introduced a Keynesian macroeconomic approach to economic policymaking, but also bound non-national governments to conform to national macroeconomic targets. The newly established Councils for Economic and Financial Planning were required to coordinate the budgeting of all territorial units. In addition, federal, *Länder,* and municipal authorities were incorporated into a hierarchical planning system (covering, inter alia, budgeting, infrastructure, and physical/regional planning). Although the introduction of legally binding planning turned out to be impossible, the objectives of federal and *Länder* governments became guidelines for subcentral policies, particularly as a basis for categorical grants.[14]

Finally, the constitutional reform of 1969 then created a new legal basis of intergovernmental relations. Joint planning, decision-making, and financing were geared to match decentralized policies with national targets, to arbitrate interregional conflicts, to avoid imbalances between regions, and to rationalize the use of resources. Federal grants were made available to help *Länder* and municipalities perform their tasks in housing, urban renewal, urban mass transport, and hospital construction. Other reform policies (for example, educational reform) were to be carried out on the basis of agreement to be reached between federal and *Länder* governments.

Expanded Incrementalism: The Era of
Adaptation and Consolidation

Adapting toward a Changed Environment (1969–1981)

These problems, however, could not be overcome by reforms of the intergovernmental framework alone. Evolving social cleavages, growing economic disparities, and a changing overall attitude toward political institutions began inexorably to challenge established routines. The Christian Democrats, who dominated the first two decades of West Germany's existence, had succeeded in absorbing right-wing parties and had formed a broad-based conservative "people's party" (*Volkspartei*), reconciling Catholic and Protestant thinking. The Social Democrats needed much longer to overcome the Marxist heritage, eventually adapting a profile that, as a consequence of the 1956 Bad Godesberg conference, approximated a catch-all party with relatively broad appeal.

The party system at large therefore developed slowly, into a choice between these two major parties, both committed to a social-market economy and economic growth, with the small Liberal Party, the FDP—dominated by economic concerns and representing the civil service and public employees—often holding the balance of power. Given the gradual convergence between the CDU and SPD, some analysts characterized West Germany's domestic political order by the early 1960s in terms of a "vanishing opposition"; under the Grand Coalition of 1966–69, parliamentary opposition was indeed to disappear almost entirely.

At the same time, social, economic, and political developments were progressing rapidly. Not only was the rate of economic change during the first two decades of the postwar period exceptional, but socioeconomic trends were reinforcing it, producing a cumulative pressure on the political system. Where continuing industrialization and technological development, aided by a traditional work ethic and stable industrial relations, helped in securing the *Wirtschaftswunder,* the social transformation of the country was hardly limited to increasing affluence. Economic growth led to a massive migration from the countryside into the urban areas, resulting in a heavily urbanized society, with a population density ten times that of the United States. The continuing decline of rural population and the growth of metropolitan areas stimulated further changes in life expectations and lifestyles.

So urbanization meant, here as elsewhere, a growing separation of the home and the workplace, a greater diversity of occupations and interests, an expanded range of career opportunities, and more geographic and social mobility. "Affluence, life-style changes, alterations in the social structure, increases in educational levels, and new international conditions transformed the social bases of West German politics."[15] Certainly, these trends were not restricted to the Federal Republic; similar changes did occur in other Western industrial democracies. In Germany, however, these trends were more pronounced because society came back from a lower general level of development, due to wartime destructions and dislocations, and because the rates of change then often exceeded those in other Western nations. Moreover, the influence of these various factors tended to overlap, thereby magnifying their impact.

After taking office in 1969, the Brandt (and later Schmidt) governments came rapidly to realize that their tasks would be more difficult than during previous decades of the Federal Republic's existence. While the international agenda did shift in a more liberal direction, so that early attempts to overcome a dogmatic East-West confrontation could meet a positive public response, the domestic political order was faced with unprecedented challenges. "Modernizing the state" as a reaction to growing functional demands, while at the same time democratizing it in response to a number of newer social cleavages,[16] posed a double challenge that turned out to be crucial both to the political fate of the government and to its capacity to adapt to a profoundly changed environment.

The first steps were nevertheless taken successfully. The government, in tune with a nearly euphoric mood for large parts of the population, announced a newly active engagement with the East, promised a number of domestic reforms, and defined new policy areas in reaction to demands raised in previous years—environmental policies, labor-market policies, policies to overcome regional disparities. But announcement of the relevant prospective reforms could carry the government for only a relatively short period; euphoria turned into disillusionment and then disappointment. It became only too obvious that the government had promised but could not fully deliver—struggling on the one hand with a "reform overload," and on the other with a rapidly changing environment, one that did not allow for policies based on excessive expectations of growth or overoptimistic hopes about international responses.

Severe economic problems, reflecting a worldwide process of structural change and leading to steadily growing unemployment, were aggravated by domestic challenges to established governmental routines and by new cleavages from the increasing differentiation of society. At the social base for politics, significant value changes within broad segments of the society led to new perceptions of the appropriate relationship between state and society. Among key political intermediaries, "alternative" groupings emerged to challenge the established organizations, while a "participatory revolution" challenged the main political and governmental institutions at the same time. Within government itself, the conscious "modernization" of its central machinery did not guarantee that other adaptations within the existing policymaking setting were easily accomplished.

In response, the parties tried to "open up" while governmental institutions sought to increase the "rationality" of the policy process. For the latter, this implied functional reforms that were supposed to achieve a substantial transfer of powers and responsibilities from the national level to subcentral institutions, in order to complement those large-scale territorial reforms that had been conducted at an earlier stage. But these attempts to improve efficiency and effectiveness failed to materialize. At the same time, growing budgetary deficits called for more substantial interventions, in the form of resource constraints and cut-back management, so that policies to secure "value for money" gained in importance.

The combination would have been difficult for any governing party, and German resilience during the economically troubled years following the oil crises and subsequent world recession was arguably comparatively successful, providing some basis for the claim to be *Modell Deutschland.*" Moreover, the West German "social market economy" continued to earn widespread admiration, as did Helmut Schmidt, who epitomized for many strong political leadership during these troubled years. Nevertheless, domestic public disenchantment with the Social Democrats grew—and eventually called for political change. Here again, normal democratic procedures worked, adding yet another version of partisan alternation in power to the postwar German experience. For this, due to a turn of the coalition partner, the Free Democrats, Helmut Kohl succeeded in overthrowing the Schmidt government in 1982.

The Semi-Sovereign State (1982–1990)

During the early 1980s, the twin pressures of a global economic crisis and of domestic political challenges led to sweeping changes in some major industrialized countries. The United States and Britain, for example, moved resolutely away from long-standing social-welfare programs and toward private-sector initiatives. France, on the other hand, initially attempted (in 1981–83) to solve its problems with a socialist program but ran up against the same constraints imposed by the international economy. In Japan, finally, a conservative party that had held office uninterruptedly since 1955 continued an essentially external response to such problems, by redoubling its export offensive on world markets to pay for the oil and other raw materials on which its economy depended, while at the same time making subtle adjustments in domestic policies to outflank its opponents.[17]

By comparison, West Germany was striking for its *lack* of new policy initiatives—as distinct from political rhetoric—despite the triumph in 1983 of a conservative coalition government. The continuation of previous policies was particularly surprising since neoconservatism struck a responsive ideological chord. Yet the conservative victory changed only the composition of the government, not its basic policy approach. The CDU avoided breaking sharply with the past, in favor of changing well-tested policies incrementally, just as it refrained from transforming a well-established institutional setting. The situation thus reminded observers of nothing so much as the *failed* political reforms introduced by the SPD/FDP government in 1969 after two decades of CDU-led federal governments. One key result was that it became a common perception in West Germany that alternation in government leads to small policy changes.

That is a conclusion linked, of course, to the over-arching hypothesis of this paper: that the political-institutional framework of West Germany's domestic political order neither required nor even encouraged the structural changes observed in the United Kingdom and the United States. Once again, it was necessary—and possible—to adapt the established framework to new needs and demands, including "soft" policies strengthening private-sector initiatives at the expense of previously public activity.[18] Indeed, analyzing the experience of the 1970s and 1980s from this perspective suggests that incremental change may have become an essential characteristic of the West German political dynamic.

In this dynamic, the institutional setting militates against overly ambitious reform attempts, allowing for gradual adaptation and avoiding abrupt shifts. The history of successive Kohl governments was also to testify to this characteristic. In the same way, as regards the party system, the principal parties, based on their moderate and pragmatic approaches along with minimization of their ideological differences, had achieved a broad electoral appeal and were likewise strongly integrative. Political strategies and electoral competition led to a centripetal party system, rather than a polarizing one.

Despite all that, the squeezing out of smaller parties did not lead to a straight two-party system, as some observers had expected and as this dynamic might appear to suggest. What resulted instead was a stable three-party system from 1971 onward, although emergence of the Greens in 1983 did intermittently threaten to change the political landscape. The constant survival of the Free Democrats, facilitated by their endorsement of both market-based economics and of libertarian social issues and civil rights, along with an electoral system that allowed voters the opportunity for "ticket splitting"—one ballot for a single-member seat and another for proportional distribution—played a pivotal role in determining the composition of coalitions. Indeed, as a result of its indispensability to the major parties, the FDP received from these arrangements an influence on governmental policy out of all proportion to the party's size.[19]

This triangular pattern of coalition politics was threatened by the arrival of the Greens, though they did not ultimately change the picture profoundly. Prospects of a new alignment on the left did not really materialize. Instead, the party system, challenged by the "new politics," underwent its own gradual "modernization" during this second postwar era, to counteract incipient divisions. The peace movement, gender issues, Green demands—all were slowly but gradually incorporated into the agenda of the main democratic parties. Interest groups followed suit: by adjusting their ways of decision-making, by differentiating their organizational base territorially and sectorally, and by carefully experimenting with new forms of interchange between the private and the public sector. With stable forms of communication and cooperation, these groups also reacted flexibly to new demands and a changing environment.

It was reasonable to believe, then, that Germany had finally overcome its latecomer position when compared to other G-7 countries. Most especially, the alternation of governments in 1969 and again in 1982 indicated that the political routines of other liberal democracies were now rooted within the West German state. At the same time, it has been argued elsewhere that, in the structural determinants of its political system, the greatest political affinities to the mature politics of this *second* West German postwar order lay not with its major G-7 counterparts, with the United States, Japan, Britain, or France, but more with the Scandinavian countries and other small but rich European states, such as Denmark, the Netherlands, Belgium, Austria, and Switzerland. Like the Federal Republic, these states favored incremental policymaking and deliberate experimentation over programs for large-scale change.[20]

The New Era: Unification and Europeanization

The late 1980s have thrown up new challenges that demand potentially more far-reaching adaptations on the part of the German political system. These involve, first of all, the impact of unification; secondly, the adaptive pressures that result from the ongoing process of European integration; and thirdly, new contextual conditions and functional demands which seem at odds with a number of established political practices. Both in quantitative and qualitative terms, these three developments, especially as seen in combination, pose a novel challenge to the German polity. This has even led to fears that the quality and scale of the challenge might, finally, overstretch the adaptive capacities of the system. What appears as a certain current disorientation, then, can be attributed to this overload, indicating that Germany has indeed entered a new era in which its domestic setting and its international role might change profoundly.

The decisive challenge of unification, Europeanization, and changed functional demands lies in the fact that they combine, at the same time, internal and external pressures, and thereby call potentially for both macro-and micropolitical reactions. Such pressures cannot, in principle, be limited to single areas or levels of the political machinery. Instead, they ask for policies which might encompass the system of governance as a whole and contain legal, institutional, and procedural elements. This challenge extends to the social base of Germany's political system as well. It has become only too apparent that political parties, interest groups, and the media were not prepared for the "shock" provided by German unification, while the impact of Europeanization had *already* been underestimated.

The Impact of Unification

In discussing the changes brought about by unification,[21] two perspectives need to be distinguished. The first refers to the (re-)establishment of democratic political structures in the five *Länder* on the territory of the former German Democratic Republic; the second concerns a need for potentially far-reaching adaptations in the political organization of the now-united Germany. Although the second aspect primarily refers to the federal administration, unification also necessitates a review of the structures of the eleven old *Länder*. Perhaps most importantly, intergovernmental linkages, the core of the system of cooperative federalism, have come under severe pressure.

In this context, unification implied, first of all, the extension of West Germany's complex legal system to the new *Länder,* which were established during the last months of the GDR's existence. The adoption of West Germany's system during this process has sometimes been criticized as a way of "colonizing" Eastern Germany. There was, however, little choice. The political pressures under which the unification process took place scarcely allowed for the development of a distinct legal and political system that would have been applicable solely to one part of the country. It is doubtful, in any case, whether it would have been politically and constitutionally acceptable to create a unified political entity in which two legal systems coexisted.

Turning from the legal to the institutional framework, one sees again a transfer of West German models to the East. By and large, West Germany's institutional structures were transplanted to, and copied in, the new *Länder*. In their constitutional and political powers, as well as their basic institutional makeup, Saxony, Anhalt-Saxony, Mecklenburg-West Pomerania, Brandenburg, and Thuringia are modeled exactly on their West German counterparts. In fact, some of the "old" *Länder* have actively sought to influence institutional development in the East to meet their own preferences.

As a result of this wholesale and largely unadjusted adoption of the West German legal-institutional framework, some of the structural problems and inefficiencies which had been identified in West German federalism before unification have now been compounded and magnified. This includes, above all, the large disparities in the size and economic potential of the *Länder*. During the 1970s and 1980s, there were already signs of the development of a two-class federal system, in which the "rich" *Länder* increasingly dominated cooperative policymaking, while the smaller "poor" states found themselves in a position of growing reliance on fiscal transfers, both from the federation and from their more prosperous counterparts.

As a result of unification, these interregional distribution problems have actually worsened, at a time when resources available for substantial equalization measures have become scarcer. Consequently, there is a fear that unification and the accession of five new states, with all their financial and economic problems, might change the structure of a new political order by giving rise to a further centralization in the federal system, with the federation assuming a dominant position vis-à-vis the financially dependent states in the East. This, in turn, has led to renewed demands for territorial reform, which many hope might result in financially, economically, and administratively more viable states.

But the relationships between the federal government and the *Länder* are further complicated by the wide disjunction that has become apparent between the political *complexion* of the federal government on the one hand and the predominant coloring of the individual *Länd* governments on the other. Both elements of this complexity and imbalance are reflected in the *Bundesrat*. Although there is no necessary correspondence between the predominance of one party or coalition in federal government and party control in the individual *Länder,* periods of sharp divergence have been few—the major exception being the SPD/FDP coalition from 1969 to 1982, when the CDU came to have control of the majority of the *Länder,* and thus also of the *Bundesrat.*

The result was a kind of "split" party system, which disappeared when the CDU regained control of the federal government in 1982. What has occurred now, from 1990 onward, is a reemergence of this split, in some cases in an additionally complicated fashion. Coalitions within the institutional *Länder* have themselves become rather more mixed, including so-called rainbow coalitions. As a result, votes within the *Bundesrat* can often not be counted as under the control of either side. Analogues to this same phenomenon are, of course, familiar to the United States and France, though not as a product of territorial expansion.

For the party system as such, it has become apparent that neither of the *Volksparteien* is likely to secure and enjoy the levels of support that they had in the past. Indeed, a long-term trend is evident in their combined vote over the span of all federal elections. This shows that the aggregate vote of CDU/CSU and SPD fell from about 90 percent (still 91 percent in 1976) to 77.3 percent in 1990. If this process of electoral shrinkage continues, even if only to a moderate degree, then the resulting volatility will add to the insecurity of the two major parties. But what might be even more important and at the same time worrying is the continuous decline in voter *turnout*. In this, growing public apathy and alienation from the political process could lead to a gradual erosion of the dominance of the *Volksparteien*.

Although the evidence of an increasing fluidity in voting patterns is clear-cut, there is more uncertainty about the cause of these patterns. Most analysts, resorting either to models of realignment or dealignment to explain processes of partisan change, are not able to provide a convincing picture. The long-term enforcements to partisanship have certainly decreased in impact among the Western electorate and remain underdeveloped among the Eastern public. Consequently, as these factors play a diminished role in electoral decisions, the political values and issue beliefs of individual voters become more important as the basis of political decision-making.

In sum, then, the establishment of a new political order on the territory of the former GDR could be described as a process of transplanting an established institutional framework and its associated organizations of interest mediation. In principle, the unification process might have offered a historically unique chance to reexamine Western experience in this transplantation, and to avoid some of the acknowledged shortcomings of the Western model in rebuilding the Eastern *Länder*. In practice, the rapid pace of unification did not permit a more gradual process of adjustment and adaptation. On the other hand, the growing acceptance of basic elements of the new political and institutional order suggests that an established institutional adaptability can work even under these historically unprecedented conditions. But does that then mean that we should expect to observe further continuity of the semi-sovereign state—tied down by checks and balances, powerful cogoverning institutions, and centralized societal organizations?[22]

The sudden exposure of the GDR economy to world markets, along with the transfer of an established polity to the East, have meant that an economic and social order characterized by a far lower productivity level, organized as a Soviet-type planned economy, and supported by a relatively egalitarian (though frugal) welfare state, has been called upon to integrate the characteristics of a democratic high-income society, a market economy, and a social-insurance-oriented welfare state. That is a tremendously demanding task, and the "big bang" approach to unification has therefore created problems which other former socialist countries did not experience to the same extent.

On the other hand, the associated problems of distribution and redistribution have, so far, been handled within the established routines of industrial relations. The transfer of basic characteristics of the West German welfare state to Eastern Germany did cushion the social costs of the transition period, aided by labor-market policies that helped to dampen the effects of economic decline. Bonn (Berlin) is indeed not Weimar. Since the political parties and most of the interest groups proved able to integrate significant parts of the East German population and its electorate, the political weight of radical parties is also still insignificant.

To date, it appears that the political setting of the now unified Germany, in particular its institutions, parties, associations, and its welfare-state policies, have functioned as safety nets and shock absorbers. Whether they will continue to do so depends largely on the ways and means to shoulder the financial costs of unification. The "solidarity pact" (*Solidarpakt*) between the federal government and the *Länder* (not to forget unions and employer associations) indicates that there is still room for broad political consensus. It remains to be seen, however, whether the overall political objectives of *Solidarpakt* will be followed by swift implementation.

Unification has certainly left intact the adaptive structural characteristics of a previous (West German) political order. It has, at the same time, caused new organizational stresses for political parties and interest groups: the requirement to bridge widely divergent interests from Eastern and Western constituencies makes interest articulation, aggregation, and representation more difficult. The available evidence so far suggests that the party system and the system of interest mediation, albeit not necessarily each party and each association, are able to accommodate most of these demands and thus to extend an older order. If the polity continues its successful attempts to cushion the social costs of unification and to engage in the unavoidable reform of German federalism, then there is every indication that the process might be hailed at later stages as a successful attempt to overcome the socialist experiment on German soil, in a new but evolutionary political era.

The Challenge of Europeanization

While struggling with unification, the impact of the simultaneous process of Europeanization on the day-to-day workings of large parts of the German political system has been rather limited. Although some critics interpret this absence of change as a failure on the part of the public sector (or even the political system at large) to adjust in organizational and procedural terms to European realities, it might also be argued that the actual adaptive pressures associated with Europeanization have been less marked so far than is sometimes assumed. In accordance with the latter view, the impact of Europeanization would be limited to a number of organizational measures and adjustments in certain key policy areas. The establishment of special units in charge of European affairs, be it in the form of European affairs ministries at the state level or the creation of "European units" in particular departments, parties, and interest groups could, accordingly, be interpreted as an attempt to adjust to European demands in the traditional manner.

In analyzing the Europeanization of the German polity, one should not, however, look solely at adaptive reactions. Europeanization is certainly a two-directional process, in which adjustment policies on the part of national and subnational governments are to be complemented by policies aimed at influencing decision-making at the European Community level itself. This involves more than the reactive adaptation of national institutional arrangements to external demands. It also refers to the attempts by national and subcentral actors to create the preconditions which allow them to take full part in the development of EC polices, according to national requirements and/or international commitments. This proactive element of Europeanization might even grow in importance, not least due to the economic weight of a unified Germany and its obligation toward Central and Eastern Europe.

Europeanization poses, therefore, as much of a challenge for Germany as for the EC itself. After successful integration of Eastern Germany into the EC, [23] today's interest centers around the impact of unification on the workings of the EC. Where foreign observers were concerned about a potential German dominance, the federal government repeatedly declared that it had no intention whatsoever of dominating the EC, and hoped for a "Europeanized Germany" rather than a "Germanized Europe." Though Germany will undoubtedly become more central than ever to European development at large, unification could be seen as accelerating further EC integration, following different approaches to tie German economic power effectively to the EC framework.

The Current Political Order Revisited

It is interesting to note, not least in comparative perspective, that even highly differentiated and interlocking political systems, such as the German, do not inevitably become structurally rigidified but are quite capable of modernizing, of adapting to profoundly changing tasks and environments. Whether this holds true under the double challenge of unification and Europeanization remains, of course, to be seen. But a look back at the basic characteristics of Germany's domestic political order allows for a number of further hypotheses.

First, while the separation of legislative, political, and administrative powers, as well as the division between central, regional, and local governments, will both surely continue, their procedural integration in program development, decision-making, and implementation is almost certain to undergo change. "Cooperative federalism" has already turned very competitive, and growing distributional conflicts among the regions *and* between different levels of government have led to intense horizontal and vertical cleavages, in which the adoption of the "solidarity pact" should not be confused with a solid intergovernmental agreement on the future of Germany's multi-tiered political system. On the contrary, it seems almost inevitable that a more serious, structured debate on "new federal arrangements," not excluding questions of territorial reorganization, will follow.

Second, functional deconcentration of state power is bound to persist. Since the high degree of departmental autonomy, along with the performance of functionally and politically autonomous bodies (not least the *Bundesbank*), helped to overcome a number of serious performance problems during the first three years of unified Germany's existence, there is growing evidence that functional differentiation, complemented by territorial decentralization, will remain distinctive features of the German polity.

On the other hand, and third, the economic system, characterized in the introduction as leaning toward "liberal corporatism," might face more serious crises during the years to come. The recession of the early 1990s certainly indicated that an export-driven German economy is not immune to cyclical fluctuations and forms part of much wider European (and world) economy, one that renders nationally adopted policies, if not obsolete, at least more difficult. Nevertheless, the gradual recovery of the East German economy could well exaggerate the strength of overall economic recovery, just as the need to integrate the East Germany economy at a crucial point in time exaggerated the recession.

Fourth, the high degree of centralization and integration in the area of social organizations, which contrasts with a functionally and territorially dispersed statehood, might undergo a number of changes, too. Indeed, both the party system and the interest groups have developed tendencies to regionalize their organizations, to allow for policies more orientated to specific problems and to target groups. The long-standing centralization of employer associations and trade unions might persist for purposes of policy formulation—their leadership continues to prefer such an outcome—yet implementation problems seem likely to induce change here as well.

Fifth, the absence of large-scale regional disparities, social conflicts, and ethnic cleavages certainly helped to improve the institutional stability that was characteristic of *West* Germany's postwar years. Under the impact of unification, economic and social disparities between the Western and Eastern parts of the country have grown in importance, and led to a number of previously unknown social conflicts. Ethnic cleavages, stemming from the enormous influx of emigrants and asylum seekers, have to be added. In comparison to other West European countries, Germany's (very liberal) immigration law had to be altered. But the country has not coped yet with the new situation. Antiforeigner protests and intermittent violence indicate a new and previously unseen social tension within German society.

Sixth, gradual institutional change and adaptation, a predominant characteristic of the domestic political order for nearly four decades, might always fail under these circumstances. The setting as described hardly allows for more than incremental steps in "modernizing" the German political system, yet the double impact of unification and Europeanization asks for more than routine adaptation. Moreover, both the coalition parties and the opposition seem ill-equipped to react to this new challenge. It should not come as a surprise, therefore, that a growing part of the population appears to be turning away from politics, as indicated by the gradual decline in voter turnout. An overall modernization of Germany's political system would thus seem to rank high on the present domestic political agenda.

Conclusion

The evolution of German political orders since 1945 suggests that forty years of stable development and unprecedented growth ought to be linked to an unusual degree of institutional stability and adaptability, characterized by incentives towards compromise and partisan convergence. The deterioration of political institutions during the Weimar Republic and the experience of the collapse of state and society under the National Socialist regime encouraged the subsequent development of a polity whose basic structural principles—following distinctive German traditions, put forward by the members of the Parliamentary Council, and enshrined in the Basic Law—reflected these experiences.

The resulting political framework proved to be extremely stable, reliable, and workable. Cooperative federalism, liberal corporatism, the consequent adoption of the *Rechtsstaatsprinzip,* and economic development based on the principles of a social market economy allowed for an evolution that served different political majorities, divergent interests, and (partly) opposing ideologies. It fostered democratic values, facilitated swift political transformations, and created identity and consensus. Though being, inevitably, subject to external pressures, it benefited for a long time from the shield—the not-unselfish protection—provided by the Western Allies and could therefore concentrate on domestic issues instead of playing an active role in international politics. These opportunities have been used to create an internal homogeneity and material well-being that contrasted sharply with the experiences in the German Democratic Republic.

New problems and demands were mostly accommodated within the given institutional framework and its constituent characteristics. The modes and outcomes of policymaking turned out to be acceptable to nearly all segments of society; a critical monitoring of ongoing policies allowed for quick adjustments in case of potential cleavages or obvious performance deficits. The forty years of West Germany's existence can thus rightly be interpreted as a case of unusual stability and adaptability. Which is to say: the era of reconstruction and growth gave way to an era of adaptation and consolidation, with clear structural differences but without major discontinuities. This ease of transition between political eras will now be put to the ultimate test, as future developments reveal whether the German polity will retain its basic characteristics and stable outcomes under the double challenge of national unification and European integration.

Notes

1. Byron E. Shafer, "Postwar Politics in the G-7: The United States," paper presented at the Annual Meeting of the American Political Science Association, Chicago, September 3–6, 1992, 1.

2. For a broader discussion of the analytical issues at stake, see Joachim Jens Hesse and Arthur Benz, "Institutional Policy: An International Comparison," Thomas Ellwein et al., eds., *Yearbook of Government and Public Administration, 1987/88* (Baden-Baden: Nomos, 1989), 377–403.

3. See Joachim Jens Hesse and Thomas Ellwein, *Das Regierungssystem der Bundesrepublik Deutschland*, 2 vols., 7th ed. (Opladen: Westdeutscher Verlag, 1992).

4. See Byron E. Shafer, "The Notion of an Electoral Order: The Structure of Electoral Politics at the Accession of George Bush," in Byron E. Shafer, ed., *The End of Realignment? Interpreting American Electoral Eras* (Madison: University of Wisconsin, 1991).

5. An official history of the German Democratic Republic, published in 1985, distinguished between periods of anti-fascist democratic transformation (1945–49); the building of the foundations of socialism (1949–61); the way to a developed socialist society (1961–70); and the further formation of the developed socialist society (1971–84). It is not without irony that the last period preceded the collapse of the socialist experiment, leaving in question the "development" that party historians assumed the GDR had already reached.

6. See, among many, Klaus von Beyme, *Das politische System der Bundesrepublik Deutschland* (München: Pieper, 1991); Eckhard Jesse, *Die Demokratie der Bundesrepublik Deutschland* (Berlin: Colloquium-Verlag, 1989); Kurt Sontheimer, *Grundzüge des politischen Systems der Bundesrepublik Deutschland* (München: Pieper, 1989); and Hesse and Ellwein, *Das Regierungssystem.*

For introductions in English, see Dennis L. Bark and David R. Gress, *A History of West Germany—From Shadow to Substance 1945–1963*, vol.1 (Oxford: Blackwell, 1993); Dennis L. Bark and David R. Gress, *A History of West Germany—Democracy and Its Discontents 1963–1991*, vol. 2 (Oxford: Blackwell, 1993); David P. Conradt, *The German Polity* (New York: Longman, 1986); Russell J. Dalton, *Politics in West Germany* (Glenview, Ill.: Scott, Foresman, 1989); Mary Fulbrook, *The Two Germanies 1945–1990* (Basingstoke: Macmillan, 1992); Charlie Jeffery and Peter Savigear, *German Federalism Today* (Leicester: Leicester, 1991); Nevil Johnson, *State and Government in the Federal Republic of Germany* (Oxford: Pergamon, 1983); Peter J. Katzenstein, *Policy and Politics in West Germany: The Growth of a Semisovereign State* (Philadelphia: Temple University, 1987); William E. Paterson and David Southern, *Governing Germany* (Oxford: Blackwell, 1991); Gordon Smith, *Democracy in Western Germany: Parties and Politics in the Federal Republic* (London: Gower, 1986).

For comparative purposes, see Renate Mayntz and Fritz W. Scharpf, *Policy-Making in the German Federal Bureaucracy* (Amsterdam: Elsevier, 1975); Yves Mény, *Government and Politics in Western Europe* (Oxford: Oxford University, 1990); Gordon Smith, *Politics in Western Europe* (Aldershot: Dartmouth, 1989); Gordon Smith et al., eds., *Developments in German Politics* (Basingstoke: Macmillan, 1993); Derek W. Urwin, *Western Europe Since 1945—A Political History* (New York: Longman, 1989).

7. For an early comprehensive history of the German Democratic Republic,

see Hermann Weber, *DDR, Grundriss der Geschichte 1945–1990* (Hannover: Oldenbourg, 1991). On the polity of the German Democratic Republic, see, among others, D. Staritz, *Geschichte der DDR 1949–1985* (Frankfurt: Suhrkamp, 1987); W. Weidenfeld and H. Zimmermann, eds., *Deutschland-Handbuch, Eine doppelte Bilanz 1949–1989* (Bonn: Bundeszentrale für politische Bildung, 1989); G. J. Glaessner, ed., *Eine deutsche Revolution: Der Umbruch in der DDR* (Berlin: Dietz, 1991); and S. Meuschel, *Legitimation und Parteiherrschaft in der DDR* (Frankfurt: Suhrkamp, 1992).

8. Among the large number of studies covering the immediate postwar development (1945–1949), see W. Benz, *Aspekte deutscher Aussenpolitik im 20. Jahrhundert* (Stuttgart: Deutsche Verlags-Anstalt, 1976); W. Cornides, *Die Weltmächte und Deutschland. Geschichte der jungsten Vergangenheit 1945–1955* (Tübingen: Wunderlich Verlag, 1957); T. Vogelsang, *Das geteilte Deutschland* (München: Deutscher Tuschenbuch-Verlag, 1966); and especially T. Eschenburg, *Jahre der Besatzung 1945–1949. Geschichte der Bundesrepublik Deutschland,* vol. 2 (Stuttgart: Deutsche Verlags-Anstalt, 1983); H. Graml, *Die Alliierten und die Teilung Deutschlands. Konflikte und Entscheidungen 1941–1948* (Frankfurt: Suhrkamp, 1985); Institut für Zeitgeschichte, *Westdeutschlands Weg zur Bundesrepublik 1945–1949* (München: Beck, 1976). Specific changes in postwar Germany are commented upon in H. A. Winkler, ed., *Politische Weichenstellungen im Nachkriegsdeutschland 1945–1953* (Göttingen: Vandenhoeck und Ruprecht, 1979) and W. D. Narr and D. Thränhardt, eds., *Die Bundesrepublik Deutschland: Entstehung, Entwicklung, Struktur* (Frankfurt: Suhrkamp, 1979). For a well-documented analysis see M. Overesch, *Deutschland 1945–1949. Vorgeschichte und Gründung der Bundesrepublik. Ein Leitfaden in Darstellung und Dokumenten* (Hannover: Niedersächsische Landeszentrale für Politische Bildung, 1989); a Marxist analysis of postwar development can be found in U. Albrecht, F. Deppe, and J. Huffschmidt, eds., *Beiträge zu einer Geschichte der Bundesrepublik* (Baden-Baden: Nomos, 1979). Of more recent publications, D. Thränhardt, *Geschichte der Bundesrepublik Deutschland* (Frankfurt: Suhrkamp, 1989) and R. Morsey, *Die Bundesrepublik Deutschland. Entstehung und Entwicklung bis 1969* (München: Oldenbourg, 1987) are worth mentioning.

9. Nevil Johnson, *State and Government in the Federal Republic of Germany: The Executive at Work* (Oxford: Pergamon, 1983). Though slightly dated, this is still the outstanding publication on the governmental system of the Federal Republic by a foreign author.

10. Gordon Smith and William E. Paterson, "The Nature of the Unified State," in Gordon Smith, et al., eds., *Developments in German Poltics,* 45f.

11. Ibid., 40. See additionally Hesse and Ellwein, *Das Regierungssystem,* chap. 3–1.

12. The era dominated by Konrad Adenauer is best documented in A. Baring, *Aussenpolitik in Adenauers Kanzlerdemokratie, Bonns Beitrag zur Europäischen Verteidigungsgemeinschaft* (München: Oldenbourg, 1969); H. P. Schwarz, *Die Ära Adenauer, Gründerjahre der Republik 1949–1957* (Stuttgart:

Deutsche Verlags-Anstalt, 1981): *Die Ära Ardenauer, Epochenwechsel 1957–1963* (Stuttgart: Deutsche Verlags-Anstalt, 1983); *Adenauer, Der Staatsmann, 1952 bis 1967* (Stuttgart: Deutsche Verlags-Anstalt, 1991). For an analysis in English, see again Johnson, *State and Government in the Federal Republic of Germany.*

13. This era is best documented in K. Hildebrandt, *Von Erhard zur Grossen Koalition 1963–1969* (Stuttgart: Deutsche Verlags-Anstalt, 1984); Thomas Ellwein, *Krisen und Reformen. Die Bundesrepublik seit, den 60er Jahren* (München: Deutscher Taschenbuch Verlag, 1989); and the specific literature mentioned in H. K. Rupp, *Politische Geschichte der Bundesrepublik Deutschland* (Stuttgart: Kohlhammer, 1982); R. Löwenthal and H. P. Schwarz, eds., *Die zweite Republik, 25 Jahre Bundesrepublik Deutschland* (Stuttgart: Seewald Verlag, 1974); A. Baring, *Machtwechsel. Die Ära Brandt-Scheel* (Stuttgart: Deutsche Verlags-Anstalt, 1982); K. D. Bracher, W. Jäger, and W. Link, eds., *Geschichte der Bundesrepublik Deutschland* (Stuttgart: Deutsche Verlags-Anstalt, 1986); W. Jäger and W. Link, *Republik im Wandel 1974–1982, Die Ära Schmidt* (Stuttgart: Deutsche Verlags-Anstalt, 1987).

14. For performance analyses of West German federalism, see "Federalism and Intergovernmental Relations in West Germany—a Fortieth Year Appraisal," *Publius, The Journal of Federalism* 19, no. 4 (1989), and Joachim Jens Hesse, "The Federal Republic of Germany: From Cooperative Federalism to Joint Policy-Making" in *West European Politics* 10 (1987); for the interaction of federalism, unification, and European integration, see *German Politics* 1, no. 3 (1992).

15. Russell J. Dalton, *Politics in West Germany* (Glenview, Ill.: Scott, Foresman, 1989), 80.

16. The situation during the 1970s and at the beginning of the 1980s is commented upon by, among others, H. v. Hentig, *Die entmutigte Republik Politische Aufsätze* (München: C. Hansen, 1980); K. Sontheimer, *Die verunsicherte Republik. Die Bundesrepublik Deutschland nach 30 Jahren* (München: Piper, 1970); *Zeitwende? Die Bundesrepublik zwischen alter und alternativer Politik* (Hamburg, 1983); M. and S. Greiffenhagen, *Ein schwieriges Vaterland. Zur politischen Kultur Deutschlands* (München: List, 1979); J. Raschke, ed., *Bürger und Parteien. Ansichten und Analysen einer schwierigen Beziehung* (Opladen: Westdeutscher Verlag, 1982); W. D. Narr and C. Offe, eds., *Wohlfahrtsstaat und Massenloyalität* (Köln: Europäische Verlags-Anstalt, 1975); C. Fenner, U. Heyder, and J. Strasser, eds., *Unfähig zur Reform? Eine Bilanz der inneren Reformen seit 1969* (Frankfurt: Compus-Verlag, 1978); S. Russ-Mohl, *Reformkonjunkturen und politisches Krisenmanagement* (Opladen: Westdeutscher Verlag, 1981).

17. See Katzenstein, *Policy and Politics in West Germany.*

18. See Joachim Jens Hesse, *Administrative Modernisation and Public Sector Reform in Germany—an Overview* (Oxford: Oxford University, forthcoming).

19. Russell J. Dalton, "Two German Electorates?" in Smith, et al., *Developments in German Politics, 1989,* 52ff.

20. Five factors seem common to this other group of countries. First is an open international economy which creates a perception of vulnerability, one that is

conducive to political compromise and finds expression in a system of social partnership between business and labor. Second are the moves by business and labor, like other major interest groups, to centralize their organizations and ingest different social and economic constituencies. Third is a process of bargaining in which political elites avoid stalemate by seeking links with other actors across diverse issues. Fourth is that ideologically moderate system of political parties. Fifth and finally are the historical origins of political accommodation, in the experiences of the 1930s and 1940s. The recollection of the Great Depression, the fear of fascism, and the experience of World War II have pushed political leaders to institutionalize a consensual political system and to seek incremental policy change within it; the question is how long this collective "social memory" can remain so influential. See Katzenstein, *Policy and Politics in Western Germany*.

21. Special aspects of the unification process are covered by Gerhard Lehmbruch, "Die deutsche Vereinigung: Strukturen und Strategien," in *Politische Vierteljahresschrift* 31 (1991), 585 ff.; Fritz W. Scharpf, "Europäisches Demokratiedefizit and deutscher Föderalismus," in *Staatswissenschaften und Staatspraxis* 3 (1992); Joachim Jens Hesse, "Das föderative System der Bundesrepublik vor den Herausforderungen der deutschen Einigung," in Wolfgang Seibel, Arthur Benz, and Heinrich Mäding, eds., *Verwaltungsreform und Verwaltungspolitik im Prozess der deutschen Einigung* (Baden-Baden: Nomos, 1992).

22. See Manfred G. Schmidt, "Political Consequences of German Unification," in *West European Politics* 15, no. 4 (1992): 1ff.

23. See David Spence, "Enlargement without Accession: The European Community Response to the Issue of German Unification," in *Staatswissenschaften und Staatspraxis* 3 (1991).

Stephen J. Anderson

Japan

Scholars disagree about the continuity of political orders for the postwar period in Japan. In brief, does Japan have one continuous order under an enduring dominant party? My short answer is no, and emphatically so after the upheavals of 1993. But at least until the election of 1993 July, when the ruling Liberal Democratic Party (LDP) lost its parliamentary majority, most scholarly studies, while they might not have used the same vocabulary, did focus on phases or shifts within a single order.[1] Now, as the postwar historical periods ends, recent splits in the ruling party and changes among the opposition parties have at last refocused attention inside Japanese politics. The following places these recent changes and impending structural reforms within a longer postwar period of divisions and transitions in governance.

My central argument is that Japanese elites themselves took steps to move from an era of bureaucratic dominance to an era of mixed governance. These adaptive steps reformed the key political structures: a national bureaucracy, a ruling catchall party, and a supportive social coalition, whose coherence gained from domestic economic growth and international stability. Moreover, Japanese elites took their steps to adapt these political structures, over time, within a domestic arena protected crucially by the stable international structures of the Bretton Woods system and of Cold War alliances. With the breakdown of these international economic and security imperatives, then, counterpart steps to adapt the domestic political order are increasingly difficult and point toward major reforms of electoral and party politics.

To assess postwar political developments, this essay avoids prolonged debate about how voters and party alignments shape political eras— simply because Japanese politics has long been dominated by the bureaucracy. Postwar political reforms and adaptive steps thus began of necessity with this national bureaucracy and moved toward empowering other intermediaries in what is here called "mixed governance." In particular, political parties dealt with shifting social cleavages under a "1955 System" of one-party dominance. Superimposed on these domestic structures was an international order that effectively separated the two great issues of economics and security—issues which were jointly so central to immediate postwar politics in most of the other G-7 nations. Economic matters alone took precedence in Japan, due to the protective security umbrella offered by a Cold War alliance with the United States. As a result, Japanese political orders could center on issues of economic growth and could resolve domestic conflicts through adaptive steps that provide the practical benchmark dates for postwar political eras.

The Backdrop to Political Dynamics in Japan

The Shaping of Governance Before 1945

What would become the basis for postwar Japanese governance actually began to take shape long before the end of the Second World War. In the nineteen century, Japanese elites overcame several crises to form a unified political order. From the outset of state formation, key decisions were made to empower the national bureaucracy and to establish some further political structures. The main point here is that the tasks of Japanese elites did not differ vastly from those faced by their contemporaries in Europe and America. Industrial change and military confrontations threw all political orders of the period into chaos. The prolonged Japanese civil war of 1853–68, for example, sparked by the arrival of American warships, ended not long after the Civil War of the United States. The last battles, when samurai blood reddened Ueno swamps in Tokyo, followed less than five years after Gettysburg and Vicksburg at the peak of the conflict between the Union and the Confederacy.

For comparable countries, central state formation in the broadest sense of creating a union from smaller political entities thus began roughly simultaneously. The point is that precedents for comparison between political structures in Japan and other countries also began long before a postwar order emerged. Yet in this regard, and more distinctively, there was also a missing comparative element: little evidence of democratic pressure from below as driving Japanese politics before 1945. Exceptions, such as rioting in 1918 over rice prices or the banning of political parties, merely prove the rule of elite dominance. In response to these challenges, Japanese elites donned the cloak of imperial ideology to enhance the power of the national bureaucracy: they acted to enforce their will through the authority of the emperor, and most especially to empower their central officials.

Central national bureaucracies across the G-7 nations faced sharply contrasting pressures in this period, especially with regard to their emerging, counterpart, political party organizations. Even in countries with similar levels of economic development, even among countries which were late developers, contrasts exist in these emerging political structures. For example, in 1866 and 1868, German and Japanese elites, respectively, began their central bureaucracies with rather differing incentives (see table 7.1). In Germany, Bismarck drew on Prussian models for a centralized German bureaucracy, one that was responsive to parliamentary politics.[2] The German ruling coalition supported the creation of this autonomous German bureaucracy, and after the 1866 victory of Prussia in the Seven Weeks War, the coalition allowed dominance by Prussian bureaucrats in the new federal government of the Confederation. Following the Franco-Prussian War and the proclamation of the German Empire in 1871, these bureaucrats still primarily controlled military and foreign matters, but domestic policy involved Bismarck's leadership in the parliamentary debates of the Reichstag, a situation differing starkly from that in Japan.

After Japan's Meiji Restoration of 1868–69, the ruling samurai-as-bureaucrats organized a national bureaucracy (table 7.1). Over time, this

Table 7.1. Dates in State and Party Formation

	Germany	Japan
Emergence of central state actors	1866	1868
Mass male suffrage (about 20% of population eligible to vote)	1867	1925
Working class party competes in elections	1869 (Social Democrat)	1947 (Socialist)
Military dominance in government	1933–45	1936–47
Competitive postwar parties reappear	1946–49	1947–55
Conservative party dominance	1949–63, 1982–93	1955–93

bureaucracy did successfully assign priorities to policies, indeed, priorities derived from the lessons of Bismarck and Krupp. Bureaucrats as well as business leaders came to accept the idea of social insurance as a means to pacify Japanese labor, and the ruling coalition aimed to deflate the threat of socialism, protect Japanese workers, and simultaneously create ways of keeping those workers in their workplace.[3] On the other hand, Japanese political development faced no counterpart impacts from any introduction of mass male suffrage. The so-called Diet, hereafter more accurately translated as the National Assembly, was not even formed until 1890, and mass suffrage came only in 1925. Japanese divergence from German and European patterns thus began with the late development of effective party politics and suffrage, and resulted in the further empowerment of the central national bureaucracy.

The wartime experience of military dominance worked to empower Japan's bureaucracy additionally. Germany, Italy, and Japan all shared this experience, of course, yet the Japanese situation brought exceptional burdens on its national bureaucrats and granted exceptional powers to these imperial officials. From the ideology of obligation to the emperor came the practical martial powers of the army, so that Japanese officials further increased their powers during wartime. Japan's "emperor system" thus managed to set extended precedents for the functioning of the national bureaucracy.

During the U.S. Occupation of Japan, civilian bureaucrats at the national level survived as an institutional group with the fewest individuals facing a purge. The military was destroyed, the industrial combines known as *zaibatsu* were disowned and reorganized, and a landlord class was disinherited. At the time of the Occupation, John Maki wrote that the postwar bureaucracy was also a threat to democracy and had remained surprisingly untouched by the American officials.[4] Yet Occupation forces saw the bureaucracy as a necessary component in the attempt to build stability out of Japan's wartime devastation—a stability which grew even more essential to an America faced with the imperatives of the Korean Conflict and the Cold War.

In the past, scholars who sought to identify adaptive political principles in Japan did not merge their work with an analysis of the resulting political structures. In a provocative synthesis, Michele Schmiegelow and Henrik Schmiegelow suggest the political philosophy of Japanese leaders as "strategic pragmatism" and identify Japanese themes reminiscent of Austrian political economy.[5] I agree that an adaptive *process* has been central to Japanese economic policymaking, but here I propose to look at specific political *structures*. The most compelling parts of work by other revisionist writers on Japan urge critical analysis of Japanese political institutions.

However, such criticism has yet to move toward synthesis and offer a more complete model of the specific structures constituting the Japanese political order and underpinning its political dynamic.

Isolating the Eras in Postwar Political History

The postwar period began with a series of structural changes that climaxed with the return of sovereignty to Japan. Historians seem most comfortable in beginning with the surrender in August of 1945, but the resulting U.S. Occupation actually took time to elicit continuing political patterns. Under the Occupation, Japanese elites at first possessed only limited powers through which to address rapid changes in society and its politics. After 1947, for example, elites faced an increasingly militant union leadership, who successfully organized a majority of the workforce through rapid unionization. By 1948, in turn, the Cold War began to be felt in Japan, with purges of the Communists and a "reverse course" for labor policies. In 1949, the Occupation moved to encourage the austere economic measures of the Dodge Line, only to turn around and stimulate growth through the procurement of goods for the Korean War.

A benchmark year for the period, however, came after the peace treaty, terminating any state of hostilities, was signed. In 1952, the Japanese bureaucracy regained autonomy from foreign control, reversed the economic disintegration of industrial groups and banks, and pursued domestic stability through regulation and administrative guidance. The consolidation in 1955 of both labor unions and party politics thus represented a culmination rather than a peak of activity in Japanese politics broadly understood. Still, the precise divisions into overall eras and the analysis of structures for bureaucratic dominance and political consolidation (as below) are likely to be controversial. Accordingly, in this section I reexamine Japan's postwar history and make a tentative statement about its major structural features.

Around 1960, Japan's major political structures faced another common, critical period of undeniable change. This benchmark year is relatively uncontroversial, in that it focused several aspects of structural change away from early postwar bureaucratic dominance. Around this time, an underlying social cleavage was bridged, in the "marriage of iron and rice" between industry and farming. Big business gave its backing to the Liberal Democrats, who acted in politics to reassure farmers with the support of rice prices, with public pensions, with national health insurance, and with other rural development projects. These activities triggered a counterpart crisis in the leftist parties, over union strategies and international postures. Unions differed over the appropriate militancy of strike tactics, and labor-backed party leaders further disagreed about the benefits of the American alliance for the exports of their industries and for foreign markets generally.

Politics then faced upheaval after a key strike failed and the United States–Japan Security Treaty passed the National Assembly. The unions and leftist parties split, and the alliance thereafter lost salience as a key factor in politics. At the same time, bureaucrats-turned-politicians suffered a decline in stature after the resignation of the prime minister, Kishi Nobusuke. Nonetheless, bureaucrats still dominated within the ruling LDP, especially as the decade brought a gradual transition in the politics associated with rapid rates of economic growth. In broad terms, the postwar era of bureaucratic dominance managed to last a further decade, due largely to the momentum of this growth.

In 1973, however, a period of true crisis brought new forms of intervention by party politicians—along with mixed governance to the political order. In the 1970s, the shifting social base of the ruling-party coalition faced erosion and the need for reconstruction. In particular, the rise of small parties as intermediaries, championing new approaches to the environment and social welfare, meant that the ruling LDP faced a challenge. A politician not of the common strain of bureaucratic elites, Tanaka Kakuei,[6] was able to meet this political challenge by staking out new positions and by recruiting new groups to the ruling-party coalition. Using a combination of opportunism, money, and genius in the budget process, Tanaka urged the ruling party to adapt its positions to attract young families, retirees, rural residents, and union members through his welfare and public-works programs. As a result, the Liberal Democrats were able to undermine and preempt other intermediaries.

International structures reinforce the characterization of 1973 as the key benchmark year of domestic change in Japan. America under Nixon began to leave Vietnam, moved to achieve economic recovery, encouraged flexible exchange rates, and recognized China without warning Japan. After 1973, Japan also went through the empowerment of big business, a period of inflation, a controversial railroad strike, and overall economic restructuring that showed the vulnerabilities of domestic and international polices. An attempt was made to form a moderate centrist party known as the New Liberal Club, and though that party failed due to financial and competitive strains, its politicians would be absorbed into the Liberal Democrats. As a result, Japan had continuous rule by a single party as the critical means of intermediation in politics, one that expanded to provide available channels for specialist politicians, deliberative councils, and media reporting as well.

Mixed governance in the 1980s, in turn, led to a steady recovery of stability in the Japanese political order. In this process, the second oil crisis of 1979 became a test of that stability, a test made worse by electoral losses of the Liberal Democrats after Prime Minister Ohira announced tax measures. This test nevertheless elicited quick adjustment from the economy, new prominence for white-collar groups and unions in technology and services, and a resurgence by the Liberal Democrats in the 1980 elections. After 1980, the conservative resurgence was strengthened through a factional coalition between leaders Tanaka Kakuei and Nakasone Yasuhiro, particularly when Nakasone moved to use his post to advance popular policies for international assertiveness and domestic administrative reform.

In the realm of international prominence, Nakasone asserted that Japan was an unsinkable aircraft carrier for the West *and* that Japan spoke for all Asia within the G-7 summit meetings of leading economic nations. In the realm of domestic reform, Nakasone faced the diagnostic policy challenge for this period with publication of the report of "Rincho," or a committee on administrative reform under the prime minster. The implementation of these 1983 reforms was to have lasting implications for social cleavages, by privatizing the large and highly unionized telecommunications and railway industries and by dividing the militant railworkers into unions under smaller regional rail companies that had to face market forces.

In the 1990s, Japan's form of mixed governance faced another incipiently critical test during the 1990–91 Gulf War. Within the political structures of the postwar order, a consensual assumption about constitutional limits on military power had long underlain the positions of various social groups, political parties, and even the bureaucracy. Fresh conflicts, even including a gender gap, emerged during the debates about a Japanese response to U.N. resolutions condemning Iraq. The leftist parties repeated their 1960 debates about foreign wars, while divisions between doves and hawks within the ruling LDP increased tensions over the future of the Japanese military. The bureaucracy was also an unspoken critic of military contributions because of latent fears of the military-industrial complex that might arise if the Japanese military was made a fully empowered cabinet participant. The difficulty, however, was that external international structures after the end of the Bretton Woods system and of the Cold War had drawn Japan fully into debates about the international political order.

To clarify this analysis of Japan's postwar history, five realms of political structure can be used to provide a broad chronology for postwar politics (see table 7.2). These structural realms underpin the political orders;

Table 7.2.   Years of Major Change in Political Structures

Benchmark Years	Political Structure				
	Governmental Bureaucracy	Political Parties	Social Cleavages	International Economics[a]	International Security[b]
1952	1952	1948–55	1947–55	1949	1948
1960	1960	1960	1959–60	1960	1960
1973	1973	1974	1972–75	1973	1972
1983	1983	1980–83	1982–86	1979–80	1980–83
1991	1989–92	1991–92	1989–93	1985	1991–92

NOTE: The most prominent benchmark year for Japan is 1973.
[a]The specific embodiment is the Bretton-Woods system.
[b]As determined by Cold War imperatives.

their changes underscore the process of transition that best accounts for standard histories. The dates of key changes in each of these five areas serve to identify assembled periods, the eras brought about by adaptive steps. The following discussion draws on the general framework of these key political structures, both domestic and international, that marked postwar political transitions in Japan. Table 7.2 reveals several periods when change occurred across areas of political structure and several common years that mark the periods of change.

The Era of Bureaucratic Dominance

The National Bureaucracy and the Postwar Period

With the end of the Occupation and the return of sovereignty, Japanese national bureaucrats possessed certain natural advantages in seizing prerogatives within the postwar political environment. Political parties saw five years of stormy competition during the Occupation but failed to establish a strong precedent for their influence. Organized interests moved to articulate new demands, with half of the workforce in unions and bank-based industrial groups seeking to set new plans. The contours imposed by American-backed economic stability packages and by the nascent Cold War set outside parameters on any new political order. Yet of all the areas of political structure likely to form a basis for stability, the national bureaucracy emerged as the critical feature of an incipient postwar order.

During the immediate postwar years, bureaucrats maintained a degree of legitimacy and took responsibility for assuring stability. There was more to government, of course, than the national bureaucracy, but the

Japanese bureaucratic traditions were well established, bureaucrats suffered few purges during the Occupation, and they maintained integrated organizations. All officials faced threats from the postwar purges, which meant that anyone identified by the Occupation as a wartime collaborator could be banned from his job and perhaps jailed. From 1945, party politics were in turmoil, so much so that from 1947, bureaucrats were even recruited into parties—leading to the rise of the bureaucrats-turned-politicians who then dominated politics through the 1960s.

In advanced industrial democracies, debate continues about the power and effectiveness of national bureaucrats. For Europeans, the power of the state is not baffling—the questions that remain are about the goals of power. Among citizens of the United States, however, with liberal traditions seeking to limit state power and deny bureaucratic discretion, questions arise both about the power itself and about its ends.[7] Japan thus represents a double challenge, both to arguments about economic competitiveness among theorists in Europe and to traditional assumptions of liberals in America.

National bureaucrats are not solely responsible for Japanese economic success through its "developmental state."[8] Indeed, scholars increasingly criticize strict attention to bureaucratic leadership because Japanese industrial policy had more mixed results than many at first assumed. Moreover, bureaucrats negotiated closely with private-sector bankers and industrial-group managers, who were just as critical for economic recovery.[9] The overall conclusions about the bureaucratic context for economic success, however, feature at least an agreement among most scholars that bureaucrats formed a skillful consensus in Japanese business-government relations. Japan began the postwar period as a defeated and devastated country, yet officials forged a clear set of goals for recovery, and Japanese public policy for economic growth had many positive impacts upon the economic miracle.

Bureaucratic dominance is a reasonable way to understand the immediate postwar rule of Japan. During the postwar Occupation, bureaucrats had the muscle both to purge Communist militants from labor unions and to apply monetary controls through the U.S.-sponsored economic reforms known as the Dodge Line. The best confirmatory evidence, however, emerges after the end of Occupation in 1952. With the return of sovereignty, officials in the Ministry of Finance created rules for highly regulated banking and strict control of foreign exchange. Bureaucrats in the Ministry of International Trade and Industry (MITI) were also especially keen to provide administrative guidance to nurture sunrise industries. At least until the ruling-party leaders sustained their challenges, bureaucrats kept a national polity intact through the start of bipolar party politics in 1955 and the later split of leftist parties after 1960.

By comparison to their European counterparts, Japanese bureaucrats also appeared relatively efficient. T. J. Pempel has made three points about this efficiency.[10] First, Japanese bureaucrats avoided the problem of "reds versus experts." They were neither too political in their use of patronage systems nor too apolitical in rewarding only technical merit based on efficiency. Second, Japanese officials avoided the extremes of being either "drones or queen bees." They were not unthinking, in hives or cells of activity, but they were not entrenched as leaders, instead transferring among posts to share a collective mission. Third, Japanese bureaucracy largely avoided the traps of "subgovernment." That is, they avoided a focus on protecting their own turf at the cost of compromising national interests.

The Japanese bureaucracy also allowed class mobility. A wide public perception remains that anyone can work his way through school into the bureaucratic elite. Of course, candidates cannot fail to get into the best high schools or fail on college entrance exams. Meritocracies leading to the bureaucracy draw on precedents from China and the Chinese examination system, as well as other places where student futures depend on entrance tests. The civil service exams are a key feature that preserves this meritocracy as a final step for entering the Japanese elite. In Japan, the bureaucracy thus combines a tradition of elitism with the modern legitimacy and acceptability of examination systems.

The bureaucrats in Japan have been at the very least a further linchpin for the support of one-party dominance, coalition building, and overall political stability. In this, there is an ironic link in ideas about national bureaucrats in Japan with the views of revisionists in Japanese studies. Revisionist writers criticize past studies of Japan, yet they share a central mission: to employ Japanese ideas about industrial policy and to emulate Japanese economic performance in foreign countries.[11] Studies of Japanese political economy and public policy now focus not on whether bureaucrats matter but rather on what, specifically, these bureaucrats do. In analytical terms, institutional studies of bureaucracy have moved from questions of autonomy to those of capacity. What Japanese bureaucrats did, in this regard, was to mobilize a full array of political actors to achieve economic success and political stability.

Structural Intermediaries in Postwar Politics

If the larger half of an explanation for the rise of the national bureaucracy in the first postwar era of Japanese politics is provided by the historical evolution of that bureaucracy itself and by the situation it encountered in the years after 1945, the other half is inevitably provinced by the situation of the main potential alternative engines for a postwar political dynamic. Indeed, the transition to a second postwar era, when it came, would consist essentially of a rebalancing in relations of influence between the rational bureaucracy and these alternatives. Interest groups, but especially political parties, are crucial to this balance (and rebalance), as are the social cleavages underneath them.

From 1955 to 1960, Japanese parties were organized in a predominant-party system. Giovanni Sartori categorizes party systems by reference to their noncompetitive and competitive aspects: noncompetitive refers largely to one-party systems of the Communist world, while competitive systems differ over their extent of pluralism and polarity.[12] Polarized pluralism, as in the Weimar Republic or Chile before 1973, was actually close to the pre-1955 system in Japan, with anti-state opposition parties and little interaction among different party leaders. Sartori also categorizes two-party systems, as in the United States, Great Britain until 1981, and even Japan from 1955 to 1960, when the conservatives and socialist opposition were more evenly matched. In retrospect, however, the category of *predominant-party system* best applies to postwar Japan, with a hegemonic ruling party and an opposition in a "permanent" position outside of government.

Scholars of Japan identify this party arrangement as the "1955 System." In 1955, conservative parties formed a coalition under the LDP and elected their party president as prime minister thereafter. The longevity of LDP rule led Robert Scalapino and Seizaburo Sato to call the Japanese party arrangement a "one-and-a-half party system" because of the permanence of the opposition.[13] More recently, a comparative project placed Japan alongside Sweden, Israel, and Italy as an "uncommon democracy," which faced specific fallout for governance and policy from long-standing one-party dominance.[14] Japanese scholars, however, tend to prefer the term "1955 System," to emphasize the formation of the arrangement of parties specific to Japan.

Nevertheless, the history of parties since 1955 has hardly lacked development. Gerald Curtis writes on thee phases of LDP rule: a two-party polarized-pluralist phase; a split of the progressive opposition after 1960; and a rise of new parties winning over a third of the vote by 1976.[15] In this progression of voter disillusionment with the leading parties, alternative organizations have increased, and they have brought about at least a new phase with the loss of a parliamentary majority of the LDP in July of 1993. But before that, these various earlier phases demand a fuller explanation.

In 1960, bureaucratic and party politics underwent a crisis focused on both economic and security issues. The central debate about the "1960 Security Treaty" with the United States divided Japanese public perceptions about the Cold War. Many Japanese felt that American ties would eventually draw the country into a genuine war, yet the bureaucratic and ruling LDP government position favored an alliance with the West. The debate also placed particular attention on Prime Minister Kishi Nobusuke.

Kishi was the quintessential bureaucrat-turned-politician, who had even been purged as a war criminal and rejoined party politics as a conservative leader. For the left, Kishi came to symbolize the old imperial official, the wartime collaborator, and the undemocratic forces of Japanese government. When Kishi rammed his treaty bill through the National Assembly with no opposition debate, Tokyo was the scene of huge demonstrations and even a death among protestors. The crisis was further fueled by clashes over leftist union responses to the militant Miike coal strike and the defection of Socialist moderates into a new Democratic Socialist party that supported the 1960 Security Treaty.

After 1960, smaller parties emerged but remained difficult to characterize. The religious party, Komeito, is an example of this multiparty splintering. This centrist religious party has many undefined views and draws on the roughly 6.5 million members of the Sokagakkai religious organization to recruit party members. Over half are women, though the party leaders are usually men. The party is controversial: in 1969, Komeito tried to stop publication of a book about the party written by a political scientist.[16] The effort was very unpopular, was condemned as undemocratic, was disliked by other parties, and led ultimately to a decline in support for Komeito itself.

Similarly, the Japan Communist Party (JCP) never overcame an early association with Stalin. The JCP was first legalized after the war, but suffered from ambiguity in its position toward Beijing and Moscow. The Communists were more popular in the 1960s as a protest party backing welfare and environmental issues and gained an ideology that attracts individual thinkers in Japan. Seen as the "happy party," the JCP achieved success in local coalitions, winning mayoral or local assembly seats. The main appeal of the party was generated by the quality of JCP publications and by the party's stance of nonconformity, and not because the JCP offered any viable hope of taking power or implementing political reforms. After the Cold War, the Communists encountered widespread disillusionment, limiting their efforts to achieve broad appeal among the public.

The larger Nihon Shakaito, the single biggest opposition party for most of the postwar years, actually changed its English name from the more accurate Japan Socialist Party to the Social Democratic Party of

Japan (SDPJ). Even this cosmetic move, however, did little to increase popular acceptance, as evidenced by repeated defeats. A victory in the 1989 House of Councilors elections did give the leftist parties a three-year majority coalition in the weaker chamber of the Parliament. Socialist Chairwoman Takako Doi then managed to raise the profile of her party, but she lost the party leadership after defeat in a House of Representatives election of 1990. The lonc Socialist victory was then further diminished in the 1992 elections to the House of Councilors and in the 1993 July elections to the House of Representatives. By 1993, the SDPJ had only seventy seats in the powerful lower house, compared to fifty-five for Komeito and close to fifty seats for each of the other conservative opposition parties.

By far the largest of the organized interest groups not primarily attached to the ruling LDP coalition has been organized labor. Yet in the postwar period, labor-based opposition groups have fragmented and declined rather than consolidating the left. In 1947, over half of the workforce was organized in unions, but this figure has since dropped steadily. Divisions began over international politics in the 1960 debate over the Security Treaty; they then extended to specific views about militant tactics and strikes. In 1991, by way of comparison, Britain still had 44.4 percent unionization, compared with just 24.5 percent for Japan. Ties to political parties also splintered, between public-sector unions that largely backed thc Socialist mainstream and private-sector unions that preferred the moderate Democratic Socialists. The extent of the overall decline is suggested by the fact that the 1987–88 consolidation of Japanese unions into a single federation (known as Rengo) has yet to help the leftist parties win favor.

Institutional Underpinning for One-Party Dominance

In Japan, the electoral system itself has effectively worked to favor one-party dominance. Indeed, the rules of the game are open to the criticism that they have operated to preserve *specific* rule by the LDP.[17] In fall of 1993, electoral reform thus became the top issue of a new (opposition) coalition government, and rule changes creating new single-member districts were implemented on Christmas day in 1994. Elections using this reform of electoral rules mark the first major change since 1925 and run parallel to reform of elections in Italy. In Japan as in Italy, prior electoral arrangements actually forced debate away from policy issues. But especially in Japan, individual candidates were often forced to respond to these electoral rules, and to district needs, in ways that moved debate toward their personal abilities to provide constituency service. The relevant features in Japan that merit attention are multimember districts and malapportionment, especially in their interaction with party factions.

An exceptional feature of Japanese parliamentary politics has been the multimember district. In these electoral districts, created in 1925, *two to six seats* were at stake, and every voter cast *just one vote* for a single name (uninomial voting). A political party that sought to form the government obviously needed to offer more than one candidate in these districts, and such a party also needed to mobilize specific groups within each. The LDP, in particular, competed principally on service rather than policy because several same-party candidates had to stand for election under its banner. In turn, each candidate had to build the support of a *koenkai* or "individual support group" and spend an enormous amount of money for services to individual supporters. Multimember districts emphasized the financial backing of these individual support groups, producing tremendous sums of money to assure constituent service. They also produced the repeated scandals that regularly shook the Japanese political scene.

Beyond that, malapportionment in districts drawn in 1925 meant that rural and center-city areas were (and are) overrepresented. Populations moved from the countryside when business concentrated in large cities such as Tokyo and Osaka, and later to the suburbs as housing stock developed. The weight of a vote now measures about six-to-one when comparing those around Tokyo with the southern Kyushu countryside. Despite repeated court challenges, the legislature has changed only the overall number of seats available in some rural areas and shifted them to urban areas. Again, the LDP has been the party best favored by the conservative countryside and the one least able to embrace substantial reform of election rules or districts.

Finally, continuing factions resulted form the long-standing arrangements that institutionalized rule by the Liberal Democrats. In turn, institutionalized factions allowed the conservatives to act *within the party* to select a prime minister, to distribute cabinet and party positions, to raise campaign funds, and to recruit additional candidates to join the factions. Except in 1947–48, the election of a party president of the ruling Liberal Democrats meant that the winner automatically became prime minister. Factions then followed the *party* rules that led to the selection of Japan's leader.

This selection process long had the following priorities. First, negotiations resulted among LDP faction heads, a process known as *hanasiai,* or "talking among the leaders." Second, elections were held within the party, which most recently involved a combination of elected National

Assembly members and regional party members. Then finally, an election might result in the National Assembly, under the formal means provided by the constitution. In the last twenty years, LDP elections seldom had any true contest, and there *has never been* a true election in the National Assembly—until August of 1993. The factions and parties preferred to negotiate about the next prime minister and divide the spoils of cabinet and key party posts on the basis of factional representation. This faction-based process ultimately underwent critical attack from splits in the LDP and from the threat of opposition coalition-building.

At the level of the individual National Assembly member, factions and their leaders reached out to nurture the support needed to rule as prime minister. National Assembly members were attached in various ways to increase the size of a faction, especially through the lure of key cabinet and party positions. Such positions provided the divisible benefits and symbolic status that voters respect in home districts. But in the multimember districts where LDP candidates could be pitted against each other, the funding of an individual support base was still critical. The faction raised campaign funds, identified likely candidates in the districts, and assured that the party headquarters recognized the new recruits. This faction-based system became highly routinized over time and remains a barrier to reform of politics, of electoral practices, and of the multimember district system. Factions were remarkably durable under the postwar system and have yet to be completely abandoned, despite widespread unpopularity among the general public.

The postwar social cleavages beneath this party system, and especially the cleavages relevant to the LDP, were initially bridged by a key coalition of groups from business and farming. Drawing on Gershenkron's work on Germany, T. J. Pempel has asserted that "marriage of iron and rice" was the explicit basis for Japan's early postwar coalition.[18] Japanese industrialists and farmers supported the conservative LDP, which acted as the intermediary in an exchange of specific policy benefits to both coalition partners. The industrialists nurtured economic competitiveness, and the farmers gained a protected rice market and high subsidies for controlled prices.

Kent Calder has claimed that the formation of these postwar Japanese coalitions resulted as well from a dynamic of "crisis and compensation."[19] Calder argues that with the rise of political crises in Japan, the ruling coalition reliably moved to provide compensation through domestic policies that met the demands of additional organized groups. When crises began, Japanese rulers approved these new compensatory measures in order to gain broader support for their coalition and to overcome the particular problem, thereby producing a ratchet effect in public policies outside of industrial or market-based sectors. During postwar economic growth, Japanese leaders thus moved to cover the gaps among shifting social cleavages. Because of the expanding economic pie, groups making vocal demands received compensation, not only in periods of crisis but also through periods of incremental change.

The national bureaucracy hardly governed unchallenged, even in its heyday. Japanese citizens at times perceived the bureaucracy as threatening to democracy and to their liberties. As early as the late nineteenth century, political parties arose under the 1890 "Meiji Constitution" to challenge imperial officials, and these parties did exercise budgetary powers . Though socialist or communist groups were banned, the parties legally allowed in the Japanese National Assembly did use parliamentary politics to seek redistribution of public works to the countryside and to criticize military rule. During wartime, the parties neither disbanded nor confronted the military openly. Various other intermediaries arose: labor unions, private schools, religious groups, business associations, and veterans groups. But the political parties were explicitly related to government and provided the focus for likely opposition.

Not until after 1945, however, did the parties even begin to prove a viable alternative that could potentially find a role in policymaking or name assertive leaders. Yet within government, Japanese leaders gradually faced the ineluctable changes in the structure of society and of its intermediaries that resulted from economic recovery. As a further result, if the immediate postwar years can be characterized by the centrality of bureaucracy, then later periods are marked by consistent challenges from a series of alternative intermediary organizations, culminating recently in coalition government. Indeed, over time, the national bureaucracy faced a decline in its prerogatives along with these increased challenges to its preeminence in the political order.

This rise of other political intermediaries led, perhaps inevitably, to a decline of bureaucratic dominance. One reason for the appeal of the Japanese Communist Party, for example, is its constant criticism of the bureaucrats and their government. The JCP has been consistent in its equation of the heavy-handed imperial state official with the postwar bureaucrat, willing to justify strong policies for the good of "Our Country" (*wagakuni*). The JCP, nevertheless, suffers from its foreign policies and from a lack of pragmatism. As a result, over time, many Japanese responded to postwar conservative government by seeking new and different intermediaries and other means of expressing their political demands.

The Era of Mixed Governance

Change in a One-Party Dominant System

In 1972–73, a challenge of a different sort arose, one sufficient to disrupt bureaucratic centrality in a lasting fashion, with the election of Tanaka Kakuei. Tanaka challenged bureaucratic dominance on many levels by building his LDP faction without regard to the (elite) origins of members as bureaucrats or university graduates. Tanaka then challenged Fukada Takeo for party leadership, defeating Fukuda, the bureaucrat-turned-politician, in a dramatic party election. As prime minister in 1973, Tanaka changed the bureaucrat-centered budget process by securing his demands for new programs in welfare and public works. With the additional onset of the oil crisis and the so-called "Nixon Shocks," Japanese politics experienced a genuine benchmark year. These major party changes were combined with 34 percent inflation from oil prices, with floating exchange rates, with embargo of American crops such as soybeans, and with the recognition of China. Nonetheless, the ruling party managed to avoid defeat, through Tanaka's policy adaptations to the changed realities facing his party.

The Liberal Democrats still benefited from the rules generally, including their rigid districts, poor apportionment, and institutionalized factions, though this situation has also led to a series of scandals involving huge sums of money. Indeed, Prime Minister Tanaka Kakuei himself was ultimately among the most prominent of postwar leaders to face indictment, for his role in the Lockheed Scandal of influence peddling. The most recent example, from 1992–93, is the Sagawa Kyubin affair, following in rapid succession upon recent Recruit and Kyowa stock scandals. In September of 1992, Niigata Governor Kiyoshi Kaneko resigned, following the August 27 resignation of Kanemaru Shin from the posts of LDP vice-president and leading figure of the largest LDP faction. This time, public criticism of Kanemaru did not actually stop until he had resigned from the Japanese National Assembly. Then on 6 March 1993 the scandal climaxed when the seventy-nine-year-old Kanemaru and his secretary were arrested for tax evasion on personal income of ¥200 million ($1.7 million) and various holdings of up to $34 million.[20]

Despite such scandals, the ruling LDP was sustained by the lack of a viable opposition, by a strong party organization of its own, and by conscious avoidance of divisions within factions. During 1992–93, the LDP remained the largest party after fresh elections, despite public opinion polls showing just 10 percent support for the Miyazawa cabinets. There is thus an especial irony in the fact that a division within the faction built by

Tanaka and Kanemaru would ultimately trigger the loss of a LDP majority and the reform of electoral politics. Indeed, a protege of Kanemaru, Ozawa Ichiro, would eventually leave the faction and engineer a coalition capable of creating the largest shift in postwar party politics.

The Japanese party system and its politics have been categorized as those of an "uncommon democracy." In postwar Japan, more than party politics has been made distinctive by this one-party dominance. T. J. Pempel compares several cases of similar party politics and identifies single parties that dominate in seats, bargaining, time, and governing.[21] One-party dominance in Sweden, Israel, Italy, and Japan shares several common traits, such as multiple-party systems, historical cycles of dominance that consolidate single-party control, as well as long-term fallout from political control under a predominant party. The last two of these cases, Japan and Italy, are additionally related, as examples of dominance by conservative parties.

In Japan under a one-party dominant regime, the party system creates "legacies" for policy processes. In the vocabulary often used with one-party dominance, the cycle and consequences of dominance influence later public policies. For example, in the emergence of national health insurance in Japan, the 1959–60 political crisis for the ruling party produced universal insurance that met demands of business groups and organized physicians.[22] In the prominence of old-age pensions in Italy, efforts made in the 1960s and 1970s by the Christian Democrats to maintain their dominance led to increasing fiscal deficits and economic disruption.[23] In the results for social-welfare policies, Japan and Italy thus offer instances of one-party dominance where the conservatives dominated the party system, pursued specific but limited welfare measures, and encouraged programs for social insurance that gave benefits to employees rather than citizens as a whole. The legacies continue, as political reform only begins to touch the structural underpinnings of one-party rule.

The policy process under one-party rule in Japan developed other intermediaries as well, in the form of deliberative councils and of specialist politicians. The deliberative councils were created by bureaucrats to seek a range of opinions during policymaking. These councils allow for a range of articulated demands, although critics charge that members are either co-opted or ignored by the bureaucracies that create them. As another intermediary, the specialist politicians (*zoku*) at times even aligned with strong coalitions to challenge party leaders. Recent studies confirm that cliques of specialists among LDP members intervened for organized interests across areas of education and welfare.[24]

However, the policy coalitions and their supporters among politicians were not always successful at blocking the leadership politicians in major administrative reforms. The party leadership intervenes mainly on major disputes and within specific limits, while the policy coalitions and their *zoku* supporters exercise significant influence over regular processes of budgeting and over incremental reform of domestic policies. Furthermore, the requirements of coalition government and opposition involvement in policymaking promise to overshadow the institutionalized roles of the ruling-party specialists.

Among other intermediaries, the media often serve both to gauge criticism and to solicit support for Japanese government. The print media long played the part of the honorable opposition, with newspapers and weekly magazines willing to publish critics. In the postwar period these newspapers ranged in political position from the *Sankei* and *Yomiuri* on the right to the *Asahi* and *Akahata* on the left, though these papers are less easily distinguished by their political stance at present. Similarly, the weekly magazines published explosive articles and investigative journalism, sometimes under aliases.

If there has been further change over time, it is in the way that television has come to occupy an aggressive and intrusive role in political debate. For example, the Sunday morning news programs and late-night investigative-report shows frequently introduce political controversy and interrogate leading politicians. A widespread disillusionment with politicians, a demand for generational change among political leaders, and the continued call for political reform stem partly from the commentators and critics who work in the media as a profession.

Changing Social Cleavages: After the Marriage of Iron and Rice

At the social base for Japanese politics, one-party dominance with prolonged conservative rule gradually changed the coalitions supporting public policies. In the first postwar era, the construction of a marriage of iron and rice was central to creating this one-party dominance. But in the course of that era, conservative dominance in turn began to cause a shift in the social coalitions beneath it. Once consequence was the splintering of the social coalition of leftist parties backed by organized labor and related interest groups. Michio Muramatsu and Ellis S. Krauss argue that, by the 1970s, Japan's ruling LDP had in effect expanded and solidified an alternative coalition of interests supporting conservative rule.

This coalition allowed partial incorporation of opposition interest groups, thereby serving to continue one-party dominance.[25] On specific issues, shifts in parliamentary strategy and party appeals were also critical to sustaining LDP rule through direct support from Japanese voters.[26] But these changes to sustain one-party dominance hinged on specific steps that adapted ruling-party positions. In 1973, for example, Prime Minster Tanaka Kakuei symbolized the critical changes that reformed Japanese politics into an era of mixed governance. If Kishi marked the decline of bureaucratic centrality, then Tanaka marked the rise of political intervention in governance.

Tanaka was the opposite of a bureaucratic imperial elitist, being a self-made businessman who asserted extraordinary controls over the budgetary and policy responses of the Japanese government. Tanaka used money to influence opponents, not just his supporters in the largest of the ruling LDP factions. In 1973, Tanaka exercised his power by shifting the budgetary process to begin child allowances, free medical care for the elderly, bigger retirement pensions, and new programs for farmers. Despite the oil crisis, Tanaka held his ground as inflation increased during the next year, imposing a cost on the economy but providing a credit to the politics of the expanded LDP coalition.

Comparativists regularly wonder about the failures of the opposition to challenge rulers and to resolve ideological differences over strategy and tactics. To venture even a tentative answer to such questions would require massive extrapolation, yet one point can be made about the ideological division between leftist opposition and centrist moderates in Japan.[27] On the one hand, the Left was pulled by the Communists, who drew on an old debate by one faction (*koza-ha*) that argued that a distinct Japanese emperor system exists, one which demands constant criticism and resistance. On the other hand, the centrists asserted that Japan was essentially capitalist, much like Europe and America (*rono-ha*), and that unionism could make gains for the workers through social-democratic unions and/ or political organizing.

Such short synopses hide great complexity about changing positions on world politics, about Stalinism, Maoism, an American alliance, and domestic tactics, all of which frustrated the Left in Japan. In any case, such frustrations splintered the opposition, distracted their debates from dealing with practical appeals to the immediate interests of Japanese voters, and sustained an electoral system favoring one-party rule, which only recently faced challenge from splintering *conservative* groups.

The societal base for political parties was simultaneously shifting further. Populations migrated to cities and left their elderly in the countryside; inner cities then lost residents to suburban areas; women who went back to work and faced new conflicts in caring for families now concentrated in the suburbs. Groups that articulated these shifting interests inevitably faced difficulties in adapting their positions. In short, coalitions demanding intermediation changed because the basic social cleavages among societal groups changed as well.

Several interpretations compete to account for the changing social cleavages that undermined the earlier marriage of iron and rice. First, some Japanese scholars assert that networks link their homogeneous society. These scholars argue that a "new middle mass" blurred distinctions among Japanese through a relatively balanced income distribution. These interpretations argue that conflict is minimal for reasons of culture, economic equality, or political organization; the combination of history, culture, and politics produces a "network society" that makes Japan the least conflictual and most stable for purposes of economic efficiency.[28] Yet these views are vulnerable to critics focusing upon periodic protests, political scandals, and economic downturns.

A different interpretation, closer to Calder's views about crisis and compensation, finds that policymaking linked groups via a compensation that redistributed income despite continuing differences of *interest*. In this, the policymaking of the 1970s and 1980s urged continuation of social and international programs that proved increasingly popular. A key result during the 1980s was the shift of younger voters toward the LDP. Japanese analysts credit former Prime Minister Nakasone Yasuhiro with articulating a sense of national pride and attracting youthful supporters through stable policies. Whether Japanese leaders will manage the balance across continuing cleavages within society remains uncertain, particularly as economic growth slows and limits the rapid pace of expanding economic opportunity. Yet this view does not explain the failures of the Liberal Democrats to preserve their unity in 1993.

A third interpretation resonates with the classic debates about realignment and partisanship that suggest voting behavior more akin to other nations. Though few scholars foresee realignment, the weakness of party affiliation increases volatility in any given election. In a large study, the authors of *The Japanese Voter* argued that partisan affiliations were far more important than previously thought.[29] These political scientists advanced the concept of "cognitive partisans" to account for Japanese citizens who were not active supporters but still identified with party images. This evidence of party identification, coupled with continuing survey results about dissatisfaction with election practices, fuels debates about possibilities for shifts in voter preferences, should political reform attack the structural bases of past stability. In these debates, the notions of dealignment or of cognitive partisans seek to explain voter perceptions that consistently return the Liberal Democrats to power despite their weak performance in opinion polls. Yet such interpretations do not explain the *structures* that limit voters' choices, structures that led to a limited change toward new conservative parties in the 1990s and yet assure relative stability in the political order.

A fourth view stresses that party dominance depends upon the factors of economic performance and strong bureaucracy. In an essay in *Uncommon Democracies,* Takashi Inoguchi emphasizes that the differences between Japan and other cases of one-party dominance hinge strongly on the context of issues that support successful intermediation by the ruling party.[30] The context of economic growth and bureaucratic activities meant that the ruling Liberal Democrats had greater opportunities to respond than elsewhere. The importance of this last interpretation is additionally resonant with *current* economic, bureaucratic, and political conditions in Japan: a prolonged structural recession, administrative inflexibility due to constraints of international openness, and scandal-filled party politics makes even Japanese one-party dominance look increasingly tentative.

Japan's intermediaries must now cope with underlying social and international change. Secured neither by the independent abilities of political parties alone, nor or by any combination of intermediary factors, the Japanese political order seems increasingly fragile in the face of sluggish growth, administrative problems, and political shifts. Two fundamental international changes face the domestic political order as a whole. These two changes are not "outside issues," but rather are fundamental structural shifts that penetrate the politics of all G-7 nations, namely, the economic structures of Bretton Woods and the security structures of the Cold War. Both have ended, and with these changes of international structure moving from outside to within the basic composition of the political economies of leading nations, Japan and its G-7 partners must make choices about the structural shifts facing their political orders.

External Shifts and Internal Adjustments: A Third Era?

Economic Changes from Bretton Woods through the Plaza Accords

Analysts of the success of the Japanese economy give major credit to postwar institutions that provided stability under the Bretton Woods system. Though the conference at Bretton Woods took place in 1944, American leadership was not fully established until the start of the Marshall Plan in Europe in 1948. Inside Japan, the specific steps taken by the American Occupation were also somewhat inconsistent and resulted in economic turmoil through 1948. Only then did Japan's "Economic Stabilization Program" (*keizai antei kyugensoku*) introduce fiscal, monetary, price, and wage controls.

From 1949 to 1951, an American banker named Joseph Dodge acted as a special adviser to implement what became known as the "Dodge

Line" of economic reforms. These reforms gave bureaucrats a strict regime for international economic policy. The finance bureaucrats kept controls on foreign exchange and foreign investment, while the trade bureaucrats managed microeconomic decisions to protect infant industries, shield markets against imports, and nurture export expansion. Therefore, the Japanese economic miracle became well institutionalized. Until the late 1960s, the bureaucrats and businessmen overcame many challenges in adopting their division of labor to modern markets and to an export orientation.

Nevertheless, domestic Japanese interests had strong reasons for wishing to escape from bureaucratic control and excessive protection. Evidence exists of the early moves of corporate actors to invest in overseas financial markets and to seek outside partners. In 1968, the Mitsubishi-Chrysler deal marked the beginning of the end of bureaucratic controls, along with the rise of transnational liberalization for Japanese business.[31] Corporate interests also led to trade imbalances over many years, with textiles as a prominent imbalance with the United States. Foreign interests then demanded that Japanese bureaucrats lessen trade imbalances and remove foreign exchange controls. In 1974, Japan floated the yen.

From 1971 to 1974, a series of economic shocks hit Japan. The fixed-rate regime of 1948–1971 pegged the yen at ¥360 to the dollar. (Note that the rate was below ¥80 briefly in April of 1995). Though the Japanese bureaucrats lost much clout, the ending of other controls from Bretton Woods were favored by Japanese business as much as by the United States and other economic observers. The mutual interests of these parties are often lost in analyses of public policies or hegemonic stability. The extent of Japanese economic shocks is also often underappreciated—an oil embargo, American agricultural embargo, and exchange rate shifts combined to force 34 percent inflation in 1974. The political disruptions of the early 1970s tested political moderates in the LDP and forced compromises over key economic policies.

Following the second oil crisis in 1979, Japan's strong economic recovery culminated in the Plaza Accords of 1985. The Plaza Accords confirmed that Japanese economic management by bureaucrat and businessman was now congruent with the notion that growth requires international interdependence. The most concrete form of this congruence includes both macroeconomic coordination and exchange-rate adjustments. On the former, the Plaza Accords proved less able to force fiscal and monetary policy-coordination, particularly due to the American budget deficits. On the latter, however, the meetings encouraged discussions of target zones and central bank intervention to influence exchange rates. Following the Plaza Accords, the Japanese yen moved against the U.S. dollar from its 1985 low of ¥263.65 to a 1986 high of ¥152.55.[32] This radical shift in exchange rates began a restructuring of the domestic economy and a surge in Japanese overseas investment.

The Plaza Accords also implicitly recognized Japan as a worldwide economic leader. On the one hand, in Asia, the bureaucrats of MITI advance a vision of flying geese in the Pacific Basin, with Japanese industry in the lead and other countries exercising their comparative advantages. This vision places Japan permanently at the head of the economic grouping and leaves other countries trailing in their technologies and abilities to provide high-value-added products. On the other hand, throughout the world, Japanese oligopolists face mounting competition overseas for investment and trade opportunities, competition that pits America, Japan, and others against one another.[33] Indeed, scholars argue that the hidden story of the Plaza Accords is the race for investment in Southeast Asia, not only by Japan but also by investors in Asian Newly Industrializing Economies (NIEs), from Korea, Taiwan, and overseas Chinese communities that rival the increases from the Japanese in Asia.

Security Changes in the Cold War Alliance with the United States

Whichever scenario emerges in the future, Japan as well as all countries of the Pacific Basin are still guarded by the U.S. Pacific Fleet. Stability in the region thus hinges on the key security alliance between Japan and the United States. Political concerns about the Cold War, however, were constant themes in Japanese politics. For security, the Cold War thrust Japanese leaders into an alliance with the United States that has prevailed for almost half a century. Especially after 1960, Japanese priorities turned to economics rather than world politics. These themes are critical issues in the overall trends of Japanese political history, and they project a new course for the second largest economy in the world into the twenty-first century.

From 1945, Japanese politicians coped with the external realities of the Cold War. Japanese leaders faced external dangers from the Soviet Union, from the Korean Peninsula, and from China, and they faced them with the backing of American troops. In effect, the American nuclear umbrella gave Japanese leaders the ability to avoid security entanglements. Simultaneously, Japan overcame internal political divisions about Cold War choices through what is known as the "Yoshida Doctrine," named after the first postwar prime minister, Yoshida Shigeru, who sought an adaptive position in order to maximize Japanese autonomy, aimed at recovery and at a return to sovereignty.

During the period from 1947 to 1954, conservatives developed the mechanism of leaving high politics to the Americans, first to General

Douglas MacArthur and later to the executives that followed, and thus assured that adaptive politics dominated Japanese foreign policy. The view that Japan is only reactive in foreign policy stems from this subordinate position in the high politics of international affairs. Japan delegated security matters to the Occupation, continued basing American troops on Japanese soil, and reacted to American concerns about military matters. In return for their bargain, Japanese leaders could shift their attention to economics and build a coalition of constituents with substantive economic needs.

A sequence of events then affirmed these security ties. In 1960, renewal of the Security Treaty tested the American alliance. Japanese citizens feared being drawn into war, as Cold War tensions were raised by the downing of a U-2 spy plane. When the Liberal Democrats and Prime Minister Kishi Nobusuke forced a vote on the treaty, Tokyo erupted with demonstrations and violence. Kishi resigned, but the treaty passed. The Liberal Democrats still ruled, and the alliance continued. In 1972, Nixon further tested the alliance by assertive initiatives without prior consultations with Japan. The "Nixon Shocks" meant unannounced changes in flexible exchange rates, the recognition of China, and an agricultural export embargo that included soybeans.

For the Japanese, foreign policy would thereafter anticipate the dangers of excessive reliance on American favoritism and search for wider-ranging relations, through multisourcing of "resource diplomacy" and "omni-directional diplomacy." Japan nevertheless experienced difficulty achieving independence in foreign relations without regard to American positions. In part, the trade relationship was followed by an investment boom, bringing Japanese investment to a total in 1991 of $155 billion in North America (compared to $69 billion in Europe, $44 billion in South America, and $53 billion in Asia). Japanese prime ministers remind audiences that the two G-7 leaders account for 40 percent of the world's gross national product. Because economic relations are deeply intertwined, a security or political rift is seen as extremely costly.

On the other hand, Japan is likely to broaden its political roles beyond the past reliance on American leadership in world affairs. For example, in 1989, almost two hundred countries were represented at Emperor Hirohito's funeral, marking the start of a new imperial era known as *Heisei* ("Achieving Prosperity"). Yet such contacts still do not mean strong influence. The Persian Gulf War fueled perceptions about the lack of personnel in the U.N. effort and the slowness of the financial response of Japan. In 1992, the Japanese National Assembly passed a reinterpretation of its Constitution to allow for cooperation with peace-keeping organizations (PKO) in Indochina by Japanese military personnel.

The resulting involvement with overseas operations is still largely sym-bolic, though Japanese politicians do have high regard for symbols and appearances. The National Assembly requires each overseas dispatch to face scrutiny in its deliberations, and the opposition opposes further such moves. In March of 1993, the deaths of a volunteer and policeman in Cambodia tested Japanese resolve, but by 1995, most experts considered the experiment to be a success. Regardless, Japanese military and civilian personnel are likely to assert themselves to represent their country over-seas. Overseas Japanese will thus be more visible in U.N. activities, in protection of various overseas activities, and ultimately in asserting the national interests of Japan.

Conclusions: Political Orders and Institutional Studies

I have argued that Japanese elites took steps to change political struc-tures and thereby preserve their domestic order. Such an approach to political history draws on types of institutional studies that focus not only on party politics but also on the array of institutions that emerge to preserve political orders in advanced industrial democracies. This institu-tional focus is akin to comparative concerns of political analysts else-where. Institutionalism focuses on how civil servants, politicians, and other officials overcome crises, resolve conflicts, adapt structures, and preserve stability. With each conflict and change—with each new politi-cal era—the terrain upon which differences are played out shifts within organized interests as well as among policymakers. Conflict and change in bureaucracy, regulation, and public policy set priorities within the agenda for institutional study.

In this, the postwar institutional shift from bureaucratic dominance to mixed governance is the key trend in Japan. One danger in using institu-tional approaches, however, lies in the risk of retreat to formal or redun-dant policy studies that repeat the shortcomings of earlier research. To avoid the excessive formalism of legalistic or descriptive institutionalism, studies must emphasize social processes—political dynamics—rather than structures alone. In the field of Japanese studies, further controversy arises over the uniqueness of the institutional differences with other coun-tries.[34] This chapter avoids formalism and rejects radical notions of uniqueness. Japan resembles elsewhere, and this review gives evidence of comparable problems and institutional responses. If the actors involved in policy processes have similarities across policy context and countries, then these findings can support cross-national generalizations.

I have pointed to five areas of political structure with ample evidence to support comparative findings and to seek common international structures shared by the G-7 countries. The trajectory of the postwar political orders nevertheless predicts a collision between domestic stability and international change. While a smaller division into five periods of political change may be discerned, this essay also finds two grand periods: one of bureaucratic dominance, peaking in 1960 and ending in 1973, and one of mixed governance, peaking in 1980 and continuing to the present. After 1993, Japan appears on the threshold of broad electoral reform and reassessment of its political structures.

Japan thus faces change within its society as well as in its relations with the outside world. In particular, agriculture has declined as the key base of ruling-party support, and new groups of small business, aging retirees, working women, educated youth, and urban singles have been courted with mixed success. Increasing apathy and cynicism about politics makes Japanese social cleavages more volatile than in the past and underscore the critical changes that face Japan in the future. If Japanese leaders choose to avoid needed reforms of existing bureaucratic and party structures, the structures that underlie the postwar order, then the danger from international conflicts over trade issues and over security commitments will surely increase.

Accordingly, a transition in both domestic and international orders requires further adaptive steps, now underway in Japan though their final form remains ambiguous. Such steps proved possible in the past, in moving from bureaucratic dominance to mixed governance. Yet past steps offer no clear prediction for changes in the political structures of the future. Most likely, the national bureaucracy will again provide a reasonable basis for stability during periods of change in party politics and in other political structures. On the other hand, the elites who mold these structures and guide evolutionary change are embattled and uncertain about their roles after the Cold War. Japan, as other members among the G-7 nations, must act through a balance of domestic reform and international coordination. Without a new type of balance, Japanese elites are well aware of the difficulties facing them in taking the appropriate adaptive steps to assure the continuance of their political order.

Notes

1. Gerald Curtis, *The Japanese Way of Politics* (New York: Columbia University, 1988). To his credit, Curtis suggested that a split in the Liberal Democrats was the most likely way that political change would occur in Japan.

2. A. J. P. Taylor, *Bismarck: The Man and the Statesman* (New York: Vintage, 1967).

210 Stephen J. Anderson

3. See Stephen J. Anderson, *Welfare Policy and Politics in Japan: Beyond the Developmental State* (New York: Paragon House, 1993), chap. 3.

4. John Maki, "The Role of the Bureaucracy in Japan," *Pacific Affairs* 20, no. 4 (December 1947): 391–400.

5. Michele Schmiegelow and Henrik Schmiegelow, *Strategic Pragmatism: Japanese Lessons in the Use of Economic Theory* (New York: Praeger, 1989).

6. Note that the convention for Japanese names puts family name first, given name last. Popularizers tend to use reverse order (Kakuei Tanaka), but scholarly style dictates that the name be given in Japanese order (Tanaka Kakuei).

7. For example, Milton Friedman, *Capitalism and Freedom* (Chicago: University of Chicago, 1980).

8. Chalmers Johnson, *MITI and the Japanese Miracle* (Stanford: Stanford University, 1982).

9. For a review, see Ellis Krauss, "Political Economy: Policymaking and Industrial Policy in Japan," and Stephen J. Anderson, "The Policy Process and Social Policy in Japan," both in *PS: Political Science & Politics* 25, no. 1 (March 1992): 44–57 and 36–44. Leading works on consensus-building are Richard J. Samuels, *The Business of the Japanese State: Energy Markets in Comparative and Historical Perspective* (Ithaca: Cornell University, 1987), and John Haley, *Authority without Power: Law and the Japanese Paradox* (New York: Oxford University, 1991).

10. T. J. Pempel, "Organizing for Efficiency: The Higher Civil Service in Japan," in Ezra Suleiman, ed., *Bureaucracy in Western Democracies* (New York: Holmes & Meiers, 1984), 1–18.

11. An example is Clyde Prestowitz, *Trading Places* (New York: Basic, 1989).

12. Giovanni Sartori, *Parties and Party Systems: A Framework for Analysis* (New York: Cambridge University, 1976).

13. Robert Scalapino and Seizaburo Sato, *The Foreign Policy of Modern Japan* (Berkeley: University of California, 1977).

14. T. J. Pempel, ed., *Uncommon Democracies: The One-Party Dominant Regimes* (Ithaca: Cornell University, 1990).

15. Curtis, *Japanese Way of Politics*.

16. Fujiwara Hirotatsu, *I Denounce the Sokka Gakkai* (Tokyo: Mainichi Shimbunsha, 1969).

17. J. A. A. Stockwin, "Japan," in V.A. Bogdanor, ed., *Elections* (Oxford: Oxford University, 1980).

18. T. J. Pempel, "From Exporter to Investor," Paper delivered at Tsukuba University, August 6, 1992.

19. Kent Calder, *Crisis and Compensation* (Princeton: Princeton University, 1988).

20. *Daily Yomiuri,* March 7, 1993, p. 1, and March 14, 1993, p. 1, when the estimate of total payment and penalty was reported to be ¥250 million (over $2 million).

21. T. J. Pempel, "Conclusion: One-Party Dominance and the Creation of Regimes," in Pempel, ed., *Uncommon Democracies*.

22. See Anderson, *Welfare Policy and Politics in Japan,* chap. 6.

23. Sidney Tarrow, "Maintaining Hegemony in Italy: The Softer They Rise, the Slower They Fall!" in Pempel, *Uncommon Democracies*.

24. Leonard J. Schoppa, "Zoku Powe and LDP Power: A Case Study of the Zoku Role in Education Policy," *Journal of Japanese Studies* 17, no. 1 (Winter 1991): 79–106, and Anderson, *Welfare Policy and Politics in Japan*.

25. Michio Muramatsu and Ellis S. Krauss, "The Dominant Party and Social Coalitions in Japan," in Pempel, *Uncommon Democracies*, 282–305.

26. Ellis S. Krauss and Jon Pierre, "The Decline of Dominant Parties: Parliamentary Politics in Sweden and Japan in the 1970s," in Pempel, *Uncommon Democracies*, 226–59.

27. On the ideological underpinnings of divisions on the Left, see Germaine A. Houston, *Marxism and the Crisis of Development in Prewar Japan* (Princeton: Princeton University, 1986).

28. Shumpei Kumon, "Japan as a Network Society," in Shumpei Kumon and Henry Rosovsky, *The Political Economy of Japan,* vol. 3, *Cultural and Social Dynamics* (Stanford: Stanford University, 1992), 109–41.

29. Scott C. Flanagan et al., *The Japanese Voter* (New Haven: Yale University, 1991).

30. Takashi Inoguchi, "The Political Economy of Conservative Resurgence under the Recession, 1977–1983," in Pempel, *Uncommon Democracies,* 189–225.

31. Dennis J. Encarnation and Mark Mason, "Neither MITI nor America: The Political Economy of Capital Liberalization in Japan," *International Organization* 44 (Winter 1990): 30–38.

32. *Japan 1993: An International Comparison* (Tokyo: Keizai Koho Center, 1992), 50.

33. Dennis J. Encarnation, *Rivals Beyond Trade: America Versus Japan in Global Competition* (Ithaca: Cornell University, 1992).

34. Karel van Wolferen, *The Enigma of Japanese Power* (New York: Knopf, 1989).

8 *Carol A. Mershon*

Italy

Byron Shafer developed the notion of a political order to deal with a two-part puzzle about the electorate and political institutions since the late 1960s in the United States: (a) an electoral realignment that was constantly expected and never arrived; and (b) divided government, the recurring outcome of—and clash between—a Republican in the White House and a Democratic majority in Congress.[1] Can the same framework help us to understand an analogous pair of outcomes in Italy: a realignment favoring the Left that gathered force in the early 1970s[2] and has since receded; and the permanent incumbency of the Christian Democratic Party, in office without interruption from 1944 to 1994?

The answer that I give here is "Yes, but." Yes, the political order framework has important advantages. Among other things, it highlights historical breakpoints, and it shows that institutions, parties, and interest groups influence how voters vote. It aids in interpreting the impact of political corruption of astonishing proportions, practiced in Italy for years but uncovered only in the early 1990s. But this framework accommodates somewhat uneasily one feature that is essential for explaining the outcomes of interest in the Italian case: the bargaining among and within parties that erects and undoes governing coalitions. For this, it requires elaboration.

I build my argument as follows. The first section of the chapter discusses what is entailed in using the political order approach to analyze

212

Italy. The second section identifies two postwar political eras and a third era that may now be emerging. Part three assesses the underpinnings of each era and the causes of shifts from one era to another. The fourth section moves some from scrutiny of Italy to reflections on cross-national research.

Italian Politics in the Political Order Approach

A provocative way to begin applying the political order approach is by isolating a key puzzle about a nation's electorate and political institutions, and proceeding to solve that puzzle by examining public opinion on major issues, intermediary organizations and elites, and specialization among institutions of governance. I echo this logic in extending the approach to Italy. My initial task, then, is to say more about the salient puzzle in Italian politics.

The Puzzling Conjunction of Change and Stability

The Christian Democratic Party (DC) perpetually dominated national government in postwar Italy, until 1994, despite massive social change and despite real shifts in election results. A look at governmental successions, at socioeconomic trends, and at electoral verdicts drives home the contrast between stability and change.

In postwar Italy, governments undergo constant change and yet remain much the same. As table 8.1 illustrates, almost no government managed to stay in office for more than a few years, and many governments collapsed after a few months. Nonetheless, the DC always held governing power between 1944 and 1994. Even the same individuals returned to office time after time. Italy exhibited the lowest turnover rate of any parliamentary democracy and, except for the defunct French Fourth Republic, the most short-lived governments.[3] How could governments break down so often and with so few apparent effects?

Italian society also has been transformed since the end of World War II. The contraction of the agrarian sector furnishes one convenient and telling indicator of the magnitude of change. In 1951, 43.9 percent of employed Italians were working in agriculture. By 1991, this percentage had dropped to 3.4 percent—the most dramatic decline found in the Group of Seven, with the possible exception of Japan.[4] The remaking of the labor force accompanied enormous changes in the quality of life, as geographic mobility rose, educational opportunities expanded, urbanization and secularization advanced, affluence spread, and printed and electronic media reached more Italians than ever before.

Table 8.1. Italian Governments, 1946–1995

Government	Date Formed	Date Resigned	Parties in Cabinet	Seats in Chamber (%)
De Gasperi II	7/46	1/47	DC + PCI + PSI + PRI	81
De Gasperi III	2/47	5/47	DC + PCI + PSI	67
De Gasperi IV	5/47	12/47	DC	37
De Gasperi V	12/47	5/48	DC + PSDI[a] + PRI + PLI	58
De Gasperi VI	5/48	10/49	DC + PSDI + PRI + PLI	64
De Gasperi VII	11/49	1/50	DC + PRI + PLI	58
De Gasperi VIII	1/50	4/51	DC + PSDI + PRI	60
De Gasperi IX	4/51	7/51	DC + PRI	55
De Gasperi X	7/51	6/53	DC + PRI	55
De Gasperi XI	7/53	7/53	DC	45
Pella	8/53	1/54	DC	45
Fanfani I	1/54	1/54	DC	45
Scelba	2/54	6/55	DC + PSDI + PLI	50
Segni I	7/55	5/57	DC + PSDI + PLI	50
Zoli	5/57	6/58	DC	45
Fanfani II	7/58	1/59	DC + PSDI	49
Segni II	2/59	2/60	DC	46
Tambroni	3/60	7/60	DC	46
Fanfani III	7/60	2/62	DC	46
Fanfani IV	2/62	5/63	DC + PSDI + PRI	51
Leone I	6/63	11/63	DC	41

Moro I	12/63	6/64	DC + PSI + PSDI + PRI	61
Moro II	7/64	1/66	DC + PSI + PSDI + PRI	61
Moro III	2/66	6/68	DC + PSI + PSDI + PRI	61
Leone II	6/68	11/68	DC	42
Rumor I	12/68	7/69	DC + PSI-PSDI + PRI	58
Rumor II	8/69	2/70	DC	42
Rumor III	3/70	7/70	DC + PSI + PSDI + PRI	58
Colombo I	8/70	3/71	DC + PSI + PSDI + PRI	58
Colombo II	3/71	1/72	DC + PSI + PSDI	57
Andreotti I	2/72	2/72	DC	42
Andreotti II	6/72	6/73	DC + PSDI + PLI	50
Rumor IV	7/73	3/74	DC + PSI + PSDI + PRI	59
Rumor V	3/74	10/74	DC + PSI + PDI	57
Moro IV	11/74	1/76	DC + PRI	45
Moro V	2/76	4/76	DC	42
Andreotti III	7/76	1/78	DC	42
Andreotti IV	3/78	1/79	DC	42
Andreotti V	3/79	3/79	DC + PSDI + PRI	46
Cossiga I	8/79	3/80	DC + PSDI + PLI	46
Cossiga II	4/80	9/80	DC + PSI + PRI	54
Forlani	10/80	5/81	DC + PSI + PSDI + PRI	57
Spadolini I	6/81	8/82	PRI + DC + PSI + PSDI + PLI	58
Spadolini II	8/82	11/82	PRI + DC + PSI + PSDI + PLI	58

(table continued on following page)

Table 8.1: (continued)

Government	Date Formed	Date Resigned	Parties in Cabinet	Seats in Chamber (%)
Fanfani V	12/82	4/83	DC + PSI + PSDI + PLI	56
Craxi I	8/83	6/86	PSI + DC PSDI + PRI + PLI	58
Craxi II	8/86	3/87	PSI + DC + PSDI + PRI + PLI	58
Fanfani VI	4/87	4/87	DC	37
Goria	7/87	3/88	DC + PSI + PSDI + PRI + PLI	60
De Mita	4/88	5/89	DC + PSI + PSDI + PRI + PLI	60
Andreotti VI	7/89	3/91	DC + PSI + PSDI + PRI + PLI	60
Andreotti VII	4/91	4/92	DC + PSI + PSDI + PLI	56
Amato	6/92	4/93	PSI + DC + PSDI + PLI	53
Ciampi	4/93	1/94	DC + PSI + PSDI + PLI	53
Berlusconi	5/94	12/94	FI [+ CCD[b]] + League + AN	58
Dini	1/95		nonpartisan	

SOURCE: Carol Mershon, "The Costs of Coalition: Coalition Theories and Italian Governments," typescript, 1995.

[a]This table always designates the Socialists as the PSI, even though the party had a different name before 1947 (when the Social Democrats split) and during the 1966–1969 period (when the Socialists and Social Democrats reunited). Similarly, the table always refers to the Social Democrats as the PSDI, even though the party used a different name immediately after its founding and immediately after its failed reunification with the Socialists.

[b]The Christian Democratic Center (CCD) allied with *Forza Italia* on the proportional representation ballot in the 1994 elections, but then constituted a separate parliamentary group.

NOTE: The table counts a new government with each change of party composition, parliamentary election, change of prime minister, and accepted resignation.

Political scientists routinely contend that just these sorts of socioeconomic trends leave a substantial imprint on choices by voters. Indeed, these factors play a prominent role in many explanations of the most obvious change in electoral results over the first three decades of the Italian Republic: the steady increase in the share of the national vote won by the Communist Party (PCI) from 1946 to 1976, which table 8.2 displays. The success of the PCI brought many analysts to announce a realignment toward the Left.[5]

The realignment, however, was transitory, if realignment it was. The PCI (today the Democratic Party of the Left, PDS) has lost votes in every parliamentary election between 1979 and 1992; the other major Left party, the Socialists (PSI), registered only slight gains over that span of time. The 1992 elections weakened the DC but still qualified it as Italy's largest party. What accounted for the persistence of the DC amid so much change?

This question becomes even more pressing in light of the bribery scandal still unfolding in Italy, which since February of 1992 has led to formal accusations against almost four thousand politicians and public officials and has prompted estimates that kickbacks may have totalled $20 billion between the early 1980s and the early 1990s.[6] How did this web of corruption help to cement a political order, and how did it finally come apart?

Starting Points of Interpretation

Guidelines for addressing this puzzle may be drawn from the original implementation of the political order framework. In the United States, otherwise perplexing patterns become comprehensible when the analyst considers the issue concerns dominating public opinion and the way those issue foci support, and are sustained by, diagnostic social cleavages, intermediary organizations, and institutional relationships.[7]

A rapid survey of the American case serves to clarify how such reasoning can work. Societal consensus on major political issues disintegrated in the United States by the late 1960s. The cross-cutting majorities that have emerged, and the outcomes they have most often produced, are given in table 8.3. On the one hand, prevailing opinion among American voters has favored traditional cultural values and a nationalist foreign policy, which conform to Republican stances. On the other, a majority of voters have preferred continuing and rather generous provision of social services, as advocated by the Democratic party. The presidency speaks most strongly to cultural issues and acts most powerfully in foreign affairs. Within Congress, these issues gravitate toward the Senate more than the

Table 8.2. Italian Electoral Results, 1946–1992: Votes and Seats Won in Elections to the Chamber of Deputies

Party	1946	1948	1953	1958	1963	1968	1972	1976	1979	1983	1987	1992
					Party Percentage Share of Valid Votes							
Rete	—	—	—	—	—	—	—	—	—	—	—	1.9
Verdi	—	—	—	—	—	—	—	—	—	—	2.5	2.8
DP	—	—	—	—	—	—	—	1.5	0.8	1.5	1.7	—
PDUP	—	—	—	—	—	—	0.7	w/DP	1.4	w/PCI	—	—
PSIUP	—	—	—	—	—	4.4	1.9	—	—	—	—	—
PR	—	—	—	—	—	—	—	1.1	3.5	2.2	2.6	—
RC	—	—	—	—	—	—	—	—	—	—	—	5.6
PCI[b]	18.9	31.0[d]	22.6	22.7	25.3	26.9	27.2	34.4	30.4	29.9	26.6	16.1
PSI[c]	20.7		12.7	14.2	13.8		9.6	9.6	9.8	11.4	14.3	13.6
PSDI[c]	—	7.1	4.5	4.6	6.1	14.5[d]	5.1	3.4	3.8	4.1	2.9	2.7
PRI	4.4	2.5	1.6	1.4	1.4	2.0	2.9	3.1	3.0	5.1	3.7	4.4
DC	35.1	48.5	40.1	42.3	38.3	39.1	38.7	38.7	38.3	32.9	34.3	29.7
PLI	6.8	3.8	3.0	3.5	7.0	5.8	3.9	1.3	1.9	2.9	2.1	2.8
UQ	5.3											
League											1.3	8.7
PM-PNM	2.8	2.8	6.9	4.8	1.7	1.3						
MSI	—	2.0	5.8	4.8	5.1	4.5	8.7	6.1	5.3	6.8	5.9	5.4
Other	6.0	2.3	2.8	1.7	1.3	1.5	1.3	0.8	1.8	3.2	2.1	6.3
					Number of Seats for Major Parties							
RC	—	—	—	—	—	—	—	—	—	—	—	35
PCI[b]	104	183	143	140	166	177	179	227	201	198	177	107
PSI	115		75	84	87	91	61	57	62	73	94	92
PSDI	—	33	19	22	33		29	15	21	23	17	16
PRI	23	9	5	6	6	9	15	14	15	29	21	27

218

DC	207	305	263	273	260	266	266	263	261	225	234	206
PLI	41	19	13	17	39	31	20	5	9	16	11	17
League	—	—	—	—	—	—	—	—	—	—	1	55
MSI	—	6	29	24	27	24	56	35	31	42	35	34
Total	556	574	590	596	630	630	630	630	630	630	630	630

SOURCES: Paolo Farneti, *Il sistema dei partiti in Italia 1946–1979* (Bologna: Il Mulino, 1983), 36–39; Martin Rhodes, "Craxi e l'area laico-socialista: terza forza o tre forze?" in Piergiorgio Corbetta and Robert Leonardi, eds., *Politica in Italia. I fatti dell'anno e le interpretazioni. Edizione 88* (Bologna: Il Mulino, 1988), 187; Giacomo Sani, "Il verdetto del 1992", in Renato Mannheimer and Sani, eds., *La rivoluzione elettorale. L'Italia tra la prima e la seconda repubblica* (Milano: Anabasi, 1994), 41.

aDashes indicated that a party did not contest the election in question.

bDemocratic Party of the Left in 1992.

cSee note at table 8.1.

dJoint slate.

eSeats won with Monarchists.

ABBREVIATIONS:

Rete	Network (anti-Mafia)
Verdi	Greens
DP	Proletarian Democracy
PDUP	Party of Proletarian Unity
PSIUP	Italian Socialist Party of Proletarian Unity
PR	Radical Party
RC	Communist Refoundation
PCI	Italian Communist Party
PSI	Italian Socialist Party
PSDI	Italian Social Democratic Party
PRI	Italian Republican Party
DC	Christian Democracy
PLI	Italian Liberal Party
UQ	Everyman's Party
PN-PNM	Monarchist Party
MSI	Italian Social Movement
League	Northern/Lombard Leagues

Table 8.3.   An Example of the Logic of Political Eras, Political Orders, and Their
              Resulting Dynamic: The Era of Divided Government in the United States,
              1968 to the Present

Issues		Public Majorities		Institutions
Cultural Concerns	}	Republican	⇒⇒⇒⇒	Senate
			→→→→→→→→→→→→→	Presidency
Foreign affairs	}	Republican	⇒⇒⇒⇒	Senate
			→→→→→→→→→→→→→	Presidency
Social welfare policy	}	Democratic	⇒⇒⇒⇒	Senate
			→→→→→→→→→→→→→	House

SOURCE: Based on Byron E. Shafer, "The Notion of an Electoral Order: The Structure of
Electoral Politics at the Accession of George Bush", in Shafer, ed., *The End of Realignment? Interpreting American Electoral Eras* (Madison: University of Wisconsin, 1991).

House. The Congress (above all the House) specializes in dealing with
social welfare issues and delivering concrete services and benefits.

Thus voters have returned Republicans to the White House, Democratic majorities to the House, and, somewhat less reliably, Democratic
majorities to the Senate. The post-1968 organizational traits of American political parties and interest groups have reinforced and perpetuated these tendencies. As chapter 2 of this book demonstrates, the
same basic explanation can be elaborated to accommodate the present-
day outcome of a Democratic president and Republican legislative
majorities.

How should these ideas be translated to other national contexts? The
institutional comparisons most fruitful to make depend, of course, on the
way that institutions are designed. Fifth Republic France, a hybrid
presidential-parliamentary system, allows for the possibility of Amer-
ican-style divided government, a possibility that became reality between
1986 and 1988 and again between 1993 and 1995, when a Socialist president "cohabited" with a Gaullist premier. In Italy and the other four
parliamentary systems in the G-7, however, the outcome of split partisan
control that is now characteristic of the United States cannot exist. Minority cabinets in parliamentary systems do not offer an analog to divided
government, for they must acquire and retain the confidence of the legislature in order to govern.[8] The array of Italian institutions thus directs
attention to a comparison of (parliament-based) national government
with two other sets of institutions: city-level elections and governments,
and nationwide popular referenda.[9]

So guided by the notion of a political order, I now turn to identifying
political eras in postwar Italy. The narrative for each era focuses on public

opinion in major issue areas, on political parties, and on the three institutional arenas just isolated.

Two Postwar Eras and a Third Era in the Making

Christian Democracy won a larger share of the vote than any other party
in the first postwar national elections of 1946, establishing a primacy that
ended only in the early 1990s. As Table 8.4 outlines, the era of clear Christian Democratic predominance stretched into the early 1970s. The 1974
referendum on divorce ushered in the second postwar era, that of unsuccessful challenges to DC dominance. Such challenges may well prove to
be successful in a third era, which opened with the municipal and regional
elections of 1990.

The Era of Christian Democratic Dominance, 1946–1974

In Italy, the cabinet, invested with authority by Parliament, sets foreign
policy and shapes the contours of the welfare state. The cabinet also han-
dles cultural concerns through such ministries as Education, which over-
sees religious instruction in public schools. Municipal governments, by
contrast, provide such collective goods as city parks, buses and subway
lines, garbage collection, and street repair; they run day-care centers,
pharmacies, and cemeteries. In the first postwar era, as table 8.4A illustrates, DC dominance of the national legislature and executive rested on
pluralities of public opinion favoring a pro-American foreign policy, a
broadly distributive (not redistributive) welfare state, and an affirmation
of Catholic values, all of which the DC championed. The same pluralities
of opinion on social welfare and cultural values underlay DC dominance
in Italy's city councils.

In the first postwar era, DC prime ministers headed three types of coalitions, as a glance back at table 8.1 confirms: (a) In *national coalitions*
(1944 to 1947), the DC governed with the Socialists (PSI) and Communists (PCI); (b) under *centrism* (1947 to 1963), the DC allied with the
Social Democrats (PSDI), Republicans (PRI), and Liberals (PLI); and
(c) in *Center-Left* coalitions (1963 to 1976), the Socialists replaced the
Liberals in governing with the DC, PSDI, and PRI.

The transitions from one type of coalition to another show how the
Cold War polarized Italian politics. The national unity coalitions pro-
longed the interparty cooperation underpinning the armed anti-Fascist
Resistance. But in May of 1947, with East-West tensions turning into Cold
War, the DC broke the coalition to force the PCI and PSI out of govern-
ment.[10] The DC soon allied with the PSDI, PRI, and PLI. For decades,

Table 8.4. Applying the Logic of Political Eras, Political Orders, and Their Political Dynamics to Italy

A. The Era of Christian Democratic Dominance, 1946–1974

Issues	Public Pluralities		Institutions
Foreign affairs	Christian Democratic	→→→→→→→→	Parliament
Social welfare policy	Christian Democratic	→→→→→→→→	Parliament, City Councils
Cultural concerns	Christian Democratic	→→→→→→→→	Parliament, City Councils

B. The Era of Challenges to DC Dominance, 1974–1990

Issues	Public Divisions		Institutions
Social welfare policy	Plurality: DC	→→→→→→→→	Parliament
	Visible minority: PCI	→→→	City Councils
			Referenda
Cultural concerns	Majority: autonomy from parties	→→→→→→→→	City Councils
	Visible minority: PCI	→→→	

C. Prelude to Regime Change? 1990 to the Present

Issues	Public Divisions		Institutions
Social Welfare Policy	Shifting plurality: DC, FI	→→→→→→→→	Parliament
	Visible minorities: PDS, League	→	City Councils
Cultural concerns	Majority: autonomy from parties	→→→→→→→→	Referenda
	Visible minorities: PDS, League	→	City Councils
Institutional design	Majority: pro-reform	→→→→→→→→	Referenda

these centrist parties publicized their rejection of the PCI as an antisystem party outside the circle of legitimate contenders for cabinet posts.

A Center-Left coalition then became an admissible option for growing segments of the DC after the PSI renounced unity of action with the PCI in 1956. The PSI's return to government was intended to isolate the Communist Party and win the government greater working-class support. It was patiently engineered by Aldo Moro, DC secretary, and was inaugurated with American consent in 1963.[11] In deliberate trials authorized by national party leaders, city-level coalitions of the Center-Left preceded the "opening to the Left" at the national level.[12]

The experience of Center-Left government contributed to challenges to DC dominance. The Center-Left coalitions promised many social and economic reforms but delivered few. The alliance "placed issues on the agenda that it could not resolve and—by its own internal divergences— provided opportunities for groups outside the polity to intervene in debates that began within it."[13] The disappointments and divisions of Center-Left government thus proved to be one of the chief sources of the wave of popular protest that spread through Italian society from the late 1960s to the early 1970s.[14]

The Era of Challenges to Christian Democratic Dominance, 1974–1990

The challenge to DC dominance fully entered the nationwide electoral arena with the 1974 referendum on divorce. By 59.3 percent, voters in May of 1974 upheld a divorce law that was enacted in 1970 over the opposition of the DC and the Vatican.[15] The DC and the neo-Fascist Italian Social Movement (MSI) were the only parties campaigning for repeal. "For the first time since the 1946 referendum that abolished the monarchy, the PCI was clearly aligned with a majority of the country."[16]

Other era-defining electoral outcomes soon followed. The PCI scored impressive victories in city-level elections in 1975. In the wake of those elections, the PCI participated in municipal cabinets in the five largest cities in Italy, eight of the ten largest cities, and sixty-five of the hundred largest.[17] In the parliamentary elections of 1976, as noted above, the PCI won unprecedented support. As a result, the PSI became the essential ally in any DC-based coalition capable of commanding a majority while excluding the PCI. [18]

How to interpret these events? Perhaps the 1974 referendum on divorce disclosed a new anticlerical, pro-Left popular majority on cultural concerns. And perhaps the Communist victories of 1975, built on a reputation for effective, responsive, reformist municipal rule, reflected the ascendancy of leftist orientations among voters in a new urban reform issue-area. This reading was probably most compelling in the late 1970s. Today, in light of the failure of forecasts of leftward realignment, another interpretation is more persuasive.

In this view, which table 8.4B provides, the majorities in the many referenda of the last two decades are best understood as asserting claims for autonomy from Italy's established political parties, assertions that would achieve their ultimate ends only in the third postwar era. In this, aspects of urban reform are best subsumed in either the social-welfare or the cultural-values issue areas. Foreign policy is also best seen as subordinate to those two overarching areas, except at the height of the Cold War. This view would define the PCI as a highly visible minority in city councils and Parliament. The existence of multiple, competing minorities is thus one foundation of DC power. The PCI challenged DC dominance but never acquired cabinet responsibilities.

Indeed, despite the accession of two non–Christian Democrats to the premiership in the 1980s, the DC weathered challenges to its primacy relatively well until the early 1990s. In the second era, the DC governed in two types of cabinets: (a) under *national solidarity* (1976 to 1979), the Communists joined other parties in supporting minority DC-based governments through parliamentary accords; and (b) in *five-party* coalitions (1979 to the 1992 elections), the DC allied with the PSI, PSDI, PRI, and PLI. Moreover, the five-party coalition "is, after all, simply the Center-Left of the 1960s with the rather irrelevant addition of the Liberals."[19]

All the same, trends were unfolding that laid the groundwork for a new era. Some of these trends were manifest—for example, the decline in the DC vote share during the 1980s, reported in table 8.2—whole others were long concealed. It was only in 1993 that a leading figure in Italian business declared to investigating magistrates: "[T]he parties' agents imposed a general condition that I could sum up briefly as 'if you don't pay, you don't work.' . . . [I]f you were not ready to pay [kickbacks], you were excluded from the possibility of even presenting bids" for a contract in the public sector.[20]

Prelude to Regime Change? 1990 to the Present

It may yet be premature to identify a new era in Italian politics. But since the municipal and regional elections in the spring of 1990, electoral shocks have become commonplace. And the corruption scandal which broke open in February of 1992 has given greater impetus to calls for institutional reform and greater success to new parties. As a consequence, fifty years of uninterrupted DC incumbency came to an end in 1994.

Debates about institutional redesign continue today. Controversies that parliamentarians have tried to avoid or finesse have gravitated toward the referendum since the early 1970s. But whereas cultural issues were put to a popular vote before 1990, *institutional* reforms have been decided by referendum in the early 1990s, as table 8.4C conveys. In turn, pressured by referendum results, Parliament approved new electoral laws in August of 1993, which combine plurality and proportional rules for Chamber and Senate elections and impose a 4 percent threshold for representation in the Chamber.[21] Before the decade is out, Parliament may well enact institutional changes far-reaching enough to constitute a Second Republic.

Of course, what the legislature does under these arrangements depends on which parties earn legislative seats. As table 8.5 documents, the Parliament chosen in 1994 under the new electoral laws has a party makeup that radically departs from the past. In the parliamentary elections in April of 1992, the DC's share of the vote dropped below 30 percent. Then, in May of 1993, Italy's first nonparty premier, Carlo Azeglio Ciampi, took office at the helm of a DC-PSI-PSDI-PLI coalition. Nevertheless, in the parliamentary elections, in March of 1994, continuing public outrage at widespread corruption inflicted devastating losses on the Popular Party (as the DC had renamed itself in January of 1994) and on the PSI. Undone by corruption, the PLI and PSDI did not even contest those elections.

Forza Italia (Go, Italy), founded in January of 1994 by Silvio Berlusconi, the media magnate, bested all other parties in proportional representation votes in its electoral debut. As a result, from May to December of 1994, Berlusconi headed a government embracing *Forza Italia,* the Lombard/Northern League, and the National Alliance (the renamed MSI). In January of 1995, Lamberto Dini became Italy's second nonparty premier, guiding a cabinet that, for the first time in postwar Italy, contained not a single member of Parliament. Moreover, the Dini government passed its votes of investiture thanks to support from the PDS (ex-PCI), among other parties. After the next parliamentary elections—and also because the Cold War is over—the PDS may even enter national government.

These sketches by themselves do justice neither to events in Italy nor to the analytical purchase of the notion of a political order. To understand how the apparent realignment of the 1970s unraveled and left the DC in place, as well as to appraise the impact of endemic corruption and of the

Table 8.5. Italian Electoral Results, 1992 and 1994: Votes and Seats in Elections to the Chamber of Deputies

PARTY	1992		1994	
	% Votes	N Seats	% Votes[a]	N Seats
Progressives				
Rete	1.9	12	1.9	6
Verdi	2.8	16	2.7	11
RC	5.6	35	6.0	39
PDS	16.1	107	20.4	109
PSI	13.6	92	2.2	14
Demo Alliance	—	—	1.2	18
PSDI	2.7	16	—	—
PRI	4.4	27	—	—
Total seats: 213				
Pact for Italy				
Segni Pact	—	—	4.6	13
DC[b]	29.7	206	11.1	33
Total seats: 46				
Freedom Pole and Good Government Pole				
PLI	2.8	17	—	—
Pannalla List	1.2	7	3.5	0
Forza Italia	—	—	21.0	99
League	8.7	55	8.4	117
MSI[c]	5.4	34	13.5	109
Total Seats: 366				
Others	5.1	6	3.6	5

SOURCES: Roberto D'Alimonte and Stefano Bartolini, "Il sistema partitico italiano: Una transizione difficile," in Bartolini and D'Alimonte, eds., *Maggioritario ma non troppo* (Bologna: Il Mulino, 1995), 320; Robert Cartocci, *Fra Lega e Chiesa. L'Italia in cerca di integrazione* (Bologna: Il Mulino, 1994), 92.

[a]Popular Party (PPI) in 1994.

[b]National Alliance (AN) in 1994.

[c]Votes on PR ballots in 1994. Seat totals for 1994 shows seats won on both PR and plurality ballots.

NOTE: The subdivisions in the table reflect the electoral alliances struck in 1994: Progressives (Rete, Greens, RC, PDS, PSI, Democratic Alliance, Socialist Renewal, Social-Christians); Pact for Italy (PPI, Segni Pact); Freedom Pole (FI, League, Centrist Union [UDC], Christian Democratic Center [CCD]); Good Government Pole (FI, AN, UDC, CCD).

DC's exit, it is necessary to examine political issues, intermediary organizations, and institutions of governance in greater detail.

The Bases of Eras and the Sources of Change

Cleavages and Issues

Ecological and survey-based studies demonstrate that religion and class have powerfully influenced vote choices in postwar Italy.[22] Similarly, content analyses of party manifestos from 1946 to 1979 show two leading dimensions of party competition: a (socioeconomic) Left-Right dimension and a (cultural) technocracy–social harmony dimension.[23] The first dimension has involved such issues as agrarian reform, nationalization, social justice, and the role of organized labor; the second subsumes Catholicism in its many manifestations.

By the late 1960s and early 1970s, the longstanding confrontation between Catholic and secular values came to include, as issues on the public agenda, such matters as divorce and abortion.[24] As in France, the Left-Right dimension seemed to give *less* coherence to voters' opinions in the mid-1980s than it had a decade before.[25] The available evidence points neither to a distinct urban reform issue-area nor to a long-lasting foreign policy issue-area independent of these two major dimensions of cleavage. The electoral earthquakes of the early 1990s prompted some political scientists to debate the existence of old-new and ideological-pragmatic dimensions.[26]

Mass Parties and Organized Interests

The Christian Democratic and Communist parties, the main governing and opposition parties of the postwar years, have traditionally been buttressed by a constellation of allied organizations, from sports associations to cooperatives to trade-union confederations. The core of these organizational networks was located in territorial subcultures whose origins trace back to the late nineteenth century: the heavily Catholic and Christian Democratic "white" Northeast, along with the "red" Center, a Socialist stronghold before Fascism and a Communist one since World War II.[27] Figure 8.3 charts how notably party strength has varied across geopolitical zones.

Figure 8.1 also attests to variation over time. Scholars agree that as small and medium-sized industries proliferated in the Northeast and Center during the 1970s and 1980s, social changes were set in motion that have eroded the subcultures. Thus the bonds of allegiance and identity that

Fig. 8.1. Variations in DC and PCI Strength by Geopolitical Area: Elections to the Constituent Assembly in 1946, and to the Chamber of Deputies from 1948 to 1987.

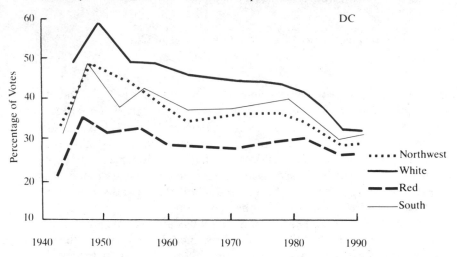

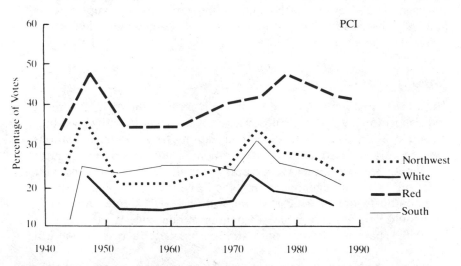

Note that for 1948, the figure shows votes won jointly by the PCI and PSI in the Popular Front. From Piergiorgio Corbetta, Arthur Parisi, and Hans Schadee, *Elezione in Italia. Struttura e tipologia delle consultazioni politiche* (Bologna: Il Mulino, 1988). Reprinted by permission.

long anchored some voters to the DC and PCI have loosened.[28] Moreover, by the late 1960s and early 1970s, several interest groups historically allied to the DC or PCI (such as unions) were attenuating their partisan ties. At the same time, new social movements—students, feminists, and environmentalists, for example—developed independently of the established parties.[29] Although the PCI absorbed militants from these new social movements, which contributed to membership growth in the 1970s, PCI membership declined again throughout the 1980s.[30]

In the 1990s, the erosion of the Catholic subculture has contributed to the success of the Lombard/Northern League and of Berlusconi's *Forza Italia*. In other words, the electorates of both parties include—though they are by no means limited to—ex-DC voters from the Northeast.[31] To be sure, the League and *Forza Italia* differ in significant ways. The League is confined to the North-Center, whereas *Forza Italia* is present nationwide and in 1994 performed fairly well in the South (in alliance with the ex-MSI). The League has appealed to localistic identities, attacking the welfare state as riddled with corruption and thus costly for the North (and redistributive in geographical terms).[32] *Forza Italia* by contrast, has exalted free-market principles and has sounded anti-PCI and (like the League) antiparty themes.[33]

Leaders of the two parties have traded vigorous criticisms, despite their alliance in the electoral campaign of 1994 and in government afterwards. Indeed, the Berlusconi government collapsed when the League withdrew. Moreover, the League has built a "new mass party," whereas *Forza Italia* looks more like a marketing firm.[34] The stories of both parties, however, testify to the dissolution of the ideological, socioeconomic, and organizational bases of traditional mass-party structures. So too do the PDS's efforts to revamp its program and "lighten" its organization.

Institutions of Governance

The records of cabinet composition and of results in Chamber elections, tables 8.1, 8.2, and 8.5, indicate that the interpretation of ears outlined above aptly characterizes the relative strength of parliamentary parties. Tables 8.6, 8.7, and 8.8 add the record of partisan office-holding in Italy's eight thousand municipalities (*communi*). Overall, Christian Democrats have dominated, despite fluctuations over time and despite the DC's marginality in the city councils of the "red" Center. All the same, the role that the PCI assumed in municipal government after the mid-1970s taxed the party's organizational resources.[35] The 1990 municipal and regional elections and, especially, the municipal elections in June of 1993 gave new prominence to the Lombard/Northern League. Finally, the municipal

Table 8.6. Party Office-Holding at the Muncipal Level: Cabinet Composition in Italian Cities, 1984 and 1991

	% of All Cities		% of Nat'l Population	
Composition of Cabinet	1984	1991	1984	1991
DC + PSI + PSDI + PRI + PLI	0.2	0.2	3.4	4.9
DC + any of PSI, PSDI, PRI, PLI	18.9	15.1	25.9	31.3
DC alone	38.3	25.6	18.1	11.9
PCI alone	5.3	2.3	7.3	2.0
PCI in any coalition excluding DC	19.9	16.4	34.4	18.4
PCI in any coalition including DC	5.2	8.7	2.5	9.2
TOTAL	8,085	8,100	56,554,000	56,556,00

SOURCES: Calculated from data from the Italian Ministry of the Interior, as reported in Arturo Parisi, "Instabilità conflittualità e alleanze tra i partiti a livello locale," in Parisi, ed., *Luoghi e misure della politica* (Bologna: Il Mulino, 1984), 136–39; Sara Romano, ed., "Appendice," in Stephen Hellman and Gianfranco Pasquino, eds., *Politica in Italia, Edizione '92* (Bologna: Il Mulino, 1992), 313–19.

NOTE: Percentages do not sum to 100 because some cabinet compositions are omitted. For 1991, data on the PCI cover the PDS. Since the table omits vague categories (e.g., mixed center-Left), it may underrepresent the presence of the DC and, to a lesser extent, the PCI and PSI.

Table 8.7. Major Parties and Independents in City Councils, 1951–1984

	% Seats in City Councils					% Members of City Cabinets		
	1951–52	1960	1972	1977	1984	1972	1977	1984
DC	48.8[a]	58.2[a]	52.6	47.7	47.8	58.5	49.9	50.6
PCI	25.3[b]	22.5[b]	15.9	20.6	20.8	12.2	18.6	17.8
PSI	?	?	11.4	14.6	14.2	11.8	16.1	15.3
Indep.	?	?	7.1	6.8	7.7	6.5	6.4	6.9
TOTAL	148,689	133,716	143,522	146,481	146, 159	46,453	47,061	47,365

SOURCES: Recalculations from Giorgio Galli and Alfonso Prandi, *Patterns of Political Participation in Italy* (New Haven: Yale University, 1970), 246; Arturo Parisi, "Instabilità conflittualità e alleanza tra i partiti a livello locale," in Parisi, ed., *Luoghi e misure della politica* (Bologna: Il Mulino, 1984), 74.

[a]DC and DC-associated.

[b]PCI and PCI-associated (including PSI).

NOTE: Percentages do not sum to 100 because some parties are omitted.

Table 8.8. Major Party Presence in and Leadership of City Cabinets, by Geopolitical Area and Size of Municipality, 1982

| | % Population Where Party Present in Cabinet | | | Party's Mayors as % of All Mayors | | | | | |
| | | | | DC | | PSI | | PCI | |
Geopolitical Area	DC	PSI	PCI	Up to 5000	Over 5000	Up to 5000	Over 5000	Up to 5000	Over 5000
N'west	44.8	64.6	53.1	57.9	49.9	11.2	25.8	11.4	18.8
White	70.3	36.2	17.1	65.5	77.8	8.3	9.3	5.4	8.1
Red	14.5	74.9	84.5	38.6	11.6	16.2	18.2	36.9	66.7
South	61.7	59.9	36.2	56.7	63.7	16.4	17.6	16.0	13.2
Italy	49.8	61.1	47.1	56.7	52.2	13.0	18.5	14.6	24.2

SOURCE: Arturo Parisi, "Instabilità conflittualità e alleanza tra i partiti a livello locale," in Parisi, ed., *Luoghi e misure della politica* (Bologna: Il Mulino, 1984), 85, 87, 95, 95, 97, 105.

231

elections of November and December in 1993 produced a string of victories for the PDS-led Progressive Alliance.[36]

Of the twenty-six referenda between 1974 and 1993 that are listed in table 8.9, only three (one on divorce and two on abortion) directly involved Church doctrine. By the early 1990s, most referenda were instead introducing institutional reforms. Although the issues submitted to a popular vote have varied, many referendum decisions do appear to have affirmed the intended autonomy of voters from the established parties.[37]

On the whole, the evidence lends support to the interpretations advanced above and suggests that 1974 and 1990 marked the boundaries of distinctive eras in Italian politics. This review also makes clear that the electoral alignments, organizational actors, and institutions of the current era are still being (re)defined. Those facts logically lead to the need for further careful reflection on the bases for descriptive and causal inferences.

The Italian Case and Implications for Comparative Research

All chapters in this book illustrate how to study political orders in different national contexts. Treatment of the Italian case invites reflection on the logic underlying the accomplishment of this common task. I first take up two questions related to the preferences of voters.

Evidence on Voters' Opinions?

To corroborate claims about public opinion that can be an integral part of the political order approach, it is helpful to have at hand a series of reliable survey data. The analyst thus has some direct sense—beyond inferences from ecological data—of what the opinions of voters are and of why they cast their votes as they do. Yet substantial numbers of Italian survey respondents do not disclose their partisan preferences, and significant bias in the surveys seems to result. The nonresponse rate for questions on partisanship, for example, is usually on the order of 30 percent.[38] The appraisal of two leading analysts of the Italian electorate is worth quoting at some length. They identify:

the following pattern: (a) "non-political" questions elicit a higher response rate than political ones; (b) broad political questions (i.e., on political parties in general) are answered more often than specific queries (feelings toward a given party); (c) questions dealing with the respondent's own partisan leanings, preference, voting intention or even past voting behavior elicit the highest non-response rate. There is no indication that significant changes have taken place over time. . . . Neither sex, nor class, nor place of residence are markedly related to the propensity to reveal or to hide one's vote. . . . The distribution of

Table 8.9.   Referenda in Italy, 1974–1994

Date	Subject Challenged	Outcome (% Votes)
1974	Divorce	Upheld (59%)
1978	Aspects of the law on public order	Upheld (77)
	Public financing of parties	Upheld (56)
1981	Public order	Upheld (85)
	Bearing arms	Upheld (77)
	Life sentence as maximum	Upheld (86)
	Abortion ("right to life"-challenge)	Upheld (68)
	Abortion (Radical challenge)	Upheld (88)
1985	Cuts in cost-of-living escalator	Upheld (54)
1987	Methods for siting nuclearreactors	Abrogated (81)
	Financing breeder reactors inItaly	Abrogated (80)
	Participation in foreign breeder-reactors	Abrogated (72)
	Judges' liability	Abrogated (80)
	Operations of Commission of-Inquiry	Abrogated (85)
1990	Laws regulating hunting	Nullified*
	Right to hunt on private property	Nullifield*
	Regulation of agricultural pesticides	Nullified*
1991	Multiple preference votes for Chamber	Abrogated (96)
1993	Proportional representation in Senate	Abrogated (83)
	Public financing of parties	Abrogated (90)
	Penalties for drug addicts	Abrogated (55)
	Treasury nomination of heads of savings banks	Abrogated (90)
	Environmental controls for local health agencies	Abrogated (83)
	Ministry of State holdings	Abrogated (90)
	Ministry of Agriculture	Abrogated (70)
	Ministry of Tourism	Abrogated (82)

SOURCE: Stephen Hellman, "Italian Politics in Transition," in Mark Kesselman and Joel Krieger, eds., *European Politics in Transition,* 2d ed. (New York: D.C. Heath, 1992), 409; Sara Romano, "Appendice," in Stephen Hellman and Gianfranco Pasquino, eds., *Politica in Italia, Edizione '92* (Bologna: Il Mulino, 1992), 302; *Corriere della Sera,* April 20, 1993.
   *Inadequate turnout.

partisan leanings among the respondents who do answer these questions [instead] tends to underrepresent rather noticeably the PCI and, though to a lesser extent, the MSI.[39]

Partly because of such reticence among Italians, it was not until the 1970s that scholars began to draw on survey-based analyses of Italian electoral behavior. Even now, "electoral research conducted in Italy remains, willingly or not, still essentially tied to the ecological method."[40] To be sure, students of past electoral eras do without survey data, and perceptive analyses of Italian survey evidence are available. But "data sets [from Italy] that tap the partisan dimension should be approached with great care. One cannot overstress the need to use caution in interpreting data that are biased in some important respects."[41]

Prevailing Opinion?

Observers of politics in the United States, Britain, or Germany can, as in chapter 2, 4, or 6, locate majority opinion on major issue dimensions. In contrast, no Italian party has ever received a majority of votes in a parliamentary election. Indeed, the DC has won a majority of parliamentary *seats* only once, in 1948. Italian voters seem to hold a relatively wide range of opinions;[42] multiple parties appeal to, and help perpetuate, these differences; and electoral laws have done little to aggregate divided opinion into majority outcomes—which is one reason why Italy's electoral laws were revised in 1993.

Previously, local majorities in the subcultural zones solidified around, and were sustained by, dense local party organizations and party-identified interest associations. These became minorities at the national level, as table 8.4 highlights. Italy's nationwide referenda, used more and more as the postwar period aged, do manufacture majorities by demanding a vote of yes or no. Yet, even they can be undone by the fragmentation of opinion: if they do not attract majority participation, they are nullified—the fate of three referenda in 1990. The political order framework by no means ignores electoral laws and ballot structure, as the chapters here on France, Japan, and Germany attest. Scrutiny of Italy underscores the need to weigh carefully what happens when electoral laws perpetuate minorities, none of which clearly prevail and some of which have privileged positions in bargaining over governments.

Bargaining among Parties

In the United States, Republican presidents and Democrats in Congress may cooperate and may collide, but they do not need to create an executive. That is precisely the task of elected representatives in parliamentary systems, as other chapters in this book have shown. In presidential systems generally, voters can launch candidates into office in a fairly straightforward fashion: (1) the concerns of voters are (2) conveyed by parties into (3) elections to public office. As figures 8.2a and 8.2b illustrate, the processes of recruitment, nomination, and election connect these steps.

In the British parliamentary system, by contrast, all postwar elections but one have at least awarded the largest party a majority of parliamentary seats. In the multiparty parliamentary system of postwar Italy, however, step (3) finds minority parties in parliament, and some of those parties then (4) bargain to constitute a coalition government or support a minority government. It takes much time (one month on average) and effort to bargain Italian governments into being.[43] Fragmented opinion and institutions that do little to manufacture prevailing opinion make room for—and even require—this fourth step. And what occurs at this step helps to explain why the PCI neared but did not enter national office between 1976 and 1979, as well as why a party that almost always obtained under 40 percent of the national vote did not leave national office until 1994.[44]

Of all members of the G-7, Italy is the country where party bargaining acquires the most importance for constituting the national executive, that is, where party bargaining flows least straightforwardly from—and is the most removed from—electoral outcomes. Britain has not seen a coalition government since World War II. Single-party governments are the rule in postwar Canada as well. In Fifth Republic France, voters elect the president directly (since the 1962 referendum), and the two-ballot electoral system induces parties to form electoral alliances. Germany has long had coalitions of only two parties, and, since 1969, German parties have announced coalition intentions before elections.[45] From the formation of the Liberal Democratic Party in 1955 until the parliamentary elections in July of 1993, LDP single-party cabinets have governed Japan.

To recast the comparison: in Italy, unlike many other democracies, governments tend *not* to form immediately after an election, and parties that are recent electoral *losers* tend to govern.[46] Why is party bargaining so crucial for the creation of Italian governments? Again, all parliamentary elections to date (except those in 1948) have made the largest party a *minority party*. That largest party—always the DC from 1946 to 1994—must negotiate with others if it is to assure the survival of a minority cabinet or to build a governing coalition capable of commanding a majority of parliamentary seats.

And why do elections have this special effect in Italy? Again, Italian public opinion is fragmented. Again too, Italian institutions preserve that fragmentation. As a distinguished research tradition has emphasized,

Fig. 8.2. Two Models of Institutions

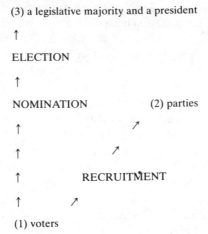

Fig. 8.2a. The political dynamic in a presidential system with plurality election laws.

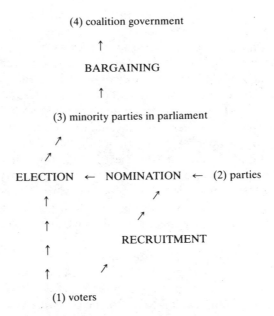

Fig. 8.2b. The political dynamic in a multiparty parliamentary system with proportional representation.

proportional electoral laws favor multiparty systems.[47] Britain and Canada (like the United States with its presidential system) have first-past-the-post electoral laws. Fifth Republic France has employed (different) runoff majority rules for presidential and National Assembly elections. In Japan, the use of the single nontransferable vote and the avoidance of redistricting have advantaged the LDP. Germany's proportional laws include a 5 percent threshold for parliamentary representation.

Until 1993, Italy had much more permissive proportional rules. Thus, for example, ten of the sixteen parties that gained Chamber seats in 1992 won less than 5 percent of the national vote.[48] Yet I should not exaggerate the distinctiveness of Italy. Governments in Fourth Republic France similarly depended on bargaining among and within parties. Governments in Japan cannot be understood without reference to bargaining within the LDP.

What structures the bargaining among parties that is so important for the emergence of Italian governments? According to the literature on coalition formation,[49] the chief influences on party bargaining are the sizes and policy positions of parties—thus, for Italy, the relatively large size and the central position of Christian Democracy—and the constraints placed on parties by formal institutions (such as electoral laws) and by informal rules (such as the long-standing rejection of the PCI as a governing ally). Taken together, those factors have produced party negotiations over new governments that are dominated by the DC and rather loosely tied to electoral outcomes; and that bargaining has yielded the record of governments shown in table 8.1.

What payoffs would await an analyst of coalitions who relied on the political order perspective rather than the large body of formal coalition theory? Compared to most formal models, this perspective devotes more attention to: (a) party organization as a constraint or resource in the hands of party leaders;[50] (b) the preferences of voters as a constraint on parties in parliament;[51] (c) the links between subnational and national governance (at least as I have translated the ideas to the Italian context); and (d) the ways that parties amplify or alter issue-dimensions.[52]

Explaining the Impact or the Origins of Corruption

As the second and third sections of this chapter have indicated, the political order approach seems to capture the recent impact of corruption in Italy: the sequence in which voters, outraged by revelations of massive corruption, launched the anti-Rome, antiparty Lombard/Northern League into Parliament in 1992 and into city halls in 1993, and then propelled the brand-new *Forza Italia* into national government in 1994. Moreover, this perspective would suggest that some voters became willing to abandon the DC with the end of the Cold War. It squares with this approach that in early 1992 magistrates moved against corruption in part because the end of the Cold War undermined the ideological justifications for "the occupation of society on the part of [Italy's] political parties"; and that many "confessions [made by corrupt politicians] . . . followed the electoral losses of the major parties in the April [1992] elections."[53]

But kickbacks and bribery were widespread long before they burst into public view in 1992. Some voters received personal favors from corrupt politicians; others were excluded from the hidden circuits of illegal exchange that linked elected officials, party functionaries, bureaucrats, businesspeople, and at times *mafiosi*.[54] To judge from recent disclosures, illegal payments changed hands wherever influence could be peddled, wherever public services were provided and contracts awarded, wherever public funds flowed.

How does the analyst of political orders treat the origins of corruption? It seems difficult—and perhaps unwise—to stretch an argument about prevailing opinion in publicly debated issue-areas to cover the forces triggering and sustaining pervasive corruption before corruption emerged as a publicly debated issue. On the other hand, because the study of political orders entails an attempt to explain who governs, it is party bargaining, above and beyond voter choices, that must be analyzed to understand who governs Italy.

Probably, then, corruption and its origins are essential components of any account of the staying power of incumbents in Italy. Perhaps, further, corruption becomes more likely in a system where party bargaining is relatively distant from voters' choices and diminishes the accountability of those who govern. What does this mean for the political order perspective? The general question posed here is the scope of the framework, the domain of phenomena that it should reach and comprehend to be considered successful.

Conclusions

Byron Shafer has advanced an ambitious agenda for research on the Group of Seven. This volume has exploited and explored his framework in diverse national contexts. The aim for each country has been to delimit political eras and map the political structures that stabilized one era or ushered in another. The research agenda is extremely stimulating, as I have tried to show for the Italian case.

Investigation of Italy also highlights, I believe, an agenda of items deserving reflection. In applying the political order framework to seven countries, our group of analysts has had to think carefully about the nature of the evidence we have needed, and have had at hand, to support our claims; about the extent of fragmentation in the electorate and in electoral outcomes; about ways to specify hypotheses about bargaining among officeholders once elected; and about ways to assess and demonstrate the comparative advantage and the scope and the analytical purchase of this framework. To implement the collective research agenda, the participants in this project have had to address the "reflection agenda" as well.

The two chapters that follow take stock of both agendas. Chapter 9 reviews the country narratives, moving additively from an initial two-country comparison to a discussion of themes and variations across all members of the Group of Seven. Chapter 10 focuses on the political order framework and the more comprehensive lessons it holds.

Notes

1. Byron E. Shafer, "The Notion of an Electoral Order: The Structure of Electoral Politics at the Accession of George Bush," in Byron E. Shafer, ed., *The End of Realignment? Interpreting American Electoral Eras* (Madison: University of Wisconsin, 1991).

2. Samuel Barnes, "Secular Trends and Partisan Realignment in Italy," in Russell Dalton, Scott Flanagan, and Paul Allen Beck, eds., *Electoral Change in Advanced Industrial Democracies* (Princeton: Princeton University, 1984).

3. For cross-national data on turnover rates, see Kaare Strom, *Minority Government and Majority Rule* (Cambridge: Cambridge University, 1990), 128. For data on government duration, see Gary King et al., "A Unified Model of Cabinet Dissolution in Parliamentary Democracies," *American Journal of Political Science* 34 (August 1990): 867. Strom defines the turnover or alternation rate for parliamentary systems as "the proportion of legislative seats by parties changing status between government and opposition," averaged across a country's governments (125).

4. ISTAT (Istituto Centrale di Statistica), *Sommario di statistiche storiche dell'Italia, 1861–1975* (Roma: Istituto Centrale di Statistica, 1976), 144; and ISTAT data in *Italian Journal* (Summer 1992): 78. Cross-national comparisons are somewhat tricky because of definitional differences (in particular, the handling of the unemployed). The proportion of the civilian workforce engaged in agriculture is reported as 40 percent in Italy and 40.2 percent in Japan for 1955 in *Agricultural Statistics, 1968* (1969), 2, and as 11.4 percent in Italy and 10.3 percent in Japan for 1989 in *Handbook of International Trade and Development Statistics, 1990* (1991), 526–30.

5. See, for example, Barnes, "Secular Trends and Partisan Realignment,"

Giuseppe Di Palma, "Christian Democracy: The End of Hegemony?" and Giacomo Sani, "The Italian Electorate in the Mid-1970s: Beyond Tradition?," both in Howard R. Penniman, ed., *Italy at the Polls: The Parliamentary Elections of 1976* (Washington, D.C.: American Enterprise Institute, 1977).

6. *Il Sole 24 Ore,* December 7, 1994; *New York Times,* March 3, 1993.

7. See chap. 2 of this volume.

8. See, for example, Strom, *Minority Government.*

9. Until June of 1993, municipal government in Italy followed parliamentary lines: city cabinets or executives (*giunte*) were formed out of the directly elected city councils. With twenty-seven nationwide referenda since 1945 (all but one since 1970), Italy holds more referenda than does any other member of the G-7. Data for 1945–80 are found in Arend Lijphart, *Democracies: Patterns of Majoritarian and Consensus Government in Twenty-One Countries* (New Haven: Yale University, 1984), 202; updates on France and Italy appear in Henry A. Erhmann and Martin A. Schain, *Politics in France,* 5th ed. (New York: Harper-Collins, 1992), 215, and Stephen Hellman, "Italian Politics in Transition," in Mark Kesselman and Joel Krieger, eds., *European Politics in Transition,* 2d ed. (New York: D.C. Heath, 1992), 409. I do not compare the Chamber of Deputies and Senate here, for they have very similar distributions of party strengths and identical formal powers—even though their constituency boundaries and their electorates differ. Citizens must be eighteen years old (twenty-one before 1976) to vote for the Chamber and twenty-five to vote for the Senate. For discussion, see Frederic Spotts and Theodor Wieser, *Italy, A Difficult Democracy* (Cambridge: Cambridge University, 1980), chap. 6; Douglas Wertman, "The Italian Electoral Process: The Elections of June 1976," in Penniman, *Italy at the Polls, 1976.*

10. John L. Harper, *America and the Reconstruction of Italy, 1945–1948* (Cambridge: Cambridge University, 1986), chaps. 7–8.

11. Paul Ginsborg, *Storia d'Italia dal dopoguerra a oggi: Società e politica 1943–1988* (Torino: Einaudi, 1989), chap. 8; Giuseppe Tamburrano, *Storia e cronaca del centro sinistra* (Milano: Feltrinelli, 1971).

12. Geoffrey Pridham, "Parties and Coalitional Behaviour in Italian Local Politics. Conflict or Convergence?," *European Journal of Political Research* 12 (September 1984): 223–41.

13. Sidney Tarrow, *Democracy and Disorder: Protest and Politics in Italy 1965–1975* (Oxford: Clarendon, 1989), 55.

14. Ibid.; Sidney Tarrow, "Maintaining Hegemony in Italy: 'The softer they rise, the slower they fall!' " in T. J. Pempel, ed., *Uncommon Democracies: The One-Party Dominant Regimes* (Ithaca: Cornell University, 1990).

15. Parliament had approved the implementing legislation for abrogative referenda in the spring of 1970. The DC favored the referendum instrument then because it calculated that a majority of voters would overturn the soon-to-be-passed divorce law. Judith Adler Hellman, *Journeys Among Women: Feminism in Five Italian Cities* (New York: Oxford University, 1987), chap. 2; Norman Kogan, *A Political History of Postwar Italy: From the Old to the New Center-Left* (New York: Praeger, 1981), chaps. 5, 7. On delays in implementing the referendum and sev-

eral other provisions of the 1948 Constitution, see Hellman, "Italian Politics in Transition"; Spotts and Wieser, *Italy: A Difficult Democracy.*

16. Stephen Hellman, "The Longest Campaign: Communist Party Strategy and the Elections of 1976," in Penniman, *Italy at the Polls, 1976,* 170.

17. Massimo Ilardi, "Sistema di potere e ideologia nel PCI: le conferenze nazionali d'organizzazione," in Massimo Ilardi and Aris Accornero, eds., *Il Partito comunista italiano: struttura e storia dell'organizzazione 1921/1979,* vol. 21, *Annali Fondazione G. Feltrinelli, 1981* (Milano: Feltrinelli, 1982), 29.

18. Gianfranco Pasquino, "The Italian Socialist Party: Electoral Stagnation and Political Indispensability," in Howard R. Penniman, ed., *Italy at the Polls, 1979: A Study of the Parliamentary Elections* (Washington D.C.: American Enterprise Institute, 1981).

19. Hellman, "Italian Politics in Transition," 405.

20. Carlo De Benedetti of Olivetti, quoted in *La Stampa,* May 18, 1993.

21. Under the new laws, each voter casts two ballots for the Chamber. One ballot is used to elect a deputy in a single-member district according to plurality rules; three-quarters of the deputies (475) are chosen in the single-member districts. The other ballot is used to vote for a party list under proportional representation (PR) rules; a party has to receive 4 percent of the PR votes to be included in the allocation of 155 seats distributed proportionally. For the Senate, similarly, 232 members are elected in single-member districts under plurality rules and 83 senators are elected under PR.

22. See, for instance, Samuel Barnes, "Religion and Class in Electoral Behavior," in Richard Rose, ed., *Electoral Behavior: A Comparative Handbook* (New York: Free Press, 1974); Samuel Barnes, *Representation in Italy: Institutionalized Tradition and Electoral Change* (Chicago: University of Chicago, 1977); Barnes, "Secular Trends and Partisan Realignment"; Paolo Bellucci, "The Effect of Aggregate Economic Conditions on the Political Preferences of the Italian Electorate, 1953–1979," *European Journal of Political Research* 12 (December 1984): 387–401; Renato Mannheimer and Giacomo Sani, *Il mercato elettorale. Identikit dell'elettore italiano* (Bologna: Il Mulino, 1987); Giacomo Sani, "Mass-Level Response to Party Strategy: The Italian Electorate and the Communist Party," in Donald L. M. Blackmer and Sidney Tarrow, eds, *Communism in Italy and France* (Princeton: Princeton University, 1975); Giacomo Sani, "The Italian Electorate in the Mid-1970s: Beyond Tradition?" in Penniman, *Italy at the Polls, 1976;* Giacomo Sani, "Ricambio elettorale, mutamenti sociali e preferenze politiche," in Luigi Graziano and Sidney Tarrow, eds., *La crisi italiana* (Torino: Einaudi, 1979); Alberto Spreafico and Joseph LaPalombara, eds., *Elezioni e comportamento politico in Italia* (Milano: Comunità, 1963).

23. Alfio Mastropaolo and Martin Slater, "Italy 1947–1979: Ideological Distances and Party Movements," in Ian Budge, David Robertson, and Derek Hearl, eds., *Ideology, Strategy and Party Change: Spatial Analyses of Post-War Election Programmes in 19 Democracies* (Cambridge: Cambridge University, 1987).

24. Moreover, surveys estimated that the proportion of practicing Catholics among Italian adults fell from roughly 70 percent in the mid-1950s to 50 percent in

the late 1960s, and to 31–36 percent from the late 1970s to early 1980s. Since the mid-1980s, the proportion of practicing Catholics has remained at about 30 percent. Giacomo Sani, "Church Attendance and the Vote for the DC: Evidence from the 1980s," *Italian Politics and Society* 34 (Fall 1991): 13–18; Roberto Cartocci, *Fra Lega e Chiesa. L'Italia in cerca di integrazione* (Bologna: Il Mulino, 1994), 162–65.

25. Renato Mannheimer and Giacomo Sani, "Themes of Mass Political Culture: A Revisitation," unpublished typescript, 1988, 13–14; Renato Mannheimer, "La natura composita dell'elettorato leghista," in Renato Mannheimer and Giacomo Sani, eds., *La rivoluzione elettorale. L'Italia tra la prima e la seconda repubblica* (Milano: Anabasi, 1994), 122–30.

26. Roberto D'Alimonte and Stefano Bartolini, "Il sistema partito italiano: Una transizione difficile," in Stefano Bartolini and Robeno D'Alimonte, eds. *Maggioritario ma non troppo* (Bologna: Il Mulino, 1995); Luca Ricolfi, "La geometria dello spazio elettorale in Italia," *Rivista italiana di scienza politica* 23 (December 1993): 433–74; Luca Ricolfi, *L'ultimo Parlamento. Sulla fine della prima Repubblica* (Roma: La Nuova Italia Scientifica, 1993); Luca Ricolfi, "Il voto proporzionale e il nuovo spazio politico italiano," in Bartolini and D'Alimonte, *Maggioritario ma non troppo.*

27. See, for instance, Mario Caciagli, "Quante Italie? Persistenza e trasformazione delle culture politiche subnazionali," *Polis* 2 (August 1988): 429–57; Paolo Farneti, *Il sistema dei partiti in Italia 1946–1979* (Bologna: Il Mulino, 1983); Giorgio Galli and Alfonso Prandi, *Patterns of Political Participation in Italy* (New Haven: Yale University, 1970); Carlo Trigilia, *Grandi partiti e piccole imprese* (Bologna: Il Mulino, 1986).

28. Reacting to these trends, Parisi and Pasquino distinguish three types of vote: a vote of belonging (*appartenenza*), which affirms an enduring social identity; a vote of opinion, motivated by a broad interest in policy; and a vote of exchange, awarded in return for patronage goods. Arturo Parisi and Gianfranco Pasquino, "Changes in Italian Electoral Behavior: The Relationships between Parties and Voters," *West European Politics* 2 (October 1979): 6–30. Mannheimer and Sani use a 1985 survey to estimate that subcultural voters constitute 60 percent of the PCI electorate and 67 percent of the DC electorate. Mannheimer and Sani, *Il mercato elettorale,* 93. See also Caciagli, "Quante Italie?"; Mannheimer and Sani, *La rivoluzione elettorale;* Gianfranco Pasquino, "La partecipazione politica fra identità e interessi," *Polis* 1 (April 1987): 3–28; Trigilia, *Grandi partiti e piccole imprese.*

29. See, for instance, Miriam Golden, *Labor Divided* (Ithaca: Cornell University, 1988); Hellman, *Journeys Among Women;* Carol Mershon, "Unions and Politics in Italy," in Howard R. Penniman, ed., *Italy at the Polls, 1983: A Study of the Parliamentary Elections* (Durham: Duke University, 1987); Carol Mershon, "Generazioni di leader sindacali in fabbrica. L'eredita dell'autunno caldo," *Polis* 4 (August 1990): 277–323; Tarrow, *Democracy and Disorder;* Sidney Tarrow, "Mutamenti nella cultura di opposizione in Italia, 1965–1975," *Polis* 3 (April 1989): 41–63.

30. Stephen Hellman, *Italian Communism in Transition: The Rise and Fall of the Historic Compromise in Turin, 1975–1980* (New York: Oxford University,

1988); Stephen Hellman, "La difficile nascita del Pds," in Stephen Hellman and Gianfranco Pasquino, eds., *Politica in Italia. I fatti dell'anno e le interpretazioni. Edizione '92* (Bologna: Il Mulino, 1992).

31. Ilvo Diamaniti and Renato Mannheimer, eds., *Milano a Roma. Guida all'Italia elettorale del 1994* (Roma: Donzelli, 1994). Moreover, 31 percent of the League's voters in the 1992 parliamentary elections voted for *Forza Italia* in 1994. Renato Mannheimer, "Forza Italia," in Diamanti and Mannheimer, *Milano a Roma,* 32.

32. Cartocci, *Fra Lega e Chiesa;* Ilvo Diamanti, *La Lega. Geografia, storia e sociologia di un nuovo soggetto politico* (Roma: Donzelli, 1993); Gianfranco Pasquino, "Meno partiti più lega," *Polis* 5 (December 1991): 555–64.

33. Mannheimer, "Forza Italia"; Ricolfi, "Il voto proporzionale"; Paolo Segatti, "I programmi elettorali e il ruolo dei mass media," in Bartolini and D'Alimonte, *Maggioritario ma non troppo.*

34. The characterization of the League is found in Diamanti, *La Lega,* 108. On *Forza Italia's* organization, see Marco Revelli, "Forza Italia: L'anomalia italiana non è finita," in Paul Ginsborg, ed., *Stato dell'Italia* (Milano: Il Saggiatore, 1994).

35. Hellman, *Italian Communism in Transition.*

36. In 1991, the Lombard League had one mayoralty and 608 (0.4 percent of 148,452) seats in Italy's municipal councils. Sara Romano, "Appendice documentaria" in Hellman and Pasquino, *Politica in Italia. Edizione '92,* 320. In the 1993 June municipal elections, held under new electoral laws, the Lombard/Northern League received 23 percent of the vote for the Turin city council and 41 percent of the vote for the Milan city council; the League's candidate became mayor of Milan, winning 57 percent of the vote in the second round. *Corriere della Sera,* June 8, 1993; June 21, 1993.

In 1993 November-December, PDS-backed candidates won mayoral positions in all six of the large cities holding elections. The PDS and its allies gained majorities on 53 of the 129 city councils elected in towns with over 15,000 inhabitants. Martin Rhodes, "Reinventing the Left: The Origins of Italy's Progressive Alliance," in Carol Mershon and Gianfranco Pasquino, eds., *Italian Politics: Ending the First Republic* (Boulder: Westview, 1995), 128.

37. Cf. Tarrow, "Mutamenti nella cultura di opposizione."

38. See, for example, the comparison of seven surveys in Renato Mannheimer, *Capire il voto. Contributi per l'analisis del comportamento elettorale in Italia* (Milano: Franco Angeli, 1989), 130. The Eurobarometer surveys, begun in 1973, illustrate the problem. The Eurobarometer nonresponse rate in Italy was 31 percent in 1980 and is typically around that figure (ibid.). In 1983, 14.6 percent of Italian Eurobarometer respondents declared a preference for the PCI and 29.1 percent for the DC. The 1983 parliamentary elections awarded 29.9 percent of the vote to the PCI and 32.9 percent to the DC (results for the Chamber of Deputies). Guido Martinotti and Sonia Stefanizzi, "Le tendenze dell'elettorato italiano: un'analisi dei dati dell'Eurobarometro, 1976–1988", *Polis* 4 (December 1990): 540.

39. Mannheimer and Sani, "Themes of Mass Political Culture," 5, 8.

40. Mannheimer, *Capire il voto,* 24.

41. Mannheimer and Sani, "Themes of Mass Political Culture," 8.

42. For example, cross-national survey data from 1976 show that the distance separating the leftmost and rightmost partisan groups is greater in Italy than in the United States, Germany, Britain, or France. Giacomo Sani and Giovanni Sartori, "Polarization, Fragmentation, and Competition in Western Democracies," in Hans Daalder and Peter Mair, eds., *Western European Party Systems* (London: Sage, 1983), 324. Canada and Japan are not included in the data set.

43. Carol Mershon, "The Costs of Coalition: Coalition Theories and Italian Governments," unpublished typescript, 1995.

44. Party bargaining also explains outcomes outside the national parliament. For example, in 1982, municipal cabinets including the PSI governed over 60 percent of the Italian population (see tables 8.6, 8.7, and 8.8), while the PSI polled perhaps 20 percent at the city level. On the nuances of computing nationwide totals of municipal electoral results, see Arturo Parisi, "Instabilità conflittualità e alleanze tra i partiti a livello locale" in Arturo Parisi, ed., *Luoghi e misure della politica* (Bologna: Il Mulino, 1984), 75–76. What does the contrast suggest? A good bargaining position, parlayed into power. The PSI could ally with the DC on its right or the PCI on its left.

More broadly, on the mix of public confrontation and hidden processes of bargaining in Italian politics, see Giuseppe Di Palma, *Surviving without Governing* (Berkeley: University of California, 1977); Joseph La Palombara, *Democracy: Italian Style* (New Haven: Yale University, 1987); Giovanni Sartori, *Parties and Party Systems* (New York: Cambridge University, 1976).

45. Jurg Steiner, *European Democracies,* 2d ed. (London: Longman, 1991), 119–20.

46. Quantitative cross-national data in Strom, *Minority Government,* 75.

47. Maurice Duverger, *Political Parties: Their Organization and Activity in the Modern State,* trans. Barbara North and Robert North (New York: Wiley, 1963); William Riker, "The Two-Party System and Duverger's Law: An Essay on the History of Political Science," *American Political Science Review* 76 (December 1982): 753–76.

48. The mixed plurality/proportional rules used in 1994 did trigger the negotiation of electoral alliances—those listed in table 8.5. Nonetheless, in a sense, fragmentation in Parliament increased from 1992 to 1994, for the number of parties (not electoral blocs) earning Chamber seats rose from 16 to 20. As D'Alimonte and Bartolini observe, the mixed electoral laws were "intentionally made so as to offer the greatest possibility of defense to all" parties. "Il sistema partito italiano," 433.

49. See, for example, Michael Laver and Norman Schofield, *Multiparty Government: The Politics of Coalition in Europe* (New York: Oxford University, 1990).

50. Alternatively, see Kaare Strom, "The Presthus Debacle: Intraparty Politics and Bargaining Failure in Norway," *American Political Science Review* 88 (March 1994): 112–27.

51. Alternatively, see David Austen-Smith and Jeffrey Banks, "Elections, Co-

alitions, and Legislative Outcomes," *American Political Science Review* 82 (June 1988): 405–22.

52. Alternatively, see Norman Schofield, Bernard Grofman, and Scott L. Feld, "The Core and the Stability of Group Choice in Spatial Voting Games," *American Political Science Review* 82 (March 1988): 195–211.

53. Both quotations from Donatella Della Porta, "La capitale immorale: le tangenti di Milano," in Hellman and Pasquino, eds., *Politica in Italia. Edizione '92.* Cf. Guido Neppi Modona, "Giustizia e potere politico," in Ginsborg, *Stato dell'Italia.* Scholars have identified other reasons why Italy's corruption scandal broke open in 1992. According to Della Porta ("La capitale immorale," 236), the costs of corruption were increasing—one politician requested higher kickbacks due to the "rising cost of living"—at the same time that industries faced the prospect of stiffer competition, above all because European economies were becoming more tightly integrated. Magistrates were better equipped to pursue corruption in the early 1990s than in the past because institutional reforms in 1989 gave new investigatory tools to them (Guido Neppi Modona, "Tangentopoli e Marti pulite: dopo le indagini, i processi," in Ginsborg, *Stato dell'Italia*). On the recruitment of new generations into the magistracy, see Carlo Guainieri, *Magistratura e politica in Italia. Pesi senza contrappesi* (Bologna: Il Mulino, 1992).

54. Donatella Della Porta, *Lo scambio occulto* (Bologna: Il Mulino, 1992); Donatella Della Porta and Alberto Vannucci, "Politics, the Mafia, and the Market for Corrupt Exchange," in Mershon and Pasquino, *Italian Politics: Ending the First Republic.*

9 *Byron E. Shafer*

Synthesis

The preceding chapters have presented seven single-case analyses of post-war politics in the G-7 nations. Each is a comprehensive portrait in its own right, of politicking in a major nation across an extended historical period, including both the influences on and products of that politicking. The challenge in producing such a portrait, both in the amount of raw synthesis and in the choice of critical elements, is itself substantial. The resulting portraits must thus be the main product of the collective enterprise, as organizing overviews but also as preliminary explanations for change. That these individual portraits also constitute the Group of Seven, so that their collective decisions can occasionally have international consequence, is, of course, a further side-benefit.

On the other hand, it ought to be possible to say something additional about the *comparative* politics of the G-7, something which might even have resonance beyond the bounds of this small but consequential group. One way to attempt this is to begin with individual comparisons among these nations, across their eras and orders, adding a nation and extending the comparison as the analysis proceeds. That is the strategy for this penultimate chapter. Such a (partially self-limiting) strategy is reinforced by the evident diversity in the postwar politics of these nations. Simple generalizations purporting to cover them all risk being desperately abstract, or simply wrong.

Nevertheless, once this is done, the effort to drive such comparisons as far as they will go—and here, of course, across all the G-7 collectively—still beckons. That is the task of the final chapter. If it seems an inherently hopeless task, then perhaps its by-products should just be enumerated in advance: a look at such concerns as the sequencing of political eras internationally; the isolation of additional, key domestic structural elements; a focus on the interaction—a mutual *and inherent* interaction—between substantive issues and political structures; the place of particular substantive issues, including the role of economic issues or foreign policy in particular; the inescapably central role of formal arrangements for government, both electoral and policymaking; the place of amorphous but powerful and parallel shifts in the larger society; the changing dynamic of politicking, a strikingly similar change, across these disparate nations; and the reasons—also mutual and inherent—that none of this will ever likely add up to "convergence" in the orthodox sense of the word.

North America

Simple and direct, concrete comparisons flow easily from the first two chapters in this analysis, on the United States and Canada. Geographic propinquity is surely involved, but it is not the main explanation. Indeed, geographic propinquity fares badly in producing similarities nearly everywhere in the G-7. Thus France and Britain are notably short of parallels, while Italy and Japan produce more than any other pair. Instead, in an analysis built self-consciously around eras and orders, the role of World War II in the politics of these nations is what makes opening parallels easy to detect. Said differently, these two nations are distinguished from the other G-7 members by the more limited—not small, just more limited—impact of the Second World War.

What this means is that unlike everyone else except France, where the counterpart effect was merely delayed, the United States and Canada *did not* feature the end of World War II as the beginning of a new substantive era in national politics, much less of a new structural order. Rather, in both, the first great political era of the postwar years stretched back before the Second World War, back, in fact, to the domestic political fallout from the arrival of the Great Depression. The political dynamics and policy responses generated by the depression did vary substantially between them. Yet both nations began the postwar years in the midst of an extended political era stretching back into the 1930s.

Not surprisingly, the central policy issues to these two earlier parallel eras were much the same: principally some policy response to the hardships of the Great Depression, secondarily some response to the conflagration that was World War II. Both stimuli were sufficiently global and sufficiently strong to command a response from governments of all the developed nations, of course. But the point here is that the war, for all its breadth, depth, and horror, was obviously *not* strong enough to have much effect on a political era beginning earlier and continuing later in both these countries.

On the other hand, the political orders associated with this (common) era did vary significantly between the two. In the United States, the Great Depression encountered a politics still organized around geographic regions at its grass roots and elicited a politics built around two broad, class-based, national coalitions instead. The majority coalition was reflected, partly by accidents of incumbency, in what became the blue-collar party, the Democrats, to be opposed by the white-collar party, the Republicans. And the Democrats gained such strong and uniform control of the otherwise very separate institutions of national government that they could take major steps toward implementing an American "welfare state."

In Canada, by contrast, the old ethnocultural and regional distinctions which dominated social coalitions at the grass roots were not powerfully disturbed by the Great Depression. The depression did sweep the Conservative party out of government and bring the Liberals in, for the duration of this first postwar era. But there was less policy difference between the two parties than between the U.S. Republicans and Democrats. The Conservatives actually began a policy response to the depression via increased provision of social welfare; the Liberals took this up, consolidated it, and expanded it modestly. Facing a parliamentary system whose governing majorities were exaggerated by first-past-the-post elections, they had comparatively less difficulty in doing so, in truth, than did their Democratic counterparts in the United States.

Similar issue concerns with different structural underpinnings implied similar policy foci but a very different political dynamic. The United States, despite the indiscipline of its individual parties, offered a dynamic approximating the classic two-party model, at least in this particular era. One party, the Democrats, found the policy preferences of a majority and became dominant. The other party, the Republicans, continued to resist the program of the dominant party, long after its implementation. Moderate Democrats thus normally controlled all the institutions of government. Moderate Republicans were nevertheless capable of doing the same. One result was that the United States took both earlier and stronger action with its incipient welfare state. Another result was that it did not carry it as *far* as Canada in the course of the postwar years.

The counterpart dynamic in Canada centered on a multiparty system but of a peculiar sort, with a dominant national party, a much weaker pretender to national opposition, and serious *regional* opposition parties. In that environment, what drove social-welfare policy was actually the programmatic goals—and numerical growth—of one of these splinters. In the immediate postwar years, this was the Cooperative Commonwealth Federation (CCF), the most explicitly socialist of the major Canadian or American parties. In order to maintain national power, the Liberals then coopted large parts of the CCF program. In order to stay potentially competitive and lacking sufficient class crystallization to block such a move, the Conservatives tagged along. In return, the CCF receded. When it did, governmental policy response eased.

In both countries, in any case, the end of this first postwar political era came with the rise of a set of individually specific cultural and national issues, to equal prominence with the economic and social-welfare issues of the first postwar era. In the nature of such developments, these new issues were accompanied by a change in political structure—partly impelling and partly resulting from this issue shift. Diagnostically, however, the shift could first have been confirmed (and is best introduced) through a change in the place of foreign affairs in domestic politics.

In the first postwar era, foreign affairs had been noteworthy, in both the United States and Canada, for the way that it did *not* change in its domestic role and impact. Which is to say: a transfer of the cross-party consensus on fighting World War II to a cross-party consensus on pursuing the Cold War was effectively accomplished in both nations, with lots of surface struggle (especially in the United States) but with no insuperable difficulties. This still represented a break with *older* eras in the political history of the United States, while it merely extended enduring divisions from earlier eras in Canada. Yet the surprising similarity was that a cross-party consensus did characterize the two nations on these issues in both wartime and the immediate postwar years.

That consensus came apart first in Canada, where the unraveling was symbolized by policy tensions arising from the Suez crisis of 1956. Yet within the framework of political eras and orders, Suez was really just a concrete if dramatic touchstone for general adjustments to Canadian foreign policy in the face of a changing international realm. These adjustments, in turn, were only indicative of a deeper tension between a *British* and an American orientation for Canadian foreign policy in the Cold War years. And that tension was still more deeply rooted in ethnic and cultural differences within Canada. As a result, it would ultimately be these latter, more explicitly domestic tensions which would most clearly distinguish this second postwar era in Canadian politics from the first.

What would in fact characterize this era was the coming of cultural as well as national issues to prominence in Canadian politics, to join the old

commercial and developmental issues, along with those intermittent
social-welfare concerns. The Conservative government whose rupture of
Liberal dominance most clearly marked the coming of a new era did shift
an old alignment on commercial policy, to favor the West over the East.
And the Liberal government which then regained power did introduce a
second postwar round of social-welfare enhancement. Those issues were,
accordingly, hardly absent from Canadian politics. But they were joined
by a whole cluster of additional issues, from international alliance behavior through domestic language policy, which involved the explicit form of
integration for the nation. It was these essentially cultural and national
issues which were to give the new era a new cast.

On the surface, partisan politics actually masked this change. The same
dominant party, the Liberals, faced the same putative opposition, the Conservatives, again with a further set of regional splinters. Indeed, the rise of
another major splinter, the New Democratic Party (NDP) which grew out
of the Cooperative Commonwealth Federation (CCF), caused the associated political dynamic to look initially much as it had before. This time,
the Liberals coopted the NDP program, through a second round of social-
welfare increase; the Conservatives then followed along; and the NDP,
while not so seriously undercut as the CCF had been, merely stabilized for
an extended period.

Yet underneath, the new order was noticeably different, and gradually
rising cultural and national issues were to play into it in a noticeably different way. At the grass roots, the mass public balance between Liberals and
Conservatives was closer, so that national governments had much less
leeway in addressing ethnocultural concerns. Moreover, the dominant
party, the Liberals, had acquired a geographically narrowed focus because ethnocultural attachments—Catholic for the Liberals, Protestant
for the Conservatives—were much sharper. Finally, and most crucially, a
previously consequential element of Canadian political structure worked
in a new way.

That element was the critical place of the province of Quebec, always
the single largest influence on electoral outcomes and governmental formation, thanks principally to its sheer size but also to its often distinctive
policy preferences. In the old political order, these preferences had involved both commercial and foreign policy. Quebec had joined Ontario in
favoring the industrial East over the agricultural and mining West; it had
differed over a more self-consciously British orientation toward the outside world. In the new political order, by contrast, Quebec had shifted to a
focus on language rights and cultural support, seeking provincial autonomy on these and making it very difficult for coherent national coalitions
to be put together: always difficult without Quebec, now difficult with it.

Foreign affairs was to be the diagnostic entry-point to a new political era in the United States as well, though the bread there came later, when the war in Vietnam served as its symbolic focus. As in Canada, economic and social-Welfare issues hardly went away in this second postwar era. As in Canada, these were, however, joined by a huge array of cultural and national issues, playing across them in consequential ways. In Canada, these issues were probably more pointed and more profound, going ultimately to the basis of national integration itself. In the United States, they included race—pointed and profound enough in its own right—but then moved on to constitute a far broader array of less encompassing concerns, ranging from crime, through abortion, to public prayer, to "permissiveness," to public protest, to sex roles, to capital punishment, and so on, all of them involving the character of national life.

These issues surely reflected a variety of background changes in American society—greater affluence, spreading education, technological development, national media. Many were brought into politics and given their specific focus, on the other hand, by way of decisions from the U.S. Supreme Court. Two structural points follow from this. In one, a court system became an important structural influence and played an important substantive role, as it would in many of the other G-7 nations. In the other, the new cultural and national issues propelled by the American Supreme Court did not so much "fragment" the general public as simply and forcefully cross-cut it. There were now two majorities to politics—an economic/welfare majority and a cultural/national majority—and they were effectively unrelated to each other.

A first-past-the-post electoral system, a decentralized party system, and, crucially, the separation of powers, then caused this pattern of preferences to create a distinctive political dynamic. In this, the two parties, nationally, offered ideologically consistent policies, liberal in both realms for Democrats, conservative in both for Republicans. The two underlying majorities inevitably bounced between—or straddled—these two parties, depending on the offices in conflict and the dominant issues of the day. Split partisan control of government was the outcome which made the new order seem most stereotypically different. Yet the underlying tension, between policies and between majorities, would surface constantly even when one partly controlled both major elective institutions of national government.

Over and around these elements of change between two political eras in two nations was a larger and more amorphous structural development, crucial to both. In abstract terms, this was a change in the essential character of political brokerage. Nothing is more integral to the story of the postwar politics in these nations than the story of this shift: the movement from a political order in which national public policy was created through bargaining among delegates from more localized communities and regions, to a political order in which national policy was instead critically shaped by national—in effect, essentially plebiscitary—processes.

That is a highly abstract description. More concretely, this change was registered by a shift in the character of the brokers themselves, again in both societies. Indeed, if parliamentary versus presidential governments or two-party versus multiparty systems differentiate these nations, a powerful parallel shift in the social character of their major partisan actors correspondingly unifies them—and coincides with the shift from the first to the second postwar political era. In both countries, local brokers, whose job was to bring national rewards home to the community or region and to hammer out some sort of national compromise on other issues, were replaced by actors motivated instead by intense policy concerns, and national concerns at that.

This second postwar era continued, essentially unchanged, into the 1990s in the United States. Thus it continued easily through the defeat of President George Bush by President Bill Clinton, and thereby through the shift from formalistically divided to formalistically unified national government. Just as it continued through the further shift to an opposite pattern of partisan division, with a Democratic president but a Republican Congress this time. The nation might mix and match partisan preferences, and then mix and match again. This did not, however, guarantee a change in the associated political order, and as long as it did not, a political era would continue—and the dynamic of American politics would continue to be of a piece.

The situation was not so clear in Canada, where the dominance of cultural issues in Canadian politics by the 1990s raised the insistent possibility of a third great postwar era. By the early 1980s, ethnocultural issues had already taken center-stage in Canadian politics. Issues of language use and cultural priority, as they defined the appropriate place of French speakers, were the cutting edge of the linguistic issue-cluster. Yet in their wake, they produced additional ethnocultural claims, for political reorganization and expanded group rights. By extension, as the linguistic issue—ultimately an issue of national integration—moved to the center of politicking, the two main parties, each in turn, attempted to solve this central problem by themselves becoming broader, intendedly national coalitions.

Yet in doing so, these parties of course became simultaneously less coherent, ingesting the elements which were both necessary to any acceptable solution *and* consecutively unwilling to accept any of the solutions on offer. Accordingly, the Meech Lake Accord went down, the Charlottetown Accord went down, the Liberal party went down, the Conservative party went down. And again simultaneously, in the face of two huge but incoherent parties alternating in the attempt to find a solution, splinters on the extremes (which *had* a simple solution) came up: the Parti Québécois at one end, Reform at the other. Their preferred resolutions promised a new order, almost by definition. Policy compromises, if they could be found, or simple public exhaustion with these issues if compromises could not be found, promised instead to mark the extension of a second postwar era.

Canada thus becomes the first of the cases—Germany, Italy, and Japan will subsequently join it—where precise specification both of temporal cuts and of structural influences for the modern era is (and must be) dependent on *further* developments. The residual tasks of any analytic framework, in the face of such an obviously indeterminate future, are to provide general building-blocks leading up to the present, along with key checkpoints for examining the change proceeding from it. In this, a framework involving political eras and the composition of their political orders can still help to highlight alternative possibilities and provide some means for thinking concretely about them. Indeed, viewed in this light, the resulting alternatives only enrich the possibilities for comparison across all the G-7 nations in the postwar years, as in chapter 10.

Anglo-America

Had it not been for the Second World War, the timing of postwar political eras in Britain might well have coincided more closely with those of the United States and Canada. After all, the Great Depression had been an equally powerful stimulus to policymaking; expansion of the welfare state was an equally plausible policy response. Yet the war did intervene, at three levels of abstraction. Most generally, it focused political attention on national survival. To this end, it demanded a government of national unity, to pursue a defense. That government, most concretely, then postponed the election of 1940, which might otherwise have foreshadowed the sharp change to come in 1945.

Nevertheless, because that election was postponed, it became the one to register the arrival of a new political era. The central concerns of this new era were to be the appropriate provision—the appropriate extension and the appropriate level—of social-welfare benefits, to insure against the disruptions, and simple harshness, of the economic marketplace. The largest single structural change underpinning this new era, in turn, was a change in the composition of the mass electorate. An entire new generation of working-class Britons grew up not just with universal suffrage as the norm but with the trade-union movement as the organizational context for its participation. It was not that they too had failed to recognize the need to subordinate social-welfare desires to the demands of national survival during the war. It was just that there had also been constant reassurances that "things would get better" when the war ended.

The war did end, and the long-delayed response to the depression came in 1945, with the massive election of a new Labor government. Major policy changes followed quickly: nationalization of utilities and strategic industries, social insurance for unemployment and disability, broader and richer pensions, socialized medicine. In no other G-7 nation during the postwar years—with the potential exception of Germany today—was raw expansion of the electorate such a decisive factor in ending one political era and beginning another. As a result, the main direct parallel with the situation in the United States and Canada was that the same basic concerns, economic and social-welfare concerns, were nevertheless to dominate the first great postwar era in all three nations.

That is half the inaugural story. Yet the other half of a complete description of the first postwar political order in Britain involves it national embodiment of the two other general factors which were also shaping politics at the time, critically, in Canada and the United States. Said differently, the same key elements—social homogeneity or heterogeneity, along with governmental centralization or decentralization—both complete a picture of the political order in postwar Britain and explain the timing and force of policy responses in these *three* nations: (a) the United States was to move first and produce the most restrained welfare state; (b) Canada was to move second and produce a larger programmatic response; and (c) Britain was to go third and deliver by far the most throughgoing reforms.

In Britain, a homogeneous society was, by its nature, less prone to generate the continual conflicts out of which individual policies might emerge. Class was by far the dominant dimension of social cleavage, unlike the United States and Canada, or France and Italy for that matter. Yet when such a society did have a policy demand, and then a party response to that demand, such homogeneity certainly facilitated policy change. When such a society was coupled with truly centralized institutions of government—a prime minister who dominated both Parliament and the majority party, without even serious alternative *layers* of government to serve as the home of an ongoing opposition—the government of the day might still resist change, as a reelected Conservative government might well have done. But that government was advantaged in moving forcefully when society (that impressively homogeneous society) appeared to demand it.

The United States was different, even opposite. There, an extremely heterogeneous society—on grounds of race, ethnicity, religion; class, occupation, lifestyle, geography, history, and on and on—was coupled with highly fragmented governmental arrangements: not just a real and strong "separation of powers" in its institutions, but a genuinely federal organization to its politics as well. One result was that widespread if varying demands for a response to the Great Depression were generated and registered early; the United States moved first among these three nations. A second result was that once the most consensually acceptable programs had been implemented, brakes upon further initiatives, or at least much greater conflicts, also followed.

Canada, then, fell neatly in the middle, as it should when these two great structural influences are the focus. On the one hand, it was closer to the United States than to Britain in terms of social heterogeneity: less heterogeneous than the United States, though with a very complicated internal patterning, but indisputably closer to the United States than to Britain. That status betokened a later start than the United States, an earlier start that Britain. On the other hand, Canada was closer to Britain than to the United States in terms of governmental centralization: parliamentary institutions buttressed by first-past-the-post elections did, on balance, clearly outweigh real federal pressures and a fragmented party system. All of which betokened a stronger policy response than in the United States, a clearly weaker one than in Britain.

These same two critical and ongoing elements of the political order—a homogeneous society, with centralized institutions of government—are also useful for emphasizing the way that the same basic structural factors can underpin quite different substantive concerns in different periods. Said differently, they emphasize the way that the same factors can work very differently under different pressures. Homogeneity and centralization in Britain did not, of course, change between 1944 and 1946. Yet when the depression, the delay in response to it caused by the Second World War, the growing body of Labour support "beneath" the wartime effort at national unity, and then the election of 1945 were all imposed on top of these two elements of the political order, a new political era (and order) emerged.

Britain, however, was very much parallel to both Canada and the United States with regard to the major aspect of the new political era which was in fact undisturbed by the end of the Second World War. This was the place of foreign affairs, and especially of conflicts over an orientation to the brave new situation in international security. In Canada and the United States, a shift from pursuit of World War II to pursuit of the Cold War, perhaps surprisingly, brought no serious shift in the domestic political order. In both countries, tensions over foreign affairs would come considerably later and would thus be important in a change to the second major postwar era.

In Britain, more remarkably, the same was true. In spite of the size of the change in public policy associated with the coming of a new Labour government, an underlying orientation to foreign affairs remained intact. A large part of the explanation was elite continuity, as it was, in truth, in the United States and Canada. In Britain, common experience in the pursuit of foreign affairs in the wartime government, for Labour as well as Conservative leaders, was buttressed at a deeper level by a common social background among those who handled foreign affairs. When there was no serious mass opposition to their acceptance of Cold War burdens, the result was even more dramatic in Britain, in that the underlying place of foreign affairs was unaffected by a huge change in the domestic political order.

The dynamic of postwar British politics, however—the way this interaction of eras and orders worked in practice—was noticeably different from the dynamic in the United States or Canada. Moreover, in this difference probably lies the explanation both for how the first postwar political era in Britain managed to last so long, in comparative terms, and for the specific character of the change in eras when it did arrive. In Canada, a second order had actually arrived by the late 1950s. In the United States, it arrived in the late 1960s instead. In Britain, it did not arrive until the late 1970s. Characteristically, when it did, no one could be in doubt about the date.

Nevertheless, when it did arrive, the new political dynamic would still be easily recognizable in terms of the old. In this dynamic, the crucial element was actually the behavior of the *opposition* party (or parties). Within a very short time, they too were competing on the same issues and programs that the turning-point election had brought into government. Thus for the long period from 1945 to 1979, the point was that the Conservatives came to argue for their version of the welfare state—more appropriately targeted, better managed, cheaper—so that Labour/Conservative competition oscillated around the same basic programs, at roughly the same midpoint. It has taken longer, for reasons addressed below, for Labour to come to argue for its version of individual opportunity and personal choice after 1979—more widely available, more humane, and no more expensive—but, at this is written, it has apparently done so.

In any case, the break registered in 1979 had all the surface hallmarks of the break registered in 1945. It had partisan change in the control of government, of course. More consequentially, it prefaced a sharp and extended shift in policy responses, as the policy aggregate known as "Thatcherism" came quickly to the fore. But below the surface, and more consequentially, it had the counterpart crucial shift in the composition of the social base for British politics. For it was the election of 1979 which registered the gradual demise of the manual working-class majority and the gradual rise of a new middle class.

When this shift was added to a continuing absence of other major principles of division in society, and to the continuing presence of a centralized government, the structural preconditions for a revised political order were all at hand. What followed was a revised version of the old political dynamic, in which the opposition either competed on the new issue concerns associated with this new order, or lost. Yet the new issue concerns around which these older structural elements recrystallized were nevertheless remarkably similar to—they were in effect the national embodiment of—central concerns that would have been very familiar from the North American context.

In the United States, when the Democratic party had moved off from the Cold War consensus on containment of Communism in the late 1960s, national Republicans had received one set of promising (foreign policy) advantages. When a spate of cultural issues had arisen, more or less independent of either party, these national Republicans had received a second set. In Canada, foreign relations had come to play the same role a bit earlier, through general questions about a Canadian orientation to the Cold War world. As in the United States, neither political party had had to look very hard for—in truth, neither had really wanted to see—a second set of newly contentious issues of language and ethnocultural rights, which then came more and more to dominate politics despite this partisan aversion.

Counterpart shifts were delayed in Britain, by social homogeneity, governmental centralization, and a dominant political dynamic. Yet they could not be delayed indefinitely, and when they did arrive, so did a new political era. Academic and journalistic debate about "Thatcherism" often focused on the fate of the welfare state, and thus (mistakenly) on the diagnostic policies and politicking of the *first* postwar era. But in fact, those were not the issue-areas which brought the Thatcher government to power, nor which sustained an era and order after Margaret Thatcher was gone. To emphasize the point: public support for the main elements of the British social-welfare program never seriously wavered across the new political period.

Foreign policy was, however, one important element of change, focusing as it did on Britain's role in the wider world. One party, the Conservatives, remained unabashed about serving as a pillar of containment in a bipolar division. The other, Labour, renounced this position, to the point of flirting with unilateral disarmament. In truth, the issue did stress both party coalitions. But majority opinion sat principally with the former pole, so that it was the Labour coalition that was principally under pressure. At the time, this fact was masked by more general debates about governing competence. Yet the perceived ability to conduct a foreign policy—a "proper" foreign policy—was inevitably a concrete referent within those debates.

At the same time, cultural and lifestyle issues came to play an even more influential role in this second postwar political era. Questions about the character of ordinary British life—public deportment, personal responsibility, criminal control—not only became more central to political debate; they also became much less consensual across the political parties. To the extent that these touched on social-welfare concerns, they involved questions of the kind of citizenry being produced, not the distribution of benefits per se. Had Margaret Thatcher presented her Conservative government as seeking instead to "cut child benefit," "restructure the National Health Service," and so on, it might never have been elected.

On the other hand, in a kind of further parallel to the immediate postwar situation, when this new era did finally arrive in Britain, it arrived with considerably more force than it did in the United States or Canada. In many ways, the underlying situation, in terms of public preferences, was really quite similar, even comparing the two extremes, the United States and the United Kingdom. In both, the public obviously approved of existing welfare-state commitments. In both, however, it clearly preferred traditionalism on cultural values and nationalism in foreign affairs. In the United States, this provided the makings for split partisan control of government. In the United Kingdom, neither the party system nor governmental arrangements could countenance that.

Forces this fundamental—underlying *and cross-cutting* public preferences, and thus underlying and cross-cutting social majorities—did call forth some related echoes, even in Britain. Thus if the Conservatives had staked out the ideological right on both dimensions, and if Labour then staked out the left on both, there was, in principle, ideological "room" for two other parties. The old Liberals actually offered one of these possibilities: liberal on cultural/national issues and conservative on economic/welfare matters. A new party, the Social Democrats, then sprang up to offer the other: conservative on cultural/national affairs but liberal on economic/welfare matters, before an amalgamation of Liberals and Social Democrats muddled the distinction.

Neither of those minor parties ultimately threatened to bring a different combination of basic preferences into the new political order. As a result, and more to the practical point in Britain, one public opinion majority ro the other—an economic/welfare or a cultural/national majority—was very likely to determine the control of national government. On the other hand, given the nature of the party system through which this was done, a party awarded control of government by one majority would be able, within some limits, to use that government to pursue its wishes on the *other* set of issues as well, despite the fact that these might be minority wishes. More concretely, a conservative cultural/national government in Britain did get to do conservative economic/welfare policies: sweeping privatization of prior nationalizations, imposition of national standards in education, introduction of "internal markets" for governmental services, a per capita tax, and so on.

That the Labour party left these initiatives effectively unchallenged for a surprising length of time was due, finally, to the national embodiment of another general trend shared with most of the other G-7 nations: the gradual shift to a politics built around partisan activists motivated by issues and ideology, rather than around party loyalists moved by organizational attachments and brokerage concerns. The rise of such "issue activists" was in fact integral to the Laborite withdrawal from the Cold War consensus and to its adoption of the progressive posture—the minority position—on cultural issues generally. By the same token, the increasing presence of these activists (though here, very much buttressed by representatives of the party's major interest group, the trade unions) was an important part of the explanation for why the party did not quickly reorient to the new era and begin to compete around a new set of concerns.

A different kind of Conservative party had done this relatively quickly in the immediate postwar years. The rise in the interim of nonbrokerage activists—set free from localized connections, motivated primarily by the national issues of their era instead, and making a partially autonomous contribution to their political order as a result—was a key element of difference between the two eras within Britain, as it was for the United States and Canada as well. By extension, this same change in the nature of political intermediation contributed toward the same overall dynamic in most of the G-7 nations, with countervailing public preferences on economic/welfare versus cultural/national issues, facing policy options from the political parties which differed from the composite preferences of the general public—with a special polarization on cultural/national concerns thrown in.

Despite all this, the parallels should not be overdrawn. For this did not ultimately imply the same characteristic political dynamic, nor the same resulting governments of the day, even in just the Anglo-American countries. The societies in which all this was happening and the institutional arrangements through which it was happening were still noticeably different, just too different for such an all-encompassing parallel. Instead, what resulted in the United States was "divided government"; in Canada, "minority government with majority rule"; and in Britain, "artificial amalgamation."

The Allies

The last of the former "Allies" in the prosecution of World War II (among the G-7 nations) is France. From the beginning, however, the war figured in yet a different way in its postwar politics. For the United States and Canada, with a few dramatic exceptions, the war had never been a directly territorial matter, and it neither marked a new postwar era nor even interrupted an old prewar order. Britain, by contrast, was under direct and sustained territorial attack, and this attack effectively postponed the arrival of a new political era until the war had formally ended, when that era arrived with a vengeance. France, however, was occupied, and the fallout from occupation was to spill over into postwar politics in a crucial way. This spillover would in fact delay a change of era (and order) which seemed otherwise destined to occur, for far longer than the war itself had delayed such a shift in Britain and with even more convulsive consequences for France when it finally came.

On the other hand, a second line is also crossed with the arrival of France in the analysis, a line which makes the appropriate comparison as much with the former Axis as with the former Allied powers. In the most abstract sense, France would still show some similarities to the United States and Canada in the immediate postwar years. These were the three nations, for example, which *resumed* a prewar political order. But in the specifics of their politics, this is patently the wrong comparison. In the nature of its postwar policy challenges, France looks much more like Germany than like Canada or the United States in the dozen years after the Second World War. And in the character of the politicking which addressed them—the disruptions to society and the instabilities in government—it would surely have been Italy, much more than Britain, which provided the apparent parallels for analysts at the time.

As a result, France sits, appropriately, between the Anglo-American democracies on the one hand and the former Axis powers on the other. Nevertheless, for a brief period after World War II, it must have seemed that none of this might ultimately prove true. Or at least, there was a serious battle within France over constitutional arrangements for postwar politics, and there was a serious strong-executive option within this battle. Had that option prevailed, a new structural order might potentially have followed from major constitutional change. Yet many of the proponents of this option were critically handicapped by associations with the war-time occupation and its Vichy regime, while more of the obvious resis-tance figures were in favor of a return to strong-parliamentary arrange-ments instead. In the immediate run, the latter prevailed.

Unsurprisingly, then, France mirrored the United States and Canada in beginning the postwar years with a political era reaching back well before the Second World War. In this, central issue conflicts continued to revolve around economics and social welfare. That fact was frequently masked by the surface drama of French politics, by the proliferation of regionally based sub-issues from one side and by constant struggles just to form a national government from the other. Yet underneath all of these was a pressing need to rebuild the postwar French economy, and it was this that would generate the defining policies—and policy conflicts—of this first postwar era.

Moreover, economic rebuilding, besides being substantively related to the concerns of the prewar political era, slotted comfortably into a struc-tural *order* reflecting prewar contours as well. That order had grown out of a heterogeneous but sharply divided and segmented society—in the latter respect unlike the United States, which was also certainly heteroge-neous. These divisions had previously gained expression through a party system reflecting, and ultimately "freezing," their major contours. The main principle of organization within this party system was still economic, along a classic Left-Right axis. But there were additional class-based fil-lips to this party system along with a heavy clerical/secular overlay. Re-gional divisions were additionally important to the actual politicking that played out within the system.

If that had been all there was to the postwar political order—fragmented society, fragmented intermediaries, fragmented constitu-tional arrangements—the same simple argument which covered the re-sponse of the United States, Canada, and Britain to these same economic/welfare issues would have made a clear prediction about France as well: that it would move early but hesitantly on extension of the welfare state. That this was nevertheless an insufficient description (and prediction) was due to one further, major, complicating element of the political order—the continuation from prewar years of a strong central bureaucracy.

Prewar France had possessed a much stronger statist tradition than the United States, Canada, or Britain. The postwar French bureaucracy found itself aided in a general sense by the fragmentation of Parliament, which made the one centralizing actor more influential than it would oth-erwise have been. At a minimum, this made bureaucratic drafting of com-prehensive economic plans much more practically possible. The bureau-cracy was also aided, in two senses, by the fact that the largest single party in Parliament was the Communists, who could not come into the government of the day. In the abstract, this did limit the kaleidoscopic character of those many short-lived governments. More practically, it gave the bureaucracy some additional leverage with the moderately conservative parties when it was pushing explicit social-welfare reforms, on grounds that the more extreme opposition had to be contained and undercut.

The resulting political dynamic was superficially still one of protest and disruption, of governmental instability and policy fragmentation, and these surface manifestations contained the larger part of the truth. Yet they also masked the rest of the dynamic, in which an indirect centralization—though not nearly, it should be remembered, to the extent that true centralization permitted in Britain—meant that many policy initiatives of this first postwar era in France were centered in the bureaucracy rather than in the elected government. Thus it was the bureaucracy that was most concerned with programs for economic recovery; just as it was the bureaucracy that managed initiatives to extend the French welfare state.

This order came apart dramatically in the late 1950s, and an obviously new era in postwar politics arrived. Decolonization provided the general issue context. Algeria provided its crucial specific embodiment, and brought on a crisis seemingly fated, by hindsight, to produce new institutional arrangements. That crisis, as it emerged, still strongly reflected the old political order. A fragmented party system inside fragmented governmental arrangements was once again being challenged by the bureaucracy in setting policy—only this time, the critical piece of that bureaucracy was the military. In any case, the crisis, as it was resolved, was to produce entirely new constitutional arrangements, albeit a variant of the same arrangements which might have been implemented immediately after World War II.

The new structure of government, *intended* as the bedrock of a new political order, was characterized principally by an executive focus among national institutions, including a separately elected president, and secondarily by a majoritarian electoral system, with two-stage (two-ballot) elections. The principal goal of this new structure was to introduce a reliably strong central executive, but to make that executive, this time, democratically accountable. Its secondary goal was to force politicking into an essentially bilateral context, so that the fragmentation and irresponsibility of the first postwar order would not be repeated. And for the next twenty-five years, remarkable as it may seem, those influences did shape a new political order roughly as intended. Thus the president, even after Charles de Gaulle, did acquire the ability to address major national issues. While the party system was reformed into two broad tendencies, a moderate Right and (eventually) a moderate Left.

The combination of these two great events—the constitutional threat from an Algerian crisis and then the imposition of a serious new constitution—probably overstates the uniformity with which cultural and national issues were to dominate this second political era in postwar French politics. Yet the theory under which French administrative arrangements had been conducted (that the colonies *were* France) meant that decolonization had to be a powerful issue of national identity. Afterward, effective implementation of a new structure of national government was likewise inevitably a central focus to politics. Part of the impetus behind the latter, and not for the last time, was also a direct comparison with *Germany,* involving the perception that the postwar German economic boom was proceeding even better than its French counterpart. Yet ironically, this latter perception was not actually to reintroduce economic and welfare issues (and conflicts) into subsequent French politics for some time.

Over time, the great cultural/national issues of the day, decolonization plus implementation of the new constitution, were successfully handled. Yet the influence of these new issues was arguably extended by the way that the great issue *undermining* substantive continuity in the United States, Canada, and Britain—a growing division over national positioning in the Cold War—was effectively circumscribed in France. The fact that one of the major political parties, the Communists, actually favored switching sides in this conflict did serve to delegitimize more moderate hesitations and realignments. Yet the further sidelining of this issue reflected additional factors distinctive to the French context. Central to these was the way that de Gaulle himself insisted on a position of individuality for France within the Western alliance, thereby defusing any argument that French national interests were being subverted.

None of this would necessarily have worked out as it did, however, had it not been for two other developments crucial to the new political order. The first of these was broadscale social change associated with a French version of the postwar economic miracle, the "thirty glorious years," which reduced many divisions in French society and actually altered others. The coming of a truly national economy, along with the growth of middle-class sectors within it, on top of a generalized economic boom, all seemed to blur the sharpness of class lines. The same underlying developments drew the regions, in effect, into a national system. These shifts were joined, finally, by an increasingly secular character to French society and a concomitant decline in the importance of the clerical/anticlerical cleavage.

The other such development, equally crucial and more pointed, was the drawing of the Socialists into the new political order, this time as *the* potential alternative government of the day. In the first postwar order, the Socialists had been frequent (and crucial) governmental partners, though they could not simply be the government. In the second postwar order, despite their initial aversion to its constitutional underpinnings, they could. The culmination of this change was the election of François Mitterrand in 1981, through a "Union of the Left." Broad societal changes in the potential electorate for such a party were central to this development. So was more than a decade of focused internal party politicking. Either way, the arrival of a broad-Left alternative, and then of an actual alternation in government, confirmed the stability of basic governmental arrangements. The vast middle of French society was thus attached to these arrangements. A dynamic of moderate competition—broad Left versus broad Right—was equally a part of this attachment.

The early years after the arrival of the Socialists in power were actually to bridge two eras in postwar politics, in as dramatic fashion as any in the postwar history of the entire G-7. From one side, this arrival affirmed the stability—the institutionalization—of an encompassing constitutional framework. In that sense, the early years of a new Socialist government helped to stabilize and extend an older political era. Yet within a very few years, this arrival would coincide with a clear break in political eras and orders—note that the break does not itself coincide with an actual election—propelled by a changing issue agenda in society at large but also facilitated, albeit perversely, by the policy aspirations of the Socialists themselves.

Accordingly, if the lesson of the second postwar era in France is the power of basic constitutional arrangements to shape a political order, then the lesson of the third era is the power of new issues and new social coalitions to make those basic constitutional arrangements work differently—and sometimes, in fact, to modify their very contents. The Socialists did begin with a truly comprehensive program for social change through governmental action, the heart of which was actually in economic and social-welfare concerns. Had they succeeded with these—with further nationalizations, expanded social insurances, new labor-management compacts—they might well have heralded a new era most closely resembling immediate postwar Britain in the substance and reach of its policy impact.

They were, however, quickly to run afoul of two major forces. One was the long-run economic cycle. Anxieties about the putative end of the thirty glorious years might have been instrumental in bringing the Socialists to power, but the factors associated with that putative end made governmental economic intervention much more difficult. The other main brake on these economic/welfare initiatives was growing economic integration with Europe, again especially between Germany and France. Ironically, this was an outcome consciously fostered by French policy in the preceding political era. Yet it was also a powerful restraint on autonomous change in French policy in the succeeding era, when Germany was not inclined to go along.

The result was to be a transition between two eras in France, a transition which possessed the greatest parallels with, of all nations, the United States. Both nations, by this time, featured not just formal but practical "presidential governance," at least by comparison to Britain or Canada. Both also featured, in effect, a two-ballot system of elections. In France, this meant multiparty competition on the first round, followed by a "run-off" between leading figures from the two general tendencies on the second. In the United States, it meant factional competition in a primary election, followed by two-party competition in the general election—for two parties which were nothing if not "broad tendencies" in the French mode.

When both political systems then encountered major new cross-cutting pressures from cultural and national issues, the stage was set for a parallel change of eras. For France, issues of European integration, and all the individual adaptations at home which they would require, were the great national issues of this new era. Just as issues of domestic social integration, especially those involving crime in general and immigration in particular, from the rest of Europe but especially from former French colonies, were the main cultural incarnations. What resulted from these newly powerful cultural and national concerns was characterized in the United States as an era of "divided government." But the more accurate term for France, divided *governance,* might really have been more accurate for the United States, too.

In this, the old Left/Right division, now moderated, still underlay the party system. Individual issues tapping into this division could still be important to politics in both the United States and France; class attachments in voting could thus still intermittently rise and not just fall; the existing parties therefore remained the main vehicle for building social coalitions. Yet new cultural and national issues, now often more central to politics, could not in principle be aligned in these same terms: the majority coalition for economic/welfare issues was just not the same as the majority coalition for cultural/national affairs. Split partisan control of national institutions, "divided government", was the signature characteristic for the result in both nations. But divided *governance,* in the sense of reliably cross-cutting majority coalitions, was really its practical essence.

Thus for both the United States and France, the diagnostic feature inaugurating the new political order was split partisanship in the American mode: Republican presidents with Democratic Congresses in the United States, Socialist presidents with conservative Chambers of Deputies in France. Yet what was really present was divided governance in the French sense. Both countries could still easily experience unified partisan control of government. But the underlying cross-alignment of economic/welfare versus cultural/national concerns did not thereby go away. France even provided a *procedural* parallel to the situation in the United States. In this, French presidents and prime ministers began to refine (and distinguish) their powers and responsibilities in the face of reliably divided governance, much as Congress and the president developed their own autonomous supporting bureaucracies in the United States to reflect that same recurrence. In this way, dominant informal arrangements began to reshape the underlying formal structures in both nations.

And at that point, the search for parallels should probably stop. For in another key respect, involving the main dynamic to politics within the new political order, France actually resembled *Canada* more than the United States (and again, much more than Britain). In the new order, in fact, the job of injecting these new (cross-cutting) issues into politics was actually played by splinter parties in France, as it was in Canada. In both countries, the established national parties preferred not to handle these countervailing issues, which did not, of course, sit neatly with their underlying social coalitions. Splinter parties then moved to capitalize on these issues, in the process injecting them into politics anyway. At that point, the major national parties had to work out a position on these emergent issues because they were now loose on the landscape. And that position was often roughly consensual *as between* these two national parties (in Canada) or tendencies (in France), precisely because such issues tended to feature a dominant majority preference.

The West

Germany is unique among the G-7 nations in the way that the benchmark events for this analysis, the end of World War II and the end of the Cold War, actually shaped the geographic boundaries—the physical definition—of the nation. The relationship between this change and change in the temporal boundaries of postwar eras and orders in German politics is, however, a good deal more complex than such a simple benchmarking might suggest. Germany did share a focus for its first postwar political era, an inescapable focus, on the same two central considerations as Japan, Italy, and, in a more uneven way, France. This was the need to create an entire governmental framework, along with the even more pressing need to restore national economic life.

France, of course, was to decide consciously *not* to adopt major constitutional change in the immediate postwar years. For Germany (and Italy and Japan), that was never an option: a new governmental framework could look back and reclaim some elements from the past, but it still had to be created afresh. Early on, however, it became clear that this would—it could—be created only for part of the former Germany. The Soviet Union was to demand a separate, nondemocratic, East Germany in its zone of occupation. It was thus the new *West* Germany that would become a major member of the G-7 in the course of the Cold War years. Within its confines, the drafting and then the practical implementation of a new constitutional framework was essential. But it would be the economic rebuilding of this (partially new) nation that was the central substantive focus for politics during the first postwar era.

The political order within which this politics played out was characterized by a strong public bureaucracy, one allowed to continue from earlier years so as to address some of the immediate service needs of postwar society. Yet unlike the situation in France or especially Japan, where an established bureaucracy was an even larger element of the first postwar order, the associated elements of the political order in Germany caused this bureaucracy to contribute to a very different overall dynamic. In France, partial bureaucratic autonomy was encouraged by a fragmented party system plus governmental instability, albeit limited simultaneously by these same factors. In Japan, a greater bureaucratic autonomy was encouraged by the fact that a dominant party, while it did ultimately emerge, was slow to do so; indeed, it grew initially under the *tutelage* of the central bureaucracy.

In Germany, by contrast, the main vehicle for connecting a rough national consensus on dominant issues with a strong and continuing bureaucracy—and thus the key intermediary organization of the first postwar order—was the Christian Democratic party, and it came together very quickly as the lead element in postwar German politics. In fact, this Christian Democratic party quickly became the main vehicle for implementing the new constitutional framework, the main vehicle for brokering economic arrangements aimed at national revitalization, and the main vehicle for making Germany a critical element in the Western alliance.

The predominance of the Christian Democrats was underpinned by a large remaining rural population and by substantial remaining confessional elements. These were joined, in loose but effective alliance, by a reemerging business leadership, as they were to be joined in Japan and as they were already joined in the United States of the same period. Party predominance was also implicitly underpinned—in reverse—by the residual Marxist heritage and more militant trade-union tradition of the main partisan opposition, the Social Democratic party, which suffered additionally from the fact that many of its best areas had been hived off to create the new East Germany. All of which was additionally reinforced by a generalized revulsion against the (extreme) ideologies of the past.

A comparatively high degree of social homogeneity along with a middling level of governmental centralization then added the key bracketing characteristics for a politics that would rapidly come to be concentrated on the establishment of nationwide frameworks for negotiating new economic relationships. Moreover, this was to be a politics concentrated additionally and especially on the development of an intricate and encompassing system of direct labor-management relations, including nationwide works councils, annual and formalized attention to working conditions, and so on. It was not that there were not also explicit debates over nationalizations; it was just that these had little programmatic outcome. Indeed, an immediate part of economic rebuilding was a structural liberalization to counteract the extreme integration of the late Nazi era. Likewise, it was not that there were not explicit public debates over social insurances; it was just that these too came to little in programmatic terms. The Christian Democrats argued (successfully) that extended social-welfare programs were just too much of a luxury for the period. Instead, economic rebuilding remained the focus, and labor-management relations gave this focus its most direct expression.

The resulting political dynamic did feature Christian Democratic dominance at the center of all this, both facilitated and personified for much of the first postwar era by the extended chancellorship of Konrad Adenauer, a predominant figure within a predominant party. Beyond Adenauer, and much more like Italy than like Japan among the former Axis powers, Germany had a substantial incipient corps of aspiring democratic politicians waiting for the resumption of postwar politics. Many of these became the key brokers for the Christian Democrats—brokering policy demands among the *Länder,* across the economy, and between voters and the bureaucracy, without serious risk of electoral displacement but also without great pressure to do more than revitalize a nation.

Historical hindsight contributes an air of inevitability to this first postwar order. How *could* something other than restarting a shattered economy have been the initial focus of postwar German politics? How could adjustments to frontline status in the Cold War not have been a major secondary focus? Indeed, given the options, how could the Christian Democratic party not have been the main intermediary vehicle for expressing (and simultaneously shaping) these policy needs? And how could public wishes *and* a continuing bureaucracy—the latter could certainly have been challenged by the Allies in principle, but possibly not in practice—not have underpinned the role of the Christian Democratic Union?

In that light, it is worth emphasizing the conditionality of even these seeming inevitables. Thus while restarting the postwar economy was a priority in the United States as well, and even more so in Britain, it produced little change in order or era for the United States, a *fundamental* change in era, order, and their public policy for Britain. Likewise, the same general policy environment was not associated with the rise of a dominating Christian Democratic party in postwar France, nor where it was associated with a similar rise, in Italy, did the other elements of the political order give that party the same character, and the same role to play. This theme of *contingent* interactions will acquire more sustained attention in chapter 10.

In any case, as with so many other breaks between political eras among the G-7 nations, the break in this first postwar German era was to be underlined most forcefully by a shift in partisan control of government. But that shift was itself only a reflection—a culmination—of changes in the issue base for politics and in the structural elements that shaped politicking. Among political issues, successful economic regeneration—a genuine "economic miracle"—was widely recognized by the late 1960s. Nevertheless, a short but sharp recession suggested that the boom was not endless and appeared to force economic and social-welfare choices. In the same way, successful integration into the Western alliance had produced a sense of strategic security, or rather, strategic stasis. Yet this was punctuated by occasional stresses and testings in the Cold War, so that a widespread desire to find some way to move beyond this partially successful stasis was equally logical and equally evident.

From the perspective of key political structures, the break was even more insistent, thanks to a partisan change in their midst. An initial "grand coalition" of the Christian Democratic Union and the Social Democratic party in 1966, itself an unprecedented event in postwar German politics, was followed in 1969 by an actual government based on the SPD, with the CDU in opposition. In the immediate sense, this confirmed the arrival of the possibility of partisan alternation in government, and hence of the single greatest test (passed successfully) of the institutionalization of postwar constitutional arrangements. But together with a change in issue themes, it also signaled the likelihood that a new order, with different key supports, had arrived.

The new era began, as the *third* postwar era was to begin in France, with a simple expansion of policy possibilities—and hence possibilities for conflict—on established issue dimensions. The initial foreign-policy consensus of the immediate postwar years, while it was never as total as in the United States or Britain, began to fray noticeably. Yet in Germany, the possibility of lessening tensions with the Soviet Union, and thus of building bridges to the East, was initially much more popular, so that the party urging a move off from the Cold War consensus, the SPD, was not obviously itself moving off into minority territory. In the same way, the initial postwar consensus on economic growth, as the main social-welfare "safety net", came under stress. Ironically, this consensus was stressed both by recognized success, which suggested the possibility of *having* more social-welfare legislation, and by economic hesitation, which argued the apparent need for same. Again—though here, very much like the situation in France or Canada at the beginning of their counterpart eras—the notion of moving toward a more generous welfare state was not obviously a minority preference when it was proposed.

Events were ultimately to prove unkind to both possibilities. Developments in Eastern Europe, with increasingly harsh Soviet responses, would make possibilities for accommodation and a more "easterly" posture look less promising and become less popular. Developments in the world economy—oil shocks, a generalized stagflation—would make major social-welfare reforms, after an initial burst of initiatives, much more difficult to offer without high associated costs. Seen the other way around, however, what these changes confirmed was that cultural and national issues had come to contribute an increasing share of the substantive backbone of the new political era, as they had in Canada and the United States and as they would in France and Britain. For Germany, this did not mean that SPD-led governments, in particular, could not produce liberalizing initiatives in areas like abortion reform or education policy. They could, and they did. It just meant that the fundamental issue basis of the new era was incipiently different—a fact which would become inescapable as Europeanization, immigration, and then finally *unification,* all appeared on the domestic political agenda.

There was inevitably a new political order associated with all this as well. Growing public divisions around the successor issues to those of the old order were the bedrock of this changed structure—except in the case of implementation of the basic constitutional framework, where a mature national consensus effectively took the issue out of politics. Yet a changing place for the bureaucracy—less the autonomous initiator of policy—was part and parcel of the same shift. The possibility of partisan alternation in government meant that a bureaucracy hewing to one party line risked setting *itself* up for reform when governments changed, while a bureaucracy distancing itself from either party was not going to drive government in a major way. All of which only emphasized the centrality to a new order of the changed role of the Social Democratic party, while focusing attention on the associated changes in the background of that party shift.

Within Germany, the long postwar economic boom had lessened the sharp edges of class lines while it reduced the possibility that an explicitly working-class party would ever again have the numbers to come to power on those terms alone. The successful implementation of a new democratic constitution also meant both that there was a reliable way to power if the Christian Democrats could be beaten electorally, and that the Christian Democratic Union would otherwise remain the government indefinitely. This produced a debate within the SPD throughout the 1950s, over an appropriate party program and over shucking the increasingly unattractive Marxist overlay in the existing one. More consequentially (though not unrelated), it produced a reaching out to sections off the white-collar middle class—teachers and civil servants were two of the earliest targets—who might share some Left-leaning ideological values and who might contribute the numbers necessary to move beyond the old blue-collar base.

All these elements have evident parallels with the situation of the Socialists in France. The French Socialists entered government much earlier in the postwar period, yet took considerably longer to *become* a government by themselves. Nevertheless, the stages of development on the way to that outcome—economic boom, blurred class lines, internal party debate, outreach to the liberal middle class—were really quite similar. They were related to the situation of the Socialists in Italy, though the parallels had inherent limitations, in that differences in other elements of the political order meant that the Italian socialists would never become an obvious *replacement* for the Christian Democrats. The situation differed, just as strongly, from the Canadian or Japanese contexts, where the Socialist party was inherently circumscribed, in permanent opposition. It differed from the American context, where there was no Socialist party to "tame." And it differed, lastly, from the situation in Britain, where a Labour party actually came to power early and thus implemented huge parts of the program common to democratic socialist parties at the time.

In any case, the result in Germany was to confirm a second postwar order. Yet the same result was to evolve rapidly into a German incarnation—or at least a clear German echo—of "divided governance", as a more comprehensive summary notion. Once again, this would feature extended intervals of superficial "split partisan control" in the institutions of national government. Yet once again, it would be the presence of cross-cutting issue preferences (rather than this split partisanship) that was particularly diagnostic. Moreover, in the German case and unlike

that of the United States or France, it was not so much the partisan balance across governmental institutions as the coalitional composition of
governments of the day that gave divided governance a distinctive further
twist.

The policymaking institutions of German government were less inherently conducive to split partisan control than were those of the United
States or France, having no independently elected executive to embody
one majority against another. On the other hand, they were more conducive than those of Canada or Britain, and indeed, for eighteen of the
twenty-six years of a second postwar era to date, the party controlling the
lower house, the *Bundestag*—and hence the Chancellorship—did not reliably control the upper house, the *Bundesrat*. Nevertheless, this was not a
central operational feature of the second postwar order. Instead, the
larger part of what gave a distinctively German cast to this incarnation of
divided governance was the coalitional structure of national governments
during this second era. The key to appreciating this, in turn, was a focus
on the critical role within these coalitions of the small Free Democratic
party.

For in fact, the Social Democratic government at the beginning of
this era, as well as the Christian Democratic government which returned to succeed it, were actually *coalitions* with these (same) Free
Democrats. More than anything else, it was this coalitional arrangement which gave a national expression to the cross-cutting impact of
cultural/national issues. Said differently: in Germany, the Social Democrats offered the moderate Left on both economic/welfare and cultural/
national issues. The Christian Democrats offered the moderate Right
on both. And the Free Democrats leaned left on cultural/national issues, right on economic/welfare concerns. They were thus potential coalition partners for either major party, depending, as it turned out,
upon which element of cross-cutting preferences was most worrisome
to the general public at a give time.

In this role, the Free Democrats could—and did—give expression to
public preferences for greater liberality on cultural/national policies
when they broke with the CDU and joined in coalition with the SPD,
while providing reassurance that the SPD would not take "dangerous"
risks on economic/welfare matters. Just as they were then the perfect
agent, when they broke subsequently with the SPD and joined in coalition with the CDU, to express public preferences for greater caution on
economic and welfare issues, while reassuring the general public that
the CDU would not do "extreme" things on cultural and national
concerns.

In the abstract, this still left ideological "space" for a party offering the alternative combination to that of the Free Democrats, that is, left on economic/welfare issues, right on cultural/national affairs. In practice, this proved to be a problematic space in most G-7 nations during the postwar years. In Britain, for example, it was filled for a short time by the Social Democratic party, which was then merged away; in the United States, Canada, and France, major parties flirted intermittently with this combination, but reliably withdrew. In Germany, the space remained empty, but for nationally peculiar reasons. In one sense, it was the Communists who most obviously offered this combination. Yet the West German Communist party was marginalized early, and the East German version was profoundly outside any Western pattern of divided governance, at least until unification brought a remnant back into the total system as the Party of Democratic Socialism (PDS).

In any case, this order (and its era) lasted well into the 1980s, when the intensification of cultural/national issues, coupled with a major change in the geographic boundaries of the nation itself, raised the possibility of a third postwar political era for Germany. The reintegration of the pieces divided by the Allies at the end of World War II would have raised this possibility in an unavoidably symbolic way. But the process of unification—the implementation of democratic governmental institutions and the extension of free-market economics—generated most of the associated, day-to-day issues of politics. On the other hand, concerns about immigration, nationality, and citizenship were already "in the air" before the reality of unification, and these concerns were almost inevitably associated with the related drive toward Europeanization—again predating unification, again given greater intensity and complexity by it.

It is more difficult to say with certainty, that is, without the benefit of hindsight, what the specific elements of an associated new political order would be, though a different general dynamic may already be perceptible. In this, the old coalitional patterns are less automatic, and the two main parties are less operationally dominant. The role of splinter parties—the Free Democrats, but now also the Greens, perhaps also the PDS, potentially even the Republicans—is to raise issues, not unlike the Canadian situation. And the role of the two major parties is then to work out a roughly consensual response, not unlike the Canadian or French situations. Such a dynamic *may* reflect the structures of a third political era for postwar Germany; it may reflect only the "growing pains" from merging the former East Germany into the second era. All that can safely be said in the middle 1990s is that even the serious possibility of a third postwar German political era does underline the open-endedness of political evolution, and political history.

Outliers

No sequence is self-evidently right for introducing the postwar politics of the G-7 nations. Yet Japan and Italy, which complete the sequence here, do share one huge formal similarity. They were the last two nations within this collectivity to secure a major benchmark in the institutionalization of democratic politics, namely, the alternation of the partisan control within government, and thus the ability to relegate the previous governing party (or coalition) to full opposition status. Indeed, these last two G-7 nations go on to share the fact that this development required more than the entire Cold War period to accomplish, and that they then accomplished it within months of each other.

More importantly, for our purposes and for both nations, the attainment of this benchmark appeared to guarantee a new political era and order, in a way that even conflict over national identity in Canada or stresses from national unification in Germany did not. For Italy, this possibility of a shift in the postwar pattern of Italian politics had been evidently (if gradually) building, to the point of inviting speculation about its eventual contours. But for Japan, the shift seemed both seismic and unprecedented. Admittedly, hindsight suggested *evidence* toward this same possibility in Japan. Yet incipient portents had surfaced intermittently before, without any subsequent effect, so that the wise analyst did not expect any given product. When the change arrived, then, a short time before its counterpart in Italy, it seemed all the more imposing.

The historical and institutional backdrop to this change, in the form of the first postwar political era in Japan, was best isolated, not so much by its underlying issue content, as by the structural character of its political order. Japan was to share with all the G-7 nations a central focus on restarting the postwar economy in these years. Yet its first postwar era was distinguished among them by the degree of effective concentration on this goal, along with the degree to which other issues, associated elsewhere with this same goal, were effectively squeezed out. It is the character of the underlying political order which best explains this concentration. And it is the centrality—really the essential dominance—of the central government bureaucracy which is at the core of that concentrated focus on the economic task.

With hindsight, it is hard to imagine a situation more conducive to a political order centered on a national bureaucracy—not on policy preferences, not on societal cleavages, not on political parties—than that of postwar Japan. This was, to begin with, a deeply traditionalistic society, without a deeply rooted democratic experience, one where established leaderships were accepted but where policymaking by open and public conflict was not. Nevertheless, the situation was much exaggerated by the way the Allies purged most of the available alternative elites, removing them as an option: the military leadership, of course, but also the wartime political elite, and even, initially, the leaders of major industrial combines.

There was no obvious "resistance" leadership waiting to fill the void, with the partial exception of antisystem organizations which were not going to be acceptable to the occupying forces. There was no strong party system waiting to be reinvigorated, to organize issue conflicts and to discipline the central bureaucracy. And in fact, the electoral system, a distinctive multimember, single-vote arrangement, was to militate against the rapid appearance of either, by fostering a highly personalistic politics of social and economic notables.

Some of the existing issues associated with this first postwar political order were not so different from those in the other G-7 nations, especially Germany and Italy. An operational framework for government was necessary; restarting the national economy was all the more so. Even more than in Germany, however, which provided the closest analogue, the diagnostic fact about postwar Japanese politics was that these underlying and consensual concerns went no further. That is, they were not joined by further economic and social-welfare initiatives, on the proper distribution of wealth in society and on provision of appropriate social-welfare services.

The central bureaucracy was not concerned with those matters at the start. Neither were the great industrial combines which became so influential as the postwar economic recovery began to happen. Nor, until its own predominance seemed threatened, was the main political party, the Liberal Democratic party, which would come to form the third coordinate element in this triumvirate. That left all these other associated themes, in what was a cluster of economic and welfare issues in Britain, the United States, Canada, or France, to be raised by the most militant trade-unions and by arguably antisystem parties.

Such a combination was still productive of a great deal of surface conflict in the immediate postwar years, but it was not to produce much actual public policy. Said differently: in the absence of widespread demand for an extended welfare state at the social base for politics; in the absence of an immediately dominant party or party system institutionalizing economic/welfare conflict; and in the presence of a strong and continuing governmental bureaucracy, with a new and at least potentially consensual "mission," the dominance of this bureaucracy was sufficient not just to describe a postwar political order but to constrict its issue content more than in any of the other G-7 nations.

There was to be one giant challenge to this bureaucratic dominance, around the ratification of the Security Treaty with the United States in 1960. In this sense, the first major division over an appropriate response to the bipolar world of the Cold War came roughly at the same time as that issue was rising in Canada, earlier than it arose in the United States, Britain, or Germany. In practice, however, the strength of the issue's associated order—almost a "machine," in the classic American sense—was already sufficient to turn this challenge aside. In this, (a) a central bureaucracy fostering economic growth, (b) helped rapidly expanding corporate businesses to prosper, which then (c) provided substantial campaign contributions to a gradually strengthening dominant party (the LDP), in order to (d) elect a parliamentary majority which could underpin the continuing policy initiatives of the bureaucracy. The resulting triumph was destined to last for another decade.

Even the strongest political order, on the other hand, could not sustain its era indefinitely, in the face of issue evolution and social change. Japan might remain an outlier in the extent to which the component parts of a shift appeared in effectively glacial fashion. Nevertheless, the break between eras, even in Japan, was clear enough when it came. That break arrived in the early 1970s, most specifically with the arrival of the Tanaka government in 1973. This time, it was the issue focus of a new government of the day which really confirmed the arrival of a second postwar era. Nevertheless, it was again the (evolving) nature of background social factors which was most crucial to this change, and change still achieved expression through a political dynamic which was in turn distinctively Japanese.

From the substantive side, it was noteworthy that there was still no single precipitating issue or crisis—some crystallizing conflict—which led on to a new political era. There was general social change, and there was personal incentive to capitalize upon (and thus crystallize) it, but that was really all. From the structural side, this change was also noteworthy—and here, perhaps more than in any of the other G-7 nations except Italy—for the degree to which all the key elements of the new order would have been easily recognizable from the old. They were distinguishable; indeed, they were obviously sufficient to generate a new order; but they were also successors to the same small set of elements, critically reshuffled.

In substantive terms, what the Tanaka government did was to bring social-welfare issues as they would have been recognized elsewhere—old-age pensions, diverse social services, along with legal protections for both—onto the agenda of government generally. Previously, these had been the province of the opposition, especially the Socialists. What Tanaka really did, then, was to seize upon them as a way to halt erosion of support for the LDP, while shifting the focus of these concerns away from labor and labor-management relations, and toward care of the elderly and of women with children.

Prosperity appeared to make these changes increasingly possible. Social shifts—urbanization, education, geographic and occupational mobility—appeared to make them increasingly necessary. In structural terms, a rural society had become urban and was on its way to being suburban, with all the changes that this implied in, for example, the ability of the extended family to provide "social welfare." On the other hand, the joining of these specific substantive gambits with those grand background forces still occurred by way of a political dynamic that was distinctively Japanese. Said differently: if these background shifts implicitly encouraged conflict over social welfare, then actual reform was produced out of explicit *factional* conflicts within the increasingly dominant Liberal Democratic party. New issues became, in effect, a way for one (or another) factional leader to distinguish and then sustain himself, along with his faction.

In this dynamic, what was most obviously changed was the balance between a central bureaucracy and a dominant party. With a limited welfare state and a focus on economic development and foreign trade, the bureaucracy had remained relatively united—and relatively unchanged. What changed around it was the growing dominance of one party, the LDP. The initial tutelage of the bureaucracy, even in this, was symbolized by the key role of bureaucrats-turned-politicians in making it happen. The coming of the Tanaka government could thus symbolize the shift in personal terms as well, since Tanaka was not only *not* a former bureaucrat, but a self-made businessman with an active distaste for the bureaucracy.

In any case, by the late 1960s, the pattern of one clearly dominant party, facing a set of smaller (fragmented) opposition parties, was established. So was the pattern of relatively stable factional divisions within that party, competing behind the scenes for influence within government. This was hardly sufficient to remove the bureaucracy from a political role. Its major business clienteles would not have wanted that, and a dominant party was certainly not averse to using the bureaucracy to pursue policies and politics. It was, however, gradually sufficient to remix the direction of influence. For in this second postwar political order, the symbiosis among these three elements shifted such that corporate support for LDP politicians helped *them* to institutionalize their actions and influence the governing coalition, which then used the bureaucracy to reward supporters and attempt to sustain factional fortunes.

Factional conflict within the LDP thus became the central political dynamic. By contrast, the social coalitions sustaining this dynamic remained relatively unchanged. At bottom, the earlier "marriage of iron and rice," a coalition between corporate business and the rural areas, continued into the second political era. It was, however, increasingly and crucially dependent, despite these other social changes, on the malapportionment of seats in the Diet, favoring rural areas, and on the peculiar nature of party competition for these seats, where multimember districts encouraged the individual factions of the LDP to pour personal benefits into husbanding favorable districts.

Such a coalition within the LDP (of corporate business and rural residents) was not in itself unusual among the G-7 nations. Roughly similar alliances had characterized the social base for the Republicans in the United States, the Conservatives in Britain, the Christian Democrats in Germany, and the Christian Democrats in Italy too, in the first postwar era in each of these nations. Yet this had remained a secondary aspect of the structure of postwar politics in the United States and Britain, while France, in keeping with the rest of its political order, had fragmented these social elements as well. Only Canada had offered no serious echoes of such a coalition, actually pitting its rural elements *against* its corporate sector.

More consequential for all these nations—and more distinguishing for Japan—was the evolution of this implicit alliance. Because rural areas were reliably in decline, the crucial question was whether the party which most directly and practically gave the coalition its expression could successfully substitute a growing middle class for this declining rural sector. In Germany, this transition occurred in apparently seamless fashion. In the United States and Britain, it actually allowed the Republicans and especially the Conservatives to return to power, and to begin to set the policy agenda. In France, a newly consolidated conservative tendency was also symbiotically successful at this maneuver, as part of a new order congealing around new constitutional arrangements.

That left Canada, where ethnocultural conflict intensified before such a coalition could ever be constructed, along with Italy and Japan, where the old coalitions were largely just rebalanced. In the kind of similarity that would more and more link two otherwise disparate nations, both Italy and Japan thus *continued* to feature the same underlying coalition as a pillar of the second postwar order, albeit with gradually intensifying difficulties. As a result, the breakup of this coalition and the breakup of the old order were probably destined to be intertwined. Seen one way, it was the substitution of a burgeoning middle class for the older rural elements which marked the transition to a third postwar order in these countries. Seen another way, this substitution was in fact essential to breaking up the second order, and its delay (by comparison to other G-7 nations) was why the old order managed to last so long.

Only in Japan was all this tied additionally and so strongly to formal malapportionment. Nevertheless, a politics based on concrete favors for the districts, one largely conducted in an individualized and private manner, did have as one by-product a continual if intermittent series of major financial scandals. Their very continuity, on the other hand, left analysts unprepared when these escalated, to interact with widespread public discontent about the character of politics generally, in a way that signaled an end to this second postwar era. Arriving only in the spring of 1993, the third great postwar era to Japanese politics cannot, in principle, be described in any definite way. Yet it is already so different as to leave little room for argument about the presence of a break-point.

The inescapable structural signal of this break was the end of LDP hegemony and the coming to power of a new, multiparty, anti-LDP coalition. This coalition and its first successor were themselves short-lived, but even the return of the LDP to government did not signal a return to the old order—coming, as it did, in coalition with its long-time postwar opponent, the Japanese Socialists! None of this change contained a safe prediction of the contours of a new political order. Yet the differences remained clear enough: there were new and serious challengers within the party system; there were factions of the LDP spinning off into additional parties (and more threatening to do so); there were factions aspiring to lead a reform movement within that (still-largest) party as well.

Perhaps surprisingly, especially in Japan, the issue contents of a third postwar era actually began to clarify earlier, at least in general terms, than did its structural contours. First, issues involving a more effective democracy—issues of democratic responsiveness in Japan—had been implicitly associated with the shift to a second postwar era and had resurfaced with every subsequent scandal along the way. In the third era, however, they produced not just a serious reform drive aimed at political finance and corruption, but serious reform conflict over the electoral system that had been so central to the first and second postwar orders. Second, issues involving the place of the nation in world politics—and thus the place of foreign affairs in Japanese domestic politics—had been growing during the second era, when independent shifts in *American* policy, from containment through currency, had necessitated growing policy responses. Now, with the Cold War over, a mature and wealthy Japan was under broad international pressure to take a more active role in world affairs in its aftermath, financially but even militarily, and this inevitably raised social and constitutional issues within the nation. Third—and on the back burner, but hardly likely to go away—were new incarnations of the old economic and social-welfare concerns. Many of these were fueled by an apparent desire to shift the nature of domestic life, away from the austerity of postwar recovery and toward a more openly consumer-oriented lifestyle. More seemed destined to receive emphasis from the dramatic aging of the Japanese population as a whole: demography seemed likely to become destiny earlier in Japan than in any of the other G-7 nations.

There were in Japan even incipient indications of the *issue cross-pressures* which characterized most of the other G-7 nations, pitting economic/welfare issues (and associated economic/welfare coalitions) against cultural/national issues (and the associated coalitions there). Thus, for example, in a new era when different governing coalitions were possible, basic social-welfare issues featured the Liberal Democrats and the old-line Socialists at opposite ends of the ideological spectrum. Yet basic issues of procedural reform actually united those two parties—the winner and the main opposition from the old order—against most of the others, who could only benefit from deliberate change in the rules of the contest.

There remained one outstanding difference in the character of Japanese politics. All the other G-7 nations, to one degree or another, had moved from a politics of local and regional brokerage to one of national, even plebescitary, policy combat. Many of the facilitating elements for such a shift were present in Japan as well. But this was the one counterpart trend which had clearly *not* been automatically registered with the end of ritualized LDP dominance. Or at least, the arrangements which followed in its immediate wake were all characterized—that is, managed—by politicians acting in a very old-fashioned, brokerage mode. Electoral reapportionment combined with financial reform might end this historical continuity too. But they did not automatically and immediately do so in the change from a second to a third postwar era.

The Group of Seven

Italy completes the reintroduction of the entire G-7, along with the partial comparisons produced by reintroducing them one by one. Some of the elements of Italian postwar politics distinguish Italy from any of the other G-7 nations: a Communist party which remained a serious domestic player throughout all these years, for example, plus a church hierarchy with a partisan role unrivaled in the other six. Some of the elements of Italian postwar politics are likewise common to each of the others: metropolitan change, from rural to urban to suburban, for example, or the rising role of courts in the political process. Yet as a composite, in direct bilateral comparison, Italy begins its postwar politics most like, not the other (former) Axis powers of Germany and Japan, but like France.

These two countries were in fact "united" by having deeply divided societies, along lines of cleavage stretching back well before the Second World War: Left/Right, clerical/secular, urban/rural, and regional as well. France did possess a prewar party system reflecting these cleavages, one which could be reflated directly, while for Italy, it had been a much longer time since prewar *democratic* politics. Yet both had serious resistance figures, with a variety of ideologies, to plug immediately into postwar politicking. And both would plug them into governmental structures which were likewise extremely similar at first: electoral arrangements enshrining full-blown proportionality, leading to policymaking arrangements embodying fully realized notions of parliamentary government.

The Italian context did add distinctive twists even here. For example, while Italy featured a number of deep and serious social cleavages, there was, at least in the earlier postwar years, a clear social plurality, in a self-consciously Catholic constituency. This became, in turn, the bedrock for a single predominant party, the Christian Democratic party, facing a fragmented opposition, a pattern foreshadowing subsequent similarities to postwar Japan rather than France. Moreover, the dominance of that party was effectively secured, even as its plurality status declined, by the fact that its largest single opponent was the Communist party.

The structures to this first order—this social base, these intermediaries, and this set of governmental institutions—were, as ever, intimately connected to the issues contributing its associated political era. Though for Italy, again like Japan, the story even of this first postwar era is much more the influence of structures than the substance of issues. Despite that, there were to be obvious and central themes to postwar policy conflict, in economic regeneration and democratic institutionalism. And there were to be obvious public ructions over a posture toward the emerging Cold War, although the practical effect of these latter conflicts was to brand what would otherwise become a comparatively national and accommodating Communist party as an impossible member for any governing coalition.

Yet at that point, the issue content of the first postwar era was essentially completed. There were to be further surface disputes over the social-welfare programs that were implemented comprehensively in Britain and piecemeal in the United States and Canada, as well as over the economic-planning programs that received major attention in Germany, France, and Japan. Yet Italy was to feature few major policy initiatives in these realms, so that what resulted was, in effect, a "welfare state by default." The governmental health service of the Fascist era was retained, as were institutional devices—even including prior nationalizations—for coordinating major sectors of the economy. But Christian Democratic policy ran largely in the opposite direction.

The political dynamic to this first postwar era was thus easily described. The numerical dominance of the Christian Democratic party, which would have made it central to governmental formation in any case, was powerfully reinforced by the second-competitor status of a party which could not enter government, the Communists. This predominance was then further reinforced—quickly cemented—through a kind of patronage dominance. A single, preponderant, Christian Democratic party would use the resources of government to buttress its electoral support across the country. In this, it benefited initially from an implicit alliance between rural areas, with their local notables as leaders, and the more diffuse population more directly concerned with economic regeneration, with corporate business as its implicit standard-bearers.

What emerged was, already by the 1950s, more akin to the Japanese "machine politics" of a somewhat later time than to French politics of the same period. This Italian version of a "coalition of iron and rice" at the grass roots was reflected in a dominant party in governmental formulation, which could then use active public works from one side and conservative economic policies from the other to reward the elements of its coalition, which could then provide reliable votes and cash contributions to sustain party control of government, and so on. What was noticeably lacking from the Japanese or French comparison was the directive role of a central bureaucracy. The Italian version had never been professionalized and autonomous, and it quickly became a kind of grand patronage resource for the Christian Democrats—and ultimately for a much broader array of parties, a fact which lessened its directional prospects even further.

There had actually been a point—one political moment—when all this might have been different. Or at least, there was a serious early effort to reform the basic electoral system, destined to be a crucial underpinning to both the first and the second postwar orders in Italy. This point gains historical interest because it was so parallel to the change which did accompany the break-up of the first order in France. It gains analytic interest from the fact that not just France but Germany, too, was deliberately forced to address the issue. Germany and Italy had in fact faced very similar stimuli in designing postwar institutional arrangements in this realm. Yet in Italy, an additionally elaborated system of proportional representation was seen as a natural move against the structures of the era of Fascism, one more effort to insure that it could not happen again. While in Germany, carefully calculated *limits* to proportional representation were viewed as a way to guard against the failures of the Weimar Republic, which had in turn *led* to Fascism there.

In any case, Alcide De Gasperi, who formed the first eleven postwar governments in Italy, did make a serious effort to change the electoral system of the country in a more majoritarian direction. When he failed, the existing system went on to underpin both the first and the second postwar political orders. What this system implied was an ostensibly precise reflection not just of party support but of factional support within parties, and especially within the Christian Democrats. And what that encouraged was a political dynamic focused on incremental, incessant, elite bargaining, a dynamic which would be fundamentally interrupted—though perhaps even then not swept away—by the third postwar era.

All this did not imply that the first postwar era was capable of sustaining itself indefinitely, and that era did draw, more or less naturally, to a close. In policy terms, the Christian Democrats could not govern forever on the issue of *implementing* democracy. Nor could they do so on the virtues of cementing Italy to the Western alliance. Nor, in fact, could they do so with simple economic recovery—though the continued presence of the Communists as a major opposition force did help with all three. Once all these had happened, however, there was only declining sustenance in serving as their guarantor.

Likewise, in structural terms, the Christian Democrats might continue to monopolize the formation of national governments. Yet society itself was changing rapidly around these governments. By the early 1960s, economic growth had already created much more of a modern, industrial, urban, integrated society, especially in the North, with two further, pointed effects. In one, Italians too were demanding more of the welfare-state programs which went with those social arrangements in most (not all) other G-7 nations. In the other, the electoral base of the Christian Democrats was being gradually but ineluctably eroded, along with the rural base of the nation as a whole.

Perhaps more than with any other G-7 nation, there was room for argument about when these general developments produced a distinctively different, second postwar era—though the argument is only between the obvious initial break-point and the point when its evolution had become inescapable. The former was 1963, when the Socialist party first entered government. The latter was 1974, when minority Christian Democratic governments returned and when Communist entry into government even seemed a possibility. Yet in this, the more important fact remains that the choice was largely one of selecting how far issue evolution and structural shift had to have gone before they signaled the indisputable break. In that sense, both are of a piece.

The entry of the Socialists into government in 1963 was meant to shore up Christian Democratic dominance, by adding an urban working-class component to it—ideally making the party itself more acceptable to such voters, at least keeping a substantial share of them cemented into the government of the day. From the other side, the "price" of adding the Socialists to the coalition was two-fold. First, there was to be a set of policy responses to increasingly insistent social-welfare demands, in realms like pension policy and industrial relations. And second, there was to be expanded access to the patronage resources of national government, to institutionalize a Socialist party presence in power, albeit simultaneously augmenting the demands on these resources and intensifying the bargaining over them.

On the one hand, then, the Italian Socialists actually both moderated *and entered the government* earlier than counterparts in Germany or, of course, Japan. On the other hand, and here much more like Japan than like Germany or, especially, France, they were never to enter government as the governing alternative. They entered only as part of a coalition whose dominant member was another party. The continued success of the Italian Communists was also part of this story. They were not to be dominated electorally by the Socialists, as in Germany, France, or Japan. Indeed, successful administration of major municipalities across Italy actually gave governing credentials (and patronage resources) to the Communists too.

By this time, the earlier postwar analogy with French politics had effectively dissipated. Or rather, France had terminated the comparison, with a new political era built around strikingly different constitutional arrangements, giving rise to a political dynamic which was to feature the serious possibility of partisan alternations in the actual control of national government. In the aftermath, politics in Italy came to look not so much like its European counterparts, but like politics in Japan. Electoral arrangements encouraging divisible exchange, the continued absence of serious partisan alternatives, a consequent political dynamic featuring unpredictable adaptations and idiosyncratic "safety values," along with an ultimate crash in the 1990s: all these unite two countries whose citizens must be as unlikely to compare themselves with each other as any pair within the G-7.

The issue contents of this second Italian era, on the other hand, were not as different from those in most other G-7 nations as this comparison of political orders might suggest. The initial issue emphases of the new political era, on economic/welfare matters, were joined quickly by cultural/national concerns, with the latter growing gradually more insistent as this second era aged—a trend not unfamiliar from other G-7 countries. In this, Italy went on to offer analogues to the "cultural issues" that would have been widely recognized elsewhere, like abortion, or crime and punishment, or the role of nuclear power. It also offered items more inherently tied to Italian society, like divorce or the role of religious (that is, Catholic) teaching in the public schools. And it included, of course, basic anticorruption thrusts, which did become more insistent as the era aged but which actually surfaced relatively early (if ineffectually) within it.

The order associated with this new political era had two central parts, superficially distinctive but practically connected, even integral. Indeed, to say the same thing more forcefully: the ability of old-fashioned, brokerage-style, Italian politicians to fashion a political dynamic amidst these cross-cutting issue pressures and across these very different structural elements is the major explanation for why the resulting order could last a remarkable thirty years. One of its main elements, in any case, was the structure of bargaining at its governmental core; the other was an evolving set of institutionalized "safety valves," to prod those negotiators—and to bypass them when they could not be prodded.

At the center of this order, a still-dominant Christian Democratic party engaged in increasingly stylized negotiations over governments of the day, shaped by certain major and recurring structural constraints. The deepest of these was self-imposed, as the defining aspect of Christian Democracy: a refusal to add either Communists or Neofascists explicitly to the government. Within the ideological space that remained, elections then served largely as a way to "keep score", though governments actually rose and fell much more rapidly than elections came and went. Old social loyalties were still sufficient to guarantee only lesser movements in the vote, in an electoral system which was designed not to amplify small shifts. What such shifts did, instead, was to register comparative adjustments among the increasingly institutionalized factions within the parties, as well of course as comparative adjustments among those parties.

On the other hand, because governing coalitions had to be built across the broad middle of economic/welfare issues, excluding the far-Left and the far-Right, such coalitions were *particularly* incapacitated by cultural/national issues, which cross-cut these other concerns and often left no residual majority. This situation was serious enough even at the beginning of this second postwar era, when the overall decline of the Christian Democrats, the simultaneous rise of their factions, and the inescapability of the Socialists had already imposed severe limits on policy responses to cross-cutting issues. Indeed, subsequent efforts at keeping policy focused on economic/welfare matters, especially in the realm of pensions and retirement benefits, were to come back to haunt policymakers in the third postwar era. In short order, however, the underlying situation—the presence of strong but cross-cutting issue preferences in the general public—

was to demand additional policy outlets. Had these not been forthcoming, they might well have consigned this era to the status of an afterward on the first postwar period.

These mechanisms were, however, found. One such mechanism was simple public protest, especially in the late 1960s and early 1970s. Protest demonstrations could force particular issues into the negotiations over cabinet formation, though they were less effective as a device for policy resolution, not least because they made these negotiations more intricate—and their coalitions more fragile. A second such mechanism was old-fashioned protest *voting*. And here, the early moderation of the Italian Communists, making them an indigenously Italian (rather than a sub-Soviet) party, coupled with their continuing exclusion from government, served to make them, ironically, the perfect vehicle for protest on cultural issues, where they offered the secular and libertarian side. Especially in the mid 1970s, this helped explain their apparent rise in public support.

A final and more curious response, becoming more and more common as this second order aged, was to turn to another aspect of the formal constitution and to use it in a new way, a way dependent on the particular forces loose in national politics at the time. This device was the referendum, a legacy of American influence in the framing of the postwar constitution. Yet it was invigorated and increasingly pressed into service in this second postwar era, especially to address cultural/national issues, the very ones which either split the governing coalition (on clerical/secular lines, for example) or united the governing coalition *in opposition* to procedural reform—which was then tackled via referendum.

This arrangement, this era and its order, appeared to be living on borrowed time for many of its later years, unlike its Japanese counterpart, which appeared capable of sustaining itself a good deal longer. Both, however, came apart within a year of each other, and in dramatic fashion. In Japan, the superficial crises precipitating the break-up involved scandals leaked by competing politicians and then amplified by the press. In Italy, similar scandals were unearthed by the magistrates instead, in yet another instance of the invigoration and refocusing of an element of the written constitution which had remained formally the same throughout the postwar years.

A new generation of judges, less knit into the evolving arrangements of the second postwar era, turned first to judicial reforms aimed at combating the influence of the Mafia in Italian politics, where reform had substantial support even among established party politicians. When they then refocused these newly energized devices on political corruption more generally, the old order proved indeed to have been living on borrowed time, and rapidly unraveled. Nevertheless, underneath the dramatic surface scandals which led most directly to this unraveling was sweeping social change, along with increasingly insistent issues of public policy which could not be effectively addressed by an entrenched "machine."

A society as radically transformed as any except possibly Japan, Italy was now urban rather than rural, educated rather than ignorant, middle-class rather than peasant, baronial, *or* blue-collar, even secular rather than sacred. More to the practical point, members of the growth areas within each aspect of this change were increasingly distressed not just at the character of Italian politics, but at their own exclusion from governmental influence. Simultaneously, the social divisions which had once been buttressed by an organizational network divided along subcultural lines and focused on peculiarly subcultural parties, to help guarantee a nearly automatic vote, were in strong decline as well.

It may be that no system of patronage disbursements would have been sufficient to keep most policy issues out of politics and to hold a national coalition together through brokerage under such changed conditions. In any case, in 1994, in the midst of an apparently unending series of corruption scandals coupled with an internal "war" with the Mafia—the latter adding insult to injury for members of the most rapidly changing sectors of society—the old order broke apart in spectacular fashion. There was a series of electoral and finance reforms, aimed at ending the contribution of proportionality and of raw cash to the maintenance of the old order; there was the promise of more to come. A remarkable share of serious national political figures from the recent past ended up either in prison or under indictment for politically related crimes. Indeed, the Christian Democrats and the Socialists, the dominant party and its lead support for thirty years, looked likely to disappear as a consequence.

All of this was convincing as evidence of the end of an era. It was much less reliable in indicating the structure of a successor. New bodies did contest the election of 1994, and new coalitions did form after it. Yet the latter still appeared unreliable as a guide, for example, to the specific intermediaries which might come to structure Italian politics. Indeed, the campaign itself—populist and only loosely brokered, featuring direct appeals to the potential electorate, on grounds of embodying general public values—looked increasingly similar to an American, or a Canadian, or even a German, French, or British counterpart, without recasting Italian politics definitively in one or another of those national modes.

10 *Byron E. Shafer*

Conclusion

Partial comparisons, with their insistent similarities and crucial differences—the focus of chapter 9—have an implicit, equivocal, further message. From one side, they do affirm the possibility of generalization, and hence the limits on national individuality. From the other side, however, they also suggest a requirement of national specification, and thus limits on generalizability too. They do hint constantly at general forces: at universal issues, universal structures, and resulting universal dynamics. They insist simultaneously, however, that these universals be embedded in specifically national contexts in order to understand their operation. Along the way, these partial comparisons do surface parallel developments—similar issue sequences, similar structural interactions, and similar patterns of conflict—while *denying* a similarity of outcomes.

At a minimum, then, it is necessary to confront this implicit proposition explicitly, by returning to see whether certain larger concerns can in fact be discerned across all the G-7 nations, at least in the postwar period. Yet the underlying logic of the analyses in chapters 2 through 8 does implicitly go a good deal further. It is possible to cut postwar history in each of these nations into political eras and to subclassify individual substantive issues within these eras into further (economic/welfare and cultural/national) clusters. It is also possible to isolate accompanying political orders and to gather their key structural influences into a small set of supporting categories (social bases, intermediary organizations, governmental institutions). Chapters 2 through 8 do nothing if they do not accomplish that much.

It is just that even when this is done, the crucial explanation of the product in individual nations is still dependent on a set of critical *interactions:* across issues to create an era; among structures to shape an order; between eras and orders to establish a political dynamic. Common elements, and thus incentives for comparison, are still central to the identification of these interactions. But so is an emphasis on the *contingent* character of any resulting generalizations, on the inherently varying interactions which make these comparisons inevitably—and appropriately—partial. The challenge of a concluding chapter, then, is to make this deeper relationship explicit.

Chapter 10 begins this effort with a consideration of postwar eras, for their substance and, especially, its sequencing. It moves on to postwar orders: to the patterning in their key structures, to the diagnostic interplay among these structures, and to the background interaction between structure and substance. Chapter 10 then cycles back to the last of these interactions, between eras and orders as they go about producing a political dynamic, to consider its reciprocal character. And the chapter closes by looking first at some allegedly common forces which impel these (contingent) interactions, then at the divergent outcomes which nevertheless follow from them. In the process, the limits on political analysis, inherent limits even on careful comparative analysis, come more fully into view.

Substantive Issues and Issue Sequences

The very first substantive concerns of the postwar period might seem to present a challenge to the notion of partial and contingent generalization. Or at least, the Great Depression and the Second World War were broad enough and deep enough, especially together, to generate the issue content—the substance—of immediate postwar politics in all the G-7 nations. By hindsight, they were to prove broader, deeper, and more temporally focused than the otherwise impressive range of incipiently political events which would generate similar pressures across the postwar years, events like the postwar economic boom, the Cold War, metropolitanization, stagflation, and so on and on. Nevertheless, this is not the same as saying that the implications even of the end of the Second World War were themselves similar across these nations.

In one group—in the United States, Canada, Britain, and at first, France—the end of World War II meant principally the chance for national politics to return to the concerns of the Great Depression, concerns with material (re)distribution and especially with appropriate social-welfare provision. In a second group, by contrast—in Germany, Italy, Japan, and later, France again—the end of war meant instead the chance to turn politics toward certain fundamental tasks of national (re)construction: founding or restarting a democratic governmental system, along with restarting a national economy. The need for some revised posture toward a changed international security situation also reached into all these nations. Yet again, for the first group, this occasioned only the continuation of a wartime political order, while for the second, it required something definitionally new.

Even such generalized and dominating substantive influences, in any case, were never destined to last indefinitely. In the case of the second cluster of these nations in particular—of Germany, Italy, and Japan—success at the initial tasks of national reconstruction, however partial that success might seem in one or another realm, did invariably sow the seeds of its own displacement. Once democratic governmental forms were institutionalized, for example, it was less and less possible for politics to continue to revolve around their institutionalization. Intermittent conflicts over governmental reform could (and did) occur, but, with one striking exception, that was all. Likewise, once an "economic miracle" had begun decisively to occur, it was less and less likely that politics would continue to revolve simply around restarting a national economy. The attempted management of a much more moderate economic cycle, while intermittently insistent thereafter, was just a much less inherently dominating focus.

In these nations, then, an initial focus on the basic integrative concerns of renewing governmental and economic life was gradually joined by the distributional and social-service concerns which had characterized post-war politics in the other G-7 nations from the start. Which is to say: for Italy by the early 1960s, for Germany by the late 1960s, and for Japan by the early 1970s, economic/welfare issues had joined cultural/national matters as joint underlying dimensions to political conflict. At the same time, those original cultural/national concerns had begun to acquire very different issue embodiments, involving central and ongoing elements of national social life—divorce, childrearing, abortion; consumerism, crime, punishment; public deportment and private morality; educational standards and subcultural tolerance; immigration, nationality, citizenship; and so on.

For the United States, Canada, and Britain, this issue evolution ran in the opposite direction. Nevertheless, an initial focus on social-service issues and redistribution may actually, here too, have generated its own limiting conditions. From one side, major tasks in the implementation of a welfare state were accomplished, albeit to a widely varying degree. While from the other side, opponents rallied reliably to combat the ostensible "next steps." This was hardly the end of such initiatives, or of the counterattack. It merely meant that they were not to be the continuing substance of some natural focus to politics, with some natural and automatic trajectory.

At the same time, cultural and national questions—as ever, involving the character and fabric of social life writ large—emerged relentlessly from the background. By the late 1950s, these cultural/national concerns had joined economic and social-welfare issues at the center of Canadian politics. By the late 1960s, the same could be said of the United States. By the late 1970s, the former issues had joined the latter to such an extent in Britain that they were arguably its predominant concerns: individual initiative, public order, international standing, national renewal. The interaction of these two great issue dimensions, in any case, of the economic/welfare and the cultural/national dimensions, came to characterize politics in all these nations.

The gradual but forceful surfacing of cultural/national issues, to coequal status with economic/welfare issues and sometimes to dominance, does invite additional speculation. Some of the roots of their rise were obviously technological. It became more and more possible, for example, to manage human life itself—birth, maintenance, extension, death—so that societal decisions on such management became more and more inescapable. Some of these roots also lay, both directly and indirectly, in postwar policy successes. The successful implantation of civil rights and liberties, plus simple—remarkable—economic growth, make social integration easier in the sense of blurring old cleavages (most particularly in the realm of social class), while it made social control simultaneously more problematic.

Some of the roots of these increasingly consequential cultural/national issues, finally, reflected little more than the return of perennial concerns, temporarily suppressed by worldwide depression and worldwide war. Without the enforced (and extreme) need to focus on personal or national survival, ethnic, religious, or regional divisions, for instance, could resume their previously "natural" role. Moreover, within a generation of the end of World War II, all six of these nations (minus France, so far) faced renewed divisions over a proper national stance toward the bipolar world produced by the Cold War. While the depth of these particular divisions varied widely among them, and while there was usually a dominant (pro-Western) position within each, the general issue did help to reinvigorate cultural/national concerns in domestic politics.

Seen one way, then, to maximize similarities, it could be said: that subgroups of these nations did experience at least roughly similar issue evolution; that a similarly dominant issue substance, when it appeared, did have some parallel implications for politics; and that all of these nations did pass through certain similar, if complex, issue stages between the end of World War II and the end of the Cold War. Seen the other way, however, to maximize differences, it could also be said: that the timing of this progression differed even within the two similar subgroups of nations; that the politics of addressing individual issues still varied enormously, depending on what else was on the substantive agenda; and that even within a roughly similar trajectory, one nation might well have left a particular issue focus (or combination) by the time another arrived.

Either way, what seemed safe to assert was that considerations of issue *sequence* were inescapably important to postwar politicking in all these nations. In the abstract, it should hardly be surprising that a focus on institutional implantation and economic regeneration lent a quite different character to politics than a focus on service provision and economic redistribution, whether the comparison was between nations or between eras in the political history of the same nation. Yet there was even more. For an issue sequence in one nation could, of course, be influenced by issue sequences in others. And here, the distinctive case, and the one thereby diagnostic of the larger place of a general issue evolution, was the nation missing from the analysis so far, namely France.

By conscious national decision, France, in the years immediately after World War II, returned (like the United States, Canada, and Britain) to prewar economic and social-welfare concerns. Yet in the late 1950s, well after Germany, Italy, and Japan had embedded their postwar governmental arrangements, France moved to revisit this substantive focus, reconstructing both its electoral and its policymaking institutions in a major fashion. Postwar French politics, then, began with economic/welfare issues, shifted to cultural/national concerns, and only in the 1980s began to focus jointly on these two underlying dimensions. Arriving at the same ultimate destination, France managed to traverse both main routes in order to get there. In the process, issue evolution—and issue sequence— did appear to matter tremendously to the specifics of politics for the nation as a whole.

Moreover, by the time the return of an economic/welfare concentration had helped the Socialists to come to power, with an aggressive agenda for economic and social change, the timing of issues not just in France but, in truth, in all the G-7 nations had probably placed inherent limits on possibilities for implementation. In the most immediate sense, Franco-German economic integration, itself the product of prior policy conflicts, now applied brakes to many of the proposed economic policies, brakes which would not have existed a decade earlier. In a larger sense, the historical trajectory of postwar economics—past the economic miracle and into stagflation, with the after-effect of oil shocks—created further and more general restraints.

In a superficial sense, France had also, most indisputably of all these nations, entered a third postwar political era by the 1980s. This was, however, more a reflection of its initial decision not to address constitutional change, rather than of some incipiently general "wave of the future" which it was inaugurating. On the other hand, Canada, Germany, Italy, and Japan were also all potentially on their way into some third postwar era, and in their cases, this possibility was not an artifact of counting or retracing. In each case, of course, they might still not arrive, so that contemporary perturbations would prove to be merely side-currents in an ongoing era. But in each case, the substance of a new era, should it follow on from current disturbances, was already evident and (across all four nations) roughly similar in its essence.

Beyond that, the arrival of a third postwar era in one or more of these (or indeed other) nations appeared likely to underline the same two basic points about issue sequence. In the first, where two initially different trajectories for issue evolution in the postwar G-7 had appeared to demonstrate some movement toward a common pattern by the 1980s, that pattern now seemed likely to feature increased divergence, with some of these nations moving off from a common focus. In the second point, if history did deliver a new political era in several of these nations, the substance of that era still seemed likely to prove clearly similar across those that moved: in every case, the shift out of an era of mixed (and cross-cutting) economic/welfare and cultural/national issues seemed likely to come by way of a dominating focus on cultural/national issues alone.

For Canada, specifically, the question was whether ethnocultural issues—the politics of language, but so much more—would produce a new Canadian politics, even a new Canada. For Germany, conversely, the question was whether the ultimate issue of nationhood, definitionally new geographic boundaries, would produce a new substantive focus to politics, and hence a new era. For both Italy and Japan, the question was whether implementing new institutional arrangements for national politics, both formal and informal, would bring newly dominant substantive concerns in their wake. The demise of the Socialists and the putative demise of the Christian Democrats argued forcefully for this possibility in Italy; a set of major alternative policy issues—involving domestic democracy, international economics, and a world role partaking of aspects of both—were already the incipient substance for such a change in Japan.

Substance, Structure, and the Nature of Politicking

The political orders of the postwar G-7—along with many of the individual structures that went to constitute these orders—could be arrayed in a fashion identical to that of their political eras, to make parallel points about partial comparison and contingent interaction. One fresh example may, however, suffice to demonstrate the parallel—and reinforce those points. Thus the immediate postwar years, courtesy of the Great Depression, World War II, and policy responses to both, were arguably the high point of bureaucratic influence, that is, of the structuring influence of governmental bureaucracies in the democratic politics of all these nations. As with the postwar issue context, on the other hand, this still left substantial room for a further subclustering among the G-7 nations, between those where the bureaucracy was a central element of the first postwar order (France, Germany, and Japan) and those where it was not (the United States, Canada, and Italy)—with Britain, this time, moving early from the second group toward the first.

Thereafter, there was again a crudely general evolution to this influence, away from an immediate postwar peak and toward a gradually diminishing role for public bureaucracies. In every one of these nations, the second postwar order offered less policy influence to the national bureaucracy than did the first. Yet again, if the trend line could be argued to be roughly similar, the end points still varied wildly. Japan at its low point of bureaucratic influence, in our time, still featured more than the United States at its high point, in the immediate postwar years. Finally, to cap this dialectic, there were even some parallel blips and counter-trends. For example, when the second postwar order in both Japan and Italy showed signs of cracking in the early 1990s, for two nations with an otherwise very different role for public bureaucracies in the dying order, the role of these (more stable) bureaucracies and their bureaucrats actually increased, temporarily and opportunistically, during the flux of an apparent transition.

If that is an evolutionary parallel between eras and orders across the postwar years, there was also an interactive parallel. In this, the interaction of public bureaucracies with other structural influences was crucial to the pattern of postwar politicking at any given time in all these nations, just as the interaction among substantive issues was crucial to that pattern. Recall that individual issues achieved different consequences in different nations, even when they were achieving major attention, depending both on the point in time when they arrived on the national agenda and, especially, on the identity of the other issues on this agenda at that point. The centrality of public bureaucracies to postwar political orders was likewise highly contingent, not just on the time of examination within

the postwar years but, again especially, on the relationship of these bureaucracies to societal cleavages, to parties and party systems, and to the
basic arrangements of government itself.

Thus, to stay with the bureaucratic example, a comparatively homogenous society with an underdeveloped party system and a nascent governmental structure—this was Japan in it first postwar order—provided
maximal deference to a directive bureaucracy. Conversely, a heterogeneous society with an established two-party system and aggressively autonomous institutions of government—this was the United States in its second
order—provided minimal deference. Yet such relationships were really
more complex and idiosyncratic than even this elaborated example would
indicate. For the combination of multiple social cleavages with fragmented party systems and weakly rooted governments was capable of
supporting a strongly directive bureaucracy in France and a much less
directive one in Italy, at the same point in time, depending on additional
elements of political structure, like a long-established statist tradition (in
France) along with a ministerial stability obscured by the overall instability of government.

Yet this still does not plumb the full interactive complexity of key
political structures, as they go to constitute a political order. To that
end, it is necessary to look back to the *substance* of politics as well, that
is, to consider interactions not just among political structures but between their resulting orders and the substance of their eras. Only then
does the additionally contingent character of the structural influences
within a political order stand revealed. At this level, structures shape
an order; issues shape an era; orders and eras shape each other
reciprocally—and two grand and complex examples can help to make
the point. The first involves the interaction of issue evolution with one
of the two fundamental elements of any democratic governmental system, its electoral arrangements. The second involves the interaction of
issue evolution with the other fundamental element of formal government, its policymaking institutions.

Nowhere does this basic interactive relationship stand clearer than with
the influence of the first of these grand categories, of fundamental and
familiar electoral arrangements. To wit: it was possible to treat the timing
and scope of postwar social-welfare programs in the United States, Canada, and Britain in terms of the homogeneity or heterogeneity of their
societies and the centralization or decentralization of their governments
(as in chap. 9) *precisely because* these three nations were linked by majoritarian rules in their electoral systems. Said conversely: one reason it
was not possible to treat the timing and scope of postwar social-welfare
reforms in Germany, Italy, or Japan in these terms—the reason this sim-

ple mode of analysis had to be expanded—was that these nations used proportional representation in their electoral systems instead.

As ever, it was hardly that first-past-the-post elections (or proportionality) generated this difference. Electoral arrangements had to be understood in connection with the society producing a vote and the institutions upon which that vote fell. Indeed, first-past-the-post electoral rules contributed differently to the presidential system of the United States than to the parliamentary systems of Canada and Britain. Just as first-past-the-post rules worked differently in the socially heterogeneous (parliamentary) Canada than in the socially homogeneous (parliamentary) Britain. Yet at bottom, *by comparison,* first-past-the-post systems allowed a much greater scope for this sort of analysis, based on social homogeneity or governmental centralization and their opposites, than did proportional systems. The latter required a look at other and additional structural factors: bureaucracies, party systems, elite ideologies, and so on.

The same general relationship—the same crucial interaction between substantives issues and electoral arrangements—can be seen in the *change* within all these nations from the first era of postwar politics to the second. In Britain, Canada, and the United States, as well as France if we focus on the shift from the second to the third era, this change was registered by a shift in partisan control of national government. Whereas in Japan, Italy, and even Germany (along with France in the shift from the first to the second era), it was not an electoral alternation, at least not directly, which signaled (and reciprocally facilitated) the change of political eras.

It is important not to overstate the impact of electoral arrangements. Changing societal demands for a different substantive focus did characterize all of these societies in the run-up to a change of political eras, so that the presence of one or another electoral system was hardly sufficient by itself either to stimulate or to blunt the force of such (era-shifting) demands. Yet in the case of the proportional nations, these demands did not come into politics by way of an electoral change in the partisan control of government. Rather, they came by way of an institutional shift within and among parties which were already elected, even in the limiting case of Germany, where a change of government (through coalitional change by the FDP) was then *followed by* a confirmatory election.

It should probably also be noted that this particular relationship shows no sign of attenuating in our time. Or at least, as Italy and Japan totter on the verge of a third postwar order, this same structural influence (from electoral systems) bids to be central to the change. Both nations in fact feature a broad if inchoate understanding that two otherwise very different forms of proportionality have heretofore worked to prevent partisan alternations in government, much less substantive successions in political eras. Electoral reform is thus an integral part of the conscious attempt to move to a new political order, and era.

An even more grand embodiment of this interaction—between dominant issue concerns and major institutional structures—appears in the question of the *product* of what often proved to be cross-cutting economic/welfare and cultural/national issues within the G-7 nations. The ultimate product of such cross-cutting preferences, of course, as they were embodied in different social coalitions from nation to nation and as they encountered different governmental institutions, was a national political dynamic, from which specific public policies emerged. But the intermediate product of this collision was a partisan approach to governing. And here, it was our second grand category, policymaking arrangements rather than electoral systems, which provided the critical structural contribution.

In the United States and France, with separately elected executives and legislatures, this intermediate outcome demonstrated the full panoply of partisan governing approaches. There was unified partisan control of government in either direction, that is, with either Right or Left in control of both the elected executive and the (elected) legislature. And there was split partisan control in either direction, that is, with different parties (or tendencies) in control of the executive *versus* the legislature. Cross-cutting issue majorities were of course central to such an available range of partisan products. But so were separately elected, nonceremonial, chief executives.

In Canada or Britain, by contrast, policymaking institutions encouraged a very different recurring response to cross-cutting preferences. Their institutions did not, by definition, allow split partisan control, in the sense of a Conservative prime minister and a Labour House of Commons. What they did allow in its place was the possibility for a party to take control of government on the basis of one of these underlying issue majorities and then to try to govern on the basis of the other. Which Conservative governments in Britain and Liberal governments in Canada did intermittently try, by addressing cultural/national issues in their election campaigns and then concentrating on economic/welfare *policies* in office. In this sense, the imposition of unelected national executives upon first-past-the-post electoral systems, as in Canada and Britain, created what is in many ways the polar opposite partisan pattern of governing to that of the United States and France.

In Germany, Japan, and Italy, cross-cutting issues then created a kind of middle course. Because their electoral arrangements fragmented (rather than concentrating) the outcome, they did not encourage simple alternations in partisan control of government through the ballot box. As a result, governments of the day tended to reflect the policy issue which had created a governing coalition or, even more commonly, the policy issues which had created an actual party system. From the other side, however, because their policymaking institutions did not encourage split partisan control in the explicit sense, they did not offer any obvious alternative way to reintroduce some major cross-cutting concerns.

Which is to say: the combination of proportional representation plus parliamentary government, when confronted with cross-cutting policy preferences on the part of the general public, in effect discouraged a shift between public issues on the part of political elites. These elites were not elected to make such a shift; they risked breaking up a governing coalition by even making the attempt. Instead, a coalition formed on the basis of one great dimension of substantive conflict, when faced with the rise of the other great dimension, had to: (a) change the composition of the governing coalition itself, as the German case; (b) find some external means of addressing this second set of issues, as in the Italian case; or (c) make some modest tactical adjustments and then "stonewall" the remainder, aspiring to be strong enough to remain focused on the previous dimension—as in the Japanese case for so long.

Eras, Orders, and Political Dynamics

Yet such examples, comprehensive as they are, *still* do not convey the full range of ways in which substantive themes and structural influences inherently interact, and thus the ways in which this interaction shapes the dynamics of politicking in these nations, as well as, of course, its outcome. The preceding examples do suggest the way in which different issues interact to produce an era and different structures interact to produce an order, as well as the way in which different substantive themes interact with different structural elements to produce different approaches to governing. What they may not yet convey is the extent to which such interactions are often inherent—genuinely reciprocal—such that it is difficult to make sense of one without addressing the other. Two further examples, a short further digression on national bureaucracies and a longer look at cross-cutting issues, will emphasize this reciprocity.

In the case of national bureaucracies, the immediate postwar peak in their structural influence was due not just to advantageous contributions from other political structures. It was due as well to the particular character of political issues at the time, and this character was in fact part and parcel of their influence. Which is to say: similar policy pressures across the G-7, growing out of the depression and war, were reinforced by national consensus, either on the further provision of social welfare (the United States, Canada, and Britain) or on governmental and economic reconstruction (Germany, Italy, and Japan)—with France showing both concentrations sequentially. Similar pressures on these general issues and similar agreements on these general policies were in turn facilitative of bureaucratic influence in policy *initiation,* and not just in implementation.

By contrast, the subsequent arrival of cross-cutting issue bases to the substance of politics, along with the changing substantive content of both economic/welfare and cultural/national issues, were to be far less facilitative. Cross-cutting issues in effect removed any simple agreement on what government (and its bureaucracy) ought to do, without creating a policy void into which bureaucratic entrepreneurs could move. Changing substance installed specific concerns to politics—nationality and immigration; crime and punishment; public entitlement and private responsibility; abortion, childrearing, divorce—which were just less inherently susceptible to administrative resolution, at least in democratic societies.

The bureaucratic example emphasizes reciprocity, with a nod to substance: this key political structure can only partially be separated, in terms of its influence, from the policy issues that it has to address. An even more striking example nods in the other direction, toward structure: at bottom, so-called "cross-cutting" (or indeed "reinforcing") issue dimensions acquire that designation—and again, most of their joint impact—in a nearly inseparable interaction with structural factors. Indeed, it is exactly this structural interaction that *makes* them "cross-cutting." And here, the case of the interaction between cross-cutting issue dimensions on one side and a very different fundamental element of political structure on the other—the social group basis for politicking—is a particularly good way to make this (reciprocal, interactive) point.

For in fact, the reason that cross-cutting cultural/national and economic/welfare issues demanded nationally specific (and not at all straightforward) results, as they fell across electoral systems and policymaking institutions, had to do only in part with the inherent substance of these issues or the operational character of those institutions. It had to do, in larger part, with deeper—and apparently also inherent—preference patterns by social groups in these various nations. That is, it was practical group preferences, not abstract substantive logic, which rendered these issues cross-cutting or not, as they surfaced in the politics of individual nations.

Said differently: there was little about these substantive concerns in themselves which created a substantive tension—and then a social cross-pressure—between one set of preferences on cultural/national issues and any other set of preferences on economic/welfare issues. The human mind could easily entertain any of the main overall combinations: liberal on both, conservative on both, or mixed liberal and conservative in either direction. Or, said differently again: many group histories or circumstances made the second pair of these combinations—liberal on economic/welfare and conservative on cultural/national, or the reverse— the socially sensible combination to hold, and not in some (socially abstracted) sense "illogical." As a result, the conservative coalition on one dimension was just not the same as the conservative coalition on the other, in nation after nation, and the same was true for the two main liberal coalitions.

The numerical balance within and between these coalitions did vary among these nations. Likewise, the tension between them, between economic/welfare versus cultural/national coalitions, could vary substantially with the particular policy issues which stimulated them or, especially, with the priority that events imparted to one or the other issue-base for a coalition. Nevertheless, a potential conservative majority in Germany on cultural/national issues was not socially the same as a potential conservative majority on economic/welfare issues, as the behavior of the Free Democrats proved so dramatically during the second era in postwar German politics. Similarly, an incipient liberal majority in France on economic/welfare issues was not socially the same as an incipient liberal majority on cultural/national issues, thereby creating the great strategic dilemma of both the broad Left and the broad Right in modern French politics. In the same way, a conservative majority on cultural/national issues in the United States could easily look like a conservative *or* a liberal majority on economic/welfare issues—fueling split partisan control of national government sometimes, but fueling "divided governance" even when one party controlled all the major governmental institutions.

It was thus the reciprocity between issue substance and social coalitions which made these issues operate in politics as they did, not the inherent content of the issues itself. The rise of this tension between issue positions and social coalitions, in turn, was also central to the evolution of party *systems* in these nations. Party systems did vary in their centrality to political orders during this period, just as the elections within their confines varied in the degree to which they actually caused one overall era to give way to another. But these systems were still a good immediate way into the overall dynamic to politics in a given nation at one or another period. And this dynamic too reflects the inherent interaction of substance and structure as it shaped postwar political developments.

Most of these nations began the postwar period with party systems built centrally around social class, and thus around Left-leaning or Right-leaning preferences on economic and social-welfare issues. This alignment was probably at its most pure in Britain and then Germany. It acquired additional class-based twists in France and Italy, overlaid with further organizing principles like regionalism and clericalism, yet the underlying alignment was still evident in those nations as well. Even the United States showed an obvious and straightforward class cut to its party system at this point, with white-collar Republicans facing blue-collar Democrats. Canada and Japan then provided the weakest approximation, with ethnicity and religion (Canada) or one-party preponderance (Japan) to cloud the picture, and with minor parties or regional off-shoots to cloud that picture additionally.

Two clear forces were to erode any such neat alignment over the postwar period, reducing the class cut between the parties in Britain, Germany, and the United States, and actually reworking the party system in a major way in France and Italy—as well, this time, as in Canada and Japan. The first of these forces was broad social and economic change, which blurred class lines in major ways in all these countries; this change is addressed below, in connection with specific notions of convergence or divergence. But the second of these forces which eroded class alignments is the same interaction between social coalitions and issue contexts as above: which is to say, the rise of *socially cross-cutting* economic/welfare and cultural/national issues in most of these nations, and the way that various social groups preferred different majority coalitions, depending specifically on the substantive issue at the center of politics.

The combination of these two influences was actually to produce demands for different electoral rules in France, Italy, and Japan, so that the new concerns (and putative new coalitions) which necessarily accompanied new issues and their socially cross-cutting prospects could more effectively gain representation—in the face of entrenched party systems built in an earlier (and simpler) era. But even without change in the formal rules, this issue (and social) tension was to produce more fluid and more contingent political coalitions beneath the parties in the United States, Britain, and Germany—as well as Canada, where this development was never braked by strong class coalitions.

It is possible, however, to go farther, at least with a little interpretive license. For in fact, it was not just that the interaction of substantive issues and social coalitions contributed a key aspect of the political dynamic, a dynamic most easily observed by way of the party system. It was also that the specific character of this interaction appeared to predispose the partisan *outcome*. The result was not absolutely invariant. But at a minimum, an emphasis on economic/welfare issues appeared disproportionately kind to parties of the Left, while an emphasis on cultural/national issues appeared equally beneficial to parties of the Right. Indeed, the substantive dominance of economic and social-welfare issues in the G-7 nations, whenever these issues were dominant, tended to bring parties of the Left to power in national government. Conversely, the substantive dominance of cultural and national issues tended, as reliably, to bring parties of the Right to power instead.

Moreover, there may well have been something inherent to this. Or at least, by dividing society into the advantaged and the disadvantaged, parties of the Left could not as easily talk, simultaneously, about the need to pull together as one indivisible unit. From the other side, by focusing upon an alleged need to pull together as one national entity—for the existing nation, which was what gave this goal meaning—parties of the Right could not as easily talk about redistribution (from one sector of society to another) at the same time. By extension, when either of these types of parties did assay the opposite tack, they were just inherently less believable. If redistribution was the priority, why not have a consistently redistributive party? If integration was the issue instead, why not have the party which *always* emphasized integrative themes?

In any case, when the dominant substantive realm involved considerations of national renewal, as it did most especially for Germany, Italy, and Japan in the aftermath of World War II, it was—it may have been destined to be?—the leading party of the Right which formed the government and addressed those problems. Just as at the same time in the United States, Canada, and Britain, with social welfare and economic redistribution at the top of the issue agenda, it was the leading party of the Left which formed the government and addressed *those* problems. When economic/welfare issues muscled their way (or were driven) back onto the agenda in the first group of these nations, the SPD came to power in Germany and the Socialists came into the government in Italy—though the LDP did stave off any such result in Japan. Just as when cultural/national issues gained renewed prominence in the politics of the second group of these nations, the Conservatives came back to power in Canada and Britain, and the Republicans back at least to the presidency in the United States.

France, once more, provided the deviant case which then confirmed both patterns. To begin with, having returned to prewar issues and alignments in the immediate postwar years, it could offer two subsequent shifts in issue dominance (and partisan fortunes). Unsurprisingly, after the Algerian crisis and the implementation of a new constitution, the issue of national renewal brought domination by parties of the Right for an extended period. Ultimately, after economic and social-welfare issues came back onto the political agenda, those concerns brought the Socialists, the leading party of the Left, back to power, with coequal partisan standing.

Thereafter, when both economic/welfare and cultural/national issues worked their (cross-cutting) ways, in our own most proximate time, split partisan control of the institutions of national government—or at least, "divided governance"—was the practical result.

Seen from the other side of the political process, the side familiar to political operatives rather than political analysts, this relationship seemed even stronger. Or at least, whenever possible, parties of the Left preferred to elevate—and emphasize—issues of economic distribution and social welfare. Likewise, parties of the Right preferred to encounter—or propel—issues of cultural and national values instead. Again, there may be something inherent to the nature of such parties which explains this, with parties of the Left emphasizing division and distribution, parties of the right emphasizing unity and integration. Regardless, it must also be said that these tactical efforts were rarely, by themselves, sufficient to enforce a focus on one or the other of the great underlying dimensions of conflict, especially not for an extended period.

Common Dynamics and Divergent Outcomes

This is a picture of continual interactions, among issues, among structures, and between them. Overarching substantive issues can sometimes dominate their eras, but issue *interactions* more often shape them. This is true contemporaneously, as when cross-cutting substantive issues work their way through a political system; it is true sequentially, as when the temporal order in which issues arise (or not) determines what must be addressed at a given point in time. In the same way, single key structures can sometimes come close to dominating their orders, though again, the interplay among a small set of structures is more often what matters. Indeed, this interplay can even make the *same* single structure work very differently in different nations, or at different times.

Interactions across this divide—between eras and orders, between substantive issues and structural influences—are more complicated but equally insistent. Here, substantive themes can drive political orders, and the sequence of those themes can even determine what structural factors will be consequential in a given order at a given point in time. Conversely, structural elements can shape the issue focus of a political era, or even the issue sequence between eras. All of which still understates the degree to which the influence of political issues and political structures is often inherently reciprocal—and thus inseparable, jointly, in conjunction. Structural elements can determine what a particular substance implies; substantive content can determine how a particular structure operates.

Contingent interactions, then, between substantive content and structural influence, between eras and orders, shaped political dynamics within all the G-7 nations during this period. This is not to say that there were not some quite similar—effectively international—pressures falling across all these nations during this same period, nor that common forces were not in some sense driving all these nations in a similar direction. It is just to say two *other* things simultaneously. First, that the policy response to these (common) forces was still dependent on a *mix* of structural influences specific to the nation in question. And second, that any policy response was likewise dependent on the mix of other issues dominating national politics at the time, and on how this common international force interacted with *it*. Moreover, to complete the picture of contingency, because a common—a transnational—policy problem could arrive in different G-7 nations at different points, the same individual nations could of course respond differently to its policy demands than they would have, had it arrived during a different era and/or order.

Perhaps the most frequent candidate for a simple contrary argument—for generalized pressures conducing toward similar responses—is international economics. All nations do have an economic life, after all, and the growth and character of their national economies is inevitably central to politics, generating political issues and political conflicts. Moreover, economic life in the whole G-7 did follow *some* clear parallels in the postwar years, becoming, additionally, more interconnected among these nations as time passed. On the other hand, such interconnections can also fall and not just rise, as new trading partners and new trading patterns, for example, emerge and develop. Moreover, the same general things can be said about cultural or social life. All nations have both of these, too; both are inevitably central to politics; each rises, falls, and interacts differently as time passes. These latter points are doubly important, since cultural and social influences may go in quite other directions to those from basic economics.

Yet just within the realm of economic life, in the face of obviously international developments, the *timing* of these developments for individual nations, given other issues on the national agenda and, especially, given differing political orders when these (international, economic) concerns arrived, did produce notably different results. Conservative party leaders in Japan decided consciously to defy them, to pay the price for taking countervailing initiatives in the face of stagflation and oil shocks in the early 1970s; conservative party leaders in Italy felt they could only temporize, and push difficult aspects into other institutional forums. In truth, nations can surely not defy economic fundamentals forever (or cultural or social fundamentals, either). Yet such an ultimate and abstract constraint should not obscure the equally consequential fact that a Socialist government coming to power in France in 1981 would still attempt—and accomplish—very different things from a Republican government coming to power in the United States in that same year.

The other obvious candidate for a contrary argument—a truly international influence, again presumably conducing in similar directions for such a "homogeneous" group of nations—was foreign affairs. And here, the Cold War in particular *was* a dominating international development, requiring some posture from every one of these nations. Nevertheless, once again, it interacted with established political orders in very different ways. At one extreme, it restructured German politics, from the start, by restructuring the German nation. At the other extreme and simultaneously, it had nearly no effect of the implementation by a new Labour government in Britain of the most far-reaching single surge of social-welfare programs in any of these nations in this entire period, the signature characteristic of its politics at the time. And in-between these two extremes, the Cold War gained its influence in Canada by interacting structurally with a basic ethnocultural divide—fueling and being fueled by it—while interacting substantively with issues like the Suez Crisis, which actually pitted Cold War allies against each other.

Moreover, the Cold War as an issue in national politics—presumably the same Cold War, when defined by an international order—evolved very differently from nation to nation. In both Britain and the United States, support for (and dissent from) a policy of Cold War containment did acquire partisan attachments over time, with reliable injury to the parties that took the dissenting line. In Germany, on the other hand, the same partisan alignment evolved, but without an inherent disadvantage to the "soft" side—until *Soviet* activities in *Eastern* Europe altered the domestic thrust of the issue. And in France, national circumstance largely marginalized the issue at exactly the point, the second postwar era, when it was gaining partisan consequence elsewhere.

The same might be said—major common elements, in highly contingent interaction—with other aspects of foreign affairs, aspects not so global in their reach but potentially more influential in nations they did affect. Decolonization is the starkest example. Here, both Britain and France possessed huge colonial empires as the postwar period began. Both would see these converted into numerous new and independent nations, with very different ties to the former colonial power, by the time the period ended. Yet decolonization, for all the tensions and adjustments which it did introduce into British politics, would essentially slot into an existing political era. While in France, the same event was effectively to terminate one era and bring on another, at least as the precipitating crisis.

The substantive nature of the issue held some of the explanation for this difference. Colonies were administered by Britain; they *were* France. Yet the character of the existing political order held more of the explanation this time. In Britain, the issue did not demand fundamental change from an executive with a simple partisan majority, buttressed by social coalitions which were not aligned with divisions on decolonization, coming on top of established dominance by civil over military leaders. In France, the issue proved indigestible instead, for a coalition-based and historically unstable executive, further undermined by coalitional fragmentation on some of the central concerns of decolonization, facing partial bureaucratic autonomy in a fragmented institutional system. Yet the larger point remains that the interaction of a substantively very similar issue with a different background sequence of issues and *very* different political orders produced a different short-run politics and a very different long-run impact.

Notions of "convergence" or "divergence" are not very helpful for such a world, even for major developed democracies with explicit institutional links over a circumscribed period of time. Contingent interactions are much more nearly the story of their postwar politics, and contingent interactions produced what was still, at bottom, a *national* political dynamic. Such interactions could, in principle, bring these nations closer together. It is just that the same sorts of interactions could obviously draw them farther apart. Indeed, the second postwar era in most of these nations, with its cross-cutting cultural/national and economic/welfare issues, certainly made their politics look more uniform than the first, with its two distinctive subgroups plus an evident outlier. Just as the *third* postwar era, as it appears on the horizon, bids to make them look more divergent again.

Which should not, one last time, be allowed to suggest that all of these nations are not strikingly different when compared with themselves in an earlier time, that is, 1995 versus 1945. Nor that the character of politics has not changed across all seven. Nor in fact that both changes have not followed a roughly similar trajectory. Such change may not constrain the grand interactions of eras and orders, certainly not so as to contribute something recognized as convergence. Yet it *is* change in a very similar direction, so perhaps it should serve as the closing note in this volume. For society has changed in every one of these nations, and the nature of politicking has changed with it. If that is still not enough to produce a uniform process—some single and unnuanced political dynamic—then that fact will perhaps serve as a final endorsement of the comparative approach.

At the social base for politics within all these nations, the country of 1995 did look very different from the country of 1945, and in ways that could be argued to be parallel throughout. There was vast economic growth. There was rising general education. There was metropolitanization, to erode local ties but to substitute new divisions. There were new media of mass communication, to knit these nations together. There was a blurring of class lines, to contribute the same effect. There was a decline in the most parochial aspects of organizational life, previously the bulwark against many of these effects. Cumulative change was naturally greatest in countries, like Italy and Japan, which were most unlike this when the period began. Just as change had still proceeded farthest in countries, like the United States and Canada, which were more like it at the beginning. But the same drift in all its elements was recognizable throughout, and its product was a recognizably different *society* at the end of the Cold War than at the end of World War II.

Inevitably, such societies acquired a different politics as well. At the beginning, there were brokered coalitions of localized subcultures, with small pieces brought together by national representatives who bargained over public policy at the governmental center. By the end, there were vague and amorphous but *nationalized* coalitions, energized by hyperactivists with their own substantive motivations or else by organized interests with a specialized focus, but built through mass media and dependent on equally vague and general popular ties for their success. Again, the United States and Canada provided the archetypal pattern. But France and Britain were not all that different. And similar developments in Germany were largely just masked by the long-running Kohl chancellorship. Italy was in evident flux, with similar incipient signs but without some distinctive resolution. Only Japan had obviously not yet made this shift, though dedicated comparativists, by this point in the analysis, nevertheless awaited its arrival.

It is tempting to flirt with an even deeper, common political *dynamic* arising from these (similar) influences. A few further sentences can sketch its outline, as well as suggest why simple notions of convergence are so misplaced in dealing with it—why common influences can arrive differently, mix differently, and produce different outcomes in different nations. In this, a composite portrait of these changing societies and the changing character of their politics might initially suggest a generalized dynamic in some sense "waiting to be born": a vague and general majoritarianism, in which a broad Left alternated with a broad Right—a politics arguably appropriate to the social change described above.

And indeed, it would be possible to tell the story of postwar politics in the G-7 nations in these very terms. At the beginning, in their first postwar era, the United States, Britain, and Canada could already have been described, in their central political dynamic, through just such a model. By the coming of the second postwar era to their politics, France and

Germany could be added to this picture—two dominant parties in Germany, two dominant tendencies in France, but able to alternate in power in both countries. And by the coming of the third postwar era, the two remaining nations, Italy and Japan, offered at least evidence of incipient motion toward the same pattern.

Such a grand overall description, however, does gloss over some important differences; it does elide developments happening at quite different times; and it thus manages to suggest parallel outcomes which are not so clearly in evidence. For example, the United States and Britain may be superficially described in these terms throughout the postwar period, but in the case of the United States, such a description actually masks the *break* from an earlier, straightforwardly bimodal, issue context to a very different, cross-cutting context instead. In the case of Canada, what is obscured by such a description is much larger. For if this is the Canadian politics of the first and perhaps the second postwar era, it is most definitely not the Canadian politics of the current world—where "alternating broad tendencies" does not come close to summarizing the surge and eclipse of the Conservatives, nor the rise of both Reform and the Parti Québécois.

Lesser fissures in a simple bimodal model, akin to the Canadian case but more restrained, could be adduced in Germany and France as well. Newly consequential third parties, and new coalitional possibilities, certainly characterize German politics. A fragmentation of the major tendencies, akin to the German case, along with sharply fluctuating fortunes for the major parties, akin to the Canadian case, certainly characterize France as this is written. Those possibilities also serve as a reminder that the breakup of the second postwar orders in Italy and Japan does not in any sense require the emergence of some simple model of alternating broad tendencies in those two nations. Indeed, if Germany and France were to continue on their current trajectories while Italy and Japan continued on theirs, the G-7 collectively would be no nearer "convergence" in their central political dynamic as a result of that continuation.

Alternatively, it is tempting to see these caveats as themselves evidence for an even larger pattern in the evolution of these national political dynamics, albeit one which makes notions of convergence or divergence effectively irrelevant. In this, a gradual movement away from a segmented society and a fragmented politics, toward two broad political tendencies competing for power, is then inherently countervailed by the difficulty that such tendencies have in retaining policy coherence and ingesting new issues. This difficulty then leads logically to *fragmentation*—and thereby causes the cycle to begin again. Societies which were once fragmented by parochialism now become fragmented instead by the range of alternative organizations and lifestyle options available to them, but change and its resolution, consensus and fragmentation, run on relentlessly.

Such an argument, in any case, goes far beyond what the postwar years can possibly sustain, and far beyond what the G-7 nations can confirm. At best, the possibility of such a larger (cyclical) movement simply affirms the underlying comparative story of these nations in this period, with issues and eras, structures and orders, in a constant but contingent interaction, producing politics (and policies) easily comparable from nation to nation, but nationally distinctive in most cases as well.

All such developments are, in turn, testimony to the final interaction characterizing the postwar politics of the G-7: between broad developments sweeping them all along, national factors which can interpret these broad developments very differently, and idiosyncratic influences running in a different, even sometimes opposite, direction. And in that interaction, sequential and contingent as it is, lies not just the story of postwar politics in the G-7 nations to date, but the story of politics in these nations in whatever the next period—the next eras and orders—proves to be.

Index

Index